Transforming
Sexuality

A C. G. JUNG FOUNDATION BOOK

The C. G. Jung Foundation for Analytical Psychology is dedicated to helping men and women grow in conscious awareness of the psychological realities in themselves and society, find healing and meaning in their lives and greater depth in their relationships, and live in response to their discovered sense of purpose. It welcomes the public to attend its lectures, seminars, films, symposia, and workshops and offers a wide selection of books for sale through its bookstore. The Foundation also publishes *Quadrant,* a semiannual journal, and books on Analytical Psychology and related subjects. For information about Foundation programs or membership, please write to the C. G. Jung Foundation, 28 East 39th Street, New York, NY 10016.

Transforming Sexuality

THE ARCHETYPAL WORLD
OF ANIMA AND ANIMUS

Ann and Barry Ulanov

SHAMBHALA
Boston & London
1994

Shambhala Publications, Inc.
Horticultural Hall
300 Massachusetts Avenue
Boston, Massachusetts 02115

9 8 7 6 5 4 3 2 1
Designed by Dede Cummings/IPA

First Edition

Printed in the United States of America on acid-free paper ⊗

Distributed in the United States by Random House, Inc., and
in Canada by Random House of Canada Ltd

Library of Congress Cataloging-in-Publication Data

Ulanov, Ann Belford.
    Transforming sexuality: the archetypal world of anima and
animus/Ann and Barry Ulanov.
        p.   cm.
    "A C. G. Jung Foundation book."
    Includes bibliographical references and index.
    ISBN 0-87773-986-2
    1. Anima (Psychoanalysis)   2. Animus (Psychoanalysis)
3. Sex (Psychology)   I. Ulanov, Barry.   II. Title.
BF175.5.A542U42   1994   94-11013
155.2'64—dc20   CIP

For Alexander

Contents

Part I

The Anima/Animus Bridge

1

Anima and Animus

I object to the term "system." If I had invented system, I certainly should have constructed better and more philosophical concepts than I am applying. Take for instance animus *and* anima. *No philosopher in his senses would invent such irrational and clumsy ideas. When things fit together, it is not always a matter of a philosophical system; sometimes it is the facts that fit together. Mythological motifs are facts; they never change; only theories change.*[1]

WE BEGIN with these words of Jung to point up the hazards of our subject. If Jung himself finds his ideas clumsy, how much greater danger must await others here, authors and readers both? If, as Jung observes, the theory itself is subject to constant change, why take it up at such length?

One answer is clear. All psychological theory, even the most elegant, is rooted in indeterminacy: its material changes just as one is drawing conclusions about it. What we can offer here are maps to orient our lived experience, no more, but also no less. The country that the anima/animus idea leads us into is volatile and deeply quiet, often explosive yet unutterable, both personal and pointing beyond our ego world to open us to claims upon us for which the ego might make the greatest of sacrifices. Maps are essential in such territory.

From our experience using anima/animus theory in lectures, in classroom teaching, and in the comparative safety of clinical relationships where it functions as a silent map rather than a topic for discussion, we have learned how bristly it can be. This material is so intimate and penetrating that it quickly reaches long-buried raw spots: rooms become crowded with the evocations of the unconscious. We feel touched precisely where we feel most violated and betrayed. Our noisiest defenses against guilt, or worse chaos, are aroused. Slumbering resentment turns wrathful. We take stands, utter pronouncements. At the same time, this material kindles our excitement at the possibility of being alive, fully awake. We are brought into the midst of our ideals, our wishes for union and reunion, for a life of love and a passion for what matters.

These reactions are collective, not simply personal, in this time of major change all around us. We hear millennial gongs ringing. All our uneasinesses gather into anxieties of gender: we find ourselves puzzled, excited, liberated, furious; released and relieved over the freeing up of old sexual stereotypes and deeply concerned about the rise of new ones. The complexity of the human person announces itself again, refusing to be frozen into anatomical definition. It is in the presence of great changes that affect everyone's experience of body, soul, and relationships to others, to government, and to God, that Jung offers his "clumsy ideas" of anima and animus.

In fact, the ideas that Jung gathered under the heading of the anima and animus archetypes are not so much "clumsy" as awkwardly expressed, and necessarily so. For what is gathered here is a series of extraordinary challenges to received ideas of gender and sexuality, a rejection of commonplaces, and an assertion of an ever-growing complexity of experience and understanding. Confident generalizations about human sexual performance do not survive the scrutiny of anima/animus analysis. For in spite of Jung's own predilection to typological reduction, it is all but impossible with anima/animus theory to make clean, clear lists of "masculine" and "feminine" qualities, even such categorical distinctions, so long consecrated in Jungian usage, as "logos" skills for the male and "eros" for the female.[2]

We do talk, in the language of anima and animus, of masculine and feminine ways of being, but not as the exclusive possession of male or female. We do insist on the appearance within the female of unmistakably masculine characteristics and ways of being and doing and of a similar contrasexuality in the male, where an abundant femininity, no matter how strenuously denied or repressed, is only too clear. But this does not add up to an androgynous creature. The more we understand of anima and animus, the more we live consciously and with ease in its precincts, the more securely we assert our defining sexual identity. Men are more masculine, women more feminine when they can not only accept but take pleasure in the complexity of opposing sexual identities constantly revealed to them in the inner dialogue that characterizes the anima/animus life.

Because so much of this life is defined by an interior conversation, we find it difficult, sometimes to the point of a bewildering inarticulateness, to give it exterior description. We are in the world now of Wittgenstein's language games without anything like a fixed set of rules or a language with a clear grammar and syntax in the particular game we are playing. What is more, much of this game is beyond the language of words or any set of gestures or postures or other habits of behavior that can be reduced to description. Still, we are in a discoverable realm. Jung has been there. Many clinicians and theorists have followed him into the dark corners and the clean well-lighted places of anima/animus, making their own discoveries in the great territory, adding their own notations, disputing this or that description, refining our knowledge of the geography—where that can be done—and worrying us with the fateful conclusion that some of this world of sexual identity is simply beyond charting.

Given the difficulties, some simply give up. Too many problems, they conclude. The theory and everything that goes with it had better be scrapped. Or, if they do not feel quite so despondent, they offer a revisionist mapping, in which anima and animus remain significant categories of sexual identity and practice but with no particular precedence in either male or female. We can all be described then as bundles of anima/animus qualities. The male does not move toward his anima counterpart with any concern different from what he feels for the animus with which he has been newly endowed in revisionist doctrine, and equally the female is as much drawn to anima as to animus. The result, in spite of some useful passing insights, is not an addition of great value to anima/animus theory, but simply a reminder that, as with all theories of such size, problems accrue with understanding. With this particular theory they must constantly present themselves, for it is centered as almost no other on the worlds, conscious and unconscious, where we experience our greatest joys and sorrows and almost all the states of being in between.

Despite its problems, Jung's theory occupies a place on a par with Freud's discovery of the Oedipus complex, Klein's of the depressive position, Winnicott's of the false and true selves, and Kohut's of the self that precedes experience of instinctual drives. Jung makes accessible to us, through image, symbol, and theoretical construct, our own sexuality, not as it should be, or even as we might wish it to be, but as it actually touches the core of our being as persons. Jung shows us that we cannot ask what kind of woman or man we are, let alone answer the question, if we are not also asking what way an *other* lives in us from a sexual departure-point opposite to our own conscious gender identity. The anima/animus is an image produced by the unconscious, usually of the opposite sex and always contrary to our conscious gender identity, that connects us to our own inner life. The person reaching toward wholeness is a contrasexual person, looking to join within himself or herself the energies of both the feminine and masculine modes of being human. We are not either one or the other, but a mixture of self and other, same and opposite. This is what anima/animus looks like from a theoretical perspective. What does it feel like from the inside? What sort of "motifs" and "facts," to use the jargon, "fit together" here?

Talking about animus and anima means talking about all the grand messes we get into sexually and spiritually, about all the experiences that mark our lives. We are talking about compulsive attachments to others, about having lost, apparently beyond reach, links to our feminine depths so that we feel we must dig under a life's pile of attitudes to a still place in an ancient forest or at the edge of the sea, in the remote mythological image of the Sumerian Corn Goddess or the great folds and fullness of Venus of Willendorf. We are talking about seeking our buried masculinity in modern forests, in aggressive activity, and in quieter attempts to reach our connection with other men.

Our discussion is about intimate sexual relations with an ongoing partner in which we struggle to learn how to fight for the best self of the other instead of always arguing in defense of our own self. How, we ask, can we live in long-term connection to the fires of passion, how avoid bogging down into flat cold patterns of codependent boredom? We are bringing into open examination the relationship with priest or teacher or analyst, already intimate, suddenly charged with sexual excitement. How do we hold to the good here? How do we deal with the danger of burning up? We all know those moments when we feel summoned forth to respond to another person in such a way that we know ourselves to be wide open, ready for anything. We also know how poorly we have dealt with such moments, have only played with them, never following them through, leaving ourselves prey to weaker and weaker repetition until cynicism sets in, poisoning our hopes of such a connection with another. We need not generalize here: we have countless everyday as well as clinical examples of anima/animus interaction between people, and within persons.[3]

EXAMPLES

At breakfast with friends, a housewife, recently returned to school to complete her college education, complains of trouble with astronomy. Her husband, a professional, tries to help her. She protests and waves her hands to indicate that she just cannot understand him as he starts explaining. A glaze comes over her eyes: she does not want to take in and work at what he says. He tries every possible way to get through her defenses. He fails. She retreats. In exasperation, he picks up the cereal bowl and says in a loud voice, as if forcing his way in, trying to penetrate her, "This is the planet!" She says, "You always did have trouble expressing your feelings." Stung, he sulks. She feels a fool.

An eighty-one-year-old woman seeks analysis for the first time. Though outwardly she has enjoyed "an easy life," inwardly, she says, it has been difficult: "There is a bigger person in me, a greater demand, that I cannot reach. Something is frozen—to do with love or meaningful work. I cannot reach it." She brings a dream in which she has lost her pocketbook and all its identifying contents. A man points to a closet, saying that it is there, and gives her a bunch of keys. She protests, in the dream, "But I don't know which key!" Thus she reveals a passivity which so captures her that she cannot take what is offered and put it to use.

An actress says that she acts out of "the male part of me," and does best in her work when she lives in good relationship with a man. Then "the female part of me has a place to live." Lacking such relationship, her work suffers because she dare not let herself succeed, fearing it will kill the female part: "I'll become a man." Thus she traces her repeated failure, always just missing getting star parts, to her panic about what they would cost her.

A man questioning whether he is homosexual or heterosexual reflects that in relation to a man he lives out of a "female part of me," but still worries whether there will be "enough room for the male part of me." In relation to women he feels he must be a performing male, which he finds exhausting. Another man, who does not accept his homosexual feelings, longs for the "manhood I don't have to rub off on me," the manhood he finds in younger, more muscular, more attractive men.

A man in his thirties finds himself compulsively attracted to teenage girls. He has worked very hard to get to his present station in life, his profession, marriage, high standing in the community. He says he has "lost his adolescence," meaning he has put behind him a dreamy, poetic, idealistic part of himself, in order to survive and solidify himself against the pull of the addiction to drugs and alcohol of his whole family. He has succeeded and has achieved a sturdy enough ego. Now the lost pieces of life compel his attention; the young girls are exactly the age at which he cut himself off from his own soul.

A woman who resists claiming all her authority, wanting to stay in a girlish mode right into her late thirties, falls in love with a man half her age. That yanks her out of her little girl, dependent mode and forces her to claim her authority as the older woman she is.

A woman scientist has worked hard on a difficult experiment, feeling she has worked "like a man." Then she looks to her close male friend to "reward" her. He misses her signal. She falls into bad moods and wants him to get her out of them, to slay the dragon of her depression and rescue her from her isolated castle. He fails again. She knows that if she were to go off alone, she could free herself. She knows that no matter what the man does it will not be enough. But she does not go off alone; she waits on him instead, and then he feels that she is acting like his mother—full of unending expectations and negative reproaches.

A woman professional, effective in eliciting energy and idealism in others, stimulating them to come together as a community, finds when she is sick and needs some encouraging energy to come her own way that she is ignored. "It is like a man giving a speech: he turns to the audience, to others, to everybody but me. He never turns toward me, to give me a helping hand. My ideals do not help me, only others."

A woman erupts in anger at a man who says he wants to see her and then acts as if she has imposed the date upon him. In his eyes she becomes the demanding woman he dreads. When she arrives, he does nothing but complain about his teeth, his fatigue, his work. If she shows little sympathy, he accuses her of hard-heartedness. She finally accepts her anger as related to his behavior, not hers.

A man finds his impulsive, even bumptious assertiveness calmed and brought to anchor in some deep place through his wife's warm, open reception of him. She in turn finds his assertiveness galvanizes her to speak out of her own views about what she thinks. Another woman's sharp, warm humor dries out her husband's soggy victimhood and blotterlike guilt. A popular radio program, through its mocking of stereotyped sex roles, alludes to a secret known only to the most intimate of couples, the amiable exchange of identities: "Lake Woebegone, where all the women are strong and all the men are good-looking. . . ."

A celibate nun finds Jesus addressing her in prayer. He wants her to want him more even than her own wholeness, because he wants her "to be a whole, passionate woman." The woman thus stumbles on the startling fact that God's version of our wholeness may be more expansive than our own.

A man drives everyone crazy in an office by making up meaningless work for them to do. He consumes other people's time and energies. "It's as if he has no penis!" one woman complains, "He sticks out nothing. He makes a big vacuum that sucks us all into nothing." His colleagues accumulate rage against him.

A creative woman stuck in her writing comes to her adviser to ask for help. She tells a dream of three appliances plugged into one socket, overloading it. She thinks she should remove one of the appliances, which means to cut something out of her life to make more room for her work. But the adviser senses an atmosphere of resentment, a stubborn refusal to receive. "Why not get an additional plug, to find additional ways to plug into the current, instead of giving up something essential to your life?" Quickly, the woman answers, "But how?" and foists every inner inclination to find connection between insight and action onto the adviser, as if to say, You be the plug. The adviser feels that this is a conversation among three people—the two of them, and a third critical voice in the woman who stands there blocking all access to ideas and their fueling energy.

A man says with great shock and pain he cannot believe he is involved in such deceit as he has been reading about in the papers, the backstairs liaisons of John F. Kennedy and Martin Luther King. To be carrying on an affair and lying to his wife—it defies everything in which he believes. Yet he feels forced to find a missing part of himself that has taken up residence in relation to the "other woman" in his own life. He has lost access to that part everywhere else, including his marriage. This part of him, young, vulnerable, and defenseless, also carries his connection to living. To think of losing it makes him feel suicidal.

Two people find each other, like animals stepping into a clearing and spotting a mate of the same stripe and fur. They never thought such love and passion possible. For the sake of it they undergo pain and upheaval of their whole lives and suffer guilt at hurting others as well, even children, in order to come together.[4]

People find themselves colluding with a government that gathers more and more power to itself. Their lack of interference exists side by side with their belief in democratic process.[5] Why such disinclination to rouse themselves to opposition? An outer enemy we know, with a stronghold of power, combats a worse, a diffuse or even unconscious fear, buried since childhood, always denied, of an all-in-all Great Mother on whom we are utterly dependent. A totalitarian government both defines and limits what we fear in such fantasy.

The examples could be multiplied with every psychoanalytic practice, Jungian or otherwise. Literature and the visual arts, film, and the theater offer examples. Even music supports the use of the anima/animus theory, and not simply from the biographies of its composers or performers. We deal here with a groping toward sexual understanding, the attempts to make sense of sexuality wherever it touches us, in body, psyche, or soul, knowing them as vehicles of ego and self. We see as we do this, as we look at the examples, how fitting these terms are—anima and animus—how their odd mixture of grandeur and indeterminateness makes sense, at least in the large, of our sexual lives and helps define the territory in which we lead those lives.

The word *anima* has a history that connects it with the mind as the dwelling place of thought and feeling and with the air we breathe, with movements in the air from small breezes to great winds that carry all before them. The anima can be read as the breath of life or the creature endowed with it. It animates us: it speaks for living being and for the life that is in love—*vos meae carissimae animae,* says Cicero, using anima in almost all its senses, "my dearest souls."

The word *animus* carries with it similar resonances. It speaks, too, for the vital principle, a word for the rational soul in human beings as opposed to or contrasted with the body. It shares with the Hebrew *ruach* all the large-scale implications of life, soul, mind, spirit, intellect, sensibility, will, mental powers, imagination, fancy, judgment, feeling, conscience, consciousness, all the refractions of meaning and association that gather around the movements of the air, the winds, our breathing.

What is significant in the application of these words to our sexual lives is that they link material and immaterial worlds. They are, as we are, compounded of flesh and spirit. They are archetypes and therefore far-reaching, extending back into history, reaching down into our lives minute by minute, day by day, as we live them, reaching forward at least by shadowy suggestion, into whatever lies ahead for us. One way to describe them, which is true of all archetypes but especially of this pair, is as rings around the human tree. From them, we can gather much about our past, how far it reaches, what its ardors have left in us in permanent markings. In them, we can see something of the possibilities that lie before us, our openings, our closings, our strivings, our shuttings down.

In anima/animus theory there is always a telic bias, a drive to account for sources, for roots, to make some attempt to name them or at least to describe them. It is not to offer final explanations but rather to identify something that smells, tastes, feels like home. As Jung said, in Delphic mood, "Life is teleology *par excellence;* it is the intrinsic striving towards a goal, and the living organism is a system of directed aims which seek to fulfill themselves."[6] The fulfillment in anima/animus life may be no more than the claiming of our egos, but what a claiming it is! For we see that our name, in relation to an inner other, is ultimately a pointing to the source, a putting down of roots, if our ego claim is firm enough, if the name we identify as our own really belongs to us. That is the indispensable beginning of self-acceptance. That is how we begin to find and organize and hold onto a self. That is when we get started on the great long march across the bridge that extends from ego to Self.

THE BRIDGE

We are all of us susceptible to the pull of the anima/animus archetypes, to their actions, attractions, and struggles and the revelations they set in motion. They occur between us and within us. They touch our sexual life, our spiritual seeking: they infuse our creative work and give energies to our pathology. They can interfere with and facilitate relations to our children, our colleagues, dream figures, whole institutions. The "facts" and "motifs" that Jung says never change are the anima/animus figures that address us from deep inside ourselves and from far outside.

Our contrasexuality, anima or animus, forms a bridge between our ego—center of our conscious identity—and the Self—center of the whole psyche, both conscious and unconscious. Anima and animus map routes to certain experiences of the Self that bring us more into life, that make it possible for us to face reality. The anima/animus figures work to build a bridge across which the contents of the Self can come to address the ego, to put questions to us about our very existence. When these questions come, they seem to issue from an Other, quite apart from us, who says, in effect, "You must deal with me, confront me, respond, receive, even reject me, but here I am and you cannot escape me."[7]

As with the man caught in compelling attractions to teenage girls or the woman whose writing was blocked from within, these "figures" cannot be talked around or reasoned away. As Jung says, "Concepts are coined and negotiable values; but images are life."[8] We cannot just dismiss anima/animus images that rear up to face us in the privacy of our dreams or the intimacy of our sexual meetings, or swim in the undercurrents of our social and cultural lives. They bring us to experiences of the Self that make us feel life really is worth living when in such moments they color our perceptions with awe at the very fact of being. These contents of Self are matters of life and death; they put the central questions to us.[9]

It makes no difference what our race or creed or class, or whether we are single or married, celibate or divorced, heterosexual, homosexual, lesbian, young or old. We all must face and answer the other who confronts us from a sexual departure point opposite to our conscious gender identity. We all share the task of putting these parts of ourselves together to compose an identifiable person for ourselves, with all its positive possibilities and inevitable tribulations.

Facing this task, we know, each of us, the differences that set us apart—accidental, fateful, idiosyncratic, our own special circumstances. Did we grow up without a father? Have we chosen a celibate life or mothered children? Are we caught in our cultural definitions of gender identity, in democratic or hierarchical conceptions of male-female relations? We do not live in a vacuum. Family history and the history of the race, the time and place in which we live, every detail of our life enters into this task, enables us or disables us for it, makes it possible for us to understand its special terms, its demands, its extraordinary possibilities.

In focusing on the anima/animus bridge, we are expanding Jung's notion of these archetypal figures as "unwelcome intruders" who compel our attention through their irresistible attractions as dream and fantasy personages and their obsessive projections onto other people. Jung says that when we bring personifications of the anima/animus archetypes to consciousness in ourselves, "we convert them into bridges to the unconscious."[10] Alternatively, "It is because we are not using them purposefully as functions that they remain personified complexes." To the degree that we actively, consciously, try to understand the anima/animus archetype, "the personified figure of anima or animus will disappear. It [then] becomes a function of relationship between conscious and unconscious."[11]

Where does the bridge take us, then? Right to the Self, bringing us, as conscious and unconscious in us move toward each other, to a meeting with reality that is available to us when our psyche is opened up in this way. We are pliable, open to ourselves, pressing something precious into the life we lead with others. There is, for example, the startling example of a woman who dreamed of a man emerging from fishing in deep waters with a cure for incurable disease. After speaking about this discovery to everyone around him, he moved to kiss the dreamer, saying he would love her forever.[12] This was an animus figure opening the dreamer to heal herself. It is precisely through such a connection to what heals and loves one that healing emerges in the world.

Jung is not alone among psychologists in recognizing these "facts" and "motifs" that he describes as the anima/animus bridge. Freud points to something of the sort in positing the bisexuality of all persons, which we live out individually in our own combinations of feminine and masculine identifications, in Oedipus complexes resolved or unresolved. Klein uncovers masculine and feminine positions that each of us not only traverses developmentally, but retains as a set of attitudes toward oneself and others. Winnicott formulates his own ideas of male and female elements that belong to all of us, and Guntrip insists—with examples—that the female element is always what gets us started as persons.[13] All these theorists speak about our need to put these parts together. Resolution of the Oedipus complex, for example, can offer a vision of wholeness. Winnicott's wholeness comes from integrating our various notions of motherhood into an understanding of the feminine ability to be at once exciting and reliable, to have passion in an abiding tension.

We need these theories to hold us to what is central to our lives, the men and women, in fact and fantasy, in the flesh and in the spirit. This theoretical focus provides some security in our actual relations with other people, both children and adults. It permits us to see ourselves in our cultural setting, in the movements of consciousness and the unconscious in our own time.

Anima/animus theory can be misused. It can lead us into the aery-faery language of generalized myths that transmogrify men and women into gods and goddesses and lose sight of the personal and historical dimensions of our lives in their earthly reality. Jung's anima/animus thinking is firmly pitted against any tendency to mythologize our early "object relations," to confuse, as Winnicott puts it, early with deep.[14] Anima and animus figures have a very clear source within the psyche, and Jung directs us to pay close attention to the fantasy images that arise inside us. They are formidable, for they embody timeless symbols that can collide with any event or thing or person in our lives and make for trauma.

Deliberate, thoughtful attention to our fantasies can free us from bondage to the so-called "bad object."[15] Take, for example, a woman who complained of men treating her as a commodity, sexual or comforting or just convenient to have around. She dared to pray the Jesus prayer of Russian spirituality, repeating, often as much as a hundred times, "Lord Jesus, have mercy upon me, a sinner." Shocked, dislocated, but freed as well, she reported, "The Spirit came into me like fire and burned me right out." She saw that she herself had looked upon men as commodities: "They were objects to me—to love me, reassure me, to make me feel safe. The whole thing was reversed, upside down. It was like a revelation."[16] Her fantasy about men fed inevitably into her disappointment in them. Seeing our fantasy for what it is does not automatically make us into angels, but it does greatly reduce our burdens.

ARCHETYPE AND STEREOTYPE

Recognizing the role of fantasy in our relationships enlarges our understanding of how anima and animus function to bridge ego and Self experiences. It also sharpens for us the difference between Jung and other theorists in this area. With Jung's anima/animus vocabulary, we have a way to talk about the spiritual component of sexuality and the connectors between consciousness and the unconscious in our struggles for identity.

To find our identity in the morass of conflicting parts with which it is faced means going down into deep, unconscious places. We must go beyond the limits of our personal histories, of our memories and the memories of those close to us, into the collective unconscious—the objective psyche—that underlies all human life. We must suffer our egos being pulled across the boundaries of their own world into Self country, that place distinguished by its own particular demands and goals. Jung defined it as "the unconscious realm of the psyche . . . the place where the living Spirit that is more than man manifests itself."[17] Anima and animus bring us, drag us, to face the Spirit.

The anima/animus figure presents itself to the ego as "other," both familiar and foreign. This "person" is human, but speaks from a sexual departure point opposite to our own. Sexuality functions as a metaphor of otherness; the spiritual hides in the sexual. We can only possess the opposite sex as an anima or animus image, never as a body part. But it opens within us a space where both sexes can meet in imagination.[18]

The anima/animus bridge functions to connect ego and Self, not to merge them. The contrasexual archetypes are border figures, taking us from one sexual departure point to another, from the personal to the collective, from the conscious to the archetypal, from the ego to Self. What seems spiritual, whether we live with a sense of meaning or of futility, for instance, shows itself as all mixed up with the sexual, the way we share existence, in the flesh, with others. What seems private turns out to be social, for our struggles to connect with an Other at our own center also reveal connections to a center far from us. In this struggle, we feel not as if we were on some isolated journey but rather were intimately bound up with other people—a woman, for example, with other women and with womanliness, and at the same time, like a man, identified with men's points of view, almost in a man's skin. In the same way, we know that the other sex, however we experience it, feels bound up with us in similar fashion.

The spiritual can expand our sexual view into a wide and flexible contemplative gaze onto all kinds of coupling; the sexual can draw the spiritual into the most specific here-and-now interaction with another concrete human being. Two terms Jung connects with animus and anima—*logos* as discrimination of truth and *eros* as relatedness to life—are helpful here. We can see that connecting to an anima or animus image can lead us to incarnate "principle" in ourselves, logos lived in the life, bodily. We know in the most direct way the truth by which we live that makes our blood quicken and our heart thump. We know that eros in the spirit as well as in the body is sexuality animated by connection to being. Sexuality thus both moves us toward incarnation and pulls us across the borders of our ego identities toward otherness, toward the center.

Sexual responses in their spiritual function act to pull us through to something larger and more encompassing than the ego, what Jung calls the Self. But here we must be careful, for this anima/animus region, where sex and spirit tangle, sort themselves out, and conjoin, can also be a place where heart and soul are broken, fall into addiction, and feel compelled to do things against their own interests. We learn to fear this place where we can be hurt so badly, where we feel betrayed. In defense, we make steely vows, not only against betrayers, but against ourselves for opening so far.

It makes very little difference what we vow, however; we have been to the fount of erotic knowledge, the place where the sexual and the spiritual meet. We can deny it, to ourselves and others. We can repress it, not simply by pushing it as far from consciousness as possible, but by that special skill of our time that reduces all experiences to the lowest possible level, so that where the spiritual mixes with the sexual we efface it from serious consideration and translate it all into physical terms. Ecstasy is glandular, no more. Doubt, incompleteness, the pain that comes when one has sought a meeting of persons and has found only an exchange of juices, all can be explained as a failure of technique, an inadequacy of experience—yours or his or hers.

But the anima/animus drive remains. Something is missing, some primordial understanding, some deeper erotic knowledge that is not known to those who live in the sexual combat zone, those for whom love can never be more than a euphemism for a bodily thrust. But even they somewhere within them, no matter how deeply buried, know that we all carry in our viscera something that cannot be laid out on the autopsy table and want to have it out in the open, to be able to identify it and make use of it, to experience it.

That is the erotic knowledge that our contrasexual dialogue brings us news of. Speaking out of our primary sexual identity to our inner opposite, animus or anima, or being addressed by it, we learn something of the complexity of our human identity. We learn it in these exchanges and accept that we are learning something of central importance to us because of the intensity of participation that this dialogue commands. It may come out of a sexual meeting with another person, at whatever level of physical engagement, with or without satisfaction to ourselves or to the other. It may come from fantasy meetings, from dream engagements, from confrontations sought or unsought. We may or may not recognize that we are involved in a significant interior exchange. What we know beyond question is that our feelings have been deeply stirred, our sense of ego or self has been piqued, our imagination has been pried open. Something beyond the achievement of physical pleasure, or the failure to accomplish it, or confinement to some drab way station on the road to or from it, has been encountered, has made demands, has surprised us with the astonishing degree of feeling it has aroused.

The urgency of this arousal is such that it overwhelms our days and nights. This, we sometimes think, is love. And it may well be. Certainly we know, on such occasions, that we have met our master, as the god of love identifies himself to Dante in *La Vita Nuova,* a figure of terrible aspect who, settled in an atmosphere of fiery mist, offers the poet's flaming heart for eating to the lady who has won that heart, a fearsome act that she then performs. At this moment in Dante's *New Life,* he has not in fact been received by the young woman who will transform everything in him. This is simply one of the young women who will catch him for a short while on the road to his jubilant meetings with

Beatrice Portinari, the blessed girl who inspired the writing of this small masterpiece and will lead him in person, in fantasy, in every known form of love's being and becoming, to the composition of the *Divine Comedy*.[19]

It does not matter that the fervor we feel will not issue forth in a work of Dantean dimension. It does not even tell against us that the experience which spurred such an intensity of response was perilously close to a mere glandular reflex. The size of this realm and the thoughts, feelings, and images it unleashes is so great that it can accommodate everything from the allegorical splendor of Dante to the minor itches of a troubled gonad. In each case questions are asked and answers are attempted, and they always go beyond surfaces. Because so much of our being has been roused, we are never content simply to let the experience fall to the side. We may not engage it in any deliberate way; our conscious life may not be troubled any more than it might be by a meal made memorable by the force of searing condiments. But within us, note is taken; our anima or animus reacts; some inner dialogue follows. We have entered the world of spirit that all along the way shares borders with the sexual kingdom, where there is a steady flow of population— which is to say of feeling, affect, emotion, thought, images, actings out— back and forth.

Scheherazade offers an instructive example. Without her help, the sultan in the famous *Arabian Nights* situation would have fulfilled his vow to execute every woman with whom he lay. She stopped him by appealing to his imagination with her thousand tales told on a thousand nights. She slowly opened in him a space of interior contemplation.[20] As long as we resist finding the Scheherazade—the helper—in each of us, we will go on reading headlines in newspapers around our world that tell of a woman who hires a thug to kill her husband, of a man who beats his girlfriend to death, of elders sexually abusing children, of a gay man murdering his lover, of rape, of contempt between the sexes. In touching our spirit and sexuality, anima and animus leave their marks on all society, sometimes bloody ones.

Critics who accuse Jung of crafting new sexual stereotypes with his contrasexual theory, or of merely reflecting the prejudices of his own cultural context, altogether miss the frightening dynamism of the archetype, against which he warned so strenuously.[21] It is easy to miss. "To understand the peculiar phenomenon of the archetype one needs a lot of practical experience," Jung explains, reminding us that "the numinous quality, so indispensable to the recognition of an archetype, is an indefinable imponderable like the expressing of the human eye, which is indubitable yet indescribable."[22]

A cursory reading of Jung might support objections to anima/animus theory as a mere recording of stereotypes. Seizing some passages out of context, we can come away with the conviction that Jung exactly equates Eros with feeling, with anima, and with women, and Logos just as precisely with thinking, with animus, and with men. The two sexes appear then to be divided up as matter and spirit, feeling and thinking, home and public life, action and passivity, penetration and reception. In isolated extracts, we can gather from Jung that women possess only a diffused Yin-like consciousness and therefore need a masculine animus spirit to counteract their passive mentality. Or, that men possess a sharp Yang-like consciousness that needs the balancing of an emotional, passive anima. These categories appear to hold regardless of a person's typology and without showing any awareness of the power of cultural conditioning to foist gender roles upon the sexes.

Jung's metaphors in such passages seem to stand as absolutes, and his own feeling reactions—such as negative responses to a woman's animus—seem to be written into definition. Animus appears to function only to disrupt, to madden, to pronounce. Confusion over relatedness and relationship makes it sound as if all females are experts at relationship and all males mere fools.

Many Jungians recognize how easily animus and anima may be reified into stereotypes. Some have suggested we think of anima and animus as two types of consciousness that we all possess.[23] Unfortunately, their attempt to free us from constricting stereotypes only lands us in another set of fixed definitions in which animus and anima represent a content that remains the same no matter where or in whom it turns up. But the anima/animus contents that cross the ego-Self bridge are insistently individual. They do not permit reduction to culture-bound prejudices or anything resembling a narrowing sexism. Reductive thinking altogether misses the epochal nature of Jung's insight, however difficult his articulation of it, or "clumsy," as it seemed to him.

In fact, as a closer reading of Jung and larger understanding of the implications of his theory might reveal, everything about archetypes combats the finality of systems and the reductions of stereotyping. If an application of archetypes approaches a typology, as with anima and animus it is only too easy to begin to do, it is a typology to end all typologies. Sexual stereotypes cannot survive the close scrutiny of archetypal analysis, which, in its mixings of symmetries and asymmetries and easy acceptance of a pairing of opposites in each of us, constantly defies simplistic generalization about men and women. Double meanings, in this way of looking at things, are always better than single ones, and a refusal to impute final meaning at all is a governing negative principle wherever judgment about sexual behavior is called for.

None of this is to say that value judgments are banned from the anima/animus world. Archetypes are often in themselves the carriers of values, but they are values that spring from or seek the truth of Being, never compliance with an ideology or a trendy reading of correctness. With anima/animus, as with all archetypal categories, we resist fixed definitions and declare preconceptions out of bounds, however much they may seem to resemble reasonable conclusions from archetypal lingerings in human behavior.

If there is a typology in this archetypal world of anima and animus, it is a common-sense one—father, mother, daughter, son, brother, sister, husband, wife. There are the obvious dream figures—hero, heroine, lover, beloved, villain, goodness incarnate, rampant carnality. Ideal images mix with a sharpened awareness of reality in this peopling of anima/animus, which is useful as a brief identification of characters in a playbill may be, never to foreclose our understanding of our actual parents or children or siblings, but simply to connect them with the millions of others who have played those parts in the past and have left us some clear directions about the ways available to us for playing them. To understand what the past has to teach us here, we must avoid all the facile sexual oppositions that flatten men and women into dimensionless categories, such as the maddening granting of intuition to women in contrast to men's intellectual skills, or the appropriation of aggression to the male and of an opposing peacemaking quality to the female. Such readings are no more acceptable here than those ancient fatuous assignments of fickleness to women and dependability to men, of a body-centered preoccupation on the part of women and a matching lack of interest and clumsiness of body on men's part, or of a feebleness amounting to helplessness in women that is compensated for by the physical strength and resourcefulness of men. The best we can say about this sort of generality is that it offers a statistical summation of the roles in which economic, social, and sexist surfaces have replaced archetypal truths.

Neither men nor women are ever any one single thing, but if they are anything, even a bundle of things, it is never their stereotyped roles. Women have been hunters and fighters; men have been feeders. Men have been ornamental, gentle, intuitive, fickle, passive. Women have been crude, clumsy, inattentive to their bodies, violent, intellectist, confident and dependable in filling those supposedly customary roles. They are as they always have been, more and less than they have been thought to be, both men and women, and far more interesting in their complex archetypal identities than in their simple stereotyped reductions.[24]

Anima and animus do not represent a set content; they display a dynamic function or process. When we slap the animus label onto people, as if it always meant the same thing, we are in fact describing a serious dysfunction of the bridge, a breakdown. The animus, in the case of woman, can never be made to fit reductive generalization; it always comes in its own highly individual textures.[25] A professional woman, whose training extended beyond the doctorate, clearly exemplifies this. She found that her animus figures—whether in dream or reality—consistently appeared as big, silent men, utterly nonverbal, who stood calmly next to her or gently placed themselves on top of her, to "earth" her, to connect her to her deeper feminine self. Another woman, who felt herself dumbly inarticulate, married a man because of his brilliant flow of words. Years later, she sought analysis because she feared that if he did not shut up and listen to her, she was going to kill him.

We share among us the same set of anima/animus functions that make the bridge between ego and Self. Where we differ is in the contents, special to each of us, which move across that bridge, though we often describe them in general terms as issuing from a departure point that is the exact opposite of our conscious gender identity.

Both June Singer and Claire Douglas, in their writing, offer the same interesting way to understand anima/animus theory and to protect its seminal and liberating substance. Using Jung's own descriptions of what he called his Number 1 and Number 2 personalities, they attribute certain limiting aspects of Jung's anima/animus ideas to his first self, the product of generations of pastors in a Swiss society branded by its own misogyny, child of a father disheartened by his loss of faith, and a complex, confusing mother, who suffered from severe depression in Jung's early childhood, but who also offered uncanny insights and, at least some of the time, a jolly, fat, maternal disposition. Where the Number 1 personality is reflected in anima/animus theory, conventional thought dominates. With Number 2, a radical originality arrives, as Jung works to free our understanding of contrasexuality from the gender stereotypes of his time, setting us the task of integrating differences into identity, otherness into wholeness, whether it fits the socially prescribed mode or not. Logos and eros both have their place. Our characteristic, most developed type of ego-functioning must be joined to our least developed, most inferior way of functioning as it is presented to us by the anima/animus figures that people our dreams, or burst out in our actions at the most inappropriate moments. Somehow we must integrate into our conscious gender identity that opposite identity that resides in our unconscious.

In Jung we see the remarkable range of the ways individuals present themselves to the world and the task we all share of putting our parts together for a psychologically true self-presentation. Jung's emphasis in this task, on the archetypal aspect of anima and animus, opens us to the primordial chthonic resources of the human psyche. New and old forces, new and old images rise up to challenge and renew forms of sexual and spiritual congress, and thus to pull us beyond the self-denying banalities of group-ego identity toward more fulfilling as well as more generous forms of community.

Jung helps us deconstruct our all-too-human tendency to reify insights into new sets of rules. We seek to incarnate what is original and fresh in our lives, but only too quickly discard what we cannot easily manage or understand. What we first receive comfortably, we fasten on, and eventually harden its behavior patterns into rules and regulations, in social, sexual, or religious life. An initial set of experiences becomes a prescribed way, the only way, and its associated symbols of masculine and feminine our defining typology.

Jung helps us confess that in thus receiving one set of signs, symbols, and experiences, we hide from the possibility of experiencing and understanding others, fearing the bright fire, the sparkling stone, the scintillae of light, the deep fruitful darkness. We take only the quickly graspable parts of what offers itself in sexual and spiritual experience and legislate those parts into the all of reality. Jung is groping here toward some annunciation of what he understands as the startling shock of that wholeness. We can realize, he is saying, that each of us is composed of *different* parts—a bundle of them that we identify and call by *different* names—and that all the gatherings of bundles of parts make up the bundle of bundles that we identify and call by the name of wholeness.

We come upon, each of us, inside the bundle of ourselves, an objective other who lives in the midst of our subjectivity. In a further identification of the textures of our complex being, we discern the objective Subject that lives in the midst of our subjectivity, sees us always, mirrors us, receives us, honors us as subjects. The separation between me and you, us and them, breaks down. We find, instead, the me–me combination, the us–us, linking the host of subjects honored and loved that the imagery and rhetoric of mystical theology try to capture. The saints write of this in their own odd and wonderful ways. Saint Teresa of Avila talks of His Majesty who takes up residence at the center of our souls. Buber talks of the Thou seen in each face, taking precedence before the I. Meister Eckhart penetrates to the great unnameable silence within and beyond the Godhead and its names. Jung talks of the Self and the anima/animus archetypes and of the bridge to us that they construct.

Seeing the anima and animus archetypes in such large terms, as the bridge of the Self to each of us, as individuals and as members of groups, Jung was returning to the original and largest meaning of the archetype. He found the word in the work of Saint Augustine and with it a great cluster of associations reaching back to the Greek roots of the word and its employment by Plato and Aristotle and the pre-Socratic philosophers. With the archetypes, we deal with starting points, guiding principles, ultimates in a sense, grounded in some *Urstoff,* an underlying essence in things.

All that is conveyed by *arche,* the Greek word that ranges in meaning and association from absolute beginnings, the origin of all things, to sovereignties and powers, corners and ends, magistracies and all commanding offices. We are in the rarefied atmosphere of Platonic ideas, at the end point of Aristotle's *materia prima,* which yearns for form, he says, as the female does for the male. There is little of basic importance that does not come under the rubrics of archetype in the ancient world—the four elements that make up the material world (earth, air, water, fire), the stages of human development from distant *archai* to present complexities, birth and rebirth, every movement of being up to the transmigration of souls.

Perhaps the richest and most useful of translations into words of the *arche* and thus of archetypes is that of Anaximander of Miletus. This "kinsman, pupil and successor" of that Thales whom we record as the first Greek philosopher was, we can gather even from the fragments we have of his thought, determined to deal with as much as he could of human experience in a systematic way, which makes all the more persuasive his understanding of the originative essence as *to apeiron*. This "principle and element of existing things," as some accounts of Anaximander have it, the *apeiron*, "contained the whole cause of the coming-to-be and destruction of the world." It is not reducible to water or any of the other elements. It is eternal and unaging; it surrounds all the worlds and is the source of all.

The beginning and fount of all things, then, is the Indeterminate, for that is what the *apeiron* stands for. We come, in this reading of things, from boundlessness, endlessness, the undetermined, the infinite, the unlimited. Those are the textures of the archetypes of the Jungian metaphysic. That is what we invoke when we move across the anima/animus bridge from ego to Self, a world without limits, not only in its origins but in its continuing being.

Anima/Animus as Complex

MAP: ANIMA/ANIMUS AS COMPLEX

People come to Jungian analysis, they or their symptoms say, because they feel unalive, frightened by a seeming inability to make intimate contact with another person or with some sense of meaning in their lives. They feel, often, as if they were falling apart, almost split in two. Some, if something does not change fundamentally, think of killing themselves. The psyche expresses these dilemmas in all sorts of images and bodily symptoms along with hints for their resolution. We ask the psyche what it is trying to bring about.

It is possible to map the territory in which these experiences occur with the special aid of anima/animus theory. This is a map, once made, of great practical usefulness, not only for the clinician but to all who are interested in the marks of human interiority in, for example, literature, the arts, and religion. It cuts through great densities, to move toward the point of it all. Vladimir Horowitz said of his performances: "I play music behind the notes. I search for it and play from this other side." We find, in relation to this theory, that we are trying to do the same—to see how anima and animus usher in the Self and lead us into that space of emptiness behind the notes of theory. There, our words and images stop and the Spirit evoked by the Self greets us.

We are less interested in proving a theory than we are in arriving at a place or entering a process that allows us to speak of what are familiarly classified as unspeakable experiences. How can we describe blazing passions that make us all feel at times that sex is a consuming madness, how communicate that total pouring out and deep taking in of self and other? How can we verbalize those moments of arrival at what it is all for, what makes it all worthwhile, that sounding, rushing of the parts to join up with the whole, that not only moves us to ecstatic pleasure but sets off a deep interior humming that lasts for days?

Jung's anima/animus theory is above all an attempt to map our living out of the kinds of situations that bring us to our center of being, to where we feel it and know that we feel it. This is it. What is here in this moment is what really matters. This is the immediate experience that Jung saw as the core of religion.[1]

Jung uses images to describe the psyche.[2] The image that best describes the anima or animus complex is a nest of interacting circles. For Jung, complexes make up the psyche's normal parts. We only notice them when they disrupt our functioning.[3] This complex in us, in its entirety, with the archetypes of anima or animus at its center, becomes the bridge to connect ego and Self. When we integrate this complex, with all its intertwined parts of our sexual identity, we do not really notice it much: it simply functions as a passageway of communication between the contents of ego and Self. We take full notice, however, when it shows itself out of sync—or, worse, breaks down. Then the affects and images, the behavioral and emotional patterns of the contra-sexual complex show themselves in personified forms that may seize or sabotage the ego, that compel projections onto other people, that do anything that will command our attention.

Like any other complex, the anima or animus one operates in compensatory relationship to consciousness.[4] It presents to us a crucial other point of view, one that consciousness has not fully admitted, but that we must reckon with. In struggling to do so, it greatly enlarges our ego worlds, personal and collective. For a personal ego example, we have a man of heavy mien, of dense conscious attitude, a serious and responsible citizen who found himself faced in dreams with elusive erotic anima figures that teased and aroused him, scenting the air with the lure of enchanting pleasures and far-off places. Once, when this cluster of psychic energies projected itself with particular force, he found himself following a strange woman home from a bus stop. To include the anima's view would balance his one-sidedness. Another man who appeared as puckish, somewhat insubstantial, always dissolving, dreamed of anima figures that made beelines to what they wanted. He needed the strength the anima offered, otherwise it lived through him in negative ways. Others complained they felt he was always scheming to get something from them for nothing.

In our late-twentieth-century culture, we constantly meet archetypal images long suppressed, of the masculine and feminine emerging to challenge and compensate for an insufficient, self-denying collective sexual consciousness. The dark feminine, not necessarily angry but darkly enigmatic, compensates for the nice, light, agreeable feminine. One woman calls it the "source feminine," another the "uterus god." A chthonic image here is of the wildly angry feminine, raging at being denied, shouting back, throwing off, shutting out the roles of consort, helpmeet, nurturer, feeder, guide. She will go her journey and the hell with you! The archetypal images of Amazon and formidable virgin emerge as dominant. The primordial masculine comes up from the dark earth in its identifying imagery, or the opaque depths of the sea in combat with the sky or sun god who descends from above. Images of a masculine wildness mix with those of a male tenderness, quiet feeling, even an impulse to nurture. We get a mixture of violence and sentimentality in our male "buddy" movies, of police or soldiers or criminals. Arnold Schwarzenegger plays a caring cyborg—an all-powerful monster with a heart. General Schwarzkopf shed tears in a television interview during the Gulf War and said he did not trust a military man who could not cry. Complex is the right name for this sort of fullness of affect, especially when compared to the simpleminded posturings of the macho figure.

In the Freudian tradition, we tend to think of the complex almost entirely in negative terms. We associate it with repression of awkward or embarrassing desires, or with trauma, some decisive event in our lives, long buried in our unconscious, perhaps, and far from easy access, but still decisive in shaping our behavior. So it is we think of that center of Freudian theory, the Oedipus complex, where a child competes, at least in fantasy, for the affections of the parent of the opposite sex and conceives, at some depth of unconscious wish-fulfillment, a murderous hatred for the competing parent of the same sex. So it is that women, in this same tradition, may be thought to be favored with a castration complex, the result of their arduous efforts to assure themselves that they have in their sexual armory something as good as a penis, even if only symbolically. Failing to find that assurance, they feel anxious, threatened, castrated.

What is clear, even in the largely negative inflection of the concept of the complex, is that conscious and unconscious elements are joined together in it in some considerable number and in constant movement. The constituents of the complex, as of any other part of our psyche's life, are almost never at rest. Moving ahead or moving backward, moving around the traumatic event or turning over the embattled Oedipal territory or running in every direction to avoid confrontation with event or territory, the psyche is always in motion, whether we are directly aware of it or not.

The complex, as Jung uses this highly charged term, is richly described by the word itself: it is a totality of many parts in intricate relation with each other. It is complicated, dense, and often as a result hard to read, a difficulty compounded by its multiple half-lives, in and out of consciousness and the unconscious. Still, its motion-filled life is at least as often positive as negative. We can get at its dynamism—indeed we must, for what moves in it is life itself.[5]

We can gather much about the complicated nature of the complex as Jung uses the term, and as we do here, from an examination of the origin, structure, and expression of the contrasexual complex. In each of these defining elements of the life of anima and animus, there are subdivisions in groups of three—three factors, three sets of images and forms drawn together in concentric circles, three modes of expression. What is significant is that these are groups of three, not two, not four. An even number invariably suggests a symmetrical balance and, in effect, a simplicity of interpretation. With three comes complexity. The possibility of unforeseen and unbalanceable permutations and combinations increases enormously with an odd number. And that is as it must be in the life of the psyche: there are always more variables than one anticipates. In their less-than-predictable and always intricate interactions, we claim our egos and move to develop a self. It is, as always with the psyche, a beckoning complexity inviting us to make what sense of it we can, and never more insistently than with the contrasexual complex.

Origin

In Jung's early contributions to gender studies, he tracked the origin of our contrasexual complex, discovering three factors that accounted for it.[6] First, biologically, we harbor recessive genes of the opposite sex in our body. Second, psychologically, we introject and fantasize about persons of the opposite sex in our own early significant object-relations. We respond as well to the more subtle but no less decisive influence of the views of our own sex toward the opposite, and the views about our own sex held by the opposite. In these processes of psychological introjection and projection, dominant cultural images of masculine and feminine play large parts. Finally, symbolically, we register the impact of archetypal images that spring from the collective unconscious—the objective psyche. They become formidable influences upon us in their concretization in our bodily experiences, and as they evolve from our dealings with others and with our culture. Archetypes for the most part transcend consciousness. But their symbols give us pictures of those contents as they are conditioned by the people and world around us.[7] The pictures change, the symbols change, but still, no matter how they change, they convey the dynamism of their archetypal core. Anima and animus persist at the center.

Structure

The structure of the contrasexual complex reveals three concentric circles of interacting images and forms to match the three sets of factors that account for the complex to begin with.[8] The outermost circle describes the personal ring of the complex—all those formative experiences with significant persons of the opposite sex in our lives, especially their responses to our sex, conscious and unconscious, which we bring with us from our first days. This is the large and fruitful realm of object relations, so imaginatively investigated by the leading theorists of the object-relations school, Klein, Winnicott, and Guntrip. Sometimes a problem an analysand brings can be seen as clearly rising from this circle of experience. A middle-aged man successful in running his own business sought analysis over his despair in managing his relations with his new wife, his second. Communication between them was nil. He felt impotent to deal with it. Analysis uncovered a barely buried rage at his father for never telling his mother "to shut up, to behave, to stop dehumanizing the atmosphere." Now, he felt hopeless about his own masculine ability to deal with the dehumanizing attitude that he had absorbed from his mother.

The influence of early object relations on the contrasexual complex can reach even beyond death. A woman in her thirties, of both keen humor and a sharp ethical sense, bewailed the fact she had fallen in love "with a man who wears only polyester!" Her treasured image of the masculine clothed itself in tweeds, her cultural group was the academic world, all the men wore tweeds—the more rumpled the better. She was appalled. And, worse, it appalled her that she was appalled. She felt picky and trite, trivialized to be so upset over a choice of clothes. She found herself shoving magazine ads for Brooks Brothers jackets under her lover's nose, or dragging him out of one store into another. She felt she was betraying their love by this obsession. Her compulsive behavior drove her to look far into herself. What confronted her stunned her. A large pocket of unmourned grief for her father, who had died when she was sixteen, bubbled into consciousness. He wore tweeds. Her personal image of her father, so formative in her construction of her image of the masculine, had disappeared from consciousness when he suddenly died. Now, when she risked intimacy in the present, her unmourned father turned up, intruded himself into her love, insisted on being dealt with. She could not give herself to this new man when part of her was still tied up with her lost father. What looked like a superficial preference in fashion led her to both a preparation for loving fully and a facing of her girlhood self, giving her finally her proper place in her grown-up self, as a woman making ready for marriage.

The collective ring of the complex forms the second circle of the contrasexual complex. Here are found all the dominant influences of our culture, the groups to which we belong that define us, our sex, race, class, nationality, even our historical epoch.[9] For years American television deluged viewers with woman as laundress, cook, and medicine dispenser; as dissipater of all small devils, of odors, of household mess, of family conflict. Man was revealed seated on a horse with a cigarette dangling from his mouth and a gun, visible or not, understood always to be at the ready. In the last years of the twentieth century, we see such simplistic reduction of masculine and feminine not merely dismissed but mocked. The masculine to many has become negative, the sexuality of a tyrannous patriarchy, characterized by rigid defensive thinking, loss of feeling, wounded body sense, responsible for hierarchical arrangements of power that dominate and even rape what is placed in subordinate positions—which is to say, the woman, the earth, the atmosphere, perhaps even the galaxy in which the earth turns. Gone is the positive masculine capacity to generate, to guide, that sticks out and sticks up for people and things, the giving masculine, the male who separates his own needs from the mass in order to reach out for the truths by which we all live. The question remains for those who reject the reductions of today as they did the stereotypes of yesteryear: What does the masculine shorn of these distortions look like?

On the opposite side, the male not at home with himself sees the feminine in his own skewed manner, as rampaging, aggressive, fanatic, as one clinging to doctrines and denials that suffocate, as a sloganeer, as inflexible, as incapable of taking hold of the complex shapes of human sexuality. And here too there is a need to ask the central question of the man who accepts and knows himself: What does the feminine really look like? Can we forget its astonishing power to uncover hidden truths, to go to the heart of things without flinching, to endure ambivalences and create new mixtures out of them, to find the sacred in the ordinary? Instead we too often get patriarchy used only as a bad word, a sort of huge negative animus, an endless retreating into windy abstractions; and the feminine, along with *feminist*—the worst of words—as a falling into a hapless unconscious, a dark sister of the female materialist who bred the rampant "consumerism" of the 1980s.

The women's movement can be understood at least in part as raising to conscious challenge reductive anima images. The experience of so many women in so many cultures of a negative animus voice, persistent in its blaming, always declaring her efforts are "not enough," "do not matter," "cannot succeed," can be understood as resulting in a massive internalization, over centuries, of an institutionalized misogyny.

The third circle of the contrasexual complex describes its archetypal sources in those timeless images that reside in us at a very deep level, often appearing archaic in contrast to the personal and collective images we harbor of masculine and feminine. One woman dreamed of a huge hole in the field of her childhood home.[10] Its gigantic depth and darkness awed her, and the enormous serpentlike snake coming up out of it mesmerized her with fear and fascination. That home was the site of trauma, of early molestation by her brother. The dream snake and its hole both touched the old injury and reached through it to the primordial powers of sexuality, as coming from another, deeper level. It gave her a sense of what moved behind her brother, pushing him to hurt her, and it gave her direct access to her sexuality, through an image of her own, uncontaminated by trauma.

Each of us gives shelter to archetypal images. They act as shelters for us, comprising, as Bachelard says, our "reservoirs of enthusiasm" for Being.[11] Because we are finite and live both in society and history, different archetypal images turn out to be dominant in each of us, shaped by our experiences of our particular mothers and fathers and groups and countries. This level of imagery both moves through our actual experiences of self and others and transcends them. We have to reckon with what "woman" or "man" means to us, what "feminine" and "masculine" connote. Examples of people describing their meetings with the archetypal image at the core of their anima or animus complex show them gathering up their most personal feelings and sense of touching a transpersonal dimension far outside themselves.

A priest seeks analysis because the persona demands of his profession have gobbled up all his life, as he sees it, leaving him nothing inside. He feels he lacks "any capacity to be." On the personal level he remembers "bringing myself up," feeling his mother's conscientiousness about doing her duty rather than any closeness to him, and feeling his father's fear of his mother, as if he too remained a boy to her. On the collective level, he maintains a successful ministry to his parishioners but allows himself no close friendship, feeling inadequate, fearing he would be devoured in anything approaching intimacy. Joking barely conceals the rancor bubbling out of him when women come up in the sessions. When asked to describe his feelings about women, he tells a heart-stopping story: A man goes fishing at the sea, casts his line, looks about him. Down the beach a charming picnic basket stands, fresh and inviting. He fishes on. As lunchtime approaches the fisherman cannot rid himself of the idea that the picnic basket is there for him. Finally, he leaves his line and goes to investigate. The sandwiches beckon to him. He thinks, Why not? He unwraps one and bites into it with pleasure. At that precise moment a fishhook lodges in the roof of his mouth; a thin fishing line, barely visible until now, stretches from the hook, taut and strong, out to the center of the ocean. Inexorably, he is pulled into its watery depths. "That is what a woman is like!" the man yells at his woman analyst. To compound the complexity of the situation, a passage from Meister Eckhart comes the way of analyst and analysand at a later date, pulling them through the patient's hideous image of woman into the Self behind it: "God lies in wait for us with nothing so much as love. Now love is like a fishhook. Whoever is captured by love takes up this hook. . . . That person must always belong to God."[12]

EXPRESSION IN BODY, EMOTION, BEHAVIOR

The contrasexual complex expresses itself in three modes: through the body, in behavioral and emotional patterns, and through images. All three circles of the complex—the personal, the collective, and the archetypal—can be manifest in these three ways, or in some combination of them.

The bodily expression of anima/animus is personal and pointedly physical. We need to reflect on how we feel living in our male or female bodies and how we have felt in the past. Are we muscular or fat, hairy or smooth, curved or flat? How were we handled as infants and by whom? What sort of body do we possess now and how does it reflect our putting together of our masculine or feminine ego and our masculine or feminine parts? One woman was dismayed, as she grew older, at the amount of body hair she possessed; she felt it masculinized her, a fear aggravated by the reigning cultural image of the feminine woman as sleek and uninterruptedly smooth. In addition, her mother and sister were untouched by the problem; only she was hirsute, like her brother and father. Not until her adult years, when she fell deeply in love and her lover delighted in her "fur," did she find another more personal standpoint from which to evaluate and claim her own body, showing how much an actual man can influence a woman's animus. A man grew up disowning illness—only women fell ill; he, a man, could never get sick. His mother constantly fell into hypochondriacal moping; his father always carried on with his work, despite colds or flu or worse. Thus this man's anima complex was burdened with the weight of physical illness. The anima made a dramatic entrance into his analysis, so to speak, when he vomited all over the floor of his analyst's office! That amounted to a violent spitting up of his burden, his anima saying to his ego, dramatically, You must integrate illness and not just push it into the unconscious. The vomiting was a giving up of the sickly mother who had contaminated his responses to the feminine. It put him for the moment in a receiving position. Depending on the analyst to clean up and minister to his illness, he could allow himself to discover that this dependence did not unman him and that sickness need not be gender-related.

The bodily expression of the anima/animus complex often comes through violent appropriations of cultural imagery that become attacks on the person. A gay man, at a pivotal period in his life, fell into active identification with his anima, so that his conscious identity displayed extremely feminine mannerisms, postures, gestures, moves. He lived collectively rather than as a person, as a caricature of the opposite sex, never integrating the contrasexual into his own personal identity as a gay man. One spring evening his work called on him to give a presentation to colleagues. He festooned himself in white suit, silk scarf, all the trimmings. Returning to his somewhat deserted city neighborhood late that night, after celebrating the success of his lecture with friends, he was attacked on his street by a deranged man who beat his head with a pipe, nearly killing him. Piecing together what happened afterward, he could only conclude that his attacker was homophobic and lit into him as an only too obviously gay man, clear in the manner of his dress and his effeminate movements. As a result of this terrifying incident, the man integrated his feminine components more securely into his own male identity. He took on some weight, stood up more solidly, carried his gay manhood from the inside, as something substantial in his identity, not a theatrical facade. He looked now like a person who could not be knocked over. He had learned a terrible lesson—that savage reaction to unintegrated feminine elements in him had nearly cost him his life, but ultimately had saved it by what it taught him.

Archetypes are often in deadly combat with bodily stereotypes. Eating disorders and obsessions with fatness, especially among women, show how intense the struggle to claim a body identity can be. A woman's animus easily falls into identification with the much-promoted media stereotype of a pencil-thin, fiber-packed, endlessly peppy body. A woman's ego, thus assailed, loses all of her actual body type, the weight, the bodily rhythms appropriate to her. A tug-of-war ensues between her ego and animus, defending the cultural stereotypes with which they have identified and her Self, which seeks out and addresses her own individual nature.[13] If she can resist succumbing to the hectoring of her collectively contaminated animus, she may be able to hear the small voice of another part of her contrasexuality appealing to a higher authority, one that might constellate a more positive animus in her.[14] Thus is a bridge formed across which comes a primordial image of the feminine rising from a deeper level of the objective psyche, an archetype to combat this tyranny. We can see how the primordial survives in the large folds and curves of the Venus of Willendorf, an image that brings comforting permission to many women to listen to the Self speaking through their body.

One woman struggled with obesity, suffering endless animus lectures on the need to diet. Emboldened by a figurine of the ancient, amply endowed Venus, she allowed herself to hear her body speak back to her animus. In response to the question, What does the body want? she said she knew just how it felt: "Big. It wanted only to lie in bed and get bigger." Resting there under her body's promptings, she remembered leaving the Midwest as a young woman, coming East, finding a profession, marrying, raising two children, leading an active and successful life. She realized now, stretched out in recollection, that she had denied all this when she returned to visit her original family, none of whom could resist commenting on her weight. But her body now would not forget her true and good size, the true and good weight of her authority.

Culture does not always thwart our opening to the larger Self. Sometimes it even encourages an open acceptance of a Willendorf-like body. Witness the popularity of the German film star Marianne Sägebrecht, of such films as *Baghdad Cafe, Sugarbaby,* and *Rosalie Goes Shopping.* She presents an image of woman unashamed to be large, one commanding for her sheer girth. She says moviegoers see her "as real—instead of actors they are used to." She continues, "Also, I think people can see how happy I am as a round lady. This is what I am. This is the form I have: my body is a genetic gift. My ancestors were farmers, and I'm very healthy and very strong, and I am liking my round form."[15] The success of an actress of such heroic dimensions gives permission to everyone to receive and live her or his own bodily shape.

We can speak of the anima or animus as straddling worlds. One part of us is planted in the personal, shaped by introjected objects and images from the significant persons of the opposite sex of our early life, from images of the masculine and feminine in our culture, and from our inherited physical constitution. Another part rests in the objective psyche, which functions according to its own laws of contiguity, similarity, association, and simultaneity, and expresses the great range of archetypes from the physical to the spiritual. In contrast, our consciousness functions according to very different laws of causality, spatiality, and temporality, always differentiating inner from outer figures, "I" from other.[16]

The contrasexual figure who confronts us may bear imagery and impulses reminiscent of our mother or sister and yet also embody a small piece of the objective psyche that is altogether other to what we think of as our personal physical and cultural life. That is why when suddenly an animus content invades our well-poised ego, we feel impelled by something wildly irrational, with tinges even of madness. We have been adapting to circumstances, talking in measured tones. Abruptly shrillness enters our voice. We may recognize its telltale rising screech and try to resist it. It sounds, we tell ourselves, just like what I hated about Mother, but we are unable to stop it. A relentless fish out of water has got hold of us, the animus that swims in the unconscious. If we can recognize what it is and understand its determination to function as an archetypal symbol, throwing opposites together, we can face even the worst screech coming from our mouths as an animus rather than a crackpot eruption or a frightening sign of madness within.

A typical pattern of compulsive emotional response to inner eruption that most of us, alas, can recognize as recurring is what amounts to quick diversion from a real to a pseudoissue. This is a trick the contrasexual complex seems mercilessly to play on the ego. We can tell when we fall prey to it because in those blasts of defensive emotion we feel so dislodged from our center. A woman in group therapy, caught in questions of large meaning in her life, felt suddenly shoved aside, away from what concerned her, in interchanges with the group. The more she insisted on asking, But what does it mean? the less related she felt to the issue and the persons before her. She got mad, the others were evading and dodging her, but she was herself making them angry because she had fled into chains of abstraction and shut them out from access to her. One man said she filled the room with a seamless ball that he could find no way into, and then complained that they had abandoned her.

A husband and wife offer similar dodges and deflections in the service of misunderstanding. He gripes. She retorts that he had used the same sneering tone of voice, with the same facial smirks, when they were arguing last September. He explodes: "What's that got to do with it?" Yes, she is maddening; she is also right. His emotional tone conveys the same contempt he displayed in the earlier argument. This makes clear that his emotions about the issue at hand have not really changed at all since then. Though it appears that they are discussing something very different from last September, *au fond* it is probably the same issue, or closely enough related, so that the husband must position himself in exactly the same way. On his side, he feels his wife is behaving in a maddeningly illogical and nasty way, refusing to stick to the terms of the present argument, dragging in old quarrels that can only poison the atmosphere. In fact, however, the wife is behaving logically, but according to the laws of the nondirected thinking of the objective dimension of the psyche instead of according to the laws of directed thinking familiar to our consciousness. She moves by association and intuition to locate his present tone in an old argument where the same tone dominated. He moves by conscious logic; he is reasonable. These are the issues; let's reach some conclusion. If a couple can learn to make use of both conscious and unconscious mentation, they may develop the skill to move quickly through argument to the underlying tensions, ancient or present. When we cannot do this, we fall into hostile polarization, not only of wife and husband, but of anima/animus and ego, of consciousness and the unconscious.[17]

The double-footed nature of the animus/anima complex reminds us just how much these are border figures. They pull us out of our familiar ego world, both personal and cultural, toward the far country of the Self. They push us from conscious styles of mentation into unconscious ones. That is why anima and animus are so useful in our attempts to understand pathologies, especially those of the borderline variety—like the borderline condition itself, narcissistic personality disorders, even some types of severe dissociation bordering on schizophrenia.[18] They stand in a liminal place, with a foot in two worlds, and confront the ego, as Jung puts it, from "a world where the pulse of time beats ever so slowly. . . . Their aspect is strange—so strange that their intrusion into consciousness often blasts into fragments the all-too-feeble brainpans of unfortunate mortals. Anima and animus contain the greater part of the material which appears in insanity, more especially in schizophrenia."[19]

Each of us knows this intrusion when we are in the grip of an emotional mood we cannot shake or feel compelled to blurt out words we know to be damaging to what we ourselves believe. Under such compulsion, we refuse to say the simple apology that would decisively end a fruitless harangue that we began. A negative animus rips to pieces the cordial connection to someone we hold dear. A negative anima sulks and fills the room with the noxious gas of resentment.

We are especially reminded of the liminal borders between conscious and unconscious when our anima presents herself, as it did for one man, as a madwoman. Either she turned up in dreams as "diseased" or "psychotic," or she announced to him that some other woman the dreamer valued was going crazy, beyond reach. Such dream figures deeply frightened the dreamer and made him reluctant to explore any further relation to his unconscious. The extremes of compulsive codependent attachment of women who, it is said, "love too much," can be understood as a massive projection of an animus image onto a man and a woman's identification of a man with her only access to the Self. A fusion of weak ego, projected animus, and the man upon whom it is projected gets going, making the woman really feel mad. A woman dreams her estranged husband comes home and changes before her eyes into a kind of monster whose skin is replaced by porcelain. He casts a spell. Then he goes to talk to the contractor who is redoing her kitchen. This dream gives a clue to the origin of the woman's compulsive renovations of her house. Was it to keep her from turning into porcelain? Or was it an expression of a transmogrification into porcelain already achieved? For the endless renovations had kept the whole family in a spell, unable to live normally.

The Psychoanalytic Fallacy

Identification with an archetypal image may be personal or collective, or move, as it so often does, from the personal to the collective. In Goethe's *Sorrows of Young Werther,* the suicide of the title figure so persuasively enacted the dreams of entering the great dark mystery of death that the young of the early years of Romanticism eagerly sought to penetrate, that hundreds imitated the act; suicide became much more than a literary ritual. It leaped from the printed page, and the luring dream turned into fact. Werther's confusion of an anima fantasy with a real woman, one who would not or could not fulfill the fantasy role he had designed for her, made suicide seem more satisfying than going on with life. It was a dramatic performance of stunning power. Certainly it seemed that way to all those who followed the literary suicide with the real act. Fairly soon, happily, the drama lost its ability to stun.[20]

But still the drama goes on. When one of the writers of this book was a visiting professor at a Pennsylvania college, Anne Sexton was giving a poetry reading in tandem with a young male poet. Clearly she found his work, his public persona, and his offstage personality engaging, even at times absorbing, but never so compelling, she made clear in conversation, as Sylvia Plath's suicide. *There* was another woman poet of unmistakable suicidal potential who had made it! Sexton admired and envied her. She had made her own unsuccessful attempt some time before. She looked forward to an achievement like Plath's. It was not long before she matched her and actualized her own suicidal potential. Werther lived again in death.

Anne Sexton proclaims again and again in her poetry her imbalance, her ego uncertainties, her fantasy selves. She longs to be both anima and animus, to achieve as an unbounded confessor of the most lurid dreams and fantasies the role of anima-woman to her own playing of the animus-male. "I am alive at night. I am dead in the morning," she says in her "Moon Song, Woman Song." In a poem about the "Other Woman," she says, "She is private in her breathbed," pointing, as everything in her confessional verse does, to the destructive subtext: breath equals death. In a tense, touching poem on "The Breast," she writes out of her animus/anima confusion,

Ignorant of men, I lay next to my sisters
and rising out of the ashes I cried
my sex will be transfixed!

Sexton's verse is a great outpouring on the analyst's couch, as, however well disguised, Sylvia Plath's was. "Catch me. I'm your disease," Sexton cries in a kind of taunting of transference and teasing of countertransference. Singing her "Ballad of the Lonely Masturbator," she taunts us all with her poorly wed, undernourished life: "At night, alone, I marry the bed."[21] Throughout her work—in her novel, *The Bell Jar,* in most of her poems, but especially in the posthumous *Winter Trees*—

Plath writes elegies not to mourn the end of life but its failure to come to an end. "When I have fears," she might well have written, "that I may not cease to be. . . ."

In "Three Women, a Poem for Three Voices," which concludes Plath's posthumous volume, there is something like a staccato insistence on death as the abiding topic and texture of a maternity ward and its surroundings. "I am ready," says the first voice. "I am dying as I sit," says the second. "I remember the minute when I knew for sure," the third adds to the litany, but tells us also that she was not ready. There are strong lines, lines of fear, lines that frighten in their hostility, a familiar element in Plath.

> It is these men I mind:
> They are so jealous of anything that is not flat! They are jealous gods
> That would have the whole world flat because they are.
> I see the Father conversing with the Son.
> Such flatness cannot but be holy.
> "Let us make a heaven," they say.
> "Let us flatten and launder the grossness from these souls."

Finally they are delivered, but not of all their burdens. They can leave behind, as the third voice does, "the clothes of a fat woman I do not know." They can contemplate their young in awe and avarice, incomparable possessions suddenly theirs. But still there is "the incalculable malice of the everyday" and the inexorable threnody of the confessional poets, "I am solitary as grass," a nagging reduction of the prophet Isaiah's "All flesh is grass."[22]

Robert Lowell was tutor to these women in the translation of the rituals of the couch and the confessional into verse. Teacher, friend, fellow traveler, Lowell fixed the molds in place in his collection of *Life Studies*. Ransack your personal life; tell it all; hold nothing back. Tell them, tell us, where you were, what you were, how it was when you were "a fire-breathing Catholic C.O." in your "seedtime," and did your time in the West Street jail, waiting for your verdict sitting alongside "a Negro boy curlicues/of marijuana in his hair," and had pointed out to you "*Murder Incorporated's* Czar Lepke" in a black T-shirt working at racking towels. Tell us about your illustrious family, your grandparents, how your father died, how your mother, fearful of a life alone stretching on too long, "mooned in a window,/as if she had stayed on a train/one stop past her destination." Complete the picture with yourself and wife: "Tamed by *Miltown,* we lie on Mother's bed."

Lowell continued the confessional saga in several editions of a *Notebook,* working not, he explains, at an almanac so much as "the story of my life." What results, he insists, "is not my private lash, or a confession, or a puritan's too literal pornographic honesty, glad to share secret embarrassment and triumph."[23] But, in fact, all the confessional poets, and the novelists and playwrights and makers of films of the same kind, do indeed put on offer something much too literal, pornographic or not, honest or contrived or simply beyond the writer's or director's or photographer's range of choice. John Berryman worked harder, perhaps, than anyone in this mode to make honest art of compulsive confession in his *Dream Songs* and several other verse sequences of the same kind. But the urge to tell it all led him too often to writing that has about it the taste and smell of the analyst's couch, whatever the margin of prosodic skill, and certainly much too of the rage, however aimed and directed, that led to his suicidal leap from a Minneapolis bridge.[24]

Case studies do not make good art. There is too much special pleading involved, a supererogation of untamed anima or animus effusion, an identification with archetypal images that edges always closer and closer to the destructive element. Mediation is called for. Some can find it in themselves; it was not Goethe who committed suicide but his fictive character, Werther, who does not fit the narrow dimensions of the *doppelgänger* the way Sexton's lonely women and Plath's voices do. Those who cannot find the necessary distance are best cautioned to seek professional guidance of some sort, or at least that wise counsel that the contrasexual self can provide, where one may discover the possibility of a positive orientation to life in anima or animus and an unmistakable aversion to the psychoanalytic fallacy, that is, to seeing clinical transcripts as art.

EXPRESSION IN IMAGES

The contrasexual invariably expresses itself in images that draw on all levels of the complex—the personal, the cultural, the archetypal. What comes across the anima/animus bridge from Self to ego most often comes in personified images. The liminal stance of the complex transcends the ego by confronting us with images of numinous power that move us to wholehearted response, positive and negative.

On the negative side, we can see how dangerous it is for an ego to fall into identification with an archetypal image, for it can compel lethal actions—like those in Brooklyn in the 1970s by the Son of Sam, who said he was instructed to murder blonde women. His identification with the polarized ego and archetypal images was so great that murderous acts seemed called for.

On the positive side, an anima carries a man's orientation to life; she personifies his animating connection to being. If he establishes a good relationship with her, he can perceive the way he is positioned toward life itself. The result may be more freedom in his responses to people and events and a transformation of daily routines into patterns with high meaning.[25] Relating to her liminal stance—one foot in ego, one in Self—he enlarges the space in between creative illusion and disillusion, the transitional space, as Winnicott defines it, of "living creatively," the space of Karl Popper's World III, the space of the mythopoeic, where all perceiving has its source, according to Ernst Cassirer.[26]

So much depends on a man's realizing the value of his anima images. When he fails to do so, they turn angry, diabolical even, and ensnare him in compulsive, pathological patterns of emotional behavior. The anima has no outlet, then, into his life, and the Self bulges uncertainly behind him. When he turns toward her to receive her, she will move to help him find the positive patterns in his day-to-day existence.

We see this in small, almost inconsequential incidents. A man brought to his analytical session a magazine picture of a beautiful blonde woman, with green eyes spaced far apart, full lips brought forward into a pout, and a small well-shaped nose. Her eyes did not look at the camera, but into the distance above the head of the viewer. Like the eyes of a big cat—lion or tiger—they settled into the unseeing look that does not seem to recognize anyone individually. "This is my anima. This is what I fall in love with," the man said. It was immediately clear what had led him years earlier into compulsive voyeurism. This anima-woman would not relate to any man personally; she was a bearer of the beyond; she was abstract beauty. For him such beauty bears the transcendent. This image caught in his voyeur's telescope is what he had long worshiped, had knelt down before, and poured out his semen into his hand in devotion. This image of beauty made the transcendent tangible, carried his religious impulse, his connection to Self. It is a religious impulse that the anima image brought this man's ego, which he needed to recognize and house appropriately. Because of unencouraging family experiences and the woeful state of the institutions where he had experienced religion in his own culture, he had turned away from any formal worship. He had not developed any satisfactory way to house his yearning for the divine. When his anima personified that yearning, he identified the image with the transcendent and fell under the anima-woman's spell.

Archetypal images of the contrasexual complex in cultural events show the same range of emphasis as dreams, from the spiritual to the instinctive, characteristic of any significant image. The example of the beautiful anima-woman illustrates the energy an archetypal image delivers, for the man was moved far out of himself, spiritually and sexually. The impact of Elvis Presley on thousands of young women, from the late 1950s until long after his death, offers a startling parallel. Like a Dionysus figure, he represented the numinosity of sexuality, its power to pull us out of banality and meaninglessness. He may seem a curious vehicle for such adumbrations of transcendence, but there is no denying the intensity or endurance of the Presley effect, or its stirrings in the young of responses far beyond the quality of the man or his music. It is useful to compare with Elvis the studied androgynous appearance of Michael Jackson. We can speculate that here the pop culture in which the contrasexual archetype is expressing itself is moving toward a more calculated mixing of the masculine and feminine.[27]

The archetypal dimension of the contrasexual figure brings to people at all levels some of their most self-searching experiences. Here, even in the trite formulations of rock culture, many find authentic articulation of the experience of intense feeling, holding forth the possibility that in loving an other they may be returned to the deepest experience of the Self that lives in them. We withdraw projections onto the other in such an experience, even a vicarious one, if we feel it strongly enough, and make them instead a means of approach to the otherness of the other. Religious people talk about this as loving God in the other and loving the other in God. Anima and animus lead us to union not only with the Self within us but with others in community.

Transformation

We call the anima and animus archetypes of transformation because their constant effect on us is to enlarge us, even if not always positively. As we must constantly reiterate, when we fall into passive or active identification with this archetype, we are impelled to act out its archaic dynamisms in the ego world, in personal relationship and social congress. This almost always throws us wildly off center. It can lead to rape and murder. Contempt is commonplace in its battery of affect, as are physical and emotional abuse and maddeningly irritating states of being and behavior. The archetype breaks apart the personal and social dimensions of our lives when we cannot contain its disruptive energies. Under the grip of an archetype we pull in one direction, it pushes in another; it drags us under, down to grim isolation. It mixes us up, it makes us feel insane, and sometimes we really lose all balance.

In large part, however, these negative effects result only after breakdown of the bridge of anima and animus between Self and ego. When it functions properly, we are enlarged in the best sense, in all directions, as the ego receives contents from the contrasexual Self. We are connected then, deep down inside, with our own sexual roots; we are made full with the unexpected enlargement that comes with the presence of the opposite point of sexual view. We are made flexible, less dogmatic, but more secure in being who we are, trusting in our identities even as, in inspired improvisation, we put together all the parts, masculine, feminine, personal, collective, conscious, unconscious, self and other. We experience what Jung calls the prospective function of the psyche in the most intimate ways of bodily life, images that arouse us, move us, establish purpose in our lives.[28] This is where we find courage in our darkest moments, our most intense suffering. When someone betrays us, besides all the pain and rage and discouragement, we can ask now, What is this catastrophe bringing me? What is the Self engineering? This question makes all the difference in the world when we are caught in addictive sexual perversion. In it we find the toughness to stand the heat of honest admission where denial is all we have been able to manage before. The question returns in this nearly masochistic self-scourg-ing: What is the Self engineering? What that is good is trying to speak to me, to reach me in this harrowing ritual?

Anima and animus enlarge our relationships with other people as they do with our inner selves, not only in the intimate connections with fam-ily, sexual partner, or close friend, but also in the greater world outside. For sexuality and its associated spiritualities reach through all the trans-actions where others and otherness may be found. Getting in touch with our own anima or animus complex puts us in touch with the graces and the prejudices that open or close the social lens of opportunity and hospitality to others, all those upon whom our projections may fall. We enlarge and help others enlarge as we face the otherness of our contra-sexuality. Equally, we ourselves are diminished, and others are too, when we turn away from the other within us.

The anima/animus complex is a formidable resource in us for good or bad. In its bridge function, it acts to connect us to the deepest being inside us and to Being itself. Our intimate sexual experiences, when they arise from a contrasexual interiority that has been well explored, mark out channels in our collective community for others to follow. As we struggle with the complex, each in our own way, we have these channels in our keeping, to clear or to muddy, for ourselves, for others, for earth itself. There, in this risky enterprise, dense with the fullness of parts of human sexuality and its informing spirit, we will find our true identity.

Part II

Anima / Animus and Identity

3

Identity

CHANGE AND CONTINUITY

Our identity is not a fixed product: it cannot be prescribed to assure a fine set content; it cannot be proscribed to avoid known pitfalls. Human identity reveals, rather, a style of being a person in which we put ourselves into a reality shared with others, not only outside ourselves but inside. It recognizes and gives evidence of a continuity felt concretely as belonging to the person—our person. Its special marks show how we gather and put together the multiple parts, the infinite variables, of our selves. We look with wonder at an infant scarcely two weeks old who already displays definite preferences for the way she should be placed in her crib, loudly exclaiming when she is on her back instead of her stomach, where she can begin to lift her head and look around. We recognize many ways of putting the parts of a person together, many styles of being man or woman, but know or hope to know the specific one that belongs to us, that we, in conjunction with others and otherness, have made our own.

Identity is not random. The parts are there—the body and all its endowments, historical and cultural conditions, particular parents, siblings, the worlds of neighborhood schools, of the buildings and rooms we lived in and dreamed in, and the architecture and interior decoration of our lives. Out of these parts we find and put together the persons we become. We elaborate on the variables of being in our multiple becomings. We help each other and wound each other in the process. We manifest our creative imagination in the way we link the parts and find symbols for them and construct the process by which we put them together or let them fall apart or bring them back together again.[1]

All of us, whether we use a philosophical or psychological vocabulary and reasoning process or simply ask ourselves questions in some everyday tongue—fragments or sentences, perhaps pieced together with grunts—seek an empirical understanding of self. We seek, within the limitations of language, of what can or cannot reach consciousness, not only a discoverable identity, but a certifiable one. For most of us, identity means what we know or think we know of a continuing, unchanging person, some set of qualities that has remained the same over the years from first consciousness, directly connected to our maleness or femaleness, what we mean when we think of ourselves as subjects, not things or objects. We look for some element inside ourselves or others, some one thing or many that we recognize as the person in the same way that a face tells us whom we are talking to or what or whom we are talking from. It may be a gesture or a particular and peculiar shape of body or way of holding or moving a body. The point is that we recognize it and accept it the way we do a birthmark or a tattoo or a dental record as a trustworthy icon of the person, and one that, on the whole, changes less with the years than the outer parts of people.

This is where the facts of experience can be gathered into a primary sorting center. This is our I-ness, where ego accumulates and where Self may grow. We can deny its findings to ourselves, others can seem to confute them, but we know that there is a core of experiential truth there somewhere within us that links us to an identity and may even proclaim it. Even if we are altogether uncertain about what this core is and how we can get at it, still we want to do so and to assure ourselves that we can do so against all the shiftings and dispersals of contingency, of our own inarticulateness or fuzzy connection to our interior life, against everything that threatens the possibility of retrieval, not only of the core facts, but of the person, the I, that recorded them.

We know beyond argument that we have recorded sets of feeling responses, speculations, and meditations out of our meetings with persons, dreams, fantasies, frustrations, and satisfactions as sexually marked persons, as men and women. We know that somewhere within us and others there is a permanent identity taking note of all this in an inner conversation, dealing with what goes on and what does not, continuity and discontinuity, change and the various ways we have of sensing it or of failing to do so.

Most curious of all and most challenging, we have some awareness of a judging mechanism within us that speaks in that interior dialogue, that bears the lineaments of an Other, of otherness itself, which more often than not takes the form of the opposite sex, with or without a discoverable personal identity to go with it. It may bear the name and familiar shape and habits of behavior of someone we know, someone in the family, someone we grew up with, someone with whom we work now or with whom we once worked. It may consist entirely of fantasy elements, drawn from daydream or book or film. It may hold only the thinnest claim to being, but there inside us, in our core identity, it is real enough; it is where the defining changes of our lives are noted and recorded and achieve the dignity of personal history. This is the realm of anima and animus. This is where archetypal possibility becomes human actuality.

The core identity, where ego forms and Self begins to form, we tend to identify with our sexual identity; it is the permanence we have been seeking, our judging apparatus, our certifiable being. The changes that assault and enlarge or diminish this permanence at the center pass through or even spring directly from the inner world of otherness that lives alongside our core identity, the world of contrasexuality. Ultimately, with the intercession of anima or animus, a fullness of sexual self, of being male or female, may emerge from this constant meeting and living together of permanence and change. We may then have something of the highest value to hold onto and know that we have it.[2]

Anima and animus affect our identity in ways central to our being. They act against stereotypes foisted onto us by the strictures of society, by people's unconscious fears and needs, by our own neuroses. They construct the bridge from the ego to Self country, acting as our threshold to the Self, leading the ego to transcend itself, to cross its own borders toward the other, and thus both to claim what belongs to itself — the ego — and to bring it into the largeness of otherness.

IDENTITY AS STYLE

Identity as it is shaped by the anima/animus archetypes veers, as almost everything in this sphere does, away from a fixed content. The bias here is toward style, put together from persons, the surrounding culture, a living mixture of sounds and sights and tastes and textures. It may express an aggressive femininity or a sagging masculinity. It may reveal a chaos of sexual attitudes and actings-out, but the presence of an identity colored by its sexuality is everywhere unmistakable.

We see the styles of anima/animus identity with particular clarity in the motion-picture totems of this century. It is not meaningless, for example, that Charlie Chaplin, a sexual shark offscreen, was such a splay-footed minnow on screen. Beneath the Hollywood aggressor there lurked a tender anima aspirant, a timid consoler of the pure waif, a nineteenth-century sentimentalist whose feelings away from the camera required the mask of a dandy as carefully designed as the tattered clothing, derby, and cane of the tramp. Buster Keaton, the Great Stone Face, rivaled Douglas Fairbanks and Rudolph Valentino and the other athletes of the screen in his anima adventures, as the shivering weakling turned into an enraged prizefighter in *Battling Butler,* as the locomotive god who all but wins the Civil War for the South in *The General,* as the empty-headed fop made over into the behemoth of the sea in *The Navigator,* opening mammoth cans designed, each one, for a whole ship's company to feed his anima beloved, braving storms, cannibals, every obstacle known to the anima fantasist.

The transformations effected by the archetypes are wondrous to behold in film. Garbo, riveting penetrator of the world of male authority, became her animus self as she moved in her devotions from Anna Karenina to Camille to Queen Christina. Women were especially enchanted because her animus style was so elegantly aggressive, in charge, on top, but never demeaning of her lovers, sure of her own views in these enactments out of an inner style outwardly caught, never reduced to a styleless shrilling. John Wayne articulated his strong-willed masculinity not with a show of muscle, usually, but with a swivel-hipped walk just short of campy caricature. His bristling patriotism caught up people miles from his views, such as his leftist costars, as a benevolent monarch might charm a cocktail-party revolutionary. He was fussy, determined, anima-ridden in his film stories as in the way he carried himself, a stylist who could be directed to archetypal effect by a John Ford, allegorist of the American West, or a Josef von Sternberg, Marlene Dietrich's tribune.

The Wayne-Sternberg collaboration in 1950, *Jet Pilot,* brings anima and animus together in the bodies of Janet Leigh as a Soviet pilot and Wayne as an American and in the planes that they fly. Both are legends in their air forces, both infuse everything around them with their body parts. The summation of the film by the French director and critic François Truffaut puts it all in archetypal space:

> We are in the realm of pure emotion, poetically expressed. The inventiveness and beauty catches in our throats. To be sure, the film's intention is stupid propaganda, but Sternberg constantly turns it aside so that tears come to our eyes in the face of such beauty, as when the male plane and the female plane seek each other out, find one another, fly one on top of the other, struggle, calm themselves, and finally fly side by side. The airplanes make love.[3]

The anima/animus proclivities of a society are always manifest in its popular culture. Where there was a Buster Keaton we have a Woody Allen, central exhibit of the psychoanalytic fallacy in film, transcribing adventures on a Manhattan analyst's couch into pretentious fables of failure. Where there were Garbo and Dietrich, there was first Monroe and then no one so commanding, just players in a socially conscious repertory, such as Meryl Streep, or figures of a masculine strength, such as Kathleen Turner or Sigourney Weaver, who stride with as much vigor as John Wayne but with something less than his swivel-hipped charm. As for Wayne's apparent successor, Arnold Schwarzenegger, he has the right politics, but his greatest success comes in playing robots. Still, if airplanes can act out an animus/anima drama, can cyborgs be far behind?

Anima and animus involve us with other people in intimate sexual ways and take us deep into ourselves and our own sexuality, laying claim to it as they help us enlarge it. The animating strength of our sexual identity comes from this inner presence we are impelled to meet, mix with, and be changed by. We discover that each of us lives as a couple, joined or disjoined with an inner other who matches us and transforms us as we transform him or her. "The supreme recognition," says Jung, "is that a man is also a woman and a woman is also a man."[4]

When we come to recognize this part of ourselves, we across its threshold into the Self, which means concretely that we accept who we are and all our idiosyncratic variations on elemental human themes. We grasp our music from behind the notes, from the other side. This is what it feels like to be accepted. It is a supreme religious moment in our lives: we accept that we are accepted as we are, and we live out of our deepest center. This feels like living according to the will of God.[5]

Charles Baudelaire, our explicator more than our predecessor, speaks for the contradictions and paradoxes, the faith and lack of faith, the acceptances and rejections of modernity as no other in the last two centuries. Saint of the open heart, surgeon of the evil visitation in the middle of the night, he reveals himself to himself as our surrogate to repudiate conventional wisdom wherever he himself feels repudiated and to accept it wherever he finds himself accepted. He goes as a matter of necessity, in endless self-probing, to his center, to find what he could not at home, at school, in society. He goes accompanied always by some anima apparition, defiling women, groaning for them, knowing the seductions and bafflements of the interior dialogue and, just often enough, the consolations. He called his poems *Fleurs du mal,* but they could just as accurately be called flowers of goodness and would just as surely have been condemned as blasphemy as they must again be condemned by that inversion of standards which he foresaw. For what Baudelaire understood from his descents into the abyss is that most of us spend most of our time in ceremonies of avoidance. We do not deal with what really matters. We waste our lives asking foolish questions. Like Pascal, whose *Pensées* his intimate journals echo in matter, in style, in splenetic outburst, and in burgeoning hope, Baudelaire wants his *semblable,* his *hypocrite lecteur,* to ask those questions that "should excite man's curiosity in the highest degree, and which, to judge from his customary mode of life, do not inspire him with any."

> Where are our dead friends?
> Why are we here?
> Do we come from some other place?
> What is free will?
> Can it be reconciled with the laws of Providence?
> Is there a finite or infinite number of souls?
> What of the number of habitable lands? Etc., etc. . . .

He has his own version of the teleological proof for the existence of God, the same God who, he assures us, "is the sole being who has no need to exist in order to reign." The argument is simple: "Nothing exists without purpose. Therefore my existence has purpose." He does not know what purpose; therefore someone wiser than he must have "appointed that purpose." Conclusion? "It is therefore necessary to pray to this someone to enlighten me. That is the wisest course."

It could be argued that these syllogisms, a kind of reverse blasphemy to the modern mind, stand behind the violences and provocations of his writing that the modern mind has found altogether agreeable. For Baudelaire, the solitary walker, as he called himself, not only confessed "a taste for life and for pleasure which is very keen," but admitted an urge to spirituality and to charity in his solitude, to "presentiments and signs sent me already by God that it is *high time* to act." That meant to find his high delight in his work, even though it was also his "accustomed torment." The torment was to carry his inner conversation with him everywhere, through the tortures of syphilis-induced aphasia, through the trials of an intensity of observation that made him, not the devil's apologist, as the frightened trimmers of his time portrayed Baudelaire, but the one who had done battle with Satan and must remind us that the devil's cleverest wile is to persuade us that he does not exist.

Seeing things as they are, as they were, as they were becoming, that was the content, far from fixed, of Baudelaire's poems in verse and in prose and his journal entries. In the best modern manner, he saw undeclared hidden interests everywhere. Guillotiners could be numbered among the opponents of capital punishment. "I want to be able to cut off your head," he heard them saying, "but you shan't touch mine." More significantly, "abolishers of the Soul *(materialists)* are necessarily abolishers of *hell;* they, certainly, are *interested.* At all events, they are people who *fear to live again*—lazy people."

Baudelaire saw not only what was and what had been but what might be, especially that bewitching anima figure he draws for us under the rubric of "The Desire to Paint." She appeared to him only rarely, he tells us in this poem in prose, and then "quickly fled, like a beautiful regretted thing the voyager leaves behind as he is carried away into the night." He had compared her in the past to a black sun, but he thinks now she is more like "the sinister and intoxicating moon that hangs deep in a stormy night, hurtled by the driven clouds." She is marked by "a tenacious will and a desire for prey," by physical features that "quiver for the unknown and the impossible," that in their allurements make him "dream of the miracle of a superb flower blooming on volcanic soil." This is not one of those women who draw you to conquer them; "this one fills you only with the desire to die slowly beneath her gaze."

She is not far, except in time, from the distant princess that seven centuries before led Jaufré Rudel halfway across the Mediterranean in inflamed pursuit, or any of the other anima figures with which every literature, like all men's dream worlds, is full. What gives her such substance for those who know and admire Baudelaire is that she is so clearly a part of the poet, not simply a nagging or hopeful phantasm in which he must believe, but the shaping force of his craft and the basis of his stubborn faith in what might be revealed through it.[6]

Pascal and Wittgenstein, so much like Baudelaire in their constant recourse to their inner voice and translation of their dialogue with it into gnomic utterance, did not have the enlivening presence of such an anima figure as the poet's, at least as far as we can see. Pascal did have his early years of carousing, to use the portemanteau word for the sinful life, the source of so much of his eloquence on the contradictions of being human: "Judge of all things, feeble earthworm; repository of truth, sink of uncertainty and error; glory and refuse of the universe"— the words are almost as familiar as Hamlet's anticipation of them in "What a piece of work is a man! . . . the beauty of the world! the paragon of animals! . . . this quintessence of dust. . . ." Wittgenstein did entertain the possibility of marriage with a Viennese woman, which she wisely declined after dallying too long with the tacit acceptance of the philosopher. He did know strong attraction to several young men and knew as well a response from two of them with something like the intensity he felt. He knew also, unhappily, a sense of impurity in himself to which he responded with a repugnance not unlike that which led Baudelaire only too often to equate love with prostitution.

The demon of opposites took up life in each of these men, fruitfully, frighteningly, instructively. Baudelaire fancied himself a mystic and came close to justifying the appropriation in his idea of *correspondances,* famous in the sonnet of that name for bringing all the senses together in a riotous synesthesia in which perfumes, colors, and sounds mix. His mystical impulse is even better illustrated by his great appeal, against the loss in the modern world of a commonality of myth and symbol, to a speculative system of universal analogies. The parallelism the poet saw as ingrained in things, in this system, brought being, becoming, identity, and change into constant relation with each other. The sheer size of this conception made the burden of subjectivity less onerous for him.

Everything was caught in startling opposition that could at any moment become analogy, an analogy which could at any moment become opposition. What the poetic phrase could do—"rise straight up to heaven without losing its breath, or fall straight down to hell with the velocity of any weight"—was a fair reflection of the antinomies and paradoxes of everyday life. We are fated to a dizzying alternation of greatness and misery, of prodigal achievement and failure of the same dimension. Against such vertigo humors Baudelaire was willing to make Pascal's wager. As his syllogism of belief makes clear, he would rather take a chance that a beneficent God exists than that he does not. If he is right and can somehow live in accordance with the conviction, he stands to gain everything; if he bets against the alluring possibility and it turns out that he has made the wrong choice, he looks to lose all.[7]

Wittgenstein, for whom understanding was not a mental process at all but rather a grasp of the circumstances in which things were said and heard and acted upon, was unable to reduce religion to a set of doctrines. Christianity is not "a theory about what has happened and will happen to the human soul, but something that actually takes place in human life." And things do happen, as ordinary people know that they do and tell us that they do in their ordinary language. We must recognize the stature and the solidity of what they report even if the words in which we and they express the recognition are not only ordinary but hackneyed. We must always be on the lookout for what is actually "the case," to use a phrase consecrated in Wittgenstein's usage. "Why is the soul moved by idle thoughts?—After all they are idle. Well, it is moved by them. (How can the wind move the tree when it's nothing but air? Well, it *does move* it; and don't forget it.)"

Ordinariness and the language in which it was communicated were supported with such stalwart good sense and warm feeling by Wittgenstein that his philosophy was sometimes called "therapeutic." He did not like the designation. Perhaps he heard the note of condescension in the word; perhaps, as the disciple of Freud he sometimes called himself, he understood how much less than curative his tracing of the linguistic "fields of force" was, or how much more than healing was involved in trying to gather and enunciate the rules of the language games into which our discourse falls and with it the behavior that occasions it. Besides, for all his attention to the ordinary, there remained in him that teasing voice, that rising feeling that he associated with great art.

Within all of it, he said, "there is a WILD animal: *tamed*. . . . All great art has man's primitive drives as its ground bass. They are not the *melody* (as they are with Wagner, perhaps) but they are what gives the melody its *depth* and power." He was quite content that the house he designed and built for his sister Gretl in Vienna, in his capacity as architect, was "the product"—and here he shows a feeling for *correspondances* among the senses like Baudelaire's—"of a decidedly sensitive ear and *good* manners, an expression of great *understanding*." But the wild animal was not in it: "*primordial* life, wild life striving to erupt into the open—that is lacking. And so you could say it isn't *healthy* (Kierkegaard). (Hothouse plant.)"

Near the end of his life, Wittgenstein could say with conviction, "My *life* consists in my being content to accept many things," or even more temperately, "What I know, I believe." But still there was the urge to the primordial, to allow the wild animal its outings, to achieve something like the quality of great art. Just a little while earlier, some five years before he died, he asked himself, "Are *all* men great? No.—Well then, how can you have any hope of being a great man? Why should something be bestowed on you that's not bestowed on your neighbour? To what purpose?!" He had an answer; he was drawing upon his own observation and experience. "And what do you experience (other than vanity)?" He went on with his catechism, and answered: "Simply that you have a certain *talent*. And my conceit of being an extraordinary person has been with me *much* longer than my awareness of my particular talent."

The simplicity and honesty of Wittgenstein's colloquies with himself are captivating in the same way as is Pascal's gathering of all his fleeting thoughts en route to that perfectly organized apologia for the Christian religion which he had planned, the equivalent of an elegant proof in science, but which he never finished. Each of these master recorders of the inner voice, like Baudelaire, is writing an *apologia pro vita sua*. Each is making his case, or showing us just what is "the case," as it emerged in interior dialogue. There was a providential ordering of the events in the three lives that left their work unfinished, far from what was originally planned, it may be, but arguably much more persuasive as a record of interiorities deeply experienced, of lives fully lived, than it would be in more formal finished order.

We return to these men so often because in each case what is complete is not a system or a thesis and a set of proofs but the revelation of a remarkable human being forging his identity and notating almost everything of value discovered in the process. As they are enlarged, we are also. As they are confused and find purpose and direction in the confusion, so do we. Talking to themselves, finding in the conversation a personage of anima- or animus-like proportions to talk with, they make their intended case, theological, philosophical, poetic.

The last recorded notations of Wittgenstein show how much may be discovered of human identity this way, and perhaps of something more. He is talking about making different kinds of mistakes in statements and acknowledging them. He cannot see how it would be possible to be making a mistake about his name being what it is. But if he were to say, "I have never been on the moon—but I may be mistaken," that, he concludes, "would be idiotic." It is less a question of trusting the evidence we are offered in such cases than of trusting the person who offers it or makes statements about it. The last examples lead to Wittgenstein's final words. "If someone believes that he has flown from America to England in the last few days, then, I believe," says the dying philosopher, "he cannot be making a mistake." Equally he accepts the word of someone who "says that he is at this moment sitting at a table and writing." Then comes the marvelous final statement, alive with the unceasing energies of an interior discourse that will not stop proclaiming the vitality of that discourse and the identity of its participants, even at the edge of the grave:

"But even if in such cases I can't be mistaken, isn't it possible that I am drugged?" If I am and if the drug has taken away my consciousness, then I am not now really talking and thinking. I cannot seriously suppose that I am at this moment dreaming. Someone who, dreaming, says "I am dreaming," even if he speaks audibly in doing so, is no more right than if he said in his dream "it is raining," while it was in fact raining. Even if his dream were actually connected with the noise of the rain.

The next day, words and consciousness ceased, some short time after he said to his doctor's wife, "Tell them I've had a wonderful life." A day later, three days after his sixty-second birthday, he died, living up to all but the last moment out of his deepest center and recording the experience in all its involuted fullness and astonishing longing for more, more, always more understanding of the subjectivity that his inner voice spoke to him about.[8]

Some of us experience that longing, which we might call a yearning for the transcendent, in terms of a love that would pull us out of ourselves into the center of life. We feel it in our gonads, our breasts and vagina; we feel it as the most potent spiritual thrust: to risk the unknown. Selma Lagerlöf, the first woman Nobel Prize winner for literature, describes such a thrusting, risking person, "the famous one," Marianne Sinclair:

> She . . . had traveled everywhere . . . received respect everywhere . . . lighted fires of love wherever she showed herself. . . . She had also loved, often . . . but that fire never lasted long enough. . . . "I wait for him, for the hurricane," she used to say about love. "Up to now he has never climbed over walls or swum moats . . . no wildness in his eye or madness in my heart. I am awaiting the strong man who will take me out of myself. I want to feel love so strong inside me that I will have to quiver in front of him; *now* I only know that kind of love my intelligence laughs at."[9]

IDENTITY AND COMPLEXITY

We do not get anywhere abstractly, however. To recognize the way the anima/animus archetype operates in our own psychology, to see the complex in which it is embedded, requires us to look to the particular images, emotions, and behavior that confront our egos. We do not meet masculine symbols in general, but a particular blond jock, say, who always appears in dreams right in front of the door we open. We do not integrate the feminine in general, but this particular girl with worms in her hair who is taking over my sessions with my analyst and making me wait forever.[10] That is why this material is so fearfully difficult to speak about, to write about. It takes us to the most intimate places in ourselves that we would rather not expose. It shows us what we must work on, even when we have not a clue as how to do so. We want to say to the jock, Get out of the way! or to the girl with disgusting hair, This is my session! But the dream shows us the fact that the guy is here, over and over again, and that the girl always goes ahead of us to the analyst.

Our identity, then, insists on opening itself to complexity, even multiplicity. The inner meeting with the contrasexual other shows us horizons that get bigger, sources of being that dig deeper. There is never a set animus/anima content. We simply cannot divide masculine and feminine into a neat pair of columnar listings. The anima and animus are archetypes and display the indeterminacy characteristic of the species, despite the ease and frequency with which people succumb to formula definitions, the "traditional" Jungian feminine as passive earth, body, irrationality, and feeling and Jungian masculine as active heaven, logic, and hierachical thinking, or the "revisionist" Jungian idea that anima and animus describe diffuse and focused kinds of consciousness, inner soul connection versus outer instrumental activity. We want formulas to make the indeterminate determined, for the sheer size and great depths of these archetypes scare us. We want to make them manageable, in a discourse we can use without uncertainty or doubt, can think and feel in and apply widely, especially to our neighbor. But then, when we succumb, the formulas box us in, prescribe and proscribe all over the place, and leave us feeling wounded in our identities.

Facing anima and animus images as they address us occasions a desire in us to respond by improvising on the basic elements of the body we live in, in this culture, at this time, coming from this family, seeking an expression of love with this other. How can we put the parts together? We feel pulled into paradox, for there is no fixed script to fulfill, yet we know somehow that for each of us a definite way exists. As persons we are open always to indeterminacy, but somewhere, we understand, one individual destiny exists that is ours alone.

It is as if we were a motley gathering of moving parts trying to establish an integrated rhythm. The ego moves toward Self across the anima/animus threshold; the Self and its contents come forward to engage the ego. A vigorous inner conversation ensues, all or some or none of which may reach full consciousness. Clearly, we do best if we can hold much of that interchange right in front of us, so to speak, to examine, to confront, to argue with, taking now one, now the other side in the great force field of feeling and thought that this dialogue represents. We have the example of Wittgenstein to pique our interest, at the very least, in how this might be done. We have Pascal as an incomparable instance of the possible profundity of our *pensées,* our fleeting thoughts.[11] We have Baudelaire as a guide to the multiple correspondences that are locked within us, in both the leading meanings of the word—as a mingling and matching of the senses, of the arts, of the disciplines, and as a kind of internal letter-writing in which we receive news from home, from the center of our being.

What we hear from home is often so moving to us that we think we know finally how we want to style our lives. Foolishly, perhaps, we fall for that grandiose term *lifestyle,* when all we can possibly mean is a way of dressing our identity, of giving it some outer recognition as film actors choose particular ways to move and clothe their bodies, to play with their faces, to manipulate their voices. At best, then, we have a card of identity fitted out with pictures. It is useful to us if we can accept that it is only the beginning of the operation in which we will learn to integrate the moving parts of our interiority. The parts come together in a mad amalgam of levers and gears that is more like one of Jean Tinguély's machines than the computer to which our interior resources have so often been likened.[12] As with the Tinguély apparatus, we must look carefully at what we have before we press the buttons or step on the treadle. There are no paradigms, only the examples of others and our own experience, but what may result is a work of art, something very different from the computer product, which at best is the constricted output of artificial intelligence.

Playing with the buttons and treadles of our Tinguély interiority will send us far inside ourselves to claim our I-ness, our ego identity, and set it reaching toward everything else within us, especially our concealed and only barely acknowledged shadow parts. This is the rich possibility of the identity dialogues. Ego may move toward shadow, and shadow, admitted to the interchange, may act to help toughen the ego to face what the anima or animus demands. That encounter changes our persona, the outer clothing of our person with which we face the world, and the world then has an impact on all these parts of ourselves. We are moved, perhaps greatly changed. With any luck, we will be transformed into persons of quality, more in touch with other persons who separately and together contribute as much as possible to the society of which they are a part, knowing that a larger center all the while secretly feeds them.

Most startling of all, the anima or animus reveals its transformative side, taking us from its elemental beginnings, in the images of father and mother, into the potentially transfiguring powers of these archetypes, with which we can develop our own particular visions of masculine and feminine and of the Holy they point to across their threshold.[13] Then it is that we come of age, as adult women and men, reaching and being reached by the center, out of the depth of our immediacies, no longer mechanically fulfilling the role of son or daughter, depending upon a parental imago to link us to reality. We can receive our own way and offer it as our personal contribution to the common good. Then we have arrived at the "still point of the turning world."

In what follows we touch upon major issues in human identity that anima and animus transform. We persist in our focus on these two archetypes and the transformations they bring about and display. For one of the dangers of this material is not only that it exposes our most intimate desires, wounds, and spiritual longings, but that in its central place in human identity and its relation to the transcendent, it covers over everything in a haze of words and images. Anima and animus possess an uncanny power to make any of us prolix, even the most taciturn among us. In conferences where anima and animus form the agenda, presenters of papers find themselves drowning in words, driven as if by diabolic contract to outline every aspect of the subject matter. We are taking a different route here, concentrating on what seem to us the central issues, issues for all their centrality insufficiently emphasized and dealt with in the literature.

Anima and Animus
and Other People

THE GRAMMAR OF THE PSYCHE

The function of the anima/animus archetype is to draw us into the world beyond the ego. Anima and animus initiate contact with people, things, and ideas that make up the psychic contents of the deeper layers of the unconscious, to which we then try to build conscious relationship. They bring to our attention—through image, emotion, and behavior—bits of the other, to which we react with desire or fear, longing or fascination. This interchange between ego and archetype constellates the core issues of our whole orientation to meaning, to what ultimately matters to us. We enter the space between us and the other, between us and the ultimate, between ego and archetype, and find there in the drama of the opposites a mirroring of our immortal soul.

The drama begins with our parents. For the unconscious has a social role, not only to people our interiority with an inner other, but to engage us with people outside ourselves. Multiple couples—ego and inner other, child and father, child and mother, sister and brother, sisters, brothers—populate our lives. Not only are we launched beyond our egos into the world of other people, but into their unconscious lives as well. There are two sets of encounters made or encounters avoided here: the unlived life of parents that falls onto their children's anima or animus, and the mutual education of anima or animus and the persons with whom we are occupied. We find the basic grammar of the psyche conjugated in terms of these anima/animus interactions or privations.

The grammar of the psyche consists of the basic terms in which psychic experience is conjugated, the essential elements through which consciousness is achieved and exercised. This is the language of the contents of the psyche, made into some reasonably orderly way of dealing with the stormy, murky, exciting sexual passions we develop for others, the sexual identities we search for in ourselves, and their intermingling. In it, we meet words and images for the contrasexual attitudes that inhabit us as they touch on ideas, political issues, art, religion, whatever passionately engages our attention. Here, our interior conversation begins, our sense of our manhood or womanhood is diminished or augmented, and with it our way of contributing to the world, in our particular languages.

"Languages," Michael Polanyi explains in his magnum opus, *Personal Knowledge,* "are the product of man's groping for words in the process of making new conceptual decisions, to be conveyed by words." For Polanyi, the range of languages offers for inspection a variety of different conclusions, "arrived at by the secular gropings of different groups of people at different periods of history." The gropings support "alternative conceptual frameworks," each with its own claims, its own "allegedly recurrent features." And what is true of languages in general is all the more true of the adaptations of language the psyche makes to formulate its own personal grammar. From childhood on, each psyche finds its tongue and discovers its ease in using it through what might be called a blind search, adding its groping after understanding to all those that came before. The search is blind and, at least to begin with, largely unconscious. But it has a context, conscious or not. Groping in the dark, we fall into historical place; we discover the resources of the mind. Polanyi describes this succinctly in this own philosophical language.

> The confident use of the nouns, verbs, adjectives and adverbs, invented and endowed with meaning by a particular sequence of groping generations, expresses their particular theory of the nature of things. In learning to speak, every child accepts a culture constructed on the premises of the traditional interpretation of the universe, rooted in the idiom of the group to which it was born, and every

intellectual effort of the educated mind will be made within this frame of reference. Man's whole intellectual life would be thrown away should this interpretative framework be wholly false; he is rational only to the extent to which the conceptions to which he is committed are true.

We may share a historical place, our contexts may have much in common, but if our interpretative vocabularies are different enough from one another, we find ourselves divided, Polanyi warns, "into groups which cannot understand each other's way of seeing things and of acting upon them. For different idioms determine different patterns of possible emotions and actions." Our beliefs may lead us to burn books or people, to build churches, or, with the sanction of an imagined master race or the conviction of a relentless class war, to persecute and exterminate whole peoples.

What remains urgent for the health of the psyche is that it recognize that it has its own idiom, that it follows a pattern of beliefs, and that it has a grammar with which to examine itself, to identify its beliefs, and to deal with them in an ongoing inner conversation. We live at the end of an era, Polanyi points out with feeling, in which the very idea of belief "was so thoroughly discredited that, apart from specially privileged opportunities, such as may still be granted to the holding and profession of religious beliefs, modern man lost his capacity to accept any explicit statement as his own belief." Belief was seen simply as one person's or another's subjective response to things, "an imperfection by which knowledge fell short of universality."

For Polanyi, this is a dubious objectivism. Speaking not only as a philosopher but as a sometime professor of physical chemistry and after that of social studies, he reminds us that "science exists only to the extent to which there lives a passion for its beauty," that our feeling for that beauty is "uncertain" and fully possessed only by "a handful of adepts." There is no way that beliefs "held by so few and so precariously" can be thought to be beyond doubt, but they remain "the source of all knowledge," gathered from our tacit assumptions and "intellectual passions, the sharing of an idiom and of a cultural heritage, affiliation to a like-minded community. . . . No intelligence, however critical or original, can operate outside such a fiduciary framework." He says we can assert our beliefs or convictions "from within the whole system of acceptances that are logically prior to any particular assertion of our own, prior to the holding of any particular piece of knowledge." This is Polanyi's philosophical approach to the structure and uses of language, as we meet it in others, as we meet it in ourselves. For us, it is a splendid opening to the reality of our psychological grammar.[1]

The terms of our basic psychological grammar are familiar: identity, identification, projection and introjection, projective and introjective identification, relating. Identity is primary, both chronologically in our infancy and in later years in any new beginning in our lives. We exist in a state of unconscious equation of subject and object, whether that object—that other—is a person, an idea, or a part of ourselves. No clear, precise separation or distinction between self and other exists. We dwell almost magically in touch and in tune with subject and object.

The very terms of identification tell us that we enjoy less than total unity with the other. As soon as we begin to entertain consciousness of self or the possibility of imitating the other, we recognize difference and at least a kind of haze of separation; we feel a conscious need for the other. We may stress samenesses between us as a defense against the fear of abandonment, or as a way of palliating any hint of hostility between us. But we know the other exists objectively out there, beyond us. With identification we move against our fears, as we contemplate the pleasures of closeness with the other, of support from the other, of effortless communication and comradeship.

In these states of being, projection and introjection occur normally and naturally. Jung makes the valuable point that projection of a bit of ourselves onto someone else—or onto a political cause, a social institution, or a religion—occurs when the initial state of identity of self and other begins to break up and we seek greater consciousness.[2] It is like a ritual in which we must first cast the psychic content of which we want to be conscious onto the face of our neighbor before we can see it as our own. Projection marks a first step toward consciousness and relationship because it links us to the other on whom we project as well as to the content we deposit there.

Introjection's role is fuzzier. We take in bits of others to use in building up our sense of self. Sometimes we must spit out the bits again, because they so clearly do not belong to us—as, for example, the degraded image of the female that women often cannot help taking in from a misogynist culture and must disown if they are to claim the worth of their own femininity. Often, too, what we introject from parents and lovers becomes absorbed into our own identities so that we can no longer tell where we leave off and the other begins. This underground feeding of each other comprises one of the most valuable unconscious aspects of self in community. Without it, selves would not exist.

Projective identification goes further than projection. Here, we not only deposit a piece of ourselves in others, we also define others in terms of that deposit.[3] We identify them with contents that we leave only for a time with others, to claim them in the future and reintroject them into ourselves. The parts so disposed of seem to stay more or less the same in the other—or we should not so easily put them there. We use the other as a parking garage; when we feel ready to manage the contents ourselves, we will pick up what we have left. Introjective identification works the same process in the opposite direction: we hold the goods (or the "bads," as the case may be) for the other. Parents know all about this, as, for example, they hold onto the future virility of their little sons, the child-bearing potential of their little daughters' wombs, the wives and husbands to come, made in the parental image ("I want a girl just like the girl that married dear old Dad!").

In this mysterious process of exchanging good and bad qualities lies the secret ethical life of a community. We carry things for each other until we are ready to take them back for ourselves. We do this silently, not seeking acclaim for our charity. Charles Williams writes about this mystery as the essence of religious life: we take up our neighbor's burden and carry it.[4] This exchange, at its far-reaching best, promotes the development of anima or animus in a partner and a deeper, fatter identity for us as men or women.

But we can project too much in our identification with the other, leaving nothing but scraps for ourselves. Then we must try to control others, because of all we have put away there and lost for ourselves. One mother sought analysis for suicidal depression following her daughter's departure for college. She had put all her inner substance into her daughter, who took it away with her (as her mother saw things) to the university. That left the mother feeling starved and, more, gutted, scooped out at her center. She became vastly overweight as she tried to make up in food for what she had given away to the daughter. In analysis, the mother came to shift the projective identification of her inner life from daughter to analyst, with the result that much of the work consisted of giving back to the mother what she had so recklessly parted with. That made the space inside her the important one, large enough so she filled it up as she introjectively identified again with her good contents, permitting her to lose weight on the outside.

Relating is the process through which we struggle to connect with each other, using all these different modes—identity, identification, projection and introjection, projective and introjective identification. We stand near to or far from each other, from ideas, from dream figures. We correspond and contrast with all of these. We weave together our modes of being and becoming into a strong, durable fabric. We know, in this process, that as we merge with objects and experience their indwelling and sameness to us, we still exist separately from them, living apart, in our own discrete center. In very strong relationships, we know we meet in a mixture of centralities, at once mysteriously deep inside us and far outside us.

How much we give, and to whom, and when and how we take back what we have given make up the intimacy of sustained relationships, not only with a human partner, but with Being itself. Do we give our all into God's hands, or do we keep certain secret parts back? Do we think that God takes things away from us, or do we know an enlarging of self through a reciprocal giving? In anima projection, or projective identification onto a woman, we may fall into codependency. We try to keep her—inner or outer woman—sure that she is under our control, sure that we cannot stay alive without her. At the other end, if a woman identifies with what she has introjected from a man, she may feel taken over inside, controlled by some force within that cannot be denied its sway, even if it is only symbolic.

Identification, especially in matters of relationship, is a kind of symbolic operation. We respond not only to a particular person but to what we have associated to him or her, symbols of personality, badges of experience, things that stand for the person. Physical facts may be involved; psychological elements are obviously present. All these are real enough. They are like data fed to a computer. But we are not computers. We do not move the symbols of the person around according to a fixed program. We respond with a complexity of feelings and thoughts, both bidden and unbidden. The anima/animus archetypes do much to determine our responses. As Jung is always quick to remind us, "The archetype does not proceed from physical facts, but describes how the psyche experiences the physical fact."

The social anthropologist and philosopher Rodney Needham, dealing with this statement of Jung's, says, reasonably enough, "We need to determine . . . what is to be understood by the crucial term 'psyche.' " Two possibilities quickly suggest themselves. One is to see it as a "formal notion," rather like an algebraical symbol, an x, y, or z that has whatever content we assign it. The other is to understand the psyche in terms of what Needham calls "symbolic vehicles," which "can be viewed as testifying to natural proclivities of thought and imagination"; their "distribution, constancy, and persistence accord them that designation." If that is true—if we understand the psyche in terms of its inner "connections"—a difficulty arises, for Needham and for us, that is put well by Wittgenstein: It is "not that of finding the solution but rather as recognizing as the solution something that looks as if it were only preliminary to it." The solution of the difficulty is, Wittgenstein goes on, "a description, if only we give it the right place in our considerations. . . . The difficulty here is to stop."

Over and over, as we examine the basic grammar of the psyche, we will be made conscious of the limitations we need to put on its connections, designations, and processes. We learn its symbolic language both as a means of expression and of silence. Often learning how to stop is the best way to go on.[5]

UNLIVED LIFE IN PARENTS

Parents influence the anima and animus components in their offspring in ways familiar to us all. A three-year-old girl will practice identification with her father—building up a picture of an animus that will later shape her adult relationships—telling her father she wants to be covered all over with hair like him and to have hairy testicles. One of the surprising excitements of mothering is to receive a proposal from one's three-year-old son.[6] With passionate seriousness he will announce, "When I get as big as Pop, I'm going to marry you!" A leitmotif through the following years is made up of the boy's responses to his mother's question, "What will you do with Pop, since I'm already married to him?" All sorts of Oedipal solutions lie at hand: "We will leave Pop at the office," or he will marry Pop, or his brother, or his sister, or one of the girls in his nursery class, or, best of all, "I will not marry, but be Batman, and have Bat girls." Finally, marriage is put aside, along with Oedipal predilections, "because I go to college."

These are innocent exchanges. The way we wound our young by allowing our unlived life to land upon them is the very opposite. One of the most serious examples is in the contrasexual longings we refuse to acknowledge and deal with. We take great comfort in the thought that we do not have to answer these interim promptings perfectly to spare our children. All we have to do is to struggle with them. But, in fact, our refusal to respond to that inner other, who addresses us so urgently and looks to transform us, ends by threatening any free-hearted living on the part of our children. The atmosphere becomes crowded with the ghosts of the parts of us that we have denied.

When we reject anima or animus and the bridge to the objective psyche it seeks to build, those archetypes flood our ego lives. Like the spirits of the dead, they take up residence in our houses and apartments, in our bedrooms, at our dinner tables, in our kitchens and bathrooms.[7] These unconscious clusters of energy, affect, and behavior crowd the spaces of our children, making their attempts to build their own identities into grim undertakings. Particularly severe consequences befall the very young child subject to such an archetypally clogged atmosphere, as in the example of the first son of a father ambivalent about his own sexual or contrasexual identity. The boy fell under the spell of his father's pleasure in siring an heir. His birth had proved to his father his own masculinity and allowed him to indulge his homosexual inclinations. As heir to a wealthy family that lived on splendid acres out in the country, this boy had no easy access to other children or other men who might have mitigated the father's influence. The father would visit his little son the first thing each morning, before anyone else had stirred. The son remembered great excitement, with erections, as he lay upon his father, who was hugging and kissing him.

David Kay, a London analyst, writes of a similar case, in which the father caught in identification with an archetype played good-mother to his son, perceived as his hero-child.[8] This father, like the other, had not sorted out his own ambiguous sexuality. In both these cases a father's intense identification with archetypal energies fell upon an infant son, foreclosing the space in which the boy could discover and create his own developmental rhythms, both in relation to his budding ego and to the archetypal world. The little boys were swamped; they fell into fused states of identity with their fathers, within an archetypal field.

In both cases, the great intense closeness came to an abrupt end. The father of Kay's patient left after six months, for business reasons. In the case of the young heir, the mother intervened, but not soon enough. Both boys were trapped in longing for their original archetypal existence, thrown into long-lived despair of ever harnessing their own energies for their own identity. In a desperate attempt to feel real, Kay's patient smashed his car at high speed and forced himself to stay awake and feel the pain while waiting for the ambulance. The other man suffered from impotence as well as from loathing of his own homosexual posture. Only after much analysis did a healing dream come that introduced in him compassion for his lost boyhood. In the dream, he and some male friends see two young boys some distance away. They look as if they are kissing. He and the other men mock the boys, make disparaging comments. But the youngsters draw closer, and one of them reveals that they had to stand so close to each other because they both suffered from faint heartbeats. Standing together made it possible to breathe, to live. The dreamer and his friends are deeply touched. For the dreamer, the full weight of his suffering came alive and with it its transforming powers. Some time later, in both cases, it was discovered that both fathers had in fact led secret homosexual lives. From clinical evidence in the sons' cases, we can conclude that the fathers' failures to deal openly with what addressed them across the anima bridge, to identify and claim their homosexual feelings, foreshortened the space of the sons and their ability to work out their own identities as altogether their own, without having to live their fathers' lives for them.

A mother can foreclose her son's space to similar sad ends through her failure to deal with her own contrasexuality. When a son is too quickly enjoined by his mother to grow up, to be responsible in grown-up ways, even to become her confidante, he develops an adult-functioning ego far beyond his psychic resources. "I can do that" and "I must do that" become his tyrannizing inner commands. Some large piece of the mother has fallen on the son—in some cases her fear of her own disordered, rowdy masculinity, her unclaimed disorganized energies.[9] She refuses openness to urgings that are her own, to be surprised, to be pulled out of herself into a grand mess-making spree or into sexual ecstasy. She refuses every aspect of the poking, arousing masculine in herself, shuts it up tight, seals it over with dutiful, efficient, and responsible accomplishments. She fashions her son under the same regime.[10] He carries his responsibility with equal if not greater propriety, and his boyish ego, long buried, is quite lost from view. At best he might develop the spiritual side of the masculine, the logos end of the archetype, but even so he would know too little about its instinctive side, the arousing eros that pushes, prods, pokes, and pounces, like a young boy figuring out how his penis works as his sexual instincts leap and bound into place. A sequence of dreams of a man who grew up in such circumstances shows how he contrived to bring the missing part back into his reach.

In the first dream he breaks in on a meeting of people engaged in the process of electing him to office. One stubborn man holds out against the majority, who try to persuade the dissenter to make the vote unanimous. In his analytical session following this dream, the dreamer reaches the idea to allow the No vote. In his next dream, a lazy, rebellious fat boy, the opposite of his own conscientious self, falls through the ice of a pool, slides under water, and disappears. The dreamer waits for the boy to come up. He hears him pounding his head against the ice, but he never breaks through. This frightening image presents him with the central missing piece of his identity and shows him how it has separated from his growing ego and frozen into immobility. It is still active in him, but under ice, on the other side of consciousness. In the third dream, the dreamer is given a large can of frozen orange juice. As he warms and thaws the frozen concentrate, a child appears at its core, almost embryonic but breathing and alive. Each time the missing piece returns, always in need of care, but rescuable. The rescuing occupied much of the grown man's analytical work as he prepared to receive all of himself.

When a father thrusts his anima on his daughter, comparable issues for the female arise. It does not matter that he may not mean to do so; if he avoids living this part of himself, his daughter is in peril. The effect is as with the beleaguered sons. The space between the ego and archetype in the little girl is crowded in upon by the father's unclaimed life. Instead of facing what comes across his anima bridge from the archetypal world, which his ego should address, he makes his daughter the bridge to his psyche. He projects his anima onto his daughter and identifies her with it. She introjects his anima and accepts the identification for her own. The result is a kind of rape, not physical but psychic. The daughter loses the creative space in which to put together the parts of her own identity, because she must always contend with this great intruder—much too big for her small identity. He thrusts into and either halts or takes over her inner conversation. Much too much of her energy must be diverted to manage this dominating archetypal piece that is not hers. As a result, a sizable part of her feminine ego—which should be integrated and consciously lived in, in her own terms—falls into the unconscious, and she develops instead a pseudofemininity, which is not hers, but her father's contrasexual side, and everywhere betrays the lack of vitality of a male's anima substitute for a woman's actual femininity.[11] This anima femininity shows its positive strengths only when it is where it belongs in the father's psyche, performing its silent bridging work, anchoring his ego in the Self. When it covers the daughter instead, it spawns a fake womanhood that may take years of the daughter's life to throw off.

Sometimes the entangling or loss of her roots in her father's un-claimed contrasexuality can drive a woman to suicide. In one such case, a terrible suicidal urge began to abate only after difficult, slogging work and a dream that struck the analyst as pivotal. In it the dreamer decides to kill herself but must wait to do so until after she disposes of the body of a girl who is already dead. The girl's body is in a place—an opera house—the dreamer associates to her father's personality. Thus in essence the dream introduces a moment of reflection in the urge to suicide. The dream ego must first perform a chore: bury, that is lay to rest, the little-girl part that lives in her father's personality and ought to be dead and buried. The dream says to her that the part she needs to be rid of is already dead. She can be free of it. She need not think of killing herself.

The danger to a daughter when her mother refuses to face the tumultuous emotions with which her own animus confronts her is illustrated vividly by another case example. The woman's husband asks for a divorce. The mother denies her rage, her terror that she might not survive without the money, status, and general security she derives from being this man's wife. She refuses to face and to receive her own suffering. Her young daughter brings it home: she nearly dies from the effects of a mysterious fall off a high ladder onto a barn's stone floor below. The daughter has felt and lived the blows of the mother's unreceived animus.

What the daughter was doing on the ladder and how she fell off are never explained. Some sort of projection or introjection seems to have occurred. In taking care of her daughter over months of convalescence, the mother vicariously nurses her own wounds. The daughter's broken bones carry (projectively) the mother's broken-up life. The mother continues to work in analysis, and a year or so later the same problem presents itself again, but now in more manageable form, for the mother has begun to relate to her own interior experience, no longer projecting away from herself onto her daughter. A dream drama is revealing. Its protagonist is a man who embodies money and power. He makes threatening gestures to a cat that the mother had given her daughter during her convalescence, and it falls many stories to the pavement from the windowsill where it had been perched, but it is not killed. The dream shows the way a dehumanized animus can crush a small feminine ego, but it also demonstrates the resilience and urge to survive of the same ego, personified as a cat. Before the dream is over, the mother reacts with her own fright and anger, now acknowledged and possessed. An unhoused animus no longer threatens her daughter's existence; girl and mother each have their own egos, able to receive and react, each on its own.

What falls out of a son's or daughter's reach when a parent's adult contrasexuality is projected onto the child is a chthonic part of the girl's or boy's own sexual identity. The daughter loses her inner witch—the only archetypal figure with the necessary cunning and craft to outwit the trap unconsciously set for the girl by her adoring parent. The witch cares not a rap for another's needs: she is ambitious for her own ends and will use any means, any sorcery, any guile to attain them. Without such a strong, archetypically chthonic feminine part of herself within reach for her defense, a loving daughter remains vulnerable to her loving father, no matter how twisted the love.[12] Similarly, a son loses the aggressive instinctive masculine, the ogre within, that might move him to roar back at the predatory anima of the mother he loves, or run off to his girl, or join the navy, anything to take him away from the projections of his overly needful, loving mother.

Recovery by grown-up children from contrasexual projection by their parents involves them in conscious claiming of the chthonic aspects of their own sexuality. This is often what they confront on the animus/anima bridge, from the ego side. The animus then may fish up not a male image but a virile female one, a witch who will take no nonsense from a man, even a beloved father. She knows her enemy and how to fight it, which is precisely what a girlish ego needs in order to enter womanhood. The anima presents a boy with a wild hairy man, what may well be the missing part of his masculinity. One adult male dreamed of a Neanderthal man, wounded and bloody, looking reproachfully at him, the dreamer. That was the piece of masculine identity the dreamer desperately needed to integrate into his sexual identity if he were ever to house the Self. One could say, technically, that this was a shadow piece, and that would be true. It would serve as an illustration of the way anima and shadow get all tangled up in each other. But the anima presents it differently to the dreamer, as the wounded chthonic part of his sexual identity without which he would not be strong enough to live in the Self.[13]

The anima or animus eventually brings up any bit of the psyche that the ego needs to enter into active daily life with the Self. The point is not to sort out one bit for the shadow box and another for the persona box, but to see and identify the pull of the Self. In this sense, the Self is rather like God pulling our marooned sailboat home, now with this current of shadow wind, now with that persona gust. Anima and animus can be understood, then, as underwater currents inexorably running toward the Self, which, to complete the metaphor, wants us to flow into it. In religious terms, this is God's love loving us, wanting us, drawing us to live in that love.

The bias of the anima/animus archetypes is toward wholeness here, but it is a wholeness that grows from awareness of the parts that make it up and all the obstacles to that awareness, parental and otherwise. "When we attend from a set of particulars to the whole which they form," Polanyi says, "we establish a logical relation between the particulars and the whole, similar to that which exists between our body and the things outside it." The philosopher-chemist-sociologist sums this up felicitously: "We may be prepared to consider the act of comprehending a whole *as an interiorization of its parts,* which makes us dwell in the parts."

This "indwelling," as Polanyi calls it, is not "merely formal; it causes us to participate feelingly in that which we understand." We rise from our bafflements and uncertainties with "a sense of mastery which enhances our existence." We live within ourselves, taking in, turning over what happens to us, accepting in the process of indwelling, not simply an interior life, but all the life that confronts us.[14]

The fullness of this experience, when we respond with all of ourselves to the pulls of anima and animus, is handsomely suggested by the phenomenologist Maurice Merleau-Ponty writing on "The Body in Its Sexual Being." He draws together the interior and exterior life of the body in a memorable phrase he quotes from Ludwig Binswanger: the body, Binswanger says, is "the hidden form of being ourself," or, Merleau-Ponty continues, we can say, "on the other hand, that personal existence is the taking up and manifestation of a being in a given situation." If then "the body expresses existence at every moment, this is in the sense in which a word expresses thought."

The body and existence, Merleau-Ponty is clear, "presuppose each other . . . because the body is solidified or generalized existence, and existence a perpetual incarnation." That understanding of our bodily being gives special meaning to the sexuality and contrasexuality that define our identity and provide the grammar of our psyche with its root and flowering. "The intensity of sexual pleasure," Merleau-Ponty concludes, "would not be sufficient to explain the place occupied by sexuality in human life or, for example, the phenomenon of eroticism, if sexual experience were not, as it were, an opportunity vouchsafed to all and always available, of acquainting oneself with the human lot in its most general aspects of autonomy and dependence."[15]

We meet in this experience of our sexual selves the endless possibilities of freedom and our ties to others. We discover, when the anima/animus currents have been strong enough and we have learned to live with them, that there is no necessary contradiction between freedom and dependence, but rather that our connections to others may be what makes our freedom endurable. The tutoring of sexual experience, even for one a lifetime removed from its conventional forms of bodily expression, can be seen in that richness of interior organization and unbroken loving dialogue within himself that Augustine reveals in a letter written to a high official who had successfully concluded a peace with the Vandals. He has learned of the "character and high position" of Darius, the man to whom he writes, through two friends, each, like Augustine, a bishop.

The fact that my bodily weakness and the twofold cold, of winter and old age, does not permit me to have converse with you face to face, has not prevented me from seeing you, for one of these friends, when present with me on a visit he was good enough to make, revealed to me the countenance of your heart, if not of your body, and the other did so by letter, so that I have all the greater pleasure in seeing the more inward man.[16]

ANIMA/ANIMUS AND ENVY

Nothing in the unlived life of parents more seriously challenges the inward man growing in their sons or the inward woman rising in their daughters than envy. Envy relentlessly combats a child's formation of an identity of its own—and it is contagious.[17] It interrupts the emergence of the contrasexual archetype in the child, regardless of sex, and the infected child offers its envy of an all-in-all parent to match its parents' envy of the child's youth, beauty, liveliness, or talent. All prevent the emergence of anything like an identifiable image of the child's own person and perhaps of the image-making inclination in the child altogether. This is no small loss, for our only clear and lasting sense of the other sex comes through images. The contrasexual archetype provides us with the image with which we invest persons, beginning with our parents. Envy blocks this process at its genesis, stops it dead; all the ordinary, inherent sexual maturational processes are prevented by envy. We stay caught in a mother-bound state or a mother/father-bound state.

If the child envies the parent in an extreme way, the envy changes the parent into a fixed, idealized object, a perfection that can never really be possessed or shared.[18] That failing, as it must, the envious child fears its own spoiling attacks of envy upon the idealized parent and so diverts psychic energy that should go into developing its ego identity into splitting off from an unpleasant reality and denying the frightful envy. If the parent envies the child, it often shows in an alternation of an "excited" love with a controlling one.[19] Giving on the parents' part may reach lavish proportions, but to the child it feels like stealing. Such giving has more to do with parents' needs to relieve themselves of excited loving laid over a denied hating of their child than with the child's actual needs or desires. This excited loving allows children to develop egos, but pseudoegos, pallid ones—caricatures, almost, of the real thing. When they attempt intimate sexual relations, they cannot develop the essential archetypal projection of anima or animus that ensures the stability of a sexual relationship.[20] The primitive phallic-breast-penis that envy blocked from becoming differentiated may break through again, to be worked on, but also may just sow sexual confusion in relationship with others.

At a quite early stage in the maturation process, boys and girls all but instinctively react against that confusion—spiritual, biological, sexual—that acts in their lives to obliterate the reality of differentiation. They develop a set of fantasies of a life lived as well-developed men and women. They associate themselves with the emotions and feelings, with almost everything in the life of affect, of the ultimate others—grown-ups. This was clear in the bobby-sox era, when thousands of youngsters, pre- and postpubescent, shrieked their appreciation of one after another of the successors of Bing Crosby at the center of popular music, Frank Sinatra, Perry Como, Vic Damone, Tony Bennett. As with Bing and his great rival, Russ Columbo, the songs that engaged the very young were ballads of unrequited love, celebrations of sexual ecstasy, or ironic commentaries on the snares and delusions of sentimental affection in the jazz-lyric tradition. With rock and all its loud and incautious derivatives, the textures changed from those of balladry, irony, and sensuality to those of protest, rebellion, and every known anodyne retreat from an unfriendly world. But again the mark of feeling on the seven- to ten-year-olds and their teenaged cohorts was an adult one. It was never too early to dream dreams of adult sexual conquest or to identify the obstacles thereto, namely adults.

Quickly enough in the development of rock, anything that assumed the configuration of an obstacle to good feeling and whatever supported it, from sexual experimentation to the drugs that made it possible to overcome failures of sexual nerve, became the enemy. Any young body's enemy became The Enemy, defined as racists, sexists, polluters of the environment. And what made it all such fun was that there were so many young who felt this way and could join hands—or whatever—in the new crusades, and all with such tangible, raucous, rhythmic support.

The forms of expression and numbers of young delighting in them have changed, but the story is not a new one. The great pleasure that young readers took for so long in works of literature in which the young not only aped the old but outperformed them is more than a vague parallel to the enthusiasm of the bobby soxers and rockers. There were all those series of tales, built around the startling deeds of prodigious young adventurers, athletes, altruists, not merely competent but ingenious in their endless foiling of villainy, from Oliver Optic to Tom Swift, from the Merriwells to the Rover Boys, from Baseball Joe to the Bobbsey Twins and Nancy Drew. More significantly, there were the elegant works clearly designed for an adult sensibility that the young for so long stubbornly insisted on claiming for themselves.

What could they have found in *Gulliver's Travels* or *Don Quixote* or even *Alice's Adventures in Wonderland?* Those who were addicted knew what they had discovered, even if words did not come to them with the ease or wit of a Swift or Cervantes or Lewis Carroll. There were those constant reductions of a glad traveling consciousness in *Gulliver,* as bedeviling in the form of oversized Brobdingnagians as in the shape of the minuscule Lilliputians. There was the sensation, known only too well to the young, of feeling ten feet tall, like Alice after the first Drink Me quaff, only to be brought down to a size smaller than ever, like Alice after the second drink. The combat with windmills and sheep, the riding off to take on the world in the cause of a raw peasant girl transformed in the imagination of Don Quixote into La Dulcinea, all the faraway princesses rolled into one, made a fine, bracingly rueful sense to the young. It was an allegory of their condition. The good, as they perceived it, was something not to be attained, or at least not until much too long a time should pass. Children did not know in that time, when Swift and Cervantes and Dickens and Hawthorne and Dumas and Fenimore Cooper made such large contributions to their ritual discontents, that what they were undergoing were in fact initiation and fertility rites; that heartening vocabulary had not yet been moved out of anthropology into common parlance.[21] What they did know was a confusion, at least as much spiritual as sexual, and a sometimes desperate separation from the good that the adult world was only too quick to confirm.

Working through this confusion waits upon the breakdown of the idealized object. It may be possible then to sort through the archaic fused object of the parts of both sexes into a differentiated claiming, of this as mine and that as the other's, with the understanding now that what I cannot have in fact I can know imaginatively. The closeness of our actual sexual parts and the imaginative space in which symbols of the opposite sex are born attests to the connection between sexuality and the life of the spirit. In any molestation of a child, sexual confusion is matched by a spiritual confusion. Children who have suffered sexual trauma grow up not wanting the parts that belong to them because they are associated with unspeakable violation of the person. They are left in sexual and psychic and spiritual disarray, without a body ego, or only a shrunken one that omits the pelvic area, anal area, or whatever, depending on the site of violation.

The space between mother and child that Winnicott calls transitional, which gradually enlarges to the space of the culture in which we live and feel alive and real, is what such molestation, sexual and spiritual in its effects, violates. As a result our inner space closes down—or, at the opposite end, never achieves boundaries. We are caught, then, in an endless falling down, never feeling firm ground under us, living without imagination or spirit. No symbols grow in us; our longing for the center seems hopeless and full of despair, or burgeons unconsciously to propel us into violence or madness. Full of crude impulse, never differentiated through successive projections and interchanges with other people, this pull to the center pulls us under. We may arrive at the center, but not with clear consciousness or gladness. We fear what we find there as death-bringing. What should feel good feels bad; salvation feels like destruction.

That spiritual confusion can mix up our relation to the good, however we define it. We may come to envy the good itself, even in ourselves, and refuse to receive it.[22] This inhibits enjoyment of our own good qualities, and of other people's too. It seems too feeble to survive our envious attacks, so we can protect it only by staying outside it.

The sexual counterpart of the spiritual confusion shows up as envy of our partner's body parts, where we should rather be enjoying and receiving them. We treat them with contempt. We project only negative emotions lest we damage the good we fear to receive. The vagina, as one man put it, oozes like a primeval hole that sucks one in; or the penis, as one woman said, feels like a dentist's drill. The accompanying inhibition may result in a woman achieving orgastic release through the fantasy in her head more than through the reality open to her with her partner.[23] Thus she can exert control against the incoming good. The question, spiritual as much as sexual, is, How much reality can we stand?

Somewhere we have known—through ancient tale or modern media enactment, or our own experience—that through our lover's embrace may ring all the bells of eternity. Can we take that? Or must we make it smaller, less important, split it into exchanges of sexual part objects, pieces of flesh, lest its fullness of body and spirit destroy us? This is the panic in the spiritual life as in the sexual, accounting for our insistence on cutting it up into rules, into fixed stages and procedures of prayer, sins and indeliberate faults, virtues and good intentions.

Our contrasexual archetypes act to still the panic by a contrary instruction. Accept the differentiation that is at the root of human identity, they say. Learn, even from the projections, introjections, false relations, and envy that represent anima/animus dysfunction. Accept even the potentiality of sexual wholeness as a spiritual blessing. See that we are accepted by Being itself when we move positively to the opening to our contrasexual presence which our inner conversation provides— when, that is, we accept ourselves.

The Ways We
Educate Each Other

THE DANGER OF HAVING CHILDREN

The danger of the unlived life of parents for their children finds a curious mirroring in the way the birth of their children may threaten the sexual and spiritual connections of the parents. How can this be? We know that having children can be one of life's most fulfilling experiences, astonishing us with the miracle of something existing where nothing was before, a person unlike any other one, God-given, as Saint Augustine indicated in the name he gave his son, Adeodatus.[1]

Precisely because of all that is so moving, and displacing, in the new presence, a child's parents may slide almost without thought into identities as mother and father, no longer woman and man. The wonder of the child, its helplessness, and the enormous, unending amount of work required for its care may combine so to preoccupy its parents that they no longer take time for the earlier wonder in their lives, the fire between them, the spiritual urgency they felt in speaking together about what had happened to each of them.

This is a frequent occurrence in a child's first months, a time that often proves exhausting to its parents. The mother may feel smashed—

tired and weakened as never before by the birth experience, whether natural or Cesarean. If she is nursing, her body continues to undergo profound changes.[2] She suffers from insufficient sleep; she is periodically in a panic about protecting the helpless baby, living in something like a state of identity with her infant.[3] The father also knows about interrupted sleep and the waves of archaic emotion called forth by the infant.

It is not too much to say that our babies offer us the possibility of new relationship to the Self, through the emotions of wonder and gratitude that the new life elicits, the lavish response it engenders to shelter it, provide for it, aid it in every distress or mere threat of illness. An infant may also open us to rage over our impotence to deal with it. Too often we read of a baby being hit or hurt or thrown out the window because the parent could not make it stop crying. A baby can arouse panic and dread in us about our future: how can we provide enough money for all the years ahead? And what if this roaring, spitting, mewling thing is that horror, a bad seed? A baby brings with it a powerful reality.

Instead of expanding to add this relation to the center to the one we already may know in our marriage, we may simply substitute the new parent–infant relationship for the old one between married lovers. Instead of the abundance of the *plenum,* the fullness of being and the generous giving it promises, we efface connection to make room for connection. The loss of any line to the center, and especially this one, is very serious. A child must grow up and claim its own life, its own lines, no longer serving as its parents' access to the Self. Where do they go then? How can they find again, under all the accumulation of years of identification with parental roles—so necessary, it seemed, and so gratifying—the joy they once knew in the power of love to unite them sexually and spiritually?

The spiritual task in this phase of life, just after a baby is born and in a sense a new family is constituted, falls mainly on the father.[4] The mother really must dwell for a time in a state of intense identification with her child. She cannot be in two places at once. She must depend on her husband to hold both poles of their relationship, the ties between two loves whose union, sexual certainly and spiritual possibly, produced the child.

Many marriages suffer sometimes irreparable fractures in this time of stress. Any number of reasons, such as the father not articulating his thoughts clearly, or the mother feeling wild, unreasonable demands, can cause a falling apart, even a bitter polarization. Some marriages never recover from the bitterness a husband feels when his wife accuses him of jealousy of the baby. He may indeed have been acting like another baby, and she must then reckon with two children. But she must not misperceive his intentions, and stoke the first fires of Oedipal rivalry between child and father, by dismissing as childishness his wish to be with her before the baby. Some marriages never recover from a husband's inability to stand by his own altogether appropriate feelings for his wife, all the more insistent in her new motherhood. He must not wimp out, accepting as too many do a wife's dismissal of her importunate mate as childish jealousy. If, on the other hand, he starts to see her as Mother and call her that and nothing more, he will have begun to fail his child. He will be doubting his own deep-seated masculine reactions, abandoning the lively old fires that used to exist between himself and the child's mother through which the child might glimpse some of the ancient mystery between man and woman. There is no substitute for that mystery in a child's background, for the zest of life that comes from having parents who know sexual joy with each other.

That is a joy that pronounces the clearest separation between the sexes at the same time it celebrates their coming together. Man and woman reach toward each other, full of each other, each knowing through the presence of a fervent contrasexuality the magnetic pull of the opposite sex. From that duality, which keeps insisting on a plenitude of equal and opposite plenitudes, comes a clear unity of purpose, but not of identities. The more one knows the strength of sexual otherness, both in oneself and in the other, the more certain one is of what it means to be oneself, man or woman. Love draws us into an ecstasy of parallels, but never an obliteration of persons.

This is the power of the animus/anima archetypes from which a joyous family life gathers its energies, in which each of the sexes in each of the generations finds its freedom and autonomy. Andrew Marvell celebrated the meetings and drawings apart intrinsic to love between the sexes in "The Definition of Love," a poem picked out with ironies typical of the seventeenth-century poet and with an exaltation that is all the more persuasive for perching on the edge of an acid wit.

The separation of lovers is assured by Fate, which looks "with jealous eye" at two "perfect loves" and will not allow them to become one, for "Their union would her ruine be,/And her Tyrannick pow'r depose." And so even when lovers enclose within their love the whole world of love, they must live apart, as far from each other, they feel, as the North and South Poles. The geometry of love is clear in all its despotic exclusion:

> As Lines so Loves *oblique* may well
> Themselves in every Angle greet:
> But ours so truly *Paralel*,
> Though infinite can never meet.

For two to become one, they must remain two. How else should they be able to unite? It is only in their separateness that they can be assured of coming together. The alternative is that external intercourse, the man forever caught within the woman, never to exit and thus never to enter, which is the punishment of the adulterous Paolo and Francesca in Dante's hell.

Separation is nothing to bewail, the poet tells us, for what Fate seals is a more exalted state, in a constant coming and going in love, than any other we can share. It is one that in its joinings and disjunctions reflects the grandeur of the universe:

> the Love which us doth bind,
> But Fate so enviously debarrs,
> Is the Conjunction of the Mind,
> And opposition of the Stars.[5]

The archetypal understanding of love that Marvell sets forth is the very opposite of the vision of Aristophanes in Plato's *Symposium*. In the ingenious, well-liquored reading of the comic playwright at that great banquet, love and original sin are both accounted for, with the misery of the latter forever dirtying the hopes and joys of the former.

For Aristophanes, the only way to explain the multiple ways of sexual identity and sexual attraction is to begin by imagining a set of round primordial creatures, each with four hands and four feet, a two-faced head capable of peering in opposite directions, with four ears to match the other doublings of parts, and two sets of genitals assigned in such ways as to produce three sexes. The child of the sun is provided with male parts only, the woman of the earth with female, and the man-woman of the moon, where sun and earth meet, with male and female parts. These extraordinary creatures of the primordium walked upright, rolled over, did all sorts of acrobatic marvels as a matter of course. When they began to take inordinate pride in their superhuman strengths, the gods punished them by splitting them in half. And so they were left with only half a head, with eyes, ears, limbs, and the like in pairs rather than in fours, and they were condemned to spend endless time looking for their missing halves, half-man for half-man, half-woman for her missing female mate, and the severed halves of the man-woman pairings for their lost other.[6]

In this fateful myth, the sexes can only ache longingly for each other, condemned as they are to wander the earth in unbridgeable separation from their lost mates. One understands the dismissal of such ways of accounting for the difficulties, the uncertainties, and the mysteries of love by Philo Judaeus in *The Contemplative Life:*

> I pass over the mythical stories of the double-bodied men who were originally brought by unifying forces into cohesion with each other and afterwards came asunder, as an assemblage of separate parts might do when the bond of union which brought them together was loosened. All these are seductive enough, calculated by the novelty of the notion to beguile the ear, but the disciples of Moses trained from their earliest years to love the truth regard them with supreme contempt and continue undeceived.[7]

The myth of the double-bodied makes good sense if love is to be understood as a kind of mechanics of sexuality, in which we work with carefully chosen tools and bonding materials to assemble and fit together our sexual parts. The archetypal understanding is the polar opposite of this reading of love. It offers both a happier prospect in which pairings are by no means so elusive or so mechanical, and a more realistic view of sexual identity, in which the full range of our experience as sexual beings, from our first days to our last, can be contemplated and dealt with.

That range of experience extends even to the most trying days of a marriage after a child is born. The mother exists in an altogether understandable state of identification with her baby. After all, she has borne the child, she is feeding it with her own body. The father must, then, take on the urgent task, spiritual as well as sexual, of calling them both back to their antecedent conjunction, the one that produced the child. The man needs all his courage and strength, right down to his glands, to do this. His willingness and ability to insist on time with his wife alone, on time sexually, on time for intimate communication at this crucial point, demand a faith in him in the enduring value of their spiritual connection. Out of that faith, he can give something priceless to his wife and child. To her he can bring the revivifying knowledge that her womanliness exceeds her motherliness; she is not to be defined as Mother. For the child, he can forecast a vision of a life that exceeds a mechanical compliance with parental roles. The feminine presence is not to be equated with mother alone, as the child's mother will show in her devotion to another commanding relationship. Thus, in the parents living their own lives with each other, the child will come to understand, at some level of consciousness, that it will one day have its own life beyond that of its parents, as a man or woman connected through another to Being. This legacy is priceless. It can carry a child through the dark moments when it begins to fear or resent its dependence on its parents, through radical behavior or tantruming episodes of any kind to get free, to claim itself.

These are the terms of a deeply founded, happy marriage. The complications grow more urgent in less salubrious marriages, where, for example, a mother may use her child to fend off the father sexually, or a father may use his wife's preoccupation with the child's arrival to absent himself more and more from intimate relationship with her, or both parents may use their love for the child to fill the emptiness they know from the loss of feeling for each other.

The man, for a time, must carry the woman's animus connection to the Self, to remind her that it too exists, in addition to the new connections of the mother–infant couple, summoning up echoes of their prior life as a couple. The two must share now the rites of two couples, lovers, and parents. Happy is the child whose parents' connection to the Self does not fall completely into identification with their parental role!

The best protection for a child is in its parents' struggle inside themselves with their own contrasexual images, and their sharing back and forth between them the contrasexual summons, now from the wife, now from the husband, in explicit terms, in the clearest possible discussion of the manliness each feels, the womanliness evoked in both.[8] The child itself, in its own growing sexuality, will give witness to the parents of the institution of sexuality in human life, will evoke memories of their experiences with their own sex and the other, offering new opportunities to contemplate and effect repair of old or new sexual wounds. Their anima or animus dialogues will be immensely enlarged. That is the remarkable thing about the gift of access to the center. It always offers more and more. The child offers chances for repair, for growth, for understanding to parents who take care in these ways not to damage their child, who respect in it the enlargement it brings them in themselves.

SINGLENESS

Not all of us find or want marriage or a mate. What then? What does contrasexuality say to the person, single by choice or chance, who is confronted with childlessness when others have children? What about older people, bereft of mate or children they once had? Often we are told there is no problem; sexuality and the family it brings do not matter after a certain age. Utter nonsense.[9] If sexuality is part of us from first to last, and a way we put ourselves into existence with others, then how does it arrange itself when we live singly?

We must all of us, whatever our state in life, struggle with our contrasexuality, because it is there inside us, part of us, because all of us want to live as wholes, because we all live with otherness, in a population of different sexes. We are bound to be drawn into dialogue with animus or anima, with the pull toward Self, even if far from full consciousness. Having children is one of life's great mysteries and momentous experiences, but it is not necessarily everyone's choice or fate. What does belong to everyone is the experience of being engineered toward an inner conversation where we can discover the place in the world our identity can make for us, where, like it or not, the Self points ahead, it mirroring us and we it.

Some of us feel, even late-teenaged youngsters, that we do not ever want to marry, because our parents' unhappy lives together have so scarred us. Some of us were mothers or fathers at twelve or earlier, because of a parent's illness or death or desertion. We mothered younger siblings while still children ourselves. Now in our adult lives we must reclaim our lost childhood. For some of us partnering or marriage threatens a merger so complete that we fear we would disappear in it. Only violence, as we see it, could rescue our sense of Self belonging to ourselves. Some of us long for a mate we never find. Even a longing for love witnesses to its reality, a longing that often reveals our particular courage and dignity. Many of us marry and still live unmated, suffering a deeper loneliness, all the more woeful because it masquerades as a union. Some of us in relationship with another choose not to cement it in marriage because we know it would not survive the stresses of daily intimacy.

Anima and animus have to do with the Self; they act as its proclaimer, as its threshold. We do not escape this proclamation or threshold because we live singly, nor is our crossing of it guaranteed because we live partnered. Single life offers the latitude to imagine and forge different combinations and timings of animus and ego interchange or anima and ego meeting; it does not spare us the commanding power of this exchange in which mutuality defines its terms. We must reckon with an inner partner, who will emerge in us with definiteness, as the *one* who addresses us. Examples abound—Hugh of St. Victor conversing with his soul; Jane Austen, with her acute perception of the dodges and the promises of meetings with one's other; women who engage in the task of regaining their own center, through the kind of multiyear parting that Shakespeare dramatizes so scarily, so winningly in *The Winter's Tale* and *Pericles;* men, as in these same late plays of Shakespeare, who discover in the rejoinings with their wives and daughters an experience of the intensity and the goodness of a resurrection of being.[10] That is what, even in a life that seems preordained to lonely isolation, the connections of the anima/animus dialogue promise. Even at the level of the imagination, they exhibit their great healing powers.

THE DIFFERENCE BETWEEN MEN AND THE ANIMUS AND WOMEN AND THE ANIMA

The anima or animus emerges from the unconscious with all the impersonal force of an archetype and all the overweening intrusive collectivity of cultural conditioning. We need to make it more personal, put it more at our ego's disposal, work to relate more to specific situations in our lives. Otherwise, for example, a woman will try to bully her polyester-loving husband into tweeds, a man will look forever to prove himself with the teenaged girls he failed to impress when he was their age. As Jung puts it, the animus thinks "gregariously, how to solve a problem if ten thousand people had it."[11] With an animus fixed at this level of collectivity, a woman drives others mad.

Interaction with people of the opposite sex is the way anima/animus develops. Mutual education is what occurs when a woman and a man's anima really meet, or a man and a woman's animus. The inner and the outer maleness or femaleness are not the same. A woman's femininity shows a force and vitality, an initiating presence far more vivid than the femininity of a man's anima, which properly is secondary to his ego. A woman's femininity shows greater range and variation, more flexibility and definiteness than the anima function that serves a man's ego as threshold to the Self. Similarly, a man's masculinity houses his whole identity, whereas a woman's animus performs the specific function of forming a bridge between her ego and the otherness of the Self; it is paler than a man's personality, less flexible and more faithful to its specific task, which, when accomplished, allows it to disappear as a personified figure and to act now simply as a threshold or bridge. A man's masculine identity, with luck and hard work, grows fuller, with greater range and sparkle, as he comes to terms with his anima.

Both anima and animus open to the indeterminacy of the archetypal world of the Self. Their bridge functions like a hyphen between ego and Self. Jung puts it amusingly: the anima "sums up everything that a man can never get the better of and never finishes coping with."[12] Our identities, in contrast, have or look to have an unmistakable definiteness, a presence. Open to change and enlargement, they do not display indeterminacy but distinctness. This quality of presence is reached through the subtle interactions between a man's anima and a woman's personality, or a man's personality and a woman's animus. The presence that a man and a woman bring to each other out of the assurances of contrasexual identity is what makes them ready for love. It is never a final presence; love is a persistent inquiry, backed by an accretion of the most absorbing and satisfying facts a man or woman can gather. But even the asking of questions, when the archetypal bridge is in place, can have a bright, defining edge. Like Augustine's restless soul seeking rest in his beloved God, never finally tranquil until it can find its repose in God, the anima-enabled man and the animus-enabled woman push on, looking for the only possible end to their blessed restlessness.

This unsettled condition is a happy one, for even its incompleteness is a kind of revelation, pointing to all that is not yet revealed about the beloved. Only hate stands a chance of discovering and articulating everything about its object, for hate is not only confined to surfaces, to what can be taken in easily and quickly by the senses, but is delighted to be so confined.

The distinction between love's search for the hidden, which is to say the archetypal thrust after depths, and hate's fulfillment in externals is handsomely stated by Hermann Broch in one of the superb little essays that light up his *Bergroman*. That unfinished novel, in some ways the most arresting allegory that has yet been made of the horrors of Nazism, may well have been beyond completion in its restless pursuit of the knowledge of good and evil. As with Pascal, Baudelaire, and Wittgenstein, old insights lead to new insights before the old have been fully articulated. The result may be a loss of a formal structure and an easy continuity, but it is a clear gain of understanding where understanding can only come in short bursts. This is in itself a reflection of the way the anima/animus dialogue works inside us, as this meditation of Broch's makes clear.

Man's prerogative is the search for the ultimate immersion of his own self, and for him love means the assumption of the fate of the loved one, love for him means the apperception of what is ultimately hidden, it means the assumption in their totality of an ungraspable future and of a past sunk in oblivion, both carried deep in himself as his forgotten past and his darkly unknown future, a hiddenness unreachable for himself and yet one which every human being yearns to reveal so as to partake of love, laying open the innermost core of his own self, that which is sunk in his deepest shaft, laying it open lovingly and ready to be loved; but while love thus attempts to descry and offer its innermost core, hatred, on the other hand, cares not for anything hidden, it cares not for the essential core, nor for any past or future, it cares not for any concealments of fate, but hates that which is, the apparent surface and the visibly real, and while love ceaselessly strives toward that which lies at the hiddenmost center, hatred only perceives the topmost surface and perceives it so exclusively that the devil of hatred, despite all its terror-inspiring cruelty, never is entirely free of ridicule and of a somewhat dilettantish aspect. The one who hates is a man holding a magnifying glass, and when he hates someone, he knows precisely that person's surface, from the soles of his feet all the way up to each hair on the hated head. Were one merely to seek information, one should inquire of the one who hates, but if one wishes to know what truly is, one better ask the one who loves.[13]

If a man tends to project all the power of his anima onto a woman, resisting the task of examining it in himself, he may find he has endowed the female with witchlike powers and fall completely under her spell. He has identified her with his projected anima image. If a woman dares to reveal her actual person to the man who has projected his anima onto her, she opens to him the possibility of seeing the reality of his projected image. He will be able to distinguish what is his, the content of his psyche, from what is hers and no part of his projection. She makes available to him then two gifts of being-in-perception: the one she is and the one his anima is. He enters and is received in the imaginative spaces between himself and his anima, and between himself and the woman. In those shared spaces, the borders of his ego and the bridge to the Self touch. Images, symbols, impulses, emotions, awe—all come together to make an inner space in him, his interiority, which graces him with a fine fat, mettlesome security at his core.

If the woman encourages his anima projection, she runs the danger herself of identifying introjectively with his witchlike anima and losing her own sense of a personal identity. She may actually fall victim to an insatiable Kali-like appetite that feeds on those who do not feed on their real selves. Identification with the man's anima replaces the woman's ego. She feels a voracious need for more and more anima projection from men to sustain her corrupted sense of the real. She becomes Harding's anima-woman.[14]

This range of unconscious interaction between men and women raises the ethical questions involved in dealing with projections. It is naive, even wrong, to say we should never project, never carry parts of each other. Invariably, we all do so at one time or another, and often that may help each other to consciousness, carrying our neighbor's burdens for them at a time when they are unconscious. Furthermore, we need some form of projection to develop emotional bridges to each other and to ideas, to social projects, even to God.[15] Thus it is that we begin to give our energies to others, to get involved with and passionate about the other. Projection functions socially; it moves us forward, into the other, into social congress. Later on, after our projective beginnings, we can sort out what belongs to whom, how much of an idea really was in the other, how much we put there, how much an other stands objectively there in its own subjectivity, how much we have invented it. That sorting through is particularly important in relations of intimacy, to human person or to divine spirit.

But we can unfortunately also do violence in this unconscious connection with others, betraying both them and ourselves. A psychologically wise film, *The Lacemaker,* shows such betrayal. A student, well placed in the world, takes up with a simple Swiss village girl for a summer of dalliance. She projects everything onto him, her whole heart and soul. As he finds his own projections faltering and the gap between their worlds widening, with summer coming to an end and school beckoning, he moves to close the relationship. She, in her almost unendurable suffering over losing him, gives new meaning to what we mean by saying someone goes quietly mad. She continues to live with him in her fantasies. She imagines the trips they take together to lands illustrated in posters on the walls of the mental institution where she is confined, working at her job of making lace, year after year after year. It is, we can see, the boy who should have claimed and kept firm hold on his projection, recognizing in the simple reality of the girl what would happen when he lured her to identify with it.

Sometimes a culture can aid men in the kind of anima differentiation that would have permitted the boy in the film to see the girl's reality and his own. The strong feeling that sexual harassment of women by men has aroused, even to the point of legislation, can exert the forces of consciousness in the man who feels caught in a helpless unconscious state of identity with his anima. To combat his inner helplessness, such a man may resort to corrosive ridiculing of a woman's body, to calling castrating any forceful expression of opinion on her part, or to lewd gestures when he passes her on the street or in a car. His fear of inner possession by a dominating anima that really makes him impotent galvanizes a sadism in defense that attacks his inner force by projecting it onto outer women. Laws or public censure that stop him acting out his projections can compel some restraint and may even lead him to discover his inner psychic content for what it is.

The great dramatization of this discovery is the relationship between Ulrich, the title character of Robert Musil's *Man without Qualities,* and his sister, Agathe. Though a character in her own right, it is as Ulrich's anima incarnate that Agathe comes alive. She achieves a relationship of the utmost candor and of a matching delicacy with her brother in the posthumous volume, Book III of Musil's meticulous examination of the way a first-rate sensibility might go about looking for, finding, and claiming those things that define or might be made to define his identity, inner and outer. The search for definition and the discovery of the complex delights of life with his sister as anima incarnation involve Ulrich in exchanges of sentiments, of attitudes, of feelings, and of desires that move from the polite to the torrential and touch almost every intellectual and emotional stop in between. Over all of them hangs the threat of incest. The cover paintings of the Picador paperback edition of Musil's three volumes, chosen from the work of that almost exact contemporary of events in the novel, Egon Schiele, strike just the right agonized sexual note—taut, intelligent, worried, reserved, thrilled.

Somehow, for the purposes of the novel, Musil keeps the tensions alive between brother and sister. One way or another, for the purposes of our understanding, those tensions are dissipated, first by shrewdly chosen words, moving in ever more engaging conversation, then by the rise of archetypes to the surface, reminding both the characters and the reader that this is a meeting of primordial elements that will be lost, perhaps forever, if acted out in compulsive sexual behavior.

All this comes into open view in Chapter 25 of *Into the Millennium,* as the third volume is subtitled. Its contradictory textures are quickly introduced, with sharp reminders in all of them of the anima/animus world. "If I were a man," Agathe pronounces, "I shouldn't have any qualms about treating women quite irresponsibly." Ulrich looks at his curiously accommodating sister lying in the bed vacated by his mistress, Bonadea, just thirty-six hours ago. "All I was trying to get at," he explains about his difficulties with self-love, "was my incapacity to have a mildly reasoned relationship with myself."

What Ulrich seeks is the ability to love an idea the way one loves a woman: "In raptures when one's returning to her. And having her always inside oneself! And looking for her in everything outside oneself!"

He looks again at his sister lying there in his bed, undefended, her face open, "simply a piece of naked body, as women are when they are together in a public bath for women only." He feels both comfort and pleasure in thinking that his sister is grown up, that she has had "all sorts of experiences; talking to her, there was no need to be on one's guard as with a young girl, indeed it struck him as touchingly natural that with a mature woman everything should be morally laxer."

Ulrich is delighted by his anima/sister. He finds no resistance, nothing repellant in her. She is incomparably the best possible fleshification of his self-love. He finds himself so much at ease with her that he tries to push open her closed eyes, though "with the most circumspect touch." Agathe does open her eyes at the touch, and responds with laughing recrimination: "Considering that I'm supposed to be your self-love, you treat me pretty roughly!"

The exchange, we are told, is like one boy trespassing upon another. Their eyes meet, "gaze exuberantly pushing against gaze, like two little boys who want to have a tussle but who are laughing too much to begin." Agathe quickly changes the tone. Do you remember, she asks him, Plato's story about the divided human beings? Of course Ulrich would, but nonetheless she presses on: "Now the two pathetic halves do all sorts of silly things, trying to join up again into a single whole." True enough, Ulrich agrees: "The point is that nobody knows which of all the halves at large in the world is his own missing half." We grab at one that seems right and perhaps produce a child and for a while we think at least we have become a whole person in that way. "But that's merely a third half, which soon shows signs of endeavouring to get as far away from the other two as it possibly can, going off in search of a fourth."

Agathe suggests, "her voice all at once husky," that it would be "reasonable to think that brothers and sisters, anyway, must have gone half the way!" They find resolution of the old Aristophanic divided-body problem, at least as it might touch their relationship, and some defusing of the thickening sexual atmosphere as well, in agreeing that they are in fact Siamese twins. They may be of different sexes and of different ages, a rare combination and an impossible one, respectively, in twins, but still that is what they are.

They are dreaming an ancient dream, Ulrich reminds his sister. To Aristophanes' myth, there might be added Pygmalion or Hermaphroditus, or Isis and Osiris: "With slight variations it's always the same thing.

It goes back a very long way, this desire for a *doppelgänger* of the opposite sex, this craving for the love of a being that will be entirely the same as oneself and yet another, distinct from oneself. . . . " This dream of "two identical-distinct" figures meeting without any of the restrictions of the body is stirred by an alchemy that every age has known. Wherever love is known, so is this: "One finds it in the stimulus associated with every change and every disguise, and in the significance of correspondences between oneself and the other, the repetition of oneself in the other."

Ulrich is left at the end of this remarkable chapter feeling a mixture in himself of "intense stimulus" and "great uneasiness." How else should it be when inner psychic contents are brought alive, in the flesh, before one's eyes, in one's head, in one's heart, in one's soul?[16]

A woman who catches a man's anima projection may be in effect a good sister to him, a good friend, a good lover. The man in chapter 1, so dense and heavy in mien, found great help in a girlfriend who embodied for him the spirit of fun. He found always in her a playful tossing back and forth of anima feelings and contents. It punctured and irrigated his denseness. He began to use his imagination; he grew less afraid of the strange, eerie nighttime ideas and fantasies that he had long experienced. When a man's anima is too passive, on the other hand, a woman may find herself automatically compensating by provocative behavior. She then may indulge in sarcastic jabs, or begin a rival sexual affair to spread the excitement around, to arouse his unconscious. She may be drawn into archetypal patterns of behavior, playing Hera to his Hercules, setting him labors to accomplish, trying to force development in him. As with the fairy-tale princess, if he solves her riddles he wins her; if not, not.

The two couples in the opening examples of the book illustrate how well a good love can repair wounds in ourselves and set us onto paths of growth. The man weighed down by soggy guilt gained perspective from his wife's gentle, humorous teasing. He came to laugh at his unconscious tendency to react allergically to other people's misfortunes, as if they were his fault or his job or duty to fix. The wife never said in so many words, You are being tripped up by your mother complex; you feel you must rescue everybody the way you felt you must cure your mother's depression. But her gaiety and pleasure in him captivated his anima, brought it to differentiate the heavy mother burden—from himself. She set both him and his anima free to be themselves. The woman whose deep receptiveness provided an anchor to her husband's ambition, so that he could focus it and develop projects in the outside world, herself gained from his aggressiveness. His challenging questions to her about where she stood on issues, about whether she would join him in effecting his projects, moved her to go far into self-examination and its inner dialogue and thus to sort out where she stood on these pivotal matters, and to what ends she wanted to use her energies. Her animus took her quickly to the wide regions of possibilities of Self. Her husband made her connect her newfound access to the All with here-and-now particularities. In full consciousness, she was able to strengthen her ego connection to what her animus put her in touch with.

MUTUAL EDUCATION

Anima/animus education goes both ways: the anima educates a woman and the woman educates the anima, and the same with animus and man.[17] The anima can spur a woman to experience her own instinctive capacities to stir up a man's imagination and with them her achievements. She finds herself pulled sometimes toward heroic, intense longing for connection to the center. Similarly, a woman's animus can call forth the hero in a man, putting him in touch with his own instinctive capacities to rescue the woman from peril, to ride off with her, to become larger than life in brave deed or magnanimous self-offering. The contrasexual archetype pulls man or woman into the big territory of the Self *in themselves,* filling out what really may be boundless potentials and rescuing them from much too narrow ego stances.

An ego identity can also pull anima or animus into more focused connection with a man or woman's ego life, to make full use of neglected capacities. One woman put a man better in touch with his chthonic sexuality by refusing his usual friendly pattings as overtures to sexual meeting and demanding a more open, conscious pursuit of his desire for her: "You must win me," she said. This is different from casting a man in the role of solver of the riddling perplexity of a woman's sexual reactions that she cannot herself unlock. This woman had her sexual response at the ready; she wanted her man to want it and to relate to her with desire specifically directed to her. Another woman, annoyed by her husband's tendency to cast her in the role of caretaker—part mother, part laundress—bit his lip when he bent to kiss her after asking her to address all his Christmas cards. He took notice! Still another woman, a practicing Mormon, who had worked hard to cook a special dinner for her husband and an old friend of his, went on strike when she heard the friend say to her husband, gesturing in her direction, "I want one of those." Immediately she stopped clearing the table and would not serve dessert. She sat down to join the men rather than serve them and waited for her husband to help with the dishes. In fact, she waited three weeks! The food, napkins, plates, crumbs, everything sat on the table all that time. Her husband's and his friend's simpleminded assumptions and passive stance triggered aggression in her animus. She connected to her deepest beliefs about what relationship meant between herself and the man she loved. She felt inwardly supported in a fight for the best between them. Her ego could wage war and endure because it was connected all the way down, through the animus and across to the Self. Eventually she did break through to her husband, quite successfully.

RECLAIMING CHTHONIC LIFE IN SEXUALITY AND CELIBACY

Breakthrough is necessary in the intersexual and contrasexual world, for what falls out of our ego identities when we are passively held in familial or traditional assumptions is our deeply grounded chthonic sexuality and spirituality. We stay "nice" boys and girls who have become "nice" matrons and gentlemen. We have not forgotten our original connection to the center, but rather than fight to stay in touch and deepen the connection, we have settled instead for childish dependence on others' experience of God and the good whether they are church-oriented, come through a militantly atheistic political ideology, or are just a bumbling know-nothing attitude we have lapsed into. We miss the spark of blazing into our own passion for another human being, which hides passion for Being itself. We lose the witch element, the ruthless life of instinct that always undergirds a daring spirit.

Our lack of housing and taming for these chthonic forces robs society too. In our niceness we leave the groups of which we are a part dangerously exposed to attack and infiltration by precisely those forces and their energies in demonic form—such as the ruthless despots who take over a government, such as a mindless racism that boils over into riots and killing, such as epidemics of prejudice and scapegoating of apparently milder kind that overrun human relationships and reduce them to bloodless civil wars. We possess no force immediately accessible to ourselves to oppose the demons and their wars and epidemics when we have failed to house the passion, the witch, or the instinct, and to learn how to use it.[18] Often enough what anima or animus brings us across its bridge from the Self is precisely those bewitching elements, those demon lovers, who can seduce us from our safe certainties into fuller living if we can identify them for what they are and make good use of them. They stand ready to support us in bursting through our boundedness and going far and deep into ourselves.[19]

Few go deeper than genuine celibates. It may seem odd to include those who take vows of chastity in a study of anima and animus issues, but of course they too must reckon with their inner voices, their inner daimons. The issue here presents itself in the form of risks of living toward Self without a mate to help mediate the ventures. The danger looms of locking oneself safely up in rule and regulation and staying there only because no better alternative offers itself. Then the religious vow lives only in superego interdictions and not as the calling of the soul in love with God. Or the threat of a special friendship presents itself, one which is technically chaste, but in fact puts the friend in place of the human lover one had presumably sacrificed.[20]

The celibate faces, just as anyone else, what comes across the anima/animus bridge to confront the ego. Celibates, like anyone else, must respond, reject, sort out what to keep or to discard of these contents, must learn how to limit their ego life in the world to what can be integrated, and following the bidding of anima or animus, connect directly to larger existence in the Self, one that challenges all comfortable assumptions, such as that fleshly passion has no place in the celibate life. The celibate differs from the rest of us only in not having an immediate, intimate flesh-and-blood partner with whom to sort out projections and reality.

If sexual love carries in it the spark of the spirit, and the lovers' task, finally, is to fan that spark into a blazing *living* fire, loving the beloved in that spirit and loving the spirit in the beloved, celibates must go even more directly to the spark. The other who partners them, the one to whom they reach for immediate contact, is the ineffable spirit. The celibate gives up only the concrete flesh-and-blood form in which the spirit is glimpsed by others, leaving open and empty the space the beloved occupies for the lover. That for the celibate is both sacrifice and opportunity. The space is empty and open for the spirit to come right in. Celibates consciously, willingly suffer the loneliness that afflicts all of us at some time. They seek regular daily communion with the unseen spirit—in prayer and meditation, yes; in fanciful image too. Theirs must be a steady alertness, like the wise virgins ready with their oil for the bridegroom's arrival. Celibates seek then to be attuned to every hint of the Self's desires.

We too easily forget that the celibate is as much motivated by self-love as any other love—not *selfish* love but self-love, which comes from and returns to love of the Self. "Our love of God cannot help being largely if not entirely need-love," Josef Pieper argues, using C. S. Lewis's word for the natural and wholesome urge he calls "disinterested self-preservation." Is it eros? Yes, he answers, going to the last book of Augustine's *Confessions* for his text. *Pondus meum amor meus; eo feror, quocumque feror,* Augustine says: "My love is my weight; wherever it goes, I go." Pieper's reasoning is as true psychologically as it is philosophically and theologically.

> We can no more govern this primal impulse, which affects all our conscious decisions, than we or any other being can have dominion over our own natures. And, once again, it is inevitable and incontestable that this natural urge for fulfillment and completion is basically self-love. "Angels like men by nature strive for their own good and their own perfection; and this means loving themselves" [Thomas Aquinas, *Summa theologica,* I, 60, 3]. Therefore, insofar as we are willing to accept the more or less established usage that defines eros as the quintessence of all desire for fullness of being, for the quenching of the thirst for happiness, for satiation by the good things of life, which include not only closeness and community with our fellow men but also participation in the life of God Himself—insofar as we do accept this usage, eros must be regarded as an impulse inherent in our natures, arising directly out of finite man's existence as a created being, out of his creatureliness.[21]

The celibate chooses that state in life—or, as some prefer, that state chooses the celibate—to achieve happiness. Love is the effective means to arrive at happiness, need-love, erotic love. In the interior conversation in which celibate love finds its most satisfactory voice, the language is often more highly charged than it is in the world of fleshly love. The self-love of the saints is unmistakable, and it is erotically triumphant.

It is unfortunate that some mystics, and even more nonmystics, writing about the mystical experience use the term "self-abandonment." Only in a very special sense do the great religious lovers abandon themselves—the same sense, really, in which all of us who are deeply in love put the good of our beloved before our own. But self-love as need-love remains the motivating urge. And the fulfillment, however different in degree, we must understand as not all that different in kind from the intensification of feeling, in spirit as well as in body, that earthly lovers experience.

So it is that celibate lovers, as confidently in many Eastern religions as in the Judeo-Christian tradition, use a highly erotic rhetoric as a way of trying to convey at least some sense of the ecstasy and exaltation they have known and are so eager to share. Bernard of Clairvaux, commenting on the most frequently used material for this rhetoric, the verses of *The Song of Songs,* explains that if we have the grace and the experience to understand the *Song,* we must recognize that "it is a joyful utterance, not of the lips but of the heart, and of harmonious wills." Only lovers in this spirit can really make it out. "Its accents are not heard abroad by everyone, but only by those two whom it concerns, the Bridegroom and the Bride, the singer and the Sung," which is to say self and Other, the world of anima and animus.[22]

Celibate and partnered persons both engage in the elaborate process of sorting through projection and reality to mark out the provinces of self and other. How much do I love the other in order to fill my own needs, to fatten my own image, and how much do I love the other in his or her ownmost life? How much do I love the best self of the other and give my best self back, and how much do I appropriate to aggrandize myself? How much of the reality of the other does my projection lead to? How much does my projection uncover unknown parts of myself? How much of divine life does my loving the other bring me to and how much more of the life in myself does the divine thus uncover?

All these questions and countless more constitute the work of lovers—whether in sexual embrace or in prayerful joinings of asceticism. This repeated process of sorting out projections and reality is like the *albedo* stage of alchemy, an endless washing and whitening in which we distinguish our complexes from reality and search through the archetypes to go beyond them, to that plane where we no longer need the language or the images of anima and animus, where words fall into silence and pictures cease to matter.[23]

The Transformative
Animus and Anima

MUCH HAS been written about anima and animus as representing the elemental life of masculinity or femininity in us. Much has been written, too, about their negative effects, and Jung has been criticized for overemphasizing the negative side of the animus and for telling us so little about its positive effects. It is true that little has been written about the way anima and animus function to transform us positively. That is our focus here. We can even see animus/anima process as part of the alchemical *albedo* stage, of washing and rewashing our complexes, anima and animus slowly differentiating our identities from the compelling behavior, emotions, and images in which they have been ensnared.

As Erich Neumann makes clear, the work of the elemental feminine is to hold us in being. We experience it positively through what Winnicott calls the "good-enough" mother whose ordinary devotion and love preside over our passage from absolute to relative dependence, and thence into independence.[1] If, however, a mother's love is blocked or diverted by the need to defend her own wounds, her children may not find the support of their inherent sexual and contrasexual processes to mature. For them, the elemental feminine will be felt as a snare, a hobbling of personality, holding children at an early stage unable to grow or leave their initial dependence on a being outside them. The transformative animus or anima may come to the rescue—like the hero freeing the maiden from the dragon attacking her castle or the heroine undertaking a risky journey to free a prince from a witch's spell.

The struggle the journey represents is primordial. It springs from the desire every people has felt to get to the roots of its being, both collectively and individually. The masculine and feminine archetypes reflect, as anything reaching to the roots must, both the collective and the personal unconscious. The Russian symbolist poet and classical scholar Vyacheslav Ivanov defines the primordial transformative journey and its conflicts in arresting terms in his study of Dostoyevsky, *Freedom and the Tragic Life.* As Dostoyevsky does, he understands the people—those for whom the journey is made and the struggle endured—as a personality, following in effect the biblical characterization of peoples as personalities and angels.

There are two principles in "the metaphysical unity" of the people, as Ivanov reads Dostoevsky, the feminine and the masculine. They pit soul against spirit in a struggle that must finally be resolved by joining the two, the feminine soul and the masculine spirit. The feminine is rooted in "the universal Mother, the living Earth, as a mystical entity." The masculine appears in "the personality of the people," as a force for leadership, like Plato's *hyemonikon,* or in apocalyptic terms as "the Angel of the people." The work of the masculine spirit is to lead a people to a free decision, either for or against God. Thus does it give a nation and its people their place in history.

It is urgent to understand that the decision made by a people is a free one. It can move toward or away from "its selfish Ego," choosing or not choosing to "bring to Earth the tidings that it bears God within itself." Russians knew this fateful decision well at the time of Dostoyevsky and know it well again now, as Ivanov would surely insist again, were he alive; for, as he says, only "by bearing God within itself can the people's Ego become universal, the Ego of the whole of mankind."

Another alternative remains. In the evolving of a people, "a temporary indecision or impotence of the masculine principle" may lead to an alienation of the Angel, a separation that will be seized upon by "the Powers of Evil" in the form of the "group-soul" of "beings inimical to God." They will become the spiritual lords of a nation, dominating its people's soul and throwing it into a "blind frenzy." Writing long before the collapse of the Soviet system was even thought to be possible, Ivanov recognized, with Dostoyevsky's help, that the communist center would not hold.

It is in these terms that he analyzes *The Possessed, Crime and Punishment,* and *The Idiot.* He sees as the agony at the core of these novels, as it was earlier in Pushkin's *The Queen of Spades,* the "cleavage" between appearance and reality and the dominance in it "of a form of consciousness—presumptuous and illusory, because its roots in the nation are snapped—which withers up man's sense of his organic union with Mother Earth, and thus of the living reality of God and of the world." A female avenger rises from the chthonian darkness to do battle with the forces of "visionary pride and rapacious high-handedness." A figure of unimaginable knowledge and power for either good or evil, she has set herself against "the wild attempt to annul by violence the decisions of eternal Themis," the goddess of law and justice.

We must understand the vision and the struggle of this "emissary of Mother Earth" if we are to understand Dostoyevsky, "for clearly all his works are concerned with man's revolt against Mother Earth, the latter's resentment and her appeasement by the expiation demanded by her and made unto her." The terms in which Ivanov describes the struggle and its participants are at the center of being, those of soul and spirit and of feminine and masculine, but Ivanov does not use this vocabulary to reduce everything to high-sounding, conflicting pairs. Ivanov's dichotomies never become a reductive dualism. His thinking, shaped by his classical training, his religious convictions, and his experiences as a poet, moves in the circles of a complex and quite concrete contrasexuality, even when his speculations are most abstract. There is always at least an oblique anima/animus angle in his work. His reflections on the masculine and feminine principles are in the service of wholeness, not of separation.[2]

His short poem "Love" speaks eloquently of the impulse to unity inherent in eros and of its transformative effects. It is a sonnet elegant in its quick characterization of the pairings of the lovers. They become two tree trunks set on fire by a thunderstorm, two meteors in the night, a two-pointed arrow with a single fate, two horses reined by one hand and goaded by one spur, two eyes with one view, two trembling wings in a shared dream, two mournful shades over the holy tomb of ancient Beauty, and a mouth with two voices for the same mysteries, each the same Sphinx for the other, and the two arms of one cross. Always in this world, Ivanov is telling us, even in its tragic conflicts, there is the promise of a transformation that will lead to wholeness, a transformation inherent in our sexual identity.[3]

The transformative anima or animus appears not only in times of trouble, but on its own in its own time. When we find right relation to its transforming powers, we can differentiate ourselves from our parents and move into our own identity. Even our shadow life is aroused by this animus/anima function, to reclaim the lost good piece hiding in otherwise worthless parts of ourselves. It provides an added path to the Self, one that is open and wide enough for us. Because the Self is boundless and its archetypes so numerous, many solutions exist for relation to it, but because we live as space-time creatures in a history and a society of boundaries, one way will emerge as unmistakably our own. The transformative animus or anima will point us to it.

If animus and anima function, as we have argued, as a bridge connecting our ego identities with the Self, they must introduce us to that liminal space, the threshold that leads from the personal to the archetypal. There, at the edge of Self, we know ourselves in all our idiosyncrasies as we touch the timeless world of responses that exists in latency in everybody.

In that threshold place, symbols arise from our ego side in the play of our imagination; the transitional place, so dear to Winnicott, becomes the place where our adult culture begins to form. There we rest from demanding ego projects and specifications of purpose that must be accomplished; we engage in only vaguely purposive meanderings, reposing in the space behind the notes of music, in intervals that accrue to us unmistakable enlargings of our sense of being alive and real and received.[4]

There, too, symbols emerge in surprising ways from the other side, the archetypal. Connections occur as if by magic. We see into an old longing with new eyes and new eyes see into us. We stand for a moment outside our skins, looking at ourselves anew. Anima or animus acts as a lens to bring into focus the Self we can see now in the other and in ourselves. To put it dramatically, we can, if only momentarily, see our husband's affair from beyond our outrage and pain, as an entry into his personality, where he is wounded, where he has sought his center. That insight rushes to consciousness to join the wound he has left and our urge to live from the heart of things. We glimpse the arc of a symbol throwing things together, good things and bad, and for an instant uniting them into something approaching meaning. Such insights engender hope for recovery from pain, hope for a life. To take a happier example, we see our husband coming toward us in a crowded street, to meet as planned, and right there, in the midst of heat and city noise and the day's fatigue, we see the immortal soul of this man, his priceless qualities, his once-and-for-allness, and gasp anew that he should ever have come into our lives. What miracle accounts for his coming to us?

The word is made flesh in these transformative meetings, made flesh in all its meanings. The incarnation of love brings joy, brings pain. We look with astonishment on the marvel that has entered our lives in this fleshified other. The sixteenth-century French poet Louise Labé, hoarding every scrap of memory of the great love of her life, is still on fire many years later with what it was like for her when she was sixteen and knew her beloved in the flesh. It was a short-lived affair; she was deserted by her miraculous man. She has since married and known feelings for others, but it is that first swift-moving, all-gathering experience that commands her being. The tense is the present; it is all still very much alive to her. Not Ulysses, nor any other man, she tells us, nor anyone else who may have yearned for "that holy face," with all its goodness and splendor, could have ached more than she for her man. She is wounded; she is poisoned by the sting of a scorpion. She would like the dawning sun to extinguish the pain, but if the desire she feels were to be burned up with the pain, she would die.

Labé's output is small, a sequence of twenty-four sonnets, three elegies, and a prose *Dialogue of Love and Folly,* but her feelings are large. In the sonnets, the first of which is in Italian, she speaks with every sort of feminine intensity, with undisguised disgust at the way she has fooled herself, lied to herself, been swept with holy fury and kept awake with human misery, with a suffering so intense there was nothing to do but scream the night away. And yet still she must toast the memory of her love, the joy of her lover's "caring face," the glow of his countenance that fills the heavens. To other women she says, No blame, no derision; I have loved. She has been transformed.[5]

Louise Labé's Italian counterpart, Gaspara Stampa, brings a similar passionate outburst to poems written in the same period. She was born two years earlier than the Frenchwoman, in 1523, and died twelve years earlier, in 1554. She, too, was deserted by her lover, and in her work also there is the constant note of a joyous suffering, of a corrosive beauty, of a thankful and a cursing and an unstoppable heart. "Do you think that I am a Hercules or a Samson to be able to bear such misery?" she asks. She never sees the day of Christ's birth come, incarnation of God himself that he was, without remembering the way Love, "stretching his net between two beautiful eyes and a smile," caught her, eyes she reminds herself that now reside far from her. Both women have too much feeling and too much honesty about it to fall easily into the clichés of Petrarchan love poetry, the dominant strain in the writing of the Lyons of the first and of the Venice of the second, however much their experience does in fact duplicate the synthetic oxymoronic freezing-burning humors of the style. Theirs is a form of recollection that verges on prayer, prayer at its best, torn from head and heart and strength and soul without protective covering. It is terrible to remember, all the high moments and the low, an almost unendurable pain, but to forget it or to throw it all away would be worse. Stampa can say with conviction that she does not envy the angels in any way their great glories and blessed life in the presence of their Lord, because her delights are of such a sort and so many that earthly hearts cannot take them in, at least as long as she has before her the serene and life-giving eyes about which she must always write. She has been transformed.[6]

Transformation, Not Sublimation

When anima and animus function positively in their transformative mode, they usher in such a seeing. They open that space between us and other, whether the other be outer or inner or both, and in so doing change the mixture of ego and Self contents. This effects transformation, not just sublimation. We feel in touch with a ruthless instinct, a surging vitality and frightening energy that brook no interference. We can well imagine an anger that pulls interior triggers into murderous action, or a devouring appetite that consumes not just a person driving off in noisy high gear in her car but the car itself. We are put in touch with images for those instincts—numinous archetypes of the power of sexuality that sometimes burst into our dreams and leave us panting and wet on the sheets, or images of power so intense and consuming that we dream of uninsulated high-voltage lines striking out after us and sticking to us when they have found us. Sex, power, hunger, survival, and more—the instincts and the images that represent them archetypally come rushing toward the ego in us, so small and personal, so hidebound and overly protected by cultural ritual.

In transformation we not only find ways to meet and channel these parts of the psyche where instincts find their images, but can see a way to escape the confinements of impulse. We look to the ego to control the instinctual archetypal force rising in us, not always realizing that without animus/anima intervention, we may just be turning the problem over or around to its other side. The maternal instinct, so strong in many women that it will burst out in illegitimate pregnancies, if not in a sanctioned form, may be restrained by the ego from conceiving children; it will then just shift its ground to some subterranean level. A woman stops getting pregnant, but instead compulsively mothers everyone in reach. That is sublimation, not transformation.

In transformation there are always changes of instinctual energy.[7] We know the size and quality of these by the changes in the images that accompany them. A woman experiences her deep longing to be a mother in vivid personal images that drive across the animus threshold to her receptive ego. The ego then brings it back—all of it, the urge to conceive, to give birth, and to nurture—across the threshold, offering it up in service to the Self. Actually conceiving or not, the woman lies in the hands of the Self—not in simplistic sentimental dreams, but in responsible, knowing ways. She feels the longing all the way down and consciously offers it to what is beyond her ordinary power to understand. In such action the tyranny of instinct over ego breaks. The instinct does not overrun the ego, does not control it or fall victim to it by identifying with its power. The ego reaches out to experience the instinct and differentiate from it and offer it to a source beyond itself and larger than it. The image of conceiving a child changes from instinct to possession to gift. Without this transformation, the ego becomes possessed by instinct and cannot face its great powers consciously. The transformation then goes in a negative direction, dragging the ego into the unconscious.[8]

Positive transformation awaits the woman closely related to her animus. Her sexual instinct to open herself, to take in, to be filled in—her "yearning passivity," as Esther Harding calls it, in an ironic play on a

Freudian commonplace—her desire to be acted upon, to have something wrought upon her, can be tamed by social restraints and by her ego freeing itself from instinctual pressure.[9] But controlling instinct is not enough. She needs actively to relate to it, to meet it and search out her feelings in it and mix its impersonal pressures with her personal aims and experiences. Otherwise, the instinctual need will continue to live in her, but estranged from her now, making her feel humiliated by its passive yearning, overcoming her, making her feel degraded by its power. She may then project this sense of shame onto a man, as if he, in wanting to engage her sexually, necessarily intended to degrade her. She projects onto him her unresolved feelings about her own sexual drive.

The transformative animus figure, joined in deliberate thoughtful inner dialogue, looks to move a woman into better relation to her instincts. She may dream, for example, of a man she consciously would have nothing to do with, but in the dream responds to with overwhelming desire. The dream surprises, even shocks her. Because she would shun such a partner in reality, never pursuing any relation with him, no matter how reserved, she must reckon on his magnetic dream appearance as a message from her own inner reality. He, as a dream figure conjured up by her transforming animus, looks to wake her up to her own sexual longings.

Sometimes such a wooing animus figure may be a male homosexual and clearly off limits for an actual sexual liaison with the dreamer, for she would not be any part of his desire. But in the dream it is *her* desire that is the issue. Becoming conscious of her sexuality through the unavailable man serves splendidly as a figure of dream rhetoric to put her in touch with the strength of her own desiring. This is one of the leading functions of the homosexual animus in woman's psychology. Because he does not threaten her sexually, she can afford to try on her own sexual feelings with him and better explore connection to her own sexual instincts. This transforms her sexuality from a fearful and repressed state to one of immediacy and potency. The change in animus-images signals the transformation her instinct is undergoing. As she moves from degrading-man whose sexual advances the woman fears and hates, to homosexual-man, with no sexual designs upon her, whom she desires without fear, she can look more equably upon her sexual feelings. The homosexual animus figure may be transformed in dream, as in actual experience, into an available heterosexual who desires her in his turn. As a valuable byproduct of this transformative process, a woman may gain appreciation for the homosexual man and all others she may have stereotyped as inexorably hostile toward women, as she confronts the masculine in herself through animus presence.

Two poems by that most modern of ancient poets, Dante Alighieri, offer a remarkable example of the wooing animus working to arouse a woman to see the masculine inside herself and outside, to bring herself to know the man represented by the poet and what moves him, to feel her own hardness, to know her beauty and her frightening destructive coldness. She is challenged, in effect, really to see herself and her defenses against herself, and to overcome them in these stirring works, two of the splendid short poems of the poet that have for too long lived in the shadows of the *Commedia* and *La Vita nuova*.

The first poem, the shorter of the two, begins in shadow, *lasso!* (alas!), in the time of year when the hills are white and color fades from the grass, in a time when the poet's desire is "rooted in the hard stone that speaks and feels as if it were a woman." She is as frozen as snow in the shade and will not warm even in the great change of seasons when she herself is garlanded in grass and holds such beauty that Love itself comes to stand in her shadow. She has qualities that exceed those in gemstones. There is no running away from such a woman, nothing that will provide sheltering shade from her piercing light. Her loveliness is such that a stone would be moved by the feeling Dante has just for her shadow. The rivers would turn back into the hills "before this soft green wood catches fire, as a beautiful woman is accustomed to do for me." He is resigned to sleeping out the rest of his time and to live on grass alone just to see where the shade is affected in it by what she wears. In the darkest shadows of the hills, her loveliness disappears into the beautiful greenery the way a man might cover a gem with grass.

The longer second poem represents a turning around, the poet affecting a deliberate hardness of tone and harsh speech to match the woman's rough nature and impenetrability. There is no arrow that springs from a quiver that could get through to her. Nothing will strip her, no weapon avails against her; there is no shield that she does not break apart, nothing that will cure him of the agony of his feelings, in which he lies with Love standing over him, the same sword in hand with which Love overcame Dido. If only this Love, which will not show him mercy, this Love which again and again attacks his heart, would get her, that murderess who assails him by day and by dark! If only he could grab those beautiful tresses that whip him, he would stay with them from matins to vespers and midnight, not in any gentle way with this switch that whips him, but like a bear at play! In revenge, he would stare coldly at her eyes from which comes the fire that inflames his heart, the heart she has slain—"and then, with love, I would allow her peace again." Go, the poet instructs his poem, go to her who has gravely wounded me and robbed me of what I want most; pierce her heart with an arrow—high honor comes through such revenge.

The power that comes through poetry of this kind, written from an apparent powerlessness, is the power of the transformative act. The poet admits his feelings, describes them at length, attacks her who attacks him and who attacks herself as well. It is not so easy to accept being *una dura petra,* a hard stone, even if one is also *una bella petra,* a beautiful one, with all the resonances of a gem or precious stone that the addition of *bella* to *petra* conveys. Frozen in snow, frozen in springtime, equally unavailable to herself and to the poet, the woman, like the dreamer above, must look to herself, must look far within herself, to find her sexual self, her living identity. Here she has the added incentive of some elegant verses from which to gather, at least in part, the transformative energies.[10]

THE RANGE OF ARCHETYPE

Another way to put the same point is that the transformative animus or anima can use the great range of an archetype, not just to one end but to many. Is the animus the father, or the son, or the wise old man? The transformative animus, as the positive examples show, moves a woman away from fixation on the negative end of the masculine, as invariably dominating and determined to shape the female entirely to his own desires. This animus figure, in his homosexual guise, presents the masculine as lover of men, absorbed in his own sexual dynamics. More, he presents the dreamer with a picture of her own absorption in her own instinct, telling her this way that she is no more available to the opposite sex than the homosexual man. That is the point he makes to her: Look to your own sexual dynamics and stop blaming men for them. That is to open her to her own desire.

A woman may really fear the tremendous force of her own sexual arousal. Its power may make her tremble. She may repress this instinctive response, which will only force it underground and may occasion a destructive frigidity in her.[11] Her unclaimed fear may act itself out by estranging her from any response as just too risky. Or she may try to control her instinctive fear by developing relation only to the logos end of the masculine archetype—all word, transcendence, and order—to avoid the eros end of active poking, pushing, arousing, opening, penetrating. A helpful animus image here will lead her to question her automatic repression of sexual feeling or overly controlling ego-attitude. In one woman's dreams this helpful animus turned wooer, became a nonverbal man, large, silent, a physical presence. She could almost smell him in her dreams, hear his breathing. The image slipped under her verbal skills, touched her through her senses, wooed her toward her fearful sexual desires. The dreams developed over time so that she even allowed herself, in them, to reach orgasmic response. What began as trembling in fear transformed into trembling ecstasy.

Fairy tales make familiar to us the similar action of the transformative anima figure.[12] When the kingdom is exhausted and the king's sons must go out in search of renewal, we always note the lack of any feminine presence in the opening of the story. The anima makes transformative connection between the father and son ranges of the archetype. Depletion of energies in the old give way to their rise in the young. And so renewal usually comes at the end of the tale, when she appears as the youngest son's bride. In real life, too, the anima often mediates between the worn-out attitude of the senex—the man's ego in need of renewal—and the too-young attitude, as yet untested by hard reality, represented in the fairy tale by the sons who must go out in the world to accomplish their fertility-producing deeds. What corresponding archetypal anima is called for then? The crone, the mother, the daughter?

One man found his renewal from a worn-out, despairing Don Juan attitude in an unexpected, even a dreaded, quarter. In one of his liaisons, the woman became pregnant, and a daughter was born. Blood tests and a court case determined that he was the legitimate father, news that came to him as catastrophe. These proceedings took time, so that it was some years before the matter clarified itself. Torn between the wish to escape and the need to face up to his responsibility, what moved the man past his suspicions was the little girl herself. She sent him short letters, asking why he did not want to know her. He met her. He claimed her. He took responsibility for her, both financially and as a father.

Slowly the girl's presence transformed him. He felt anchored in reality. His playfulness met comfortably with his responsible side; in making a home for his daughter, he came home to himself. His ambivalence about women—as wonderfully desirable creatures or as creatures "who eat you until you die"—found a third alternative in his daughter. Here was a little one who depended on him for steady, reliable support and affection. This disciplined his own wild swings of emotion between giving all or nothing.

His psyche also made use of this new female as a young supporting anima figure, acquainting him with the great range of the archetype. Instead of the holding maternal side of the feminine, which he had either played up to or fled from as a snare, the dependent-daughter image evoked a tougher side of his own masculine identity. In one dream he and his daughter dug up pictures of him in company with a man who displayed "effortless virility," something the dreamer always feared he lacked and compulsively tried to prove in his Don Juan conquests. Then, in the dream, they found an old room with a huge gun in it that could only be fired by two men together. The dream commanded, with this accompanying anima figure, that he make contact with his much-wanted shadow virility.

THE CONTRASEXUAL EGO

The transformative effect of the positive animus or anima changes the ego too. It becomes contrasexual because it has at its disposal masculine and feminine modalities of being and doing.[13] Some analytical psychologists insist that everybody has both anima and animus consciousness. Thus, in Jungian terms, we do not have to equate the feminine, and thus the anima, with feeling or the masculine, and thus the animus, with thinking. While sympathizing with the desire to avoid sexual stereotypes, we think the evidence and the very nature of the contrasexual archetype say something else. To make an anima and animus conscious-

ness universal in men and women is once again to assign to these archetypes a set content and a fixed role. But clinical experience constantly
underlines an enormous variety in the contrasexual archetypes; they
change very much from sex to sex as they do again from person to
person. Further, animus/anima are not just qualities of consciousness
but pull our egos out of familiar territory toward the deep, unknown
Self.

When we struggle to meet, integrate, and differentiate our animus or
anima, our ego is challenged, changed, rescued. We gain access to an
opposite way of ego functioning. What the opposite will be depends on
what our initial ego-orientation has been, male or female. One man,
with a lunar, earthy, feeling-oriented ego, dreamt of endless anima figures framed in bright sunlight, clearly conveying to him the need to
move toward the light, into more expansive and imaginative self-asser-
tion. Shine like the sun, the anima bid him.[14] Another man with an ego
disposed toward conceptual thinking by years of tough medical school-
ing, where the teaching was conducted in a clearly hierarchical manner,
dividing student from doctor, dreamed at the start of his analysis that
his female analyst sat facing him in the bath and that their sessions were
conducted in easy intimacy, less sexual than a soothing informality. His
anima, personifying the analysis, pictured the work as the *solutio* operation of alchemy, dissolving into fluid connections the hard-edged disciplines of his ego stance.[15] How different from the anima that cried out,
Shine! The sun-framed woman brought into play the *calcinatio* of alchemy—to dry out a moist ego and usher it toward a warm, clear, sun-
like consciousness.

We offer the terms "ego-as-spacemaker" and "ego-as-instrument" to
describe the modalities of being and doing that belong to all of us.
Masculine and feminine, solar and lunar provide comparable terms. We
acquire these modes of ego functioning as a result of wrestling with our
anima or animus as counterpoise to our given sexuality; in them we
meet another point of view, opposite to our customary one. Anima and
animus do not form our consciousness here, but rather provide the
means by which an ego can enlarge and become more conscious.

Traditionally, in analytical psychology, the ego has been defined as an
instrument and consciousness characterized as masculine.[16] The notion
of spacemaking as a principal ego function has developed from analytical work on such nasty problems as obsession with weight, attacks of

envy, and an animus that overpowers a woman's ego, all but smashing it. In each such problem, our instrumental ego attitude, though it could understand and even struggle to master the conflict, ends only by inflaming it. The patient understands everything but can change nothing. Thus a person feels the problem extending into every psychic nook and corner, making him or her feel humiliated by the compulsion to act against personal ego values and intentions.

A different attitude needs to be developed to relate to the experience one is already having rather than to fix it, or deny it, or quickly acquire new experience to replace it. This spacemaking attitude has nothing to do with being "spacey" or "spaced out" but rather very specifically with how to live within boundaries we have already formed.

Spacemaking is a style of relating to contents that arise in the ego, both from the unconscious and the outside world. It has the mark of feminine symbolism in being defined by particular personal and unmistakably precise boundaries, as we make room in consciousness for what is happening to us. This style of consciousness is attentive and very different from the usual ego-functions, where we abstract, conceptualize, and generalize to avoid being confined to the terms of our personal experience. Here, accepting its own real space, the ego finds its way to others, to perhaps unfamiliar or hitherto unacceptable values, to fresh cultural symbols, to a religion through personal experience, beyond verbal concept and generalized precept.

The spacemaking ego offers a commodious residence for new contents—not to *do* to them, nor to *become* them, but to *make room* for them in consciousness. The ego expands in this much as the womb does—to house, to hold and carry what comes into it, to contemplate and enlarge with it. The hallmark of the spacemaking attitude is really to mark what is there, never to repress it, identify with it, project it, assimilate it, or change it. The ego contemplates, noticing what is there and what is not. In this way the ego provides rest without relinquishing its more familiar role as agent. In this sort of activity, the ego holds and beholds, maintaining a durable and permeable place of awareness, into which dreams, images, symbols, people, events, and every kind of feeling and thought can enter, be attended to, really be seen.

We open our eyes and ears. What we see and hear go together, as we accept the ego's complex mixtures of movement and rest. We see rhythms. We hear visual patterns. Basil Bunting, that preternaturally sentient poet of modern England, of new worlds and old, offers some materials drawn from such contemplation in his long poem *Briggflatts*. Hear and see, see and hear—"Starfish, poinsettia on a half-tide crag,/a galliard by Byrd"—and be moved again by "Asian vultures" in dusty formation, or another beast that suggests other Renaissance sounds—

> swift desert ass startled by the
> camels' dogged saunter
> figures sudden flight of the descant
> on a madrigal by Monteverdi.

We taste and touch and smell the world. We join the behaviorists' favorite beast, in Bunting's capacious mixing, with the Viennese master of twelve-tone modernity—

> and rat, grey, rummaging
> behind the compost heap has daring
> to thread, lithe and alert, Schoenberg's maze.

Bunting calls his poem *An Autobiography* but makes clear that he has not written "a record of fact." What he offers is a fullness of the senses, alert especially to his piece of England, Northumbria, in poems that sometimes seem a series of tag ends to a life lived with distinction in his sounding, seeing craft, at other times a sustained response to his inner light, whatever that may reveal at any given time. *Briggflatts* is the name of a Quaker meeting house, and what emerges in the poem named after it is of a piece with it, as it is with his understanding of the East and the Near East, Persia particularly, from whose literature he has translated handsomely, as he has also from Horace and Lucretius and Catullus, sometimes with a fine, mischievous wit.

What makes Bunting's work so compelling as an example of the performance of the contemplative ego is the way it moves and then pauses. We often hear the stops before we see them on the pages; they are latent in the verse as they are in the man. He makes the point in an early poem: "Dear be still! Time's start of us lengthens slowly." He makes it again out of Horace: "Please stop gushing about his pink/neck smooth arms and so forth, Dulcie; it makes me sick." He puts an end to the crabbing pedantry, the nagging irrelevancy of so much of the criticism of Ezra Pound's *Cantos:* "There are the Alps. What is there to say about them?" And then once again, in the last lines of this eight-line riposte: "It takes some getting used to. There are the Alps,/fools! Sit down and wait for them to crumble!"

No confessional poet, he. He will give you what is there, in him, around him, after thinking, feeling, meditative selection. What he presents he knows very well, having identified with it and then gone well beyond identification. In this respect, he stands on the other side of Ezra Pound, with whom he is so often associated. In his economy of thought and of style, he is very much like the composers he favors.

> It is time to consider how Domenico Scarlatti
> condensed so much music into so few bars
> with never a crabbed turn or congested cadence,
> never a boast or see-here.[17]

What Winnicott and Guntrip call the "pure female element" comes to mind in such contemplative activity, except that here the ego moves beyond the initial state of identity with the object, where the other exists only with reference to the self, as a subjective object for a nascent ego.[18] Here the object exists in its own right, just as the ego does, and the ego holds the object well within the boundaries of awareness. The ego acts as a presence, immediate and responsive, but not in identification with the object. We do not stand back and look from afar at the other, plotting what to do. The ego functions more like a harbor where ships pass in and out.

Like a flexible container, the ego feels neither flooded by the contents of its contemplation nor greatly let down when the contents withdraw. The ego companions its guests, who take up residence in the awareness provided for them. For example, the antidote to an invasion of envy, which can so pillage one's resources, is simply to make space for and attend to what is happening to us, good or bad, to dwell upon it at suitable length and take good notice of it, even if it is only to see what few crumbs we possess in contrast to our neighbor's whole loaf.[19] These small personal experiences need to be held firmly, even lovingly, on the ego's lap, protected there by a calm attentiveness that does not run off and hide, no matter how strongly the gales of envy blow.

The inestimable importance of exposure to the arts for psychic growth applies here. Looking at colors—reds, blues, yellows, purples, greens—or lines and shapes in a painting, not doing anything to the work, just contemplating it, taking it in, letting it live in us, builds our capacity to house psychic contents. Another example is the man in chapter 1 who was attracted to teenaged girls and at the same time suffered enormous self-loathing and the fear of being caught. When the adolescent girls showed up in his dreams as minor figures, rather than the living girls on whom he had fixed his projections, he could begin to make space for this troubling attraction in his consciousness, neither to act on it nor to condemn it. He did not "know" about it; he did not yet see that he sought in young girls his own lost young soul, with all its idealism, tenderness, budding life, and taste for fun. He just sat now with this driving desire, as if pushing back the furniture in his mind to make space for the forbidden compulsion to sit down and reveal itself. Finding such room, he could cease to fret. His ego allowed him a resting place in which to look at his problem from different angles, to let it be, to hold it in awareness, to come into relation to it.

This capacity to make room in consciousness for different parts of us, different points of view, to sit, hold, and contemplate, helps build what Jung calls the transcendent function, the bridge-building between opposites that lays the foundation for new attitudes that can both include and surpass the old. The instrumental ego, with its capacity to master, solve, remember, propose, cope, fight, flee, create, stands in strong contrast to the spacemaking ego, with its power to hold, appreciate, companion, contemplate, and house. If we describe this capacity and this power as masculine and feminine, respectively, as by tradition they are denominated, we must also recognize in them central symbols of the human, representing the place of disjunction and conjunction in our lives.[20] We exert in our egos the modes both of being and doing and when they separate and where they come together.

One man was startled to discover this double vision in himself, in his customary way of doing things, and alongside it a new way where he really saw his anima point of view.[21] He comes to his analytical session furious with his wife. She has been haranguing him about all the things he should be doing. They have been locked in argument for three days. He finds her walled up, impenetrable to logic, barricaded against his feelings. In his session he reaches a new insight: he sees where she is, trapped in these defenses, helpless to free herself because imprisoned for the moment by combativeness that he only aggravates in his criticism of her bullying. He sees that some unconscious force is in fact bullying her. Greatly struck by seeing *her,* as distinct, separate from what imprisons her, he feels moved to reach out and help, a prince riding to her rescue to free her from her dragons. He wants to fight for her, to win through to her and for her, no longer to fight against her.

But. He cannot hold and contemplate his insight. He cannot house it and give it space to see what it may tell him about himself. He goes home and immediately wants to use his insight with his wife. He explains to her about the dragon and the prince. Enraged, she returns again to the attack. Instead of appreciating the insight as his own, he wants to plant it in his wife, to put it into words and change her with them. Thus, he himself becomes a trapped princess, who cannot be seen because the prince is so busy talking, explaining, doing helpful things. The crucial anima figure is left out, just projected onto his wife. To make space for the insight involves a slower process of carrying it around, turning it over, now in reference to his wife, now in reference to his own anima. Such a consciousness pulls in, fills out, and enlarges his ego contours. He becomes the princess, his wife turns rescuer, in one reading. In another, that part of him that needs all his own attention to be rescued receives it. In still another, he really stops to see his wife and she, in time, responds. All the lively possibilities circulate in him.[22]

Holding insight means appreciating it, but not identifying with it. Developing such a sense of space, where inner conversation can flourish, is to generate new energy and arrange the parts of oneself in new patterns. Best of all, the ego recognizes that it does not have to identify with any of its contents. Its function is to mirror them in a long spacemaking, contemplative gaze, not to become them.

A further mirroring remains in which the ego's holding of contents is reflected in the way the ego is held by the Self. The ego retains its own point of view. We are moved by experience and deeply committed to what we value. But with space comes paradox. Though utterly committed, the spacemaking ego sees even commitment as open-ended, as something to be looked upon as just one part of a larger whole. We are both firmly possessed of identity and at the same time disidentified from it too, recognizing it through the larger being of which it is a part, seeing it itself contemplated, held in the gaze of the Self.

Musil's Ulrich, his *Man without Qualities,* is a definitive example of an identity grounded in disidentification, a product of the spacemaking attitude. He is a man capable of doing an incalculable number of irresistible things yet identified with none. Ulrich's spiritual reach shows in his receptivity to what is, to being as it lives in many different types of people, places, activities, and skills, and especially in his living anima figure, his sister Agathe. His ego beholds being in thought, in feeling, in the flesh; it moves toward everything and yet keeps its distance. Ulrich personifies the essentially religious nature of the spacemaking attitudes.[23]

Persons who join in themselves the feminine spacemaking ego and the masculine instrumental ego know here on earth, in the ordinary events of daily life, the mystery of a concrete personal identity living over an abyss of space. How that space is imaged depends on each person and his or her culture. It may reveal itself as death, as God, as mindlessness, as Self. The ego that lives fully, ever open to the oceanic tides of Being, experiences not just one, but a succession of transformations.

THE PERSONAL

What effects such transformations is the ego meeting with the transformative anima or animus. Here we face in a personal way whatever comes across the contrasexual bridge. We do not move here in abstract collective categories, as *the son,* or *the man,* but rather as a particular son of a particular mother, a particular man facing with all his assets and defects a particular dream image. The unconscious does not yield here to a generalized approach. The anima/animus problem is not solved on an impersonal level or by general principle, but only in our own special individual way of being. Marie-Louise von Franz narrates with humor her own failures in active imagination because, with her as with everyone, the unconscious at first displayed such pompous, theatrical, collectivized communication. She would set to the task industriously, but every time a figure from the unconscious would greet her with "Hearken!" she quit in disgust. She needed courage to take her animus seriously and to move with it to a more personal interaction.[24]

Unlike the unconscious in general, and very differently from the mother or father archetype, the transformative anima or animus steps forward to address the ego personally. We must try to answer back out of our own individual ego identity. The transformative animus asks a woman for immediate personal reaction. One woman was astonished at the results of her efforts to deal imaginatively with a destructive animus figure. In a dream he appeared as a great thug with metal teeth who trashed a roadside cafe, scaring the dreamer out of her wits. To her surprise, she found herself screaming at him never to terrorize her like that again. He yelled back that he would keep doing it to get her attention if he couldn't get it any other way. A slanging match ensued. But eventually she heard and identified the primitive aggression trying to reach consciousness. She never would have touched it if she had referred to it as "primitive aggression"; she needed to scream her wholehearted fear in the face of his metal teeth and bullying.

The transformative animus or anima addresses us personally to promote us to ourselves in some way—to develop, to listen, to retreat, to open. We are none of us a genus, but each a specific other to this contrasexual figure. Therefore we must face what comes to us across its bridge as a personal message. Thus a middle-aged homosexual man who dreaded anyone at work knowing about his sexuality dreamed of the version of it he hated the most intensely. Across the anima bridge came an extravagantly effeminate version of his conscious identity—a man, womanlike, looking like a witch, with sequins on his face, which confronted him boldly and forced him to sort out what it meant for him.[25]

The man whose beautiful anima left him stunned in dream, immobilized in mute gazing, was given the push by his dreams into life. His ego needed to relate to the beautiful creature, to be active with it, to give and take. In one dream the woman's nose began to bleed. Was it from being elevated too high? When he projected this anima beauty onto a lady friend, she would complain he was too silent, too unrevealing of himself, too ungiving, whereas he felt all but poured out before her. Both the actual woman and the inner anima delivered the same message in the same process: respond, react, initiate, from your own center.

The process is succinctly stated by the preeminent modern philosopher of process, Alfred North Whitehead. "Attention yields a three-fold character," he says, in dealing with things that matter, involving totality, externality, and internality. "There is the totality of actual fact; there is the externality of many facts; there is the internality which lies within the totality." We bring together in Whitehead's view of what he calls a civilized universe "the self-enjoyment of others melting into the enjoyment of our own self." This is the way we face "actuality," which we do most explicitly in "our realization of those other actualities which we conceive as ourselves in our recent past, fusing their self-enjoyment with our immediate present. This is only the most vivid instance of the unity of the universe in each individual actuality."

To know that our individual actuality is one in a world of actualities is "the gift of aesthetic significance." If we fail to perceive that significance consciously, so much the worse for us. It is available to us, Whitehead says, in very small as well as large experiences: "Our intuitions of right-ousness disclose an absoluteness in the nature of things, and so does the taste of a *lump of sugar*." We may not be able to make sense of the range of our experiences, but the element of the aesthetic "in any factor of experience carries its proof of existence beyond present immediacy." The conclusion is inescapable, and richly supporting: "The ego enjoys an importance stretching beyond itself."[26]

We must accept this importance as an act of faith, coexistent with the responses, the reactions, the initiations that we at least allow and at best encourage to rise from our center of being. C. H. Sisson, perhaps the most philosophically and theologically secure of modern poets, mixes all his problems of identity and faith in this manner. He is secure enough in his faith to allow his uncertainties their voice; he is insecure enough about the nature of his identity to ask all the questions about it which, in the mere asking, assure a kind of stability. In "Dialogue of the Soul and God, or of Psyche with Cupid," he says ruefully to the Holy Spirit, "Lord Wind/I am your patience so I am not I." That is a play on words, but a serious one. If he *is* patience, a gift of the Spirit, then that surely is enough. In the same spirit, at the end of this part of a superbly condensed poem, he remarks, "I rise upon the wind," and comments with the same mixture of certainty and uncertainty, "I, I?" He shows us that when we pray, it is the Spirit that prays in us and through us, moving us to our knees. Finally, in the last lines of the poem, he offers an act of faith in the persona of the most fitting anima figure with whom to gather up the *complexio oppositorum* he has been posing for us:

My hair
Mops up your feet as Mary Magdalen's did

Slut, I am there.

In a poem on the Eucharist, Sisson speaks for himself and the sacrament and the experience of both self and sacrament. He is uneasy about the persona the dual task now seems to have imposed upon him. He prays to have taken from him the compulsion to speak for Christ:

Holy Father, Almighty God
Stop me before I speak

—per Christum.

How can he measure up? The plays on words continue, and so does the *mysterium tremendum* of both identity and persona. He receives the sacrament; he knows how much he is enlarged by it, so much that no one can accept what it is that really has entered him. There is a shattering pun in the next line:

Lies on my tongue. Get up and bolt the door
For I am coming not to be believed
The messenger of anything I say.

He waits in the cold night, servant of the host he carries on his tongue, like it or not an *alter Christus,* another way of reading and living the *Ecce homo.* "Beware, I am the man, and let me in."

He is pursued by his doubts, which turn into affirmations, and his affirmations, which turn into doubts. Only the certainty of someone who is far inside himself could speak with such a mixture and meeting of confidence and diffidence. He turns from God because he blinds him, though he knows that nothing exists without God—"And I am nothing as I turn away:/Nothing is what I am, therefore I turn."[27]

What finally happens to us when we meet the transformative anima or animus is that we are changed like the poet receiving God. We come into dialogue with the unconscious in a very particular way. The man struck by the links of a woman's beauty to the transcendent must wrestle into words and action his own perception of the transcendent and actively relate to the feminine in his own terms. The woman with the animus of iron teeth must look for ordinary ways in her daily life to use her aggression, to stand by herself, and with whatever animates her connection to being, to bring into the world the seed the animus hurls into her. Transformation means change in the way we live, here, on earth. We claim our name, different from our parents', our own idiosyncratic vision of the whole.

Can we imagine anyone really doing this, really embodying this? When we think of our own struggles, we often pull a blank, unable to see that we have moved at all. But with a little distance, we can see it in others, if not ourselves; people do come to mind who show forth a transformed presence. Winnicott says this wonderfully of Jung in his own version of the anima: "It is the part of me that I always knew was a woman!"[28] Winnicott himself writes with such animating effect on his readers that we feel our own connection to being through his "free heartedness."[29] Yet he is always insistently himself, making us aware of his feelings, his suffering, not only in the pain that is obvious, in his divorce, in his coronaries, but also in the great openness that he could not always accept, which sometimes left him its victim in a kind of distress. All these idiosyncratic details bring him into focus in his very own identity, secret at the core, generous in the giving. He stands forth as a man at home with his anima.

Melanie Klein offers an example of a woman who went far to integrate her animus. She brought her fresh, controversial views into play in the world and stood her ground against her critics. She supervised or analyzed many other original, creative minds, such as Winnicott, Adrian Stokes, and Wilfred Bion. Each time, after writing still another original paper for yet another psychoanalytic congress, her first instinct was to rush out to buy a new hat.[30] She, too, impresses us with her candor and her individuality, sharing the dreadful suffering she felt fighting in public for her theories for more than thirty years, with even her own daughter ranged against her. We can trace the fierce dogmatism in defending her theories, which made Winnicott despair, to an unintegrated bit of animus.[31] We can speculate that she could not herself accept the full weight of her authority, and so her animus kept forcing that unclaimed bit of her out into the open through her authoritarian insistence that her theories were always right. To the end, she insisted that she had merely brought the master's, Freud's, the father's, theories to their logical sources, in the first months of a child's life, denying that she had in fact inaugurated a new school of depth psychology.[32]

Jung offers a third example of a man who wrestled to earth his contrasexuality, to bring it in relation to his ego, in his courageous following of his anima, even in "the house of the dead."[33] Again we see how individual an identity is, how idiosyncratic its path, including in Jung's case his suffering a simultaneous living out of relationships with two women, with all the guilt and disease that aroused in all three of them.[34]

Idiosyncrasy in the service of contrasexuality can transform the most painful guilt and suffering into something positive. The German poet and novelist Elisabeth Langgässer offers a triumphant case in point. A Catholic convert, she was sent to do forced labor by the Nazis because of her Jewish background, with no consideration for the multiple sclerosis from which she suffered. She survived the Nazis long enough to write two novels, *The Indelible Seal,* a bringing together of theological themes and surrealist treatment that Broch greatly admired, and *The Quest,* an eccentric and moving story of pilgrimage on the heels of the Second World War. She also lived to see her daughter released from the concentration camp at Auschwitz, which she celebrated in a poem titled after the season and the date, "Spring 1946."

Holde Anemone, she greets her daughter, lovely Anemone, associating her with one of the most beautiful of spring flowers. She asks the girl wonderingly if she really is here now, with her shining calyx, to console her parent for all that has oppressed her, as a Nausicaa would do. It is an extraordinary identification of her daughter with the Phaeacian princess who met the shipwrecked Odysseus as he rose from sleep on her island shore, where he had been thrown up, his nakedness covered only with a leafy branch. The poet becomes an *alter* Odysseus as she goes to meet her Nausicaa, each home from the worst of war and pestilence. Free at last from her own terrible burdens, the Odyssean mother rises from the "Reich of Toads," the burning redness of Pluto still under her eyelids, with the flute of the *Totenführer,* Hitler as leader of the dead, still rasping horribly in her ear. Like Odysseus, she had met the eye of the gorgon, hard as iron, and heard in whispers the lie that the monster could do her in. "Anemone!" she cries out to her daughter, "let me kiss your face, unmirrored by the rivers Styx and Lethe, without knowledge now of *Nein und Nicht,*" of No and Not.

Still playing the role of Odysseus, the poet-mother says to her princess-daughter, again in wonderment, "You really are here, unseductive, to warm my heart but not to inflame it—child Nausicaa!" We are stirred with Elisabeth Langgässer as she takes her child into her arms, each transformed by her Homeric associations, the shipwrecked heroic mother, the innocent, good-willed daughter. Odysseus' is a fitting ani-

Anima/Animus and Religious Experience

THE POSITIVE anima or animus exists in all of us, however much suppressed or repressed. It exerts its transformative effect, when it emerges, as sooner or later it does in most of us, by ushering us into its threshold space. Our meetings with it create a ritual space where we undergo preparation to experience the Self. Our contrasexuality is very pointed in its positive effects: it leads us to what we feel has life-and-death importance for us, to where we can see our center, know it exists, believe in it, and begin to make our way to it. Whatever we hold dear, our system of values defines its goals in these experiences. Here we discover hopes and intimations of reality that transcend our egos, both personal and collective. Anima and animus lead us to religious experience, to whatever we revere or call holy. That is the function of the contrasexual archetype for our identity: to make the bridge across which we forge a link with a living Self and receive its substance in our daily life.

This possibility of religious experience is one we share with others, but what we have in common here is our differences, and thus we each reckon with the experience differently. How, then, can we understand this contrasexual bridge to the Self in a way that will make room for all our differences? Perhaps by the fact that the defining element in human identity is its complexity. We can expect then great, almost endless variation in the way we enter this domain.[1]

SAMENESS

We share in common the shock of our anima or animus figure confronting us with an otherness that entirely sets it apart from the ego, from what we identify as "our own." The contrasexual figure and the mood it brings with it—or the thought or the impulse—appear strange, dissimilar, unfamiliar. Thus it opens us to otherness itself, not in the abstract but in concrete experiences of our body, our emotions, our sexual desires.

One introverted woman, often anxious and self-doubting in her consciousness, felt continual astonishment before the "personality" of her animus figures. They added up for her to an aggressive, pushy presence, entirely caught up in its own views and interests and quite bored by others. In sharp contrast to her conscious enthusiasm to listen to others' stories, experiences, and ideas, this part of her could not care less. Vigorous, passionate, even self-absorbed, her animus stood boldly against her customary shyness. Extraverted, and not so much confident as bumptious, he often blurted out through her whatever he felt like saying. Even if she was quiet, others, particularly those who did not like her, reacted now to an attitude of superiority or self-involvement they found oozing from her. She found men who matched this animus type entrancing and looked forward to taming them. She ran from her animus's opposites, especially despising the man who "circles around nothing in himself," as she put it, exerting a kind of "sucking emptiness" on others. She knew now, in this animus opposite, a maleness contrary to her femaleness, an extraverted attitude opposed to her introversion, a confidence that controverted her self-doubt. His exhibitionistic procedure was to "stick it right out there," as she put it, where she used to hide herself. How could she harbor such a stranger within herself?

With just a little forthright self-examination, we can all know such surprising contrariness in ourselves. Each time this surprise overtakes us, this sudden awakening to the presence of a stranger within us, we experience a little annunciation. We are, with some small degree of awareness, saluting the astonishing fact that all of human sexuality exists there within us. In each of us there is another being, an opposite, a stranger who is at the same time our intimate. We know him or her, whether or not we admit the knowledge to consciousness. Sometimes we actually do permit the knowledge open entry into the great body of thoughts and feelings that is our interiority, and even do so with a celebratory flourish. Then we hail the stranger. We rejoice in the presence of this alien being that most of the time we cannot easily, comfortably identify or live without.

The mysterious annunciation of Gabriel to Mary, which so fascinated the amateur artists of the back alleys of Rome that they drew their versions of the archangel kneeling to the woman up and down their walls, is more closely related to our little annunciations than most of us dare to think. How can that be? We do not give birth to God in human flesh, do we? Don't we? We are not impregnated by the Spirit, are we? Aren't we? We do not have within ourselves our sons and brothers and fathers, our daughters and sisters and mothers, do we? Don't we?

The terms of the annunciation that marks the conceiving of Jesus are so large and mysterious that we cannot bring ourselves to compare what happens within us to Mary's experience or even Joseph's as foster father to the movement of ultimate Being in a human womb. But it is just such grandeur that our sexuality in its double being asks us to accept as our own, belonging in different surprising ways to each of us. Even the mad, awesome twistings of the generations in this generative act are ours to seize upon and claim, at some level of participation and understanding, as our own.

Think, feel, claim—with the necessary substitutions for sex, age, time, and place—the prayer of Bernard of Clairvaux that opens the thirty-third canto of the *Paradiso,* the hundredth and last canto of the *Commedia.*

> Virgin mother, daughter of your son,
> humble and exalted more than any creature,
> determined end of the eternal plan,
> you are she who so ennobled
> human nature that its maker did not scorn
> to be himself made by it.[2]

We are each of us the fixed purpose of creation, if we understand the annunciation as made to all of us, for we each bear the history of the race within us, its design, its aims, its successes, its failures. If we see within us as John Donne saw in his version of the Virgin Mary in his annunciation sonnet, we open ourselves as she did at the moment of conception, to all possible conceiving. In fantasy, in prayer, in reasoning through the potentialities of the human, even in sifting through the tangled processes by which we bring ourselves to religious faith or reject it, as we conceive God, if only as an idea or hope or foolish fancy, we can read Donne's lines as addressed to us:

> yea thou art now
> Thy Maker's maker, and thy Father's mother;
> Thou hast light in darke; and shutst in little roome,
> *Immensity cloysterd in thy dear wombe.*[3]

Perhaps women see this more easily and claim it more fully because they know the quickening of the womb, with or without pregnancy. But Dante and Donne were men and spoke with that blessed fullness of projection that allowed them some place in the unceasing conception. If we accept all of ourselves, inner and outer, then we must contrive the same conception and carry it, men or women, to term. We must in our acceptance return to our *Terre origenelle,* our "Original Earth," as the French-Canadian poet Anne Hébert calls it in the poem of that name. Woman or man, we can say out of our fullness of being,

> My soul tastes of sea and green orange.
> Alerted forests, unleashed rivers singing time's primal waters
> A whole continent under a wind storm.
> And starting out, handsome love, the world founds itself
>   like a city of linen.
> Let the heart's wild resemblance
> To its original earth be accomplished.[4]

Yes, we can hold all that within us, for all that is instinct in all creation, its mark from the first day to the last. Each of us bears that mark in the simple fact of our sexual identity. We are progenitors, conceivers, birth givers. In one hushed moment, Beatrice explains this to Dante. She does so near the end of the *Commedia,* in the twenty-ninth canto, near the end of what can be put into words. By comparison, the angelic hierarchy, which Beatrice has just finished describing for her lover, is easy to explain.

Dante has not asked Beatrice to make creation clear to him, either the original or any of its mirrorings. She is not asking him what he would like to hear, she says; she is telling him. That alone should give us pause. This is the mystery of Beatrice, that she has such prescience, that she can hear Dante's question before he asks it and answer it. But it is also the simple fact of Beatrice that she is part of Dante, his exalted anima, and all the more so because her original earth was his, in Florence, where he knew her in her childhood and youth.

She can tell him what he wants to know because she has seen *it*, creation, at the source, "there, where every *where* and *when* is appointed." In a lovely inversion, which reads like all the modern poets, such as Eliot and Pound, who have imitated Dante in their creating, she says of the Creator, "Not to acquire any more good for himself, which could not be, but so that his splendor in shining back [to us] could say 'I am,' beyond time, beyond every other understanding, as it pleased him, the eternal Love showed itself in new loves."

Specifically, Beatrice is describing the creation of angels, who do indeed, in this reading of the unreadable, mirror creation back to the Creator. But the angels are the messengers of creation. They shine back and forth, to Creator and to creatures. The new loves consist of all being that ever was, or is, or shall be. That is the great weight that our creative spark, our sexuality, carries, that in our maleness and femaleness we can conceive creation itself and all its parts and all its wholeness, that we, all of us, can conceive. That is a great weight indeed, but in its ineffability it is lighter than air.[5]

Anima and animus constantly make great weight out of little things. They carry in us what Jung calls our "inferior function," that way of looking at the world, at ourselves, and even at God, which is least developed in us.[6] It opposes our customary, which is to say our most developed, way of seeing things, our "superior function." Our inferior function may lag behind, but we exist in partial identification with it so that when it bursts out it carries us along with it on its full tide. Because we have differentiated ourselves from it so little, have been conscious of it so rarely, this way of being and doing stays archaic, primitive in its intensity, just withdrawing from conscious reach, carrying us only in its wake. Yet precisely because we do not bring our inferior function under ego control, it can renew our consciousness. We see things through it in a new way, for it brings something bewitchingly exotic to the ego, utterly other to its accustomed way of looking at things.

We can see, then, how an animus figure will appear both bad and good. In an introverted thinking woman, the animus carries all her inadequately developed, inferior extraverted feeling, often causing her to erupt in anger or bawdy humor and then to feel wounded if others take offense, and herself to feel appalled at her behavior.

Although Jung asserts that universal human traits are not gender specific, and offers in his typology at least eight different modes of functioning, nonetheless he often speaks as if feeling defines the anima, perhaps because of the dominance in him of his own intuitive thinking function. Such an overtopping role for feeling by no means holds true for all men's animas. In fact, depending on his conscious development, a man's anima may appear in countless guises over the years. The differences in anima/animus theories can be understood as expressions of the different ego stances of their authors.[7] If, for example, someone insists that the anima has only to do with soul and never with ego-reality, we can speculate that such a theorist is subject to tremendous ego demands, ambitions, inflations. If the anima is described as dwelling only within us, never to be projected onto a person, we can speculate that the theorist may be suffering from overinvolvement with others or fear of falling under their spell. Our own emphasis on anima and animus as bridge between ego and Self, our focus on the in-between middle space, may compensate for our concern not to be pulled too far to either side, ego or Self.

Even in constructing our theory, the radical otherness of anima/animus confronts us. It introduces into our deliberations a relativism that demands more space for differences, not only to be tolerated, but to be applauded. We understand that to see many ways to the center is not to conclude that it does not exist, nor to exclude passionate commitment to the way we have chosen.

The point is that anima or animus always presents otherness, difference, and does so in the most intimate terms, terms that move us to reverent reaction, to an experience worthy of the name "religious." A cogent example is that of a thinking type, a man subject to far-flung negative intuitions about the ultimate precariousness of human values. He found himself carried right out of himself into ecstatic states by what seemed to him a numinous suppleness in a woman's skin. The immediate, concrete, literal feel of the flesh—like "butter-lamb leather," he said—promised a bliss unimaginable in his philosophy. He felt truth through his senses, embodied by his anima, to counter his hitherto gloomy intuitions about the nature of being. A woman comedian, an extravert of electric energies and snappy repartée, found herself plunged into depression by an animus figure that ruthlessly attacked her writing. "Nothing but shit," he exclaimed and berated her for emptiness inside herself, for possessing no interior life. With near violence, he dragged her into introversion and nonverbal, meditative silence. Once there, she found prayer a suitable counterforce to the animus's negativity; it delivered her into a wider sense of being, a deeper support for her place in the larger scheme of things. She discovered she could have a philosophy of her own. The woman of chapter 1, who married her husband because she so admired his ability to talk and display his creative vision and then wanted to kill him to get him to shut up and listen, recognized that what she saw in him was her own undeveloped extraverted capacity to originate and risk creative venture for herself.

Anima and animus provoke each other. The woman who tried to shut up her husband, so she could articulate her own inner dialogue with the animus, found her voice first by falling into identification with the animus, so that only her views and ideas absorbed her. She lost all interest in her husband's talk, and, now altogether identified with her animus, triggered an anima attack in him. He went as far as he could, under attack, identifying with his negative anima. The wife now holds forth with the pomp and circumstance of an inflated animus state, and the husband withdraws, mopes and sulks in his anima identification. Four persons, two couples, occupy the room: husband and wife, the bombastic animus and resentful anima. One spurs the other, now to negative effect, at another time to positive.

A woman identifying with a long-neglected animus needs sooner or later to join, receive, and challenge her animus inflation, to allow her to feel connected rather than vamped by the contents the animus ushers into her ego life. She needs to give her inner partner the attentive, spacemaking listening she so often gave her husband in the past. She will feel the more balanced, able to bring her own insights alive.[8] This is work to be done imaginatively by fantasizing inner dialogue between ego and animus, which ultimately means wife and husband. At another point, she may fantasize the reverse, needing a warriorlike determination to challenge an all-consuming malaise that the animus brings on, to uncover with persistent, penetrating questions the specific painful content her animus is bringing across the bridge.

The dance of masculine and feminine carries on, it is clear, between us and within us, between ego and anima or animus. One constellates the other. We know in consciousness our alternation between space-making and instrumental ego attitudes, and we know, between conscious ego and unconscious anima or animus, alternation of identity and difference, person and archetype, reality and fantasy. This dance of mixings and distancings, of joinings and separations, creates in us another of the middle realms of transformation. We experience this way what Jung, Solovyov, and others call syzygy, that coupling of masculine and feminine that runs throughout mythology, religion, literature.[9]

Experiencing syzygy pulls us into the dramatic spaces that exist between parts of ourselves, between people, between the human and divine. Here we find the linkings of relationships. Here we live in the space of *I* and *other,* one full of energy and numinosity, where everything seems to partake of and return to unity. This ambiguous but omnipresent syzygy space is not set in one mold, for all its sense of unity. It goes through many forms, separating to reunite, pulling away to come close, coming close to pull apart.[10]

We can see the appeal of the figure of the hermaphrodite or the androgyne to characterize syzygy space, for it encloses and combines all sexual permutations and variations.[11] But actually we cannot enter this space or live there securely without a firm hold on our sexual identity and knowing reach to the contrasexuality within us opposite to our gender identity. Syzygy space is all around us and between us, and we repeatedly fall into it. What it offers is not ambivalence but clear identity as women and men, and stable connection to anima or animus.

Androgynous and hermaphroditic images offer to some an appealing release from the straitjacket of sexual stereotypes, but to accept them is not to work to construct relation between the sexes, but to deconstruct it, and to turn from integration of all our sexual parts into a whole identity.[12] Then syzygy space functions as a substitute for mundane reality and identity, and we become spaced out. The concrete life misleadingly called androgyny is in fact that which we live as contrasexual persons.

To think of contrasexuality as androgyny is to make something much more orderly of our sexuality than it can sustain, something more balanced in its mixing of the sexes than it is, something finally that is false to life in its dissipation of mystery. Anima and animus provide stability in our lives when we are clear about their large archetypal presence and at ease with it; they do not offer neat chains of causation or arithmetical balancings of the male and the female. Our sexual identity is always to some degree in motion, always delivering a sense of Self to us as we live through and accept the constancy of change in our outer and inner worlds.

In the summary chapter of his *Essay on Man,* Ernst Cassirer characterizes culture in terms that apply to our sexuality, as they must if they are true, for the complexity that defines the human condition takes its character as much from our outside world as from our inside. As much, but no more, for the "functional unity" that our inner/outer lives represent is, as Cassirer insists, "a dialectic of unity, a coexistence of contraries." This would not be the case if one side were so much stronger than the other, if, as historical and dialectical materialists have for so long asserted, we were the pawns of economic and social agents with only minimal interior resources with which to resist the pushing around on the board.

Cassirer takes his leading metaphor in the concluding chapter of his *Essay* from Heracleitus. "Men do not understand," says the pre-Socratic sage, "how that which is torn in different directions comes into accord with itself—harmony in contrariety, as in the case of the bow and the lyre." Those primordial instruments may be so far from frontal consciousness in us that we miss for a moment the force of Heracleitus' rhetoric. The bow is the weapon from which arrows are shot; the lyre is the small stringed instrument that provided the ancient bard's accompaniment. Aggression and creativity confront each other and resolve the confrontation in harmony: "In order to demonstrate such a harmony we need not prove the identity or similarity of the different forms by which it is produced."

Whatever balance may exist among the elements of our culture, it is a dynamic equilibrium, not a static one: "It is the result of a struggle between opposing forces." The disorder in our lives, of which we are only too conscious, does not shut out the "hidden harmony," which, in Heracleitus' words, "is better than that which is obvious." All of our lives—and especially that which is central in them, our sexual identities—reflect the struggle and the resultant disorder *and* the hidden harmony in it.

It is in the attention we pay to the consonance that is concealed beneath the disorder—the harmonious order beneath the skin—that we achieve our creative ends. These may be no more than an awareness of an underlying intentionality in our lives, with no specification of aims or the means to achieve them, what Kant calls purposiveness without purpose. We have a general sense of sexual purpose even without specific ends. That is enough. That is how our sexual lives find positive definition. The range and complexity and baffling inconsistency of performance of our sexuality, we can come to understand, do not indicate a defeating discord. "The dissonant is in harmony with itself," as Cassirer says of human culture; the contraries are not mutually exclusive, but interdependent: "Harmony in contrariety, as in the case of the bow and the lyre."[13]

The amazing possibility the image of syzygy holds out to us is of living simultaneously in ordinary reality and the middle realm within us and between us, which our inner conversation constantly speaks out of. There we experience a tangible community with others, a subtle, exciting dwelling together in a large field of energy where our individual identities function as parts of a great, densely populated whole, not to set those who make it up in a rigid hierarchy but to expose them to each other as moving parts of a large living reality. Such a vision shows us infinity dwelling in the finite. But the finite must be sturdy to enter this dance, to be inspired to new steps because it knows the old ones, to be moved across ego boundaries into transcendence because the boundaries exist firmly in place.

Vladimir Solovyov, writing about *The Meaning of Love* in the early 1890s, apologized for his use of the "neologism" *syzygetic* to describe the "bond" between personal love and its many collective incarnations, in small communities, in the nation, in the world. Solovyov makes a remarkable doctrine of *syzygy,* linking it directly or by implication to his experiences as poet, philosopher, theologian, mystic. The syzygetic union of sexual and spiritual love corresponds in his thinking to "the true unity of the two fundamental sides of [human nature], the male and the female," to which, he says, "the mysterious divine image was joined from the outset, in agreement with which man was created."

It is that image that we need to restore within us, but because of our imperfections we cannot do so except in that mutuality which is, for Solovyov, the meaning of love. We accomplish this when the complementary strengths of male and female are united in support of the creative principle that springs from the creative power of the Godhead. He foresees puzzled readers. "Why," they might ask, "do you climb to such inaccessible and fantastic heights over such a simple thing as love?" He answers that if he thought "the religious norm of love" fantastic, he would not have proposed it, and if he were considering only *simple* love—"the ordinary commonplace relations between the sexes"—he would just keep quiet. But love, as he sees it, is, "on the contrary, an extraordinarily complex affair, obscure and intricate, demanding fully conscious analysis and investigation, in which one must be concerned not about simplicity, but about the truth." The poet ends the discussion: "A rotten stump is undoubtedly simpler than a many-branched tree, and a corpse is simpler than a living human being. The simple relation to love is completed by that definitive and ultimate simplification that is called death."

The "absolute norm" of Solovyov's love is the "restoration of the integrity of the human being." When that norm is infringed, in no matter what direction, the result is an aberration, contrary to nature and characterized by a purposelessness such as occurs when the spiritual aspires to a separation from the sensual, a separation that can best be accomplished by death. Solovyov mocks a "pure spiritual love from which all genuine content has been removed by other inferior devotions of the kind that reduce it to a dreamy and sterile sentimentality without any real task or purpose in life." This sort of "spiritual" love reminds him of the little angels in old paintings that have only a head and wings and nothing else. Better a physical love, however shameful, that at least knows what it is about, or a family union, however mediocre, that at least accomplishes its indispensable purpose.

True love, which is based on faith, brings us the possibility of the "reunion of the individual human being with God and the restoration in him of the living and immortal divine image." It is in its pairing of body and spirit, "both ascending and descending *(amor ascendans et amor descendans),* or in those two Aphrodites whom Plato excellently distinguished, but wrongly separated *(Aphrodite Ourania* and *Aphrodite Pandemos)."* The heavenly and the earthly, which is to say the spiritual and the human, will not suffer separation in Solovyov's understanding of love: "In sexual love, understood and realized as it should be, the divine essence finds the means for its definitive and ultimate incarnation in an individual human life, the means of the most profound and at the same time the most outward and tangible and real union with it."

Syzygy for Solovyov leads to restoration, to connection, to integration. Here is where society finds its "perfect likeness of the all-one idea," where individual and collective existence come together. "If the root of false existence consists in impenetrability," he explains, with a fine appropriation of a sexual image, "i.e. in the mutual exclusion of creatures by each other, then true existence is to live in another as in oneself or to find in another the positive and unconditional completion of one's own being." And make no mistake about it: "The foundation and type of this true existence remains what it will always be, sexual or conjugal love."

It is a vision that can be realized, Solovyov thinks, at least as a goal for society and for the individual to contemplate and move toward. "The power of this spiritual-corporeal creativeness," which is what sexuality in the syzygetic bond represents, "is only a transformation or *turning inwards* of that same creative force which in nature, directed outward, produces the infinity of multiplications of physical organisms."[14]

So what we share in common in anima or animus is not only its differences from our egos, not only its carrying to consciousness little-known or suppressed functions, not only its bridging capacity to Self, but the creation of a syzygy reality that links us with one another. There is our community in the great field of energy that extends from the human to the divine. Anima and animus give the ego a lens through which to perceive Self in the other.[15] In addition to all our projections of ourselves and what we desire in a mate, we see through animus or anima the true self of the other, the other's capacity to live in and out of the Self as it addresses him or her. We are thus enabled to relate to persons as others, to greet them with curiosity, wonder, even awe in the center of being we share.

This is the reality of the syzygy, which we experience while at the same time we live in our diurnal reality with all its anguish, anxiety, and possibility. This is the experience of transcendence in immanence that connection to anima or animus makes possible.

DIFFERENCES

What makes one person's anima or animus different from another's is the tell-tale accent of the individual life it carries and its reflection of differing social, cultural, and historical climates. A woman who loses her girlhood at the age of nine in the Second World War, because as the oldest in the pediatric ward she must act the adult and lead all the other children to safety when the hospital suffers a bombing raid, grows up with a very different relation to her animus from that of a child for whom peacetime conditions afford the luxury of a gradual, slow maturation. A woman remembers her adoption at the age of three and knows her adoptive father as the truly mothering one in her life, who provided refuge from her actual mother, who was always critical, always demanding perfection. This woman, as a result, never reached Oedipal reaction to her father until her adult years, when she entered analysis. She discovered she was using her idealized version of her father as a way of dealing with and fending off sexual responses. Imagine her fright when she dreamt of making sexual approaches to her adoptive father, who was, after all, no blood relation.

Such a woman's animus poses very different problems and possibilities from that of a woman who as a little girl always saved her father for the last good-night kiss. On warm summer evenings, when her family sat outside, she would run across the lawn in her seersucker nightie, long hair streaming behind her, to wrap her slender arms around her beloved father, with a passionate "Oh, good night, Daddy, good night!" We must be careful here: the difference is just that—difference; it is not a matter of better or worse.

Where we come from and how we have been brought up determine which archetypal images will assume dominance in our anima or animus complex. The Jungian analyst Manisha Roy says that for Indian women, whose culture imbues them with a sense of being part of a goddess in their femaleness, the animus wears Indian clothing, speaks a local idiom. The Indian animus is like Shiva, whose energy is passive and calm and whose job it is to tame fierce female energy, and also, like the god, derives his power to perform this task from female energy itself. The animus of the Indian woman, Roy argues, does not lead her to the Self; she is already connected to it by virtue of her femaleness. Yet like her Western counterpart, an Indian woman knows the dancelike ego-animus interaction. Her animus defines her connection to the center, aiding her in keeping her energy from turning destructive.[16]

Bou-Yong Rhi, a Korean Jungian psychiatrist, argues that in his country the change in education and religion over the last fifty years poses particularly difficult problems for women. Under Japanese rule, the young received a "conservative Confucian-oriented education," whereas now they have the benefits of a more liberal education. In the old rule, women were taught to be modest and to sacrifice personal desires for the extended family; now women are taught to expect that they can actively pursue their own fulfillment. But after marriage, men still return to ancient customs, which the new woman cannot endure. One woman, for example, fell ill because she could not conceive the son the entire family awaited impatiently. Inwardly, a son image dominated her animus; it carried all her unlived power to be and to do. Denied a male infant, she felt excluded from her own inner life as well as her family.[17]

Jae Hoon Lee investigates the notion of animus in relation to the female Korean shaman Bari, and especially in terms of the reality of *han*. Lee argues that *han* is not only negative suffering which afflicts all Koreans, but also the source of creativity for both individuals and their collective culture. *Han* is comparable, in fact, to the collective unconscious. When Bari meets her animus figure, she discovers that her vocation is to care for the souls of both the dead and the living by bringing them the "medicine water," an unmistakable symbol of the Self. The shaman is "the administrator of *han*," argues Lee; she tries to lead the stray soul to its proper dwelling place. By transforming negative *han* into positive creative energy, the shaman creates a new person.[18]

An American Indian tale depicts the work of the animus in vivid terms, as ripping the killing teeth out of a woman's vagina. A witch, posing as the woman's mother, put the teeth in place to unman the daughter's suitors. The daughter tells her lover of the hidden teeth and so saves his life. Coyote, the animus lover of the tale, kills the woman's sister and the witch mother in his determination to marry the woman, who plays heroine to his hero. How can I do so? she asks; the teeth in me live in the wrong place. Simple: he knocks out the teeth in her vagina, "except for one blunt tooth that was very thrilling when making love." Coyote functions much like Shiva, to tame and direct a woman's energy into creative channels and to disarm all the destructive elements in her being.[19]

These three examples illustrate the strong, sharp cultural edge in the anima or animus complex. We can see that, whatever the differences of color or accent, the place of animus or anima between ego and Self remains much the same across cultures, as does the function to form a bridge across which the psyche's energy may flow to bring life in the world and devotion that goes beyond it. Any anima or animus will reflect a culture's conditioning, all of it, from its insights to its prejudices, which rather enhances than interferes with the powerful psychic functions of the archetype.

Because of the determining influence of cultural conditioning, we can appreciate the problems created in women when their culture adopts misogynist views. Because we build up our animus or anima partly from dominant images of the masculine and the feminine, such misogyny burdens a woman's animus with inner disparagement and detraction, from which she must differentiate herself in an interior dialogue that is as doggedly determined on its ends as the outer culture is on its own. This adds enormously to her personal task, just as it does a man's task in comparable circumstances, but the end result is worth the great struggle called for.

We can count on anima and animus to fish up for ego response whatever belongs to us that is other than our conscious gender identity, but the content will vary according to the way we lead our sexual lives. Whether we are heterosexual, homosexual, or celibate, all of us must come to terms with the contrasexual opposite living in us, which—in the anima/animus function as bridge to the Self—will affect, out of sexual beginnings, the way we come to spiritual expression.

One man, trying to discover in analysis whether his way was homosexual or heterosexual, found the numinous other presenting itself to him in images of a perfect male body. His images of women were barely visible and often mangled. He dreamed of a woman's scream as she was thrown from a rooftop. This grim picture stood in sharp contrast to his conscious liking of women and enjoyment of their company—as long, that is, as things did not turn sexual. Then he felt obligated to perform, under constant pressure to play the male. The numinous clothed itself for him in the archetype of the double, of one like him but also different in its astonishing degree of bodily perfection.[20] The man had to reckon with a personification that addressed him, male to male, and had also to take up the task of rescuing his inner female image from damaging violence.

The task of recognizing the constituent elements, gathering them together, and constructing identity from them remains the same for all of us, regardless of sexual practice, but the specific contents and the burdens of linking their parts vary greatly among us. Where the archetype of the double presides over entry to the Self, we are faced with the possibility of a strong narcissism and the likelihood that our narcissistic wound will then provide the shortest route between ego and Self. Narcissism often emerges here as a block to our choice of a love object: we seek in the other as close as possible a reflection of ourselves. Our greatest fear is the nearness of death, visible in our aging. But the archetype of the double also brings a potential for unity of being, making two into one, healing splits within one's own spirit, and forming a community based on kinship libido, in the understanding that we all finally make up the One. Reliance on relating through identification and identity, though it may initially impede our growth as persons, may also strongly inform and enlarge our relationship to otherness, as we develop an inner dialogue around the experiences that reliance inevitably brings to consciousness.

For heterosexuals, entry to the Self is likely to fall under the archetype of the other. We usually imagine otherness—which is to say difference—in terms of the anatomy of the opposite sex and find fascinating and engrossing every variation and permutation that otherness brings in a body and psyche so like and so unlike our own. Anyone who lives intimately with a person of the opposite sex knows the subtle and influential differences of psyche and body—the anxiety about getting pregnant or over menopause, about getting and keeping erections or losing sexual drive. These are not the exclusive property of one sex or the other when they are experienced together; the differences are of nuance. These differences, sometimes minute, often glaring, we can also experience in like to like, in sister or brother or even identical-twin relationships. They go to make up the mystery of the person, and we marvel that we can ever satisfactorily join at all. The same would hold for lesbian or gay couples, for striking differences exist there that convey themselves in intimate moments, often astonishingly. But the foreignness of the opposite sex proposes the greatest risk at the same time that it offers the longest sexual journey.

Where the archetype of the other presides over entry to the Self, schizoid splitting and projective identification are always in the air, either to pull us away from differences or to lead us to deny them. We must learn to relate to others, even to those with whom we identify. To do so is to see the potential for unity that exists even in self-evidently different parts and persons in sexual meetings, an incomparable model for a social community which celebrates differences while containing them, knowing that unity of Self arises out of the multiplicity of others.

Depth psychology confirms, either through clinical experience or inspired theorizing or a combination of both, an earlier wisdom about self and other. We can understand better now the reach, almost beyond words, of the dissertation on self-consciousness in Hegel's *Phänomenologie des Geistes*. Whether we think of his subject as Spirit or Mind, all but inescapably the philosopher's ruminations attach themselves to the psyche. The use of unconscious and consciousness as words today, as concepts, as ways of entry into the mysteries of human interiority, reflect with or without return to Hegel's text the sheer force of his understanding of the centrality of self-consciousness in a world of otherness.

We deal in Hegel with refractions of our grasp of the "I" that represents our sense of self, in our own individuality and in others. "With self-consciousness," he says, "we have entered the native realm of truth." It is true that when Hegel speaks of the subject or Ego, as J. N. Findlay explains, he means "not what we ordinarily understand by a personal thinker, but the logical function of universality in a peculiar sort of detachment from its species and instances." The Hegelian *Geist* is "a bustling Agora" of forms, as in Aristotle, "involved in endless transactions and conversations" that touch us in individual ways in our individual lives, but achieve their identifying character and force in a world of essence where Self and other find their source. The prevailing winds are Greek; we deal either directly in Hegel's ruminations about consciousness or in the adaptations of these aspects of the *Phenomenology* of Heidegger or the related thinking of Gadamer, with addenda and corrigenda to Plato and Aristotle, to Pythagoras and the pre-Socratics. Being is illuminated; but for all the differences of emphasis and of vocabulary, so is our understanding of the psyche.

For the philosopher, the Hegelian dialectic of self-consciousness offers rich metaphysical rewards. For the psychologist, the understanding of the drama of desire as an exchange of othernesses, either completed or thwarted or left hanging somewhere in mid-act, is at least as much enhanced. As Gadamer sums it up, "The self-consciousness of desire knows itself to be dependent on the object of desire as something other than itself." But this is no simple animal pointing to a longed-for appropriation: "If self-consciousness is to become true self-consciousness, then it must stand on its own and find another self-consciousness that is willing to be for it." The conclusion is pivotal: "Thus, the doubling of self-consciousness is a necessary consequence: self-consciousness is only possible as a double." Once again, we meet the archetype of the double and, pressing on its heels, the archetype of the other.

The essential is reciprocity. Even in the most conventional process of greeting someone, we look to be seen by the other reciprocally: "Think of the feeling of humiliation when a greeting is not returned, be it because the other refuses to take cognizance of you—a devastating defeat for your own consciousness of self—or because he is not the person you thought he was but someone else and hence does not recognize you—not a very nice feeling either." A whole series of jokes, dating from a time long after Hegel's, hang on that observation, as for example the meeting of two psychoanalysts. "Hello," the first greets the second. "I wonder what he meant by that?" the second worries to himself.

Hegel's characterization of the separated self-consciousness, one that is without the required reciprocity of relationship to the other, is an eloquent argument, for all its negative emphasis, in favor of a social reading of self-consciousness. It also argues, we think, for the richness of understanding of the anima/animus world, where archetypal textures join us not only to the contrasexuality within us but to the universe outside ourselves, where we find our confirmation of being-in-itself through our being-in-the-other, the other who returns our understanding and confirms our experience of the support that arises from reciprocity.

Consciousness itself is the *absolute dialectical unrest,* this medley of sensuous and intellectual representations whose differences coincide, and whose identity is equally again dissolved, for it is itself determinateness as contrasted with the non-identical. But it is just in this process that this consciousness, instead of being self-identical, is in fact but a purely casual, confused medley, the dizziness of a perpetually self-engendered disorder. It is itself aware of this; for it itself maintains and creates this restless confusion. Hence it also admits to it, it owns to being a wholly contingent, single, and separate consciousness—a consciousness which is *empirical,* which takes its guidance from what has no reality for it, which obeys what is for it not an *essential* being, which does those things and brings to realization what it knows has no truth for it. But equally, while it takes itself in this way to be a single and separate, contingent and, in fact, animal life, and a *lost* self-consciousness, it also, on the contrary, converts itself again into a consciousness that is universal and self-identical; for it is the negativity of all singularity and all difference.

We do not have to share Hegel's metaphysic to recognize the wisdom of a reading of self-consciousness that hangs on reciprocity and holds as inimical to self that "splitting-up," as he calls it, which leaves us in "the dizziness of a perpetually self-engendered disorder."[21] We move against singularity and difference as marks of separation, toward an interdependence in which the existence of the other is at the very least a pointer toward self and at best its guarantor. The movement starts, we are saying, with that consciousness of an interior reciprocity of self and other that springs from our relationship with anima or animus and issues in a lively inner conversation in which we keep finding and claiming more and more of ourselves.

The person whose conscious gender identity embraces celibacy as the major sexual commitment presents different configurings of anima and animus but to similar interior ends. Here the ego makes radical sacrifice of a sexuality lived out in fact. We reach the other, whether the same sexually or different from ourselves, across a consciously maintained gap in intimacy. The celibate forgoes the closeness that includes the solace of enduring intimate companionship in the flesh. Across the sexual gap, celibates live with heightened attention, alert to the approach of the spiritual Other. They must seek the Divine directly, without the mediation, most of the time, of a human partner. Anima or animus must carry that gap, then, that empty space, honoring it by offering it up. The perils are unmistakable: of suffering turning masochistic, or of withdrawal into denial of the suffering the offering engenders, or of the breaking of the celibate vow by intimate friendships, which may bring a further and even more dangerous denial. The potential also exists of transforming the sexual gap into a middle space where the engendering is entirely positive. There one may perceive the abundance of grace that surrounds everywhere and always, there be conscious of that animating *circulatio* bestowed by Creation, from which everything comes and to which everything returns. Anima and animus figures people celibates' dreams as they do everyone else's and bring projections, but they can at all times be dissolved back into the gap, burned up in the fiery void of ultimate Being.

Working in analysis with such persons may bring into play a quite intense sexual energy, but one sees quickly that it is being lived very differently. In transference–countertransference dynamics, sexual energies are often transmuted into a spiritual force that is handed back and forth, defining the void, which is also the offering. The sexual energies between two women or between a woman and a man present themselves and change into spirit because the gap that always exists in the genuine celibate steps back from concrete sexual manifestation, as if to allow God to step forward. The anima or animus bridge for the celibate is where full human longing for intimacy is conducted into consciousness, where the celibate can hold it as a discriminating and precious yearning to be offered up to the God who enters the flesh as well as the spirit, who resurrects being from the void into presence, on earth, so very near, so unmistakably other.

Finally, in noting anima and animus differences, we must see how the differences are reflected in the contrasexual bridge. Generalizations are particularly questionable here, where every individual suggestion of accent or nuance articulates a significant contrasexual element. That is the way these archetypes work.

In Western culture, insofar as the feminine is demeaned, we should expect the anima to function to bring a man down to meet the feminine through a lowering of consciousness. She would, we might reason, entangle him in her life, pull him into experiences both compelling and murky, in marked contrast to his association of the masculine stance with objectivity, mastery of facts, easy abstraction and conceptualization. The anima might need to make him feel undone to reach him. He needs to submit to her.

In contrast, a woman would need to rise above her animus contents, to stand at some distance from them and look at them probingly, not allowing them ever to swamp her sense of person. She would need to reserve to herself the power in the contents the animus ushers toward her, never to give it to her animus, but to harness the energy to serve her precise perceptions of truth and value. What she needs from the animus is ardent support for her values, anything that would build self-confidence in her. The animus functions to bring her close to the truths by which she lives, where he serves both as psychopomp and *logos spermatikos*. The parallel function of the anima is to bring a man his animating connection to being, what makes him feel alive, abundantly himself in a tangible reality. Meaning and life attend both archetypes.[22]

A woman feels the need to discriminate among the many seeds the animus inseminates, to know which ones to plant. Then she can nurture this inner nucleus until it is time to give birth to it in the outside world. She creates, then, out of the wholeness of being which a joining of consciousness and the unconscious represents. She can move to discover transcendence in immanence, spirit in everyday life.[23] A man's need is to open to the anima, to let it inhabit him with its sense of enlivening presence, even if it comes in the guise of restless searching for repose in a goal to which he can devote himself. For a man, transcendence arises outside him, as something he reaches to beyond himself.

In general, then, a man needs to yield to the anima and at the same time to resist being hoodwinked by it, for its blandishments can be deceptive. A woman needs to stand up to her animus and not be bullied as she listens to the secret intimations of truth he imparts. Conversely, in making the journey of individuation, a man may need to fight heroically to win through to the Self, and the woman may need to endure a descent to the underworld to connect instinctive vegetative depths of fecund wisdom with her spiritual aspirations. The anima engenders in a man appropriate emotional attitudes with which to engage his nature. The animus helps a woman determine her goal and go straight to it. In contrast to the bodies of men and women, an anima may be all curves, reconciling and containing opposite things; an animus, all linearity, an arrow penetrating right to the source.

A fourteenth-century prayer to the "source" recalls the urge of anima and animus to creativity and to mystery, to harmony in contrariety, to the syzygy and the reciprocity that assure an undivided self-consciousness.

Give then yourself to me, O best of givers and giver of the best; for, as for yourself, you are mine, and nothing can be mine nor can I be my own, unless you be mine first. Be mine, be mine, therefore; for so alone shall I be mine, and yours; but, if you are not mine, nothing is mine.

With what then shall I purchase you or compare you? With nothing, save yourself. You must then give yourself to me, that with you I may buy you. Anticipate yourself, therefore, and make me ready to receive you; and, when you are received, speak for me to yourself and hearken to yourself on my behalf. Ask from yourself your gifts for me, and on yourself, asking yourself from me, bestow yourself. Now, O most sweet, I see what you would have from me.[24]

The interdependence of our sexual and contrasexual selves, with themselves and with the selves of others, could not be better invoked than in this prayer to the Spirit. If we remember some of the ancient meanings of anima—as a current of air, a breathing out, the rational soul, mind, spirit, life—and of the animus—the intellect, the sensibility, will, consciousness, recollection, self-possession, passion, imagination, belief—we must surely see in the fourteenth-century words the large reach of these archetypes across human experience, understanding, and prayer.

Anima/Animus in
Full Pursuit

THE FULLNESS of attention of the animus/anima archetypes to our inner lives does not cease with age. Quite the contrary, for nowhere is their shaping and reshaping of the marks of our identity more evident than in our later years. Assiduously they pursue us in the minutiae of our sexual and spiritual lives as we grow older. We feel their stinging presence as we look for signs of aging in our bodies. We imagine taunting comments, mocking gestures, rollings of the eyes of our contrasexual selves as we contemplate the inevitable—the sagging and eventual loss of our sexual and spiritual energies. Boldly, they stand in for the key members of the opposite sex in our lives, telling us what men will think of us as declining women, or women as they note our vanishing virility. And even if we have not yet lost our powers, our inner conversation has almost certainly begun to sag and droop with the anticipation of failure at the core of our being. If it has not, isn't there something wrong with us? And we really think we still possess our youthful vigor, and show that we do, not simply in short skirts and high heels and bright ties and dashing jackets, but in the rhythms of our lives, aren't we out of order and appallingly unrealistic about who we are and where we are?

No, says Goethe, speaking for men of genius and, what is more, speaking as a man nearly eighty years old. If the entelechy, the defining force in a person's life, is of "inferior quality," says Goethe in 1828, in one of his notable conversations with his devoted companion Eckermann, it will be able to do little to halt the body's decline. "But if the entelechy happens to be powerful, as is the case with all men of genius, it will not only permeate the organization of the body with an invigorating and ennobling quality of life, but, by virtue of its spiritual dominance, it will also be tending to assert its prerogative of eternal youth." That, he adds, speaking from personal experience as well as a fullness of historical example, is why "the pre-eminently gifted" show such bursts "of special productivity even in old age," and still more, he goes on, bursts of "rejuvenation," evidencing nothing less than "a recurrence of puberty."[1]

Are we condemned, then, if we are not men or women of genius, to sag and droop, to sexual and spiritual decline? A lifetime is contained in our answer to the question, the long history of our dealings with our entelechy, our vital agent, in the form of our animating contrasexuality. We may for long have persuaded ourselves, in inner deliberation about the resources that define the quality of our lives, that we are hopelessly second-rate and doomed to lose energy with our falling hairs, to give up significant presence with our faltering memory. It does not require advanced years for us, with such a history, to say Yes to the question of inevitable decline and No to the possibility of rejuvenation. Our answers have been with us for years. Go back to puberty! What an idea!

We may be surprised to find here, as in so many other areas of our sexual and spiritual lives, that our pursuing animus/anima archetypes are not satisfied with those bedraggled answers. They may not be content to taunt us with failure; they may insist, in a contrariety that is sometimes mocking, sometimes courtly, and in all its states of being somehow supporting and inspiriting, that in our later years we enter a new set of strengths alongside or even within the unmistakable physical changes. We are not the same; that is clear. We are also not, as a result, necessarily diminished. Nothing presents the complexity of the question better for us, and nothing the foolishness of simple answers, than women in menopause; nothing shows more thoroughly what may develop in us, men as well as women, when we contemplate so formidable a change of life under the tutelage of our contrasexuality.

THE ANIMUS AND MENOPAUSE

The end of her monthly blood ritual says to a woman, in the most intimate and dramatic way possible, that death approaches, that it has taken residence in her own body and she must find an attitude to deal with it. Once again images are called for in building the bridge to the unknown, images of the meeting of life and death. Menopause for so many women is the crucial crossing point. Their body changes make them aware of the power of the animus as their entelechy, the vital agent in them that can wound or heal.

The physical discomfort of menopause brings immediately to a woman's consciousness how little any of us control our own lives. She feels cracked open by this reminder of the fragility of being that comes through shocking intrusive hot flashes that live in a terrible intimacy just beneath her skin. No medicine, no breathing exercise, no correction of psychological attitude will deter these sudden eruptions of heat and their accompanying feverish perspiration. One feels skewered. It helps to get a hormonal map to combat the panicky feeling that one's body thermostat has been blown out of control—trembling chills, trembling burnings, up, down, rapid changes, slow changes, sleep constantly interrupted by the high temperatures. One woman complained that even her skull sweated.

Medicines help a lot to restore physical equilibrium, but nothing removes the sense of loss over all that is gone. One woman said she felt gutted, left with an empty black hole where her reproductive organs used to be. She still had all the organs, but their food, the blood, no longer pumped through them to nourish new life or even the prospect of it. The cycle on which a woman depends, even in her suffering and revilement of it, has disappeared. Much of her body's youthfulness, she is sure, has gone with it. The drying up of her juices, thinning of her membranes, coarsening of her skin, confirm her in her convictions and presage her death. Relief from menstrual pain is matched by a new metaphysical pain.[2]

One woman said she felt filled to the top with grief. She knew what it was like not to know what her body was doing. She could no longer interpret its signals. It spoke a foreign language now, not the one she learned and lived with for so long, with its familiar and comfortable physical and spiritual grammar. She described her experience of ovulation as carrying a sense of intense excitement, where boundaries melted to make her feel porous, open to life's juices and filled with them. At each ovulation she experienced countless insights, so many seeds of new actions to be taken, new ideas to think, new feelings, new projects, new truths to meditate upon. She saw connections and linkings everywhere. As her menstrual period approached, she felt herself go down into herself, a denser person, weighted with existence. She did not resent her heavier breasts, sore belly, or the slowing of her pace. She felt it was time to realize one of those creative impulses, as if her monthly period was her food flowing out of her into the world.[3] With the approach of menopause this same woman felt robbed of her body language; she became mute. Was this, she wondered, what people felt when they became deathly ill? The body lets you down; it betrays you. Her body was leaving her while she was still perfectly healthy and quite up to holding onto it.

Another menopausal woman aimed her complaints and resentments at American culture: it offers nothing to older women except ways to disguise themselves as younger women. Society makes you feel in menopause, she said, like a dead flower, something that must be thrown out. For another, menopause introduced irreversible changes and discontinuities. She could never go back to what she was. Her womb had closed and with it her old life.

Clearly experiences like these lay women open to nasty attacks by a negative animus. Lingering sexual problems must surely be intensified. Self-doubts must increase; sexual self-confidence is hardly possible. The animus of the woman who identifies with her culture's standard images of the female throws up to her the nubile youngster of pop novels and films and television, mocking her every new bulge, wrinkle, gray hair, and all the profound tissue and hormonal changes that menopause introduces. One woman fought hard against these pressures by trying to discover what her body was opening her to, not just succumbing to her body's closings. But then she was laid low by her husband's middle-life confusion, evidenced in the changed image of woman he now held before him. In a fantasy version of himself, he saw himself always with a sexy young woman on his arm, never an aging, menopausal wife.

When menopause touches men, as it does most of the time, it raises a stern question: Can a man's anima imagination stretch to include an older woman whose change of life points toward death? What the animus does in this confrontation of animus and anima is critical for a woman seeking to navigate the menopausal storms. In the most immediate way possible—in madly alternating body temperatures and hormonal shifts, in dream images that reflect the biological changes, in little emotional melodramas, in up-and-down sexual desire—everything seems to forecast death. It is quite the opposite of the woman's younger life, where her reproductive potential, acted upon or not, with its regular monthly reminders of the conceptual power in her blood, bespoke nothing but life to her.

A woman has an extraordinary opportunity here to live her mystery in its entirety, first life, then death, and to share what she learns with the rest of us. Perhaps that is one reason wise old women, even hags and crones, received so much honor in ancient cultures.[4] To live her mystery, to know it and make sense of it, a woman needs more than distant cultural respect; she must have the support of her animus in its transformative role, and, if possible, that of a good man.

All involved must ask themselves, relentlessly: What purpose does menopause serve? Why does it happen to women when they have so many years still to live? How does it equip a woman to live the remaining decades of her life? What new kind of living is being engineered?

These questions, at least to begin with, must be answered in solitude. They must be looked at in concrete personal terms. The problems cannot be looked at as those of women in general but rather as belonging to one particular woman sharing the destiny of all her sex. Any universal truth about menopause must quickly be translated into the special needs, rhythms, difficulties, possibilities of this woman in this place at this time.

The solitude in which she chooses to take up these problems will greatly influence her way of dealing with them. If she looks at her situation through a screen of depression and despair, emphasizing her sense of having come to the end of any significant sexual life, feeling with keenness the loss of her childbearing strengths, her solitude will be a nagging one, breeding despondency, a retreat from life. If she looks instead for what positive sense this change of life represents, what enlargements of view and supporting energies it might offer, the affirmation of sexual power that might lie in it, then she will be glad to be alone. She will not feel assailed by her situation in the time she spends by herself. She will look forward to the opportunities to reconnoiter the territory for sexual resources long hidden from sight that a new inspection, unhindered by the constraints of youth and the narrowings of limited experience, might reveal. In a positive solitude she will discover the meditative and contemplative reach that a seasoned sexuality provides and begin to feel grateful for this extraordinary new development.

Out of such a use of solitude comes a great sharing with others. One has been stripped naked before oneself and made to look and see what is there. Simple self-gratification is not so easy any more. One has been pointed away from the beginnings of life toward its ends, with all the meanings of the word. How much longer will one live? With what sense of purpose? With what ease with oneself and others?

We may not at this juncture want to use the portentous language of Heidegger, thinking of our mature being as a *Sein zum Tode,* a Being-toward-death, but if we have used our menopausal solitude well, we will not be affronted by the suggestion and may even find in it some of the movement toward authenticity that Heidegger, following Hegel, sees in this construction of one's being. Authenticity is a corollary enhancement of the *Sein zum Tode* proposition. Like the solitude that enables us to accept such conclusions, it is an inflection of the positive, even in the face of our finitude, perhaps especially in the face of finitude. We discover that we can practice the presence of death without tremor or distaste. We feel neither imprisoned by the body nor confined to it, but glad to have it still, to use it still, to make more of it, not less, because of our change of circumstance.[5]

In *Man and People,* the grand summation of his views of society that he wrote near the end of his life, José Ortega y Gasset describes a "radical" difference between the female and male ego. "Normally," the philosopher observes, "we men forget our brother the body; we are not aware of possessing it except at the chill or burning hour of extreme pain or extreme pleasure. Between our purely psychic I and the outer world, nothing seems to be interposed." Not so with woman. She is always conscious of her body, carrying it before her, "at once as a shield of defense and as a vulnerable hostage." For her, body and soul live in a high degree of "interpenetration."

The connection of woman's body and spirit is close, knowledgeable, an alliance rather than the sorry thing man makes of the two: "In man, comparatively speaking, each normally takes its own course; body and soul know little of each other and are not allied, rather they act like irreconcilable enemies." Understand, Ortega is telling us, what started in woman's "remarkable culture of the body" as great attention to ornamentation, developed in cleanliness, and "ended in courtesy, that inspired feminine invention, which, finally, is the subtle culture of the gesture."

We might be moved to dismiss these well-turned phrases as simply the product of the courtesy that Ortega, the *hidalgo* of philosophy, learned from women or perhaps more accurately from his own fully lived anima life. It would be a mistake. We would miss then an essential emphasis upon woman, and in archetypal terms, upon anima presence, as soul.

> The result of this constant attention that woman devotes to her body is that her body appears to us from the first as impregnated, as wholly filled with soul. This is the foundation for the impression of weakness that her presence creates in us. Because in contrast to the firm and solid appearance of the body, the soul is a little tremulous, the soul is a little weak. In short, the erotic attraction that woman produces in man is not—as the ascetics have always told us in their blindness on these matters—aroused by the feminine body as body; rather, we desire woman because her body *is* a soul.[6]

With this understanding, menopause is exactly what its name indicates—a pause in a life rhythm effected by a cessation of a major bodily function, but not of the body itself, or the soul with which it is "impregnated." Soul does not have mass. It is neither diminished nor augmented by a loss or gain of body weight nor made smaller or less significant by a change of body rhythm. The shift, like one from 4/4 to 3/4 time in music, represents a change of emphasis, an opportunity for a more leisurely, more graceful, more rounded sort of motion in one's life. The *rallentando* effect is a deliberate slowing down, not a running down but a running with, to take in more, not less. It is the occasion in a woman's life to ask the central questions.

Women who bring such questions into analysis mixed with their menopausal suffering have something to tell us. One woman, a theologian, contrasted what she knew of the female experience of continuity with the male. She was born of woman, and as woman could herself bear children. A man remains always as he began, just one. In menopause, woman suddenly knows radical discontinuity, an approaching end; a man grows more gradually toward death. The woman theologian wondered if out of this breaking of her life cycle, a woman was not being asked to speak to others about all the different ways available to women to experience the nexus of body and spirit. First she knew spirit embodied in her sense of continuity with past (mother) and future (child). Now, in menopause, she experiences spirit disidentified from body, or in process of disidentifying from fleshly existence, a significant preface to death and the afterlife. In her menopause, a woman knows daily recollected thought about death. Menopause works its way silently through the body; no matter how medical intervention slows its course, it advances inexorably. Thus, the theologian mused, we gain a chance to experience consciously and fully in life the disengaging process we experience in dying, which is almost always more traumatic, sudden, and painful, obliterating any chance we might have to dwell on its meaning for us and those around us. Furthermore, she reasoned, menopause is followed by life, not death. A woman can experience now both being in her body and yet not of it, being possessed by the body while being dispossessed of it.

Another woman in analysis found menopause recapitulating her whole sexual history. She dreamed her way back to its beginnings in puberty and looking back saw herself sorting out where she was male, where female. She dreamed again her sexual trauma, of a sibling assaulting her. The dream brought something new: she behaved differently from the way she had in the actual event, with angry defense now and accusation, and refusal. Most important of all, she said, she found her old sexual fantasy no longer held any potency. It configured a woman yielding to her own sexual desire. She said that plot was too juvenile for a woman going through menopause. Instead, she felt gathering in her a feminine force that flowed in her, which she could house and honor and pass onto her partner and to the world.

Still another woman found inestimable support for opening herself to what she called the shift from bearing children to bearing a differently specified being, which came from the good man in her life and through him to her own supportive animus. Her man showed keen interest in the changes happening to her and how as a result their sexual meetings would be affected. He insisted that these changes were taking them somewhere for good purpose. She took in this attitude and developed it in herself. The searching meditative attentiveness to her body processes that she now found in herself allowed her to explore rather than to judge her menopausal changes. Like the other women, she hit upon the paradoxical experience of both being in her body and yet not of it, a kind of disidentifying that always gives wide scope to one's spirit. To her surprise, the initial slackening of her sexual desire changed too; she picked up pace and heat and discovered orgasmic responses that "scooped her out" entirely, as she put it, a letting go of restraint to flow into the river of being. Just as she used to feel life pulsating in her, now she felt life running through her, making her a part of its universal course.

Menopause is as decisive a point in the spiritual connection between a man and woman as the birth of their child. The man is as pivotal here as before. The couple can go the way of death, settling into fear, depression, and resentment at the dissolution of the body and their sexual congress, or they can go the way of life, following the lead of the body to experience a new conjunction of flesh and spirit, an enlargement of their resources to embrace this life and the next.

The support of a woman's animus proves the turning point in conjunction with the support of her mate. Together, they uphold the approach of Self in the midst of body turmoil. A woman is privileged to rehearse death this way and tell us out of her experience how to construct images that will bridge life here with the ultimate dwelling place of Self. For as von Franz says, "The fear of death is thereby in the last analysis a fear of the Self and of final confrontation with the Self."[7]

A woman at menopause can bring to her rehearsal of death an equal and opposite rehearsal of life. She can see herself as a painter might, as a woman of a certain age who bears the marks of her life in her face and body, her choice of clothing, the way she makes up her face and wears her hair, the motions of feeling she brings into her posture, her movements, her gestures, her gaze, her repose. She has a chance, in her positive solitude, in her preparation to meet people, on her return from meeting people, to examine the life she presents to people. How would I look, she might ask herself, to a Berthe Morisot, an Edgar Degas, an Edouard Vuillard? Would I reveal as much solidity of life in the hunching of my shoulders as Vuillard's mother sewing, reading, moving toward a doorway? Could I justify in my singularity of being what Vuillard found so satisfying in a woman's head? "A woman's head just gave to me," he said, "a certain emotion; the emotion alone must be enough for me and I mustn't struggle to remember her nose or her ear, all that doesn't matter in the least."

The anima power that Vuillard drew from the women around him and transformed into the images of his art is much more, clearly, than material for a painter's exercises. It is something of such intensity that he could make of a nearly abstract version of woman, caught in a sea of fin de siècle all-over designs, a gathering place for a serene contemplation of being: being-toward-life in maternity subjects, being-toward-death in older women. His sister with child, his mother at work or rest, a cook, a dressmaker, a society matron, all pique a meditative response in the painter, so different from his response to men as subjects—in them "I always see burdened wretches, I have only the feeling of ridiculous objects."

What we see in Vuillard's paintings of women is an inner world of an anima-fixated man translated into color and composition, flattened into such concentrated speculative vision that one glimpses the two dimensions of the Cubist picture plane all but settled into place. These pictures can be viewed as art objects, as a stage in the development of modern painting, as a movement toward Cubism, or as a record of that self-styled prophetic group, at the edge of twentieth-century painting, to which Vuillard belonged, the Nabis. They can also be seen as a tutelage in the iconography of contrasexuality, not in contradistinction to their place in art history, but as an extension and a deepening of it. They stand before us as guardians of that tutelary spirit, reminding us, as men, of how far an anima vision can go to show us what really matters in a life, even one that on the surface looks to have little distinction, a corset maker's, a cook's; telling us, as women, of the possibility of drawing from one's own animus life an inspection of a fullness approaching Vuillard's, which assures the least of the sex of a confrontation of substance with the Self.[8]

A woman can tell us of the meeting with Self as it exists in a nonincarnated timeless eternity with the Self incarnated in her own physical-spiritual personality. Menopause forces that detachment from the here-and-now which is necessary to permit us to see the ever-and-always beyond us. This transformation takes place literally, in her body and in meetings of the flesh with her lover. Is it too much to say that menopause gives us in these experiences a foretaste of resurrection? For a woman can feel uniting in herself two usually separated elements of Self, its universal center that exists far outside the psyche, and the objective center that resides deep inside her own personality. But she cannot reach that union of the small feminine with the large Self without the warm, firm support and farsighted vision of the masculine—whether as animus or mate. If she has both, as the fortunate woman analysand described above did, she will learn from her experience that menopausal changes change our leading question from one of life and death to one of an even larger dimension: How do we achieve a lasting inner wholeness? We do so, we learn, by taking the opportunity menopause offers a woman, and through her a man as well, to join the little Self in us to its transcendent Source.[9]

BARTH, FREUD, JUNG, TILLICH, AND THE SPLIT ANIMA

Anima and animus touch the life of the spirit in us as they do the life of the body. They pursue us boldly in things spiritual as they do in things sexual, especially, as with menopause, where we are most strenuously engaged and most vulnerable. If they find us in pensive solitude, they rejoice. Human interiority is their native hunting ground, where they work with what looks like Aristotle's conviction that perfect happiness is a contemplative activity. They know us here, as in the speculations that frequently accompany our sexual life, as deeply concerned with issues of being and especially with the finitude that orgasm proclaims so wantonly that it has become a commonplace to call its conclusion "the little death." Once again, our contrasexual dialogue acts to set us on the bridge that leads to the center of being. Contemplating our mortality, in our solitude, we approach the Self and find in this activity of the spirit some of the same tensions of our life with each other as men and women that we found in the activities of the body. If our inquiries take us far enough, we will discover that in our time men of genius have shown themselves particularly vulnerable to these tensions.

It is a curious fact about this century that so many of its seminal thinkers in depth psychology and theology lived in a split anima situation.[10] They drew their insights from one or another kind of solitude, in which they developed an extraordinary facility in the dialogues of interiority notable for the place in them of a feminine presence reflecting the high place of women in their lives. Freud, Jung, Barth, and Tillich, our cases in point, all experienced much of what they knew of the feminine in what convention calls "irregular" sexual liaisons. The feminine, both within them and in the remarkable women to whom they were attached, was a constant preoccupation for them. In cases of this kind, a split invariably exists between the feelings, attitudes, dreams, and fantasies engendered or not engendered by the "regular" partner—usually, as in these cases, a wife—and the outsider, the "irregular." The woman at home may remain, as these men's wives did, steadily available, aware in some way of what is going on, but still reaching out to their men. They may argue, protest, show their great discomfort, but they abide like a grounding earth, a secure foundation for a widely adventuring life.

An apparently conventional marriage goes on side by side with unconventional attachments, sometimes just one other relationship, and perhaps the significant one, the real inner marriage, as was apparently the case with Karl Barth. The unconventional partners seem present to unbounded fires of passion, leaps of erotic imagination, sudden spiritual excitement. The arrangement seems also to produce inspired work, but not without great cost to all the participants. We only have to think of the brilliant mind of Charlotte von Kirschbaum, Barth's secretary and major collaborator—it was she who wrote the profound and voluminous sections that appear in fine print in the great thick volumes of Barth's *Church Dogmatics*—who descended into the no-man's-land of Alzheimer's disease for the last years of her life.[11] Or the howling pain of Hannah Tillich, quieted finally by the discipline of yoga and the solace of accompanying meditation.[12] Even Freud, who seemed to lose interest in overt sexuality and proclaimed an end to it early in his marriage, nonetheless surrounded himself with intimate relationships with women other than his wife—inside his household his wife's sister, Minna, and his daughter, Anna, and in his work a number of radically different, highly intelligent, sexually unconventional women, such as Lou Andreas-Salomé.[13] Jung's simultaneous relationship with his wife, Emma, and his longtime companion, Toni Wolff, cost all three much suffering and greatly affected his children, who, it is said, had a chapter devoted to Wolff removed from Jung's autobiography.[14]

Attitudes and insights, speculations and conclusions forged in the inner conversations of solitude tell us much about these large figures. They reflect in many ways the determining role of an anima presence, even in the life and work of a Freud, whose doctrines seem to proclaim an inherent inferiority in everything feminine, starting with the ritual place assigned woman in which to become aware of and mourn for her missing piece, the penis.

Freud's discovery of the unconscious, by his own proclamation the third of the three giant "blows to human self-love," following those of Copernicus and Darwin, was developed in a necessary solitariness. Though the founding father of psychoanalysis, he was never analyzed by anyone else. His transferences and countertransferences were to himself. What he elicited about the nature of the human psyche came, to begin with, from forays into his own interiority. The antimetaphysical bias of early depth psychology, the spurning of religion as projection erected into dubious myth, the inversion of life process postulating the emergence of being from becoming, the assertion of a sexual determinism—all may be said to have sprung from Freud's colloquies with himself. Psychoanalysis can rejoice in the fact that the container was so large and its contents so fruitful. It also must take account of the problems created by its long reliance on one man's experiences and understanding of those experiences as the basis for what that same man insisted was a scientific discipline, with all the precision and openness to close inspection of a hard science.

The special irony of Freud's achievement, enormous as it is, is that the science it proposes and the facts upon which it constructs its propositions must be revealed, by the procedure he himself insisted upon, in the course of analysis with a professional analyst, just that experience he himself never had. It has been left to others to draw the inferences about his own psyche from his life and works that must serve in effect as analytical judgments about him, not because his writings and his methods and practice should not be judged on their own, but because so much of what they offer rests upon elements in his doctrine that only analysis can reveal.

There is no escaping the odd anima life Freud lived as a way into the substance of his theory. One may dismiss the dominance of male associates in his organization of a psychoanalytic movement and the publication of psychoanalytic ideas as a reflection of the patriarchal society of the *Mitteleuropa* in which he lived. But the curious exceptions to this dominance in the women he did bring close to him, and the contrast between his treatment of his daughter, Anna, and the adopted sons he wooed and cast away—Jung, Rank, Adler, Stekel, Tausk, Groddeck— demand serious reflection. Everything must be referred back to him, as the disciples who stayed the course came to understand. François Roustang speaks to the point:

> What Freud himself experimented with in an exemplary way, however, and what some of his disciples recognized in their own experience, could never be a decisive criterion. Personal obedience was not enough to guarantee faithfulness to the Freudian way of thinking nor to sustain what was necessary for the analysis. When one considers on the one hand the mysticoclinical ideas of Lou Andreas-Salomé, which Freud hardly criticizes and even encourages, and on the other hand the reductions of Anna Freud, which subvert psychoanalysis in the most decisive way, one is convinced that the confidence Freud had in these women is equal only to their admiration of him and their submission to him. They explicitly questioned neither Freud nor his work, thanks to which they could transform psychoanalysis into a Russian novel or a school textbook.[15]

Freud's aim was always to establish psychoanalysis as a science, but as he grew older, his writings show, he came to recognize what must have emerged in his interior dialogues with particular force and clarity, that what had seemed satisfactory to speak of in a positivist language was better discussed now in philosophical terms just this side of the textures of religious discourse. And so by the time of the *New Introductory Lectures* (1932) he could admit, "The theory of instincts is so to say our mythology. Instincts are mythical entities, magnificent in their indefiniteness. . . . We have always been moved by a suspicion that behind all these little *ad hoc* instincts there lay concealed something serious and powerful which we should like to approach cautiously." That is not the language of hard science, or at least not the positivist brand with which he had grown up. It is closer to the indeterminacy of quantum physics, a world in which metaphysical speculation brings no offense.

In 1927, Freud was adamant about metaphysics: "In secret—one cannot say such things aloud—I believe that one day metaphysics will be condemned as a nuisance, an abuse of thinking, a survival from the period of the religious *Weltanschauung.*" A year later, writing to his friend Oskar Pfister, a Protestant pastor, he spoke of his recently published books, *The Question of Lay Analysis,* in which he argued for the credentials of analysts like his daughter, Anna, who was not a medical doctor, and *The Future of an Illusion,* his most forthright attack on religion. He confessed to a hope that suggests the role he fulfilled in his interior colloquies: "I do not know whether you have guessed the hidden link between 'Lay Analysis' and 'Illusion.' In the former I want to protect analysis from physicians, and in the latter from priests. I want to entrust it to a profession that doesn't yet exist, a profession of secular ministers of souls, who don't have to be physicians and must not be priests." Freud's anima life, one cannot help concluding, casts him not as the secular Moses of frequent fantasy, but as Sarastro to Anna's Pamina.[16]

Jung, like Freud, analyzed himself, but unlike him looked everywhere to expose himself to exchanges that would challenge and deepen his probings of the unconscious. It seems fair to say that no one in depth psychology ever sought so earnestly conversation with authorities in and practitioners of the religions of the world. He did as much again with anthropologists, specialists in mythology, philosophers, quantum physicists, anyone who might enlarge his understanding of the workings of human interiority. Practiced as few others in "rigorous self-examination," he invited others to look over the territory with him, seeking always greater understanding of its depths. He was not fazed by learned disagreement or the imputation of being unscientific: "Psychic events are observable facts and can be dealt with in a 'scientific' way."

Jung saw himself as following the time-honored steps of so-called scientific method—observing, establishing "relations and sequences between the observed data," and even hazarding "the possibility of prediction." He was not quick to assume "principle," he explained. With the collective unconscious, for example, he was simply giving "a name to the totality of observable facts, i.e., archetypes." But he was stubborn about the "scientific" nature of procedures like his that went beyond physical or physiological methods. "Psyche is the mother of all our attempts to understand Nature, but in contradistinction to all others," he explained, "it tries to understand itself by itself, a great disadvantage in one way and an equally great prerogative in the other!"

That is Jung's way, as to some extent it is the way of Freud and all others who draw upon interior dialogue for their leading insights into human nature. Their conclusions will always be questioned and often dismissed by those who think anything unscientific, as Karl Popper insists, that is not falsifiable. There is no objective scale, true enough, but there is human history. There is no neutral outside observer, but again, there are the wise men and women of the past, against whose experiences to check present-day findings or observations. Only another who has had a like experience or clinical observation or a sedulous inspection of the experiences of those who have gone before us can confirm the methods of interior converse.

Jung's understanding of human interiority, gathered from his own experience and the wisdom of the past, permitted him to deal with the extremes of belief and unbelief. Because, as he said, his psychology dealt with modern man, who "has lost or given up . . . his traditional beliefs and has to find out for himself what is going to happen to him in his impoverished state," his method was directed to see "the uncertainty of all human postulates" in that state. "Nothing of the things I describe comes to life unless you can accompany or sympathize understandingly with beings that are forced to base their life upon facts to be experienced and not upon transcendental postulates beyond human experience."

Such convictions did not distance Jung from those in the past who had experienced the transformation of instinct in the "ritual anamnesis of an archetypal figure" in renewal or rebirth mysteries. He understood at first hand, as might a Rabbi Akiba or a John of the Cross, "the hermeneutic conception" of the Song of Songs, with the added inflections of analytical psychology, seeing Christ as fulfilling the role of "the 'spiritual ancestor' or archetype of man (as *Adam secundus*), while the fundamental instinctive basis is represented by an indubitable erotic situation."

So it was that he would understand from clinical data and records of the past the kind of dissociation "which consists in a splitting-off of the feminine element in the unconscious, which in Western languages is designated by anima, psyche, and their associates." When consciousness has "strayed too far from its natural basis and gets into conflict with its natural preconditions," dissociations of this kind follow as they have done forever in human history. To heal them, reconciliation rituals were devised that often "took the form of the *hierosgamos*," in which Christ and the church were united symbolically or, as in Judaism, the Shekhinah, conceived as feminine, was united with the Tifereth (Beauty), the sixth of the Cabala's ten Sefiroth, thought of as masculine. For Jung, the history of the psyche, wherever one could gather it, was an indispensable resource. The records of past experiences, in religion, literature, philosophy, prepared one, often in great detail, for clinical observation and healing treatment. Furthermore, as his patients and those of others constantly testified, the past persisted in archetypal deposits, in dreams and fantasies and actings out.

A man meets an anima figure personified as a very large version of Dante's Beatrice, doing some strange things. What should he do? "Start a dialogue with your anima," Jung advises. "Anybody who feels natural about such things would follow his surprise and put a question or two to her: why she appears as Beatrice? why is she so big? why are you so small? why she nurses your wife and not yourself." Accept her reality, is the point. Poke at all the oddnesses of appearance and behavior, "treat her as a person, if you like as a patient or a goddess, but above all treat her as something that does exist." Thus did Jung deal with his anima experiences; thus did he elicit wisdom from his positive solitude.[17]

The split-anima condition reflects in its sexual triangles a man's efforts to unite in himself what has been split apart, the tending, holding maternal and the exciting, transforming feminine. That requires separate treatment.[18] Here we must speculate about the purpose of the suffering occasioned by split-anima situations like those of Freud and Jung, Barth and Tillich. These were people not only of exceptional consciousness and brilliance but also men and women who gave much of themselves to help others as analysts and teachers and clergymen and founders of inquiry into the nature of being. What is it that struggles to evolve in such mixings and meetings and divisions? Is there an archetypal image of the feminine and of the masculine-feminine relationship from which we must learn something? Perhaps these women and men struggled to surpass the customary oppositions of personal goal and suprapersonal value, of objective fact and interior narrative. They may have been impelled to reach toward the feminine as a being in its own right, not just a supporter, a mate for the masculine. Certainly in these relationships of the feminine and masculine two centers of being are held in a larger ground, an *Ungrund*, as Tillich would put it, following Jakob Boehme, that embraces and unites old oppositions. Then a personal goal well might be construed as a means to the suprapersonal, and objective and subjective as joint perspectives into the same reality.[19]

These speculations may lack conviction or even offend, for the women and men involved all suffered terrible strain as they lived through their unconventional liaisons in public view. They worked on the projections of anima and animus openly, constantly exposed to the projections and censure of other people. It is easier to analyze the pathology here and its causes than to glimpse what purpose might be unfolding. But even a larger view must include pathology as part of the picture.[20] At the very least, because of these men and women we now can better identify and take apart the split-anima condition and look to its healing from the point where they left off.

Take Tillich as an example. He knew in himself the excruciating tension between faith and anxiety, being and nonbeing, to use his theological categories. He lived those categories in the flesh of his own entrapment in his compulsive feeling about women and actings out, and in his facing compulsion and finding a place for it in his theology. He struggled to receive the feminine in himself and sought out women to tell him about their experiences of being. He felt that through women he was listening in on what made being tick. This was the way he turned the threat of the void in him, the compulsion to the demonic, into a liberating word about the depths of being that threaten to grasp and overwhelm each of us. He stayed on his boundary line, one he himself had denominated, with the help of his woman friends, and saw from that vantage point how we all struggle to receive being in the tangled nets of our lives.

Tillich was fed by the women who carried his anima for him. Their reception of being fed his abstract thought. He used his understanding and experience of woman to make explicit his intuitions and attraction to her, as he found in her revealing words and actions that showed him the nature of her being. His moving of those receptions into abstract conceptual formulation was his way of overcoming the power of the abyss and of living with the inevitable anxiety and guilt it aroused in him. His wife wrote that he asked her forgiveness before he died, which she was able to give him. The other women, all that we know about, say they felt called forward by Tillich, taken seriously, affirmed, recognized each in her own dignity as one connected to being, embodying it in both sexuality and spirit.[21]

Tillich leaves us his questions to be asked again and answered in our terms: What is the role of anima and animus in bringing us to understand the depths of being available to us, to experience the abyss? How does the animus/anima bridge, pathology and all, connect us to the ground of being, to the consuming fire? Must we be caught in compulsions, and, if we are, how can they influence our lives and our work for the good? Must we descend to such frightening places, or is that just part of the compulsion?

The Animus and the Female Ancestors of Christ

Scripture anticipates and prepares the way for depth psychology in its pursuit of the truths and strengths of human interiority. The four women named in the genealogy of Jesus Christ, as recorded in the Gospel of Matthew—Tamar, Rahab, Ruth, and Bathsheba—offer moving examples of women who make use of animus energy, drawn from lives lived with a kind of solitary determination, under fearful circumstances, to reach truth and justice. They demonstrate the power of women who in this way integrate the animus in their sexual identities and from it take counsel that speaks specifically to their condition, particularity by particularity. For each of these female ancestors of Jesus differs from the others, thus showing us how animus integration supports and develops individuation. We come in such transformations more fully into the selves we were given to be, gathering from our interiority the strength to do whatever we were meant and were equipped to do. For the female ancestors of Christ display a range of personality from across the full spectrum of the feminine that fits, in one remarkable form or another, what might be expected of a precursor of the incarnate God as a model for lives lived in circumstances very different from theirs.

These women burst the bounds of health as they move into their places of strength, displaying in themselves problems as well as a tremendous potency. All exhibit the capacity to live a belief rather than simply accept it in reason. That is in itself a definition of faith. As Ortega says, "We have *ideas,* but we inhabit *beliefs.*"[22] They draw their strength at the source. Hence each woman affects her society in central ways that spring from belief inhabited and the possibilities for religious experience that arise as a result. Each one scoops out a deep place to show how and where the divine and the human meet.

Tamar, obsessed with having the child she judges is hers to have, employs the most devious trickery to reach a just end. According to Jewish law, her father-in-law, Judah, dealt with her unjustly in not pro-

viding her his third son as husband after the first two sons died following sexual intercourse with her. She lures Judah himself into her bed by
posing as a temple cult prostitute, thus weaving into the pattern of Jesus'
ancestry the iconography of the female deity. Tamar resists and defeats
the male dread of the *vagina dentata* and wins through to a male child
who carries the sacred line to David and thus to Jesus.

Rahab, by profession a whore of Jericho, shrewdly sizing up the comparative military strengths of those invading and those defending her
city, chooses the invader and his God, Yahweh, for her own. She inter-
cedes with the invading army on behalf of her very large family and wins
its safety and her own by lies, by trickery, and by betrayal of her country.
She poses in her animus strengths the rough demands of faith. Her
actions ask, in effect: When grace comes, do we correspond with it no
matter what and snatch it boldly, even if we must pay the price of breaking loyalty to what have been our highest ideals? She too weaves rich
material into Jesus' cloth through immediate association with flax, under
which she hides the invader's spies, and by application, with the female
deities under fealty to whom her strong faith was first formed.

Ruth, out of devotion to another woman, Naomi, rescues the salvific
line. Out of the force of her love for her mother-in-law and armed with
an animus strength, she leaves all that is known and comfortable to
travel into a threatening unknown world. With Naomi, she begins a new
life in a society permeated with masculine power. She seduces Boaz with
her own kind of virility and at the same time elicits a mothering kindness
from Yahweh, who shelters her as a female bird might her young under
her wing.

Bathsheba, the fourth ancestress, we see only through David's anima
projection. We never hear her own voice, except when she announces
her pregnancy and when, much later, she asks that Solomon, David's
and her second son, be made king after his father's death. One might
say that hers is entirely a reflected glory, arising from her pivotal association as wife and mother to Israel's greatest kings and the major royal
figures in Jesus' lineage. But there is more that is Bathsheba's own. We
see the enormous strength for goodness the image of such a woman can
hold for a man, for David changes altogether as a result of his adulterous
cohabitation with her and his slaying of her husband. From a warrior
king, he becomes a penitent one; from a governing monarch, a religious

figure of monumental size, fit to hold a place alongside his son as a legendary Psalmist of the Lord.

All four of these women secure the line, through David, down to Jesus, except for a radical transformation at the end of the genealogy. For their line leads to Joseph, not to Mary, and it is the Holy Spirit that fathers Jesus onto his mother, not Joseph. So we see in the genealogy of Matthew a mystical transfiguring of continuity between the human and the divine rather than a straightforward factual history. Once again, a woman secures the lineage, as before, just when it threatens to break.

Each one of these women displays the virginal quality of the feminine as one-in-herself—yes, the incestuous daughter-in-law, the whore, the widow, the woman taken in adultery—initiating a compelling bringing of order and continuity out of what looked to be a disorder without any healing resource. Each finds the requisite strength in her complex contrasexuality rather than in simple, bold reaction against manmade laws and customs. Each does what she does in the service of truth as she experiences it, not for power, not to please, not to win security. All four chance scandalous behavior—as deceiver, traitor, seducer, adulterer. From such ambiguous, confusing, confounding sources, the figure of Christ inherits the strengths of the feminine. We see here, one after another, women securely anchored in their feminine selves and their masculine contrasexuality and through these to what informs and transcends them. Each has in herself a firm hold on her energies and the resourcefulness to attach them to ultimate purpose, thus giving scriptural sanction to the journey from ego to Self and making exalted sense of the pursuit of the archetypes.[23]

Part III

Breakdown

The Collapse of the Anima/Animus Bridge

Breakdown
The Ego's Side

WHEN THE anima and animus function well, an inner conversation gets going, on one side an abiding sense of our identities, on the other what is newly emerging in us. The archetypes look to open up space between our conscious ego and deeper Self. Sometimes a personification represents the archetype; sometimes it is not so clearly signified, but the procedure is clear. The animus, for example, will lead us to the contents of the Self; the anima is noted for bringing with her a whole *Weltanschauung* of the unconscious, appropriating large territory for it.[1] So it is that the ego converses, not with just another point of view but with the possibility of a different way of life, a new orientation. The anima may persist over the years of a man's life in manifesting itself as a young girl. Then the man must accept that part of himself looks at things from the perspective of youth. The anima may be loudly pagan to a man's conscious religiosity, or religious to his conscious indifference to faith.

Anima and animus move now to the ego side, to confront it with Self demands, now to the Self side, to bring to it ego concerns. If we take these interior motions seriously, our bridging space will grow wide, deep, and durable, constructing for us a realm in which symbols are born, support for identity accrues, and our talking to ourselves becomes more accommodating to matters of substance.

This inner conversation at its best feels like a spacetime continuum, in which anything is possible, at least to contemplate. We rarely speak of it, though those we call mystics confide visions that come to them here, and lovers often discover this secret place in each other as the abiding source of their passion. Mothers woo this space into being in their babies as they talk as much to themselves as to their infants about their new life.[2]

We know in a minute when this space is closing in ourselves; we are without inner conversation that hums along. We feel out of sorts, off center, estranged. And when others lack the dialogue in themselves, we know it too. Things fall flat between us; a settled ennui kills inner life. People caught in its emptiness speak to dominate rather than to communicate, to assure themselves that they exist. But as for the inner dialogue—*that* they deny. Totalitarian governments ritualize the denial with predigested material for thought and even thought police. Their citizens react with apathy, with rage, with chronic drunkenness, just waiting for the signal to break out, as in the August 1991 Moscow coup or Tienanmen Square. It is not just outer events that spur such revolt, but perhaps even more the breakdown of inner conversation.

The point at which archetypes penetrate the psyche in inner conversation is the point where we discover the size of our personal identities, where our small self moves toward the Self of being. Anima or animus brings archetypal energies, imagery, a sense of a vital agent moving in us to conscious ego inspection, and the ego responds by thrusting its needs, aims, hopes, possibilities into the anima or animus. The ensuing conversation incarnates spirit in our lives, assures us of our personal presence in the world around us.

When the bridge of archetypal conversation breaks down, for whatever reason, we fall apart. Wounds seem irreparable. We have been betrayed—our lover has gone; our country has gone. Nothing remains for us; goodness does not exist, nor our capacity to give or to receive anything of substance. Cynicism offers its dubious solace as we make steely vows never to let anything or anyone mean that much to us again. We sin against the Spirit, as Kierkegaard says, by denying its existence in the three-way conversation of Self, ego, and Spirit, and by denying that it has gone sour in us.[3] To lose the Self is serious. The Self in conversation with the ego breeds Spirit. The Self in us is not God but is that in us that knows about God.

The loss of connection between ego and Self and Spirit can be a terrifying experience. Ingmar Bergman made his own kind of horror movie from the experience in *Winter Light,* the middle film of his trilogy of the early 1960s, which begins with *Through a Glass Darkly* and concludes with *The Silence.* The setting articulates the mood: "It is twelve o'clock, midday, a Sunday at the end of November. Over the plains, a grey half-light. A dark cold wind is blowing off the marshes to the east." In a medieval church, with a fine sixteenth-century Flemish altar and a large stove "hissing softly to itself," the Lutheran mass begins. We hear a "bang and rumble" when the congregation sits down. We see the officiating clergyman's feverishness and hear it in his strong intake of breath. We are shown an all-but-grotesque hunchback in the pews and a troublesome five-year-old girl, yawning, kicking her legs, moving "like a regular pendulum." The priest sings, "The peace of God be with you. . . ."

The drama comes solemnly through the gray winter light. We learn that the priest, Tomas, has been without a housekeeper for five years and that the schoolteacher, Marta Lundberg, would gladly supply her services, keep house for Tomas, and not only replace his dead wife, but with her love fill the emptiness left in Tomas by his loss of faith. Right there, in the fine old church, she protests her love to the clergyman and attests her honesty. She would make a good wife for him and a faithful one, she argues: "After all, I'm not exactly beautiful, so you can have me to yourself." She is interrupted by the organist, back for his music and for a hasty mocking glance at the clearly uncomfortable Tomas and the earnestly wooing schoolteacher: "His laugh," the screenplay explains, "is faintly libelous." Marta seizes the moment to assert her own intense unbelief as an answer to Tomas's impatience with the deity: "God's silence, God doesn't speak. God hasn't ever spoken, because he doesn't exist." But God will be back, and so will she.

Tomas reads a letter from Marta, full of ancient and present miseries—her eczema of last summer and its open sores, Tomas's avoiding her after the eczema reached her forehead and her scalp, her unbelief. In spite of all, she prayed ("God, I said to myself . . .") to be relieved of her indifference, prayed for meaning and for something to do with her strength. And she was answered. She wanted a clear mind and now she has it: she knows she loves Tomas and will live for him.

Jonas Persson, "a tall, thin fellow with a face that might be carved out of wood" (the young Max von Sydow), will not live. He has been deeply troubled. As his wife has explained to the priest, it began the previous spring: "Jonas had read in the papers about the Chinese." What? They are being taught to hate and it is only a matter of time before they have the bomb. After an anguished interview with the priest, and listening, like it or not, to Tomas speaking about his own indifference and fright in being so much alone, "poverty-stricken, joyless and full of fear," Jonas goes off and kills himself. Tomas, left to himself before the news comes of Jonas's death, moans in a feverish state the words of the Cross, "God, my God, why have you abandoned me?" On his knees, echoing Marta, he proclaims that God no longer exists. That brings him back to his feet, exultant in his discovery—"At last, free"—to face Marta where she is standing, behind the pulpit. Now he can bear with the fact of Jonas's suicide.

The duel between Marta and Thomas moves in and around Jonas Persson's family, sitting in a space in which the last bits of afternoon light "are not strong enough to light up the oblong room with its bulging wallpaper and dirty stairs." Priest and teacher go off together, back to the church, to a sexton's insistence that out of his own suffering he has finally come to understand Christ at Gethsemane: "To understand that no one has understood you. To be abandoned when one really needs someone to rely on. A terrible suffering." All that Tomas can muster in reply is "Obviously."

But that was not what was worst, the sexton goes on: "The moments before he died, Christ was seized with a great doubt. Surely that must have been his most monstrous suffering of all? I mean God's silence. Isn't that true, Vicar?" "Yes, yes," Tomas agrees impatiently, turning away from the sexton's insistence and his own interior echo of it. He goes off to leave Marta with the organist, who makes clear to her that the vicar's dead wife was no more than a "proper woodlouse," in whose fatal illness no one would believe. But Tomas loved her "like a lunatic. She who hadn't a genuine feeling in her whole body, not an honest thought. That's what you can call love, if you like! Jesus! But it put an end to the vicar, it did. And now he's done for." Which just leaves time in the film for the beginning of mass, with the church empty, except for Marta in the pews, the sexton to give the signal to the organist to begin, and Tomas at the altar: "Holy, holy, holy, Lord God Almighty. All the earth is full of his glory. . . ."[4]

Unrelieved gloom? A bitter screed directed at the faith and the faithless? A great sounding of despair in a world of eczema and lunatic love and believers with hunchbacks and feverish unbelievers in clericals and so real a threat of the atom bomb in the hands of a huge, hating people that a fisherman in Sweden, with family and pregnant wife, must kill himself? Yes, all of that. And no, none of that. Yes, because as Bergman has shown with an austere finality, life is like that when the bridges to the interior break down and the ego cannot descry the Self as even a distant possibility in the darkening winter light. No, because even the firmest of Bergman's nonbelievers has felt the urge to pray and known an answer to her prayer and found the unmistakable possibility of Self and even of Spirit.

The strength of Bergman's gray allegory is in the trust the writer-director displays in Marta, his anima figure. His clergyman, as always with Bergman's figures of uncertain faith, plays the ancient game of "I do believe, I don't believe, I do, I don't. . . ." pulling leaves from the Bible rather than from some hapless Swedish flower. His woman, unhandsome in her eyeglasses, prone to the minor mischiefs of the body and the major griefs of the soul, somehow finds the strength to begin the reconstruction of the bridge. The anima, Bergman's invariable refuge, provides the necessary illumination.

When the anima/animus bridge breaks down at the ego side, inner conversation collapses because there is no ego there to partake in it. Our ego falls into a secondary, passive position instead of remaining a responsive participant in our inner conversation. Then the contents that come across the archetypal bridge flood what is left of the ego, or stand in front of it so that it has no access to anything, or split away from it, so that it has no contact at all with the substance of Self.

IDENTITY AND IDENTIFICATION

We are easily flooded by contents that come across the anima/animus bridge when our ego has not emerged from its nascent state of identity with our parents or a cause or body of ideas, an institution, a job, or a social environment on which we depend for nurture and from which we have not yet differentiated ourselves. Held within this larger container, we have not yet found our own point of view, our own person. We stay locked within the parental circle, marooned in the flat world of the literal. We paint the landscape and all that shows is the landscape. A photograph would do just as well; there is no mixing of landscape and our attitude toward it. We produce nothing but carbon copies. We speak what the boss says, what our cause decrees. We develop no originality in our work, no distance from which to inspect ourselves and our world. We live in stereotypes because we cannot connect in a personal way with archetypes.

When our ego remains in a state of identity with a parental container, anima or animus does not emerge in its own right but stays dependent on the opposite sex to carry it, mirroring its original parental form. Woman still looks like Mother, man like Dad. Anima and animus remain collective, without personal images. We live collectively, in our choice of friends, loves, dress, vocabularies even, if not tied to parents, then to a political movement, a sexual cause, a predetermined set of convictions and actions that follow from them.

Archetypes, like the human unconscious, can be personal or collective. We do not often enough make room in our consciousness for the collective forms of the contrasexual archetypes. They are very much with us in groups, in institutions, on campuses, in organs of government, in churches, any one of which may display an unmistakable sexual character. We are talking here about something that goes well beyond the nominal association of certain collective structures with gender, such as Fatherland, or Motherland, ships as women when pronouns are required ("She rode through the swells . . ."), Mother Church. We mean that insistent proclamation of a contrasexual identity that leads us to react to a political movement or party, a religious or psychological attitude, a philosophical or aesthetic position, as man to woman or woman to man. It becomes our contrasexual opposite number, and, as we do with the personal anima or animus, we identify with it.

Getting out of this state of identity usually requires aggression—on somebody's part. A man in group therapy angered the women in the group, because, they said, he would plop his dream down without taking any attitude toward it, expecting them to produce a useful response to it and then give it back to him, exactly what he himself needed to do. One woman complained that he brought his dream like a letter addressed to no one. He saw that he made the women into a mother collective, to take care of his psyche, to substitute for his ego connection to his own psychic process. When they refused to go on with it, he inaugurated inner conversation with his dreams. His ego became more active; his anima began to emerge from the mother world.[5]

But that may not always work. We may develop our ego and still get flooded by what anima or animus brings. We may now, instead of reacting to it on the inside, fall into identification with the contents and act them out on the outside. A woman acknowledged with mortifying chagrin the truth of her husband's criticism that she behaved like a fool at a party. She was dimly aware she always felt compelled to speak, filling up every pause with stories, questions, speculations. Inundated with her contents, she simply spewed it all out. In analysis she faced up to the fact that she thought the level of conversation at such parties boring and impossibly slow. Instead of admitting that to herself and contemplating the unconscious contents that rushed to fill her inner emptiness, her ego just fell right into the stream itself and everything gushed out of her. She saw she might have asked whether lurking in the boredom was someone's attack on liveliness, or whether the slow pace was making room for people to say something of quality. Instead, she said, a sort of phallic strut took over. The animus wanted to stir up, to display dazzling Self-items. Because her ego did not choose to receive and discriminate among them, her animus simply ran over her ego and put on his razzle-dazzle display for the party.

This kind of animus identification frequently inflates our devotion to causes. Archetypal energy fills our ego, and we dutifully broadcast the terms of our cause at full length, insisting everyone identify with them, just as we ourselves have done. When we do not receive great gusts of affect in response, we may explode with our substitute for the warmth that should have greeted the justice and wisdom of our cause. Our identification may fall on a theorist who touches a profound truth for us. Instead of relating to the truth we see, and differentiating our reaction from it and its progenitor, we suffer inner breakdown: the animus bridge between our ego and the truth collapses. We open our mouth and, say, Jung, speaks through us, and we bridle if someone challenges us: "That's Jung you're questioning! Do you realize that?"

Vasily Rozanov is a splendid example of someone who strutted, cringed, attacked, defended, identified, and disidentified not only with ego and Self a thousand times over in his life and writings in the late nineteenth and early twentieth centuries, but with whole religions, whole peoples. The animus/anima bridge in breakdown summons him to the attack; in reconstruction, to loving tribute and support. Though he had more than an ordinary sense of meetings with the personal anima, he was caught up, as so many Russians were in his revolutionary time, in encounters with the collective contrasexual archetypes.

In his attacks on both Christians and Jews, Rozanov is sometimes deeply offensive. In his testimonies to the ancient splendor of the Jews and the central place of his own faith as a believer in and practitioner of the Russian Orthodox church, he is often profoundly moving. In his struttings and cringings, attacks and defenses, no matter which side he takes, he remains a brilliant observer of the follies of the old regime and the new, as Russia makes its way from the czars to the commissars. Breakdown has had few better chroniclers.

He writes with the plangency of a practiced victim, but the shouting and the drumbeating are never so loud or disturbing that they muffle his insights, especially as they proceed from his readings of the author of *The Brothers Karamazov.* He admired Dostoyevsky above all men and wrote in support of his enthusiasm a long, thoughtful analysis of the Legend of the Grand Inquisitor. He was the first to see the richness and multiplicities of meaning of that parable, without ever losing sight of its central *aperçu:* "the doctrine that came to save the world has through its very loftiness destroyed it; it has brought into history not reconciliation and unity, but chaos and hostility."[6]

That was in 1891. By 1912, with more than a little experience of revolution and the revolutionary, he noted about the species, in one of the shrewd musings that make up his *Solitaria,* "The dreamer walks away; for he loves his dream more than he loves food. In revolution there is no room for the dream." Perhaps, he speculates, "just because revolution has no room for the dream, it will fail." He sees the revolution strangling its Michelangelos and Leonardos "at the age of eleven or thirteen, when they suddenly discover 'something of their own in their souls,' " and he concludes his *pensée* with a prediction that the end of this century has more than supported: "And the new edifice, with its donkey face, will crumble to pieces in the third or fourth generation."

A year later, in his next set of maxims and reflections, *Fallen Leaves,* he describes the two tiers of revolution. The "bottom—the genuine one, its *animus agens*—is composed of bitterness, spite, poverty, envy, despair." The top is made up of "sybarites, who have a secure existence and *do not work;* loungers, idlers; *with no occupation.*" Revolution is two-dimensional, lacks depth, "will never produce a *ripe and tasty fruit,*" will never be fulfilled, "will always be agitated and will have hopes only in tomorrow."

By the time of the 1917 revolution, Rozanov had seen enough to know how accurate his observations had been. Separated from his family, ill and without sufficient food, housed with a priest, he tried to make some sort of living from the pamphlets that made up what he was able to finish of his bittersweet vision, *The Apocalypse of Our Time.* In it, under the heading of *La divina commedia,* he presents his summary judgment:

> With a clang, a creak, and a scream the iron curtain drops on Russian history.
> "The performance is over."
> The people get up from their seats.
> "Time to put on your fur coats and go home."
> They look around.
> But the fur coats and the houses have all vanished.

This is *echt* Rozanov, famous, if anything in his work can be said to be famous. His use of the phrase "iron curtain" so many years before Churchill adopted it to describe the separation of the Soviet-dominated countries from the rest of Europe has been noted — by one or two. That is his fate, to be perceptive in quick flashes of insight, to find wisdom in his passionate leaps, but not to find many readers. It is a fate deliberately chosen and carefully prepared; passion must be served.

In his anima life, as in so much else, Rozanov was so identified with Dostoyevsky and his passions that when he was still a university student and met Apollinaria Suslova, the great man's "infernal Polina," he was overwhelmed. She was in her forties; he was twenty-four. He must marry her. As Dostoyevsky's anima mistress, she had made his life miserable. As Rozanov's anima wife, she did as much for him.

Fortunately, the woman distinguished for the quality of the men she made miserable left her young husband after a six-year reign of terror. They were never divorced, but Rozanov did find peace in a liaison with a good and loving woman, an attachment that produced many children and the support of accommodating priests whose blessings gave more than just a superficial gloss of marriage to the relationship. It supported his pronouncements of the joy he found in breasts and pregnant bellies: "I was always desiring to see the whole world pregnant." Sexuality and the spirit, sexuality and God are indissolubly connected for Rozanov: "The relationship of God to sex is closer than the relationship of God to mind, and even closer than the relationship of God to man's conscience." Asexualists—Rozanov's word for the disagreeable species— show themselves to be atheists, who are as little interested in sex as in religion or countries and cultures distant from them such as the Argentine.

Rozanov lived in endless witness to breakdown: "I carry literature as my coffin, I carry literature as my sorrow. I carry literature as my disgust." Technology has "crushed the soul," left it " 'a technical soul' with only the mechanism of creation and without the inspiration of creation." That is inevitable in a time the "essence" of which "is that it transforms everything into a cliché, a copy, a phrase." A somber truth remains: "One only has a *true* relationship to *oneself.*" Thus the necessity of publishing his solitary musings.

He is not charmed with himself. His name repels him. "I always have a strange feeling when I sign my articles: V. Rozanov. I wish it were 'Rudnev,' 'Bugayev,' anything." Even the common name "Ivanov" would do. Bryusov "must be perpetually delighted to have such a name." As for his own, why, he has even seen a sign, "Rozanov, German Baker." A winning manner and behavior, like one's name, are inherited, not to be taught. In effect, Rozanov sums up, "My soul is in the way I walk." He shakes his head: "Unfortunately, it seems my walk is very repulsive."

But even such dismal reflections can be countered by a man so thoroughly in his flesh, the flesh blessed by God and open to sharing in the love of woman. "Everything is *limited* and *finished* except the sex organs," Rozanov explains. Compare them to anything else and they look like a mistake, "a vagary . . . which encounters and unites with the error, the vagary, of another organ. And then—both are complete." Don't people find the sight of them disgusting, Rozanov asks, because of this incompleteness? And then see what follows—"ecstasy in the moment of completeness." Rozanov's theology hinges upon this: "It is as if God wished to accomplish the *act,* but He failed to execute the movement and instead bestowed its *element* in man and in woman. And it is they who complete that primordial movement. Hence its sweetness and irresistibility."

Even at the very end of his life, when he repudiated all the worst of his effusions, all his attacks on persons and peoples, everything that he found questionable in himself, Rozanov would not have denied his convictions about sexuality and the Godhead. He knew from his endless ruminations and from both his ugly experiences and his blessed ones that the collapse of truth and the breakdown of the person were answerable if one knew love as he had known it:

> To love means "I cannot live without you," "I suffer without you"; "it is absolutely boring without you."
> This is an external description, but completely accurate.
> Love is not at all fire (as they often define it), love is air. Without it one cannot breathe, with it it is easy to breathe.
> That is all.[7]

Identification with the anima or animus can wreak lethal results. Rebecca West, in her story "The Salt of the Earth," presents Alice Pemberton, who thinks herself generous to a fault when in fact she regularly speaks murderous things to others and ends up herself being murdered by her husband because he cannot make her see what she does. She creates a beautiful face and house but cannot make friends or keep servants. Like a little girl, she wonders why people are so mean to her. She does not see that she makes everyone feel haunted, hunted down, by her ideals. Her mother leaves the village where she lives to escape her. Her brother avoids her because her solicitous concern always reminds him that his war injury will shorten his life. Her sister hides her fatal illness from her lest Alice blurt it out to the sister's husband, who is desperate over his failing finances. Alice's husband sums it up when he says to her: "You are the salt of the earth. . . . The point is that nobody likes having salt rubbed into their wounds. . . . That's the worst of you, Alice. You find out what people live by, and you kill it." No better description can be found of the negative animus.[8]

PROJECTION

When we identify with something, we project it. If we do not sustain the anima/animus bridge inside ourselves, we ourselves become the bridge for other people, in interminable actings out.[9] We feel compelled to engage in animating conversation with others, to make them feel linked up to the truths we have decreed for them, because we do not conduct the conversation waiting there to be started within ourselves. One man, terrified of "going dead" inside, felt driven to wake women up sexually. And indeed he did so, and then each time left peremptorily. He played the bridge for them. They felt victimized for a time by his abandonment, but he was the real victim, the lasting one, as a grim dream image showed: "I'm made into a plow. A woman holds each of my legs and my penis is the rudder; they push me along like a plow."[10]

Another man felt enjoined to make contact with the souls of the women he courted and bedded. He woke them up to the life of the spirit, by getting them to reflect on their daily lives in relation to what really mattered *sub specie aeternitatis*. He too succeeded in doing what he planned. One woman reentered her church. Another woman began therapy and eventually gained both education and a career. But the women who really wanted relation with him felt bitter, saying that he opened them up for relationship and then ran away. He would not let them in. But he felt he either did not know how or would not dare to do so.

Identification with animus or anima can take active or passive form.[11] A man may passively become his anima bridge and play at being it for others. This allows him to be unusually tuned into some aspects of women but woefully out of range of an actual woman's daring. He can connect her to her depths, but because he does not house the feminine in himself, he fears her bold risk to make passion permanent in a love relationship lived in real time and space.[12] He must run away. We see a very different response in the gay man cited in chapter 2, who was nearly murdered on the street by a homophobic attacker; he learned that he had to relate to the anima inside himself, and not simply identify with feminine characteristics on the outside in persona behavior.

A woman saw through a dream that she needed to increase her connection to the power her animus brought her: she and her man were eating supper and were told Hitler would drop in. She had no choice, because he was a tyrant. She was terrified. In a dream years later the power configured by the dream Hitler has become more humanized, though still not enough. In this dream she sees set before her all her favorite foods in a hotel dining room. But the waiter, black-haired and with a thick mustache (reminding her of the Hitler figure), stands before her, forbidding her to eat.

PROJECTIVE IDENTIFICATION

When we identify with anima or animus, we easily find ourselves projecting it onto others, and then we discover we desperately need them to become the bridge to the center for us. An Asian woman loved a man who was obviously, she saw, a double-dealer. He told her his marriage was sacred, still another woman was sacred for him, and she was too. How can I be so crazy? she asked herself. To see this mad scene for what it was was not enough to extricate her; it only made her feel all the more hooked to a humiliating obsession. The man was her Self and her animus. Without him, she felt exiled from all meaning and happiness. But the impossible outward situation kept telling her: You cannot find what you want here; you must take yourself back, retrieve from him your own connection to the center.[13]

Literature abounds with examples of such projective identification. The *locus classicus* is Dorothea Brooke in George Eliot's *Middlemarch*, "whose mind was theoretic, and yearned . . . after some lofty conception of the world . . . and her rule of conduct there." She is indefatigable in the hunt for the right projective object, "enamored" as she is "of intensity and greatness, and rash in embracing whatever seemed . . . to have those aspects." As her omniscient chronicler tells us early on, she is "likely to seek martyrdom . . . and then to incur martyrdom where she had not sought it." Dorothea suffers terribly because she projects all her undifferentiated yearning to connect to lofty truth onto the Reverend Edward Casaubon, who promises to produce the "Key to All Mythologies," no less.

All is projection in Dorothea. "The really delightful marriage," she muses, "must be that where your husband was a sort of father, and could teach you even Hebrew, if you wished it." Dedicating herself to Casaubon's monumental work, "though only as a lamp-holder!" she discovers none of the grand "Key" exists, only its sham prospectus, behind which Casaubon hides from the world, from his wife, and from himself. When she withdraws her help, seeing herself as colluding in his fraud, he feels betrayed. In a sense he is, for it was she who had puffed him up to demigod proportions, failing to see his reality as a petty pedant and hers as a projector and both as coconspirators: "She filled up all the blanks with unmanifested perfections, interpreting him as she interpreted the works of Providence, and accounting for seeming discords by her own deafness to the higher harmonies."[14] Though his is a more obvious display of aridity at the core than hers, both have suspended for too long serious engagement in that inner conversation that their dreams and ambitions demand. Though Dorothea may elicit our sympathy, she remains a figure of gestures and postures, doomed to be caught up in the grandeur of rhetorical promise in all her relationships. We cannot rid ourselves so easily of our responsibility to engage directly in inner conversation with the center. We cannot substitute projections onto others for our own interior struggles.

BLANKNESS AND WOUNDS

The contrasexual bridge collapses at its ego end when we just go blank, withdrawing instead of reacting, feeling, thinking, receiving, challenging what anima or animus presents. Our blankness is like dead air space where contents should be. Into the blankness steps anima or animus. It speaks in place of the withdrawn ego, demoting it to nothing better than secondary effect.

We get these blank spaces when a wound has been inflicted on our psyche and has not healed.[15] It lives on in us, but in dissociated state. Blank with hurt, we are susceptible to further hurt; any pressure on the deep bruise to our ego will make it bleed again. All we can do is endure its pain.

The animus/anima archetypes act like encasing shells around the wound, sealing it in place. We try to put up our guard, often through denial, but the pain always gets through. One man, living with long-standing wounds to his sense of self, did not register his hurt when his lover told him she had had a phone call from an old boyfriend. His ego went blank to the hurt he felt, and the anima slipped in. Filled with jealous rage, he started quizzing her in a public restaurant about her past romances until she broke down in sobs and fled the place. Examining the events in analysis, he discovered that the mere fact of the phone call was enough to make the old bruise bleed again—feeling insufficiently appreciated and respected. Instead of receiving that wound into his ego to care for it and keep it from bleeding again, his ego had gone blank with the pain, and his anima had taken over in a hysterical, jealous manner.

Sometimes the wound may go back to childhood. One woman, molested by her brother many times before the age of eight, found herself in dreams wanting to be the one with the penis. Identifying with the aggressor, she hopped over her painful confusion at being molested by one she loved; feeling both pleasure and so much guilt, she became incontinent and had to hide her soiled underwear to avoid discovery. She projected onto her beloved sibling her budding capacity to be connected to the Self. His violation of her nullified her projection; she lost connection to the Self. When such projections work well, the other person can carry them for a while and return them to us intact, or we can take them back again, enriched by clear differentiation from the other person. But here she could not get it back, for it had splintered in the confusion. This left her wounded, in body and soul. Her adult love relations with women foundered on her being at once too beseeching and enraged, and her work was constantly interrupted by embarrassing blankings out when she could not speak or do much of anything. Her courage in seeking, in analysis, to respond directly to the wound behind the blank ego and to restore her inward bridge to the Self testifies to the power latent in this ego/animus instrumentation for constructive as well as destructive purpose.

Split Anima and Split Animus

One of the most severe breakdowns the anima/animus bridge suffers is when it splits into pieces. Our ego gets part of the contents coming from the Self but not all; so it too is split. A well-functioning anima or animus will help us, often unconsciously, choose a mate who connects with our identity where it reflects our parents and culture, and where it shows a capacity to change and grow into its own individuality. When anima or animus splits, we cannot find that guidance. We choose the wrong partner because we do not see either ourself or the other for who we are.

We may find part of what we need with a partner and miss everything else. Marital triangles rise from the split anima or animus condition.

One man found in his wife the companion and friend he depended on for security and continuity of his values, but his sexually ecstatic responses were altogether outside his marriage. The woman-out-of-bounds awakened a dead part of him that had always turned up in his dreams as corpses. He felt split between a secure situation without ecstasy and an ecstatic situation without security. The split anima is akin to what Winnicott calls the split between the "environment mother," who holds us in being, and the "instinct mother," who excites us.[16] In holding on to marriage and the affair, this man expressed his split and tried to house in himself both his ego and his instinctual life. But the stalemate the triangle represents tells him he had urgently to repair the anima bridge inside himself. Juggling two women did not work.

Other times the split may show up not as between two people, but between an inner fantasy and an outer partner. This also reflects a split in the archetype. A woman marries her husband because of his staidness and stability, then complains of his dullness. "He's too much like a father," she says. In fantasy she happens on a boyish kind of man whom she finds alluring. Marriage problems arise when she tries to foist onto her actual husband some of the fantasy youth's liveliness. She is trying to forge together in her husband the father and the son aspect of the animus image that is in fact split apart in herself. She could not see the liveliness that really was in her husband because she had not located the split in herself.

Another woman feared her wild sexual fantasies and defended against them by splitting up her image of her husband. She loved his sensitive intellect but rejected his hairy body, even though her fantasies concocted far-out primitive scenes that exactly dovetailed with a hairy partner. Her ego could not yet receive all sides of her animus imagery.

A man felt split between his image of himself as a successful businessman and an emotional cripple where his wife was concerned. He could win her but not stand to be with her. He saw himself as a burn victim: "If she comes anywhere near me, the pain is excruciating."

Another man felt split in his sexual behavior: rough sex with one woman, tender sex with another; lusty drunken revelry with the first type, spiritual conversations with the second. He could not unite himself or his partners into one, which left him lonely, at a far distance from himself.

A woman never liked the men who sought her and suffered rejection from the men she herself sought out. She chose unsuitable partners, who were either unavailable or put her through great pain, and left her with hours spent ruminating obsessively on why, for example, one man flirted with the waitress when she was with him, what could be the matter with her, and so on and so forth, far into the night.

When our ego receives only part of what anima or animus brings us from the Self, we get caught up in splits between our principles and our behavior. A man may know what he believes, but in an argument his unclaimed feeling sneaks in to change the facts so that he can get his way. A woman says her personnel director simply rewrote a job description that had been agreed upon to secure his own candidate. She faces him with this, and he attacks her personally. Fortunately, her animus bridge supports her right there, at the moment, and she does not crumple with hurt. She faces him with the objective facts and wins.

More subtle splittings concern our inner conversation. We may split the life in our body from our religious life. We find we cannot connect our instinctive life with moments of ecstasy where we feel we touch the heart of Being at a concert, or the theater, in a painting, a poem, prayer. We may then denigrate the life of our body in its appetite for sexuality or food or rest, or hold in question the demands of the life of the spirit, as if we could have only one, never both. We feel split off from the deep flow of Being that seeks to incarnate all.[17]

Sometimes the splitting sets us a false problem; we must choose between outer action and inner realization. One woman struggled with a nasty fight at her work, not knowing whether to stand up against her opponents or inwardly to analyze what the conflict meant psychologically. She transformed the impulse to fight into inner conversation, asking in it what the impulse wanted of her and how her ego felt about it. She submitted the debate to the deepest center she could reach in herself, asking what it wanted. The answer came in what seemed like a paradox: Do both. She learned she had in fact to do both, to act and to reflect, in order to do either one effectively.

CULTURE

We are endowed with anima and animus to introduce us to living with others. When the contrasexual bridge collapses from the ego side, we close to otherness and just cannot respond to people around us. Without ego initiative, no way exists for the Self energies to come into the world of shared existence in relatable human proportions, in which the person is served. The contents and energies of the Self remain collective, impersonal, and flood into the society we keep with no clear channels or direction. We feel invaded and answer in kind, seeing the unconscious and nature as resources to be plundered for our own ego purposes, say for money-making, for political power, or for all sorts of self-gratification. We give the place of the personal anima or animus to a collective contrasexuality in which there is no room for clear delineation of ego or Self. The ego consciousness we share in a society splits away from its source in the nonego world of the unconscious and the transcendent. We must take strong measures, move great distances to survive as persons in possession of ourselves.

Emily Dickinson moved away from the negative forces of contrasexuality, especially the cohesive animus in the arenas of money, visible personal gratification, and social life, moved indoors to stay at about the same time that the American Civil War began, in 1861. From her upstairs room in Amherst, all but sealed off from the outside world, she made herself a poet's life unlike any others, except perhaps those of the English metaphysical poets Donne, Herbert, and Cowley in its perfect merging of sensibility and poem. All sorts of events in an apparently eventless life have been conjectured to account for the drama of the poems. They miss the point. The drama is the drama of the animus. The events are countless interior conversations, enough to produce more than seventeen hundred poems. Emily Dickinson did not need a failed love affair, a demon lover, or even a phantom one, to produce such work. She was her poetry. She inhabited it, as Ortega says we do our beliefs. And poetry was her belief, her animus, her life.

We do not have to choose from a very small list of candidates to find the "man" in her poems. Her animus figure is the familiar compound, part father, part clergyman friend, part neighbor, part literary correspondent, part literature. She was uncertain about how well she worked; she declared utterly against publication; she had no distance from which to view what she was doing. When she wrote Thomas Wentworth Higginson, whom she judged from his writing in the *Atlantic* to be a sympathetic reader of an apprentice poet, she asked him to say "if my Verse

is alive." More to the point, she explained, "The Mind is so near itself—
it cannot see, distinctly—and I have none to ask." He, just as sympathetic as she hoped, was simply not in her world; he lived too much
outside, though with distinction, as commander of the first all-black
regiment in the Civil War, as a Unitarian minister, an ardent abolitionist
and proponent of women's suffrage, and as a writer of occasional essays.
He confirmed her as a poet, but one who needed "corrections." She
wrote him from her sickbed "pillow" to thank him for his "surgery."
We have not all been equally thankful, for we had to wait until 1945 to
read her poems uncorrected and thus to meet her genius unimpeded.

Higginson meant well, but he was neither a good reader nor open to
animus duties. He removed many of the dashes that give so much life
to Emily Dickinson's poetry, that provide the oblique angles, point to
the experience at the bone, which she told him about in the same letter
in which she curtsied to his scalpel. She has other poems to send him,
about which she says, "While my thought is undressed—I can make the
distinction, but when I put them in the Gown—they look alike, and
numb." She has further explanation of the same sort, to be understood
only by a motion of interior grace, and clearly not to be corrected: "I
had a terror—since September [this is seven months later]—I could tell
to none—and so I sing, as the Boy does by the Burying Ground—
because I am afraid—."

She lists her "Books": for poetry, Keats and the Brownings; for prose,
Ruskin and Sir Thomas Browne and Revelation. As a little "Girl," she
tells Higginson, explaining much in a very few words, she "had a friend,
who taught me Immortality—but venturing too near, himself—he never
returned—" This is Benjamin Newton, her father's law student, who
encouraged her to read widely and to write her poems, and died very
early in his life—and hers. As with the move of her good friend, the
minister Charles Wadsworth, to San Francisco, the widely told violences
of the Civil War, and the passing not long after this of Nathaniel Hawthorne, everything supported an apocalyptic view of human events.[18]

"View" is not exactly the right word. She did not look over events;
she lived them in her upstairs room and made them into brilliant poems
of an unequaled compression in our literature. "Tie the Strings to my
life, My Lord," she commands; "Then I am ready to go!" She knows
that "we must ride to the Judgment—And it's partly down Hill." This

is a poem to be read in tandem with its more famous mate, "I felt a Funeral, in my brain, And Mourners to and fro." This is the metaphysician of Amherst, who declines to claim her ego and still, in the very act of refusing, asserts her poetic substance:

> I'm Nobody! Who are you?
> Are you—Nobody—Too?
> Then there's a pair of us?
> Don't tell! they'd advertise—you know!
>
> How dreary—to be—Somebody!
> How public—like a Frog—
> To tell one's name—the livelong June—
> To an admiring Bog!

One sounding image—of that most public creature, the loud, love-swollen, brazen frog—is enough. It makes a point made a hundred times over in her poems: "I think to Live—may be a Bliss To those who dare to try—" But the greater bliss may be the Bliss of Death, which is "Life's Bliss," extolled in imitation of its end. More and more in Dickinson's poems, Death takes the animus role, but not forbiddingly. She is conscious in her upstairs chamber of "a shapeless friend—" It is her old companion, Immortality, which, under that accustomed name or as Eternity, makes tolerable "Life's low Venture." Suicide troubles her thoughts, or more accurately courses through her sensorium; a trigger is "Caressed . . . absently," and then he who had "Groped up, to see if God was there—" and "Groped backward at Himself" simply "wandered out of life."

She knows with a certainty the chafings and roilings of life at the center, in the genius of her solitude:

> To try to speak, and miss the way
> And ask it of the Tears,
> Is Gratitude's sweet poverty,
> The Tatters that he wears—

She knows the unravelings of a consciousness so close to extinction, to that "awful stranger Consciousness," which no one is bold enough to face directly in lonely solitude, where every news of a death brings

>the chance of Life
>Afresh annihilating me
>That mightiest Belief,
>
>Too mighty for the Daily mind
>That tilling its abyss,
>Had Madness, had it once or twice
>The yawning Consciousness

She could, finally, face the abyss, as fully alive for her as it was for Baudelaire, the presiding spirit of the interior glooms. She would, out of her colloquies with Death and its shadow, Immortality, "Tell all the Truth but tell it slant"; that was her creed. There was no social life for her as most of us understand it. Her friends were those to whom she could write letters as stubbornly oblique as her poems and whom she could trust to read the poems and to press on for meanings. Her refuge remained, not simply the room that she had made so much her own, but within it an interiority that needed no supervising editor, no corrections from outside, no intercourse with anyone at all except her true ruler, her soul. With it, for all its troublesome self-contradictions, its menacings, its monarchical power, she could identify, she could be content, she could write her poems, she could allow herself to be:

>The Soul unto itself
>Is an imperial friend—
>Or the most agonizing Spy—
>An Enemy—could send—
>
>Secure against its own—
>No treason it can fear—
>Itself—its Sovereign—of itself
>The Soul should stand in awe—[19]

Sometimes, like Emily Dickinson, we must withdraw into an upstairs room. We must admit to ourselves that an indefinable malaise infects our capacity for shared joy. We find no pools of shared meaning easily accessible to us. We get caught up in means with not enough energy or clarity of purpose to come to an end, an other beyond ourselves. We experience difference as polarization: us against the establishment, us against the government, the homeless against us, the rich against us, whites or blacks or men or women or Asians or Hispanics against us. Our spacemaking ego function contracts to fit imagined or real threats and exchanges that seem inextricably hostile: if there is more for them, then there is less for us. We feel no growth to truth or animating connection.

We lose the transformative power of the feminine and masculine modes of being. We lose sight of the indeterminacy of the archetype and help perpetuate sexual stereotypes instead. The chthonic feminine, committed to a vast variety of kinds of people and ideas and experiences, and to the ennobling strengths of change, become something fearful to us. It splits away. When it comes back, it does so with an undertow of materialism: if we will not seek what matters, matter will pull us under into acquisitiveness, overspending, a manic preoccupation with money for everyone and everything—all good causes—to pay all debts, for people and banks and institutions of any kind, to tend to the needs of the homeless in every city in the world. The denied feminine that supports being returns in the demand for an all-purpose collectivity that will assuage all needs, all wants that can be budgeted. The chthonic masculine, equated with a misogynist patriarchy, can offer no hope. Its ancient drive to know, to penetrate to the heart, to stir up emotion and encourage action, to dare confront the numinous without fear of looking foolish, has not many servitors and runs the risk of being a dubious machismo that were better depotentiated.

At such moments of breakdown from the ego side, we need to follow the example of a Rozanov or an Emily Dickinson. With the Russian, so prescient in his reading of the revolution, we must look for more air for our persons, to replace the deadening fires. With the American we must open, in our carefully cultivated upstairs room, to the Self that tells the ego to stand sovereign with itself, to stand with the soul in awe.

Breakdown
The Self Side

COLLAPSE OF the contrasexual bridge at the ego side results in our ego being made passive, of secondary importance; collapse at the Self side results in an unlived life. Unlived life persisted in brings death: the Self's energies do not flow into our ego, we find ourselves at odds with our persons and with our culture. The bridge is broken; the Self has no way to cross over and evolve into incarnate form. It roils and burgeons, creating anxiety of ontological proportions. We look not just for acceptance but for sure means to keep ourselves in being. We barely endure depressions of a magnitude that stuns us into immobility and leaves us sleepless night after night. An unlived life invokes a burning envy, particularly in things sexual. Women in its toils derive scant support from each other, always suspect treachery, fight over men, or over the quality of their femininity and feminism. Men compare sizes—penises, income, reputation, sexual exploits, power over women.

We see others living where we have failed to do so and attack them in just these places where we are most envious. Unlived Self energies project massively onto a whole sex. They are inordinately primitive because unmodified by ego interaction; they explode into contempt, gross discrimination, hatred, exclusion, rape, murder. Headlines speak of a woman hiring a thug to kill her boyfriend; of college boys getting a coed drunk just this side of extinction, sodomizing her, and then denying that anything other than friendly sexual games was involved; youngsters gang-rape a woman jogger, hitting her with a brick when she protests, and leave her for dead.[1]

The Wrong Foot and the Negative Voice

When the bridge collapses at the Self side, we cannot find right relation with anima or animus. We have no way in, no crossing point. One woman, as far back as she could remember, always felt that life was "too hard." Her energies never flowed back to their source. Everything was always uphill, a struggle to turn choice into accomplishment, a prolonged muddle. In despair, she fantasized running away from her work in research science; she would become a clerk in a small town where no one knew her. She would run back this way to where she would feel connected to life again.

When we do not live our animus or anima energies, they turn negative. Almost always it is because we begin with a wrong premise. When a man's anima is unlived, it exerts a "possessive influence," fastening him to stubborn emotional convictions that his actual experience is impotent to change.[2] For one man it was simple: she doesn't like me; she has contempt for me. Another man believed his work was no good, leaving him entirely dependent on others for any value judgments about it. One man was held fast to an image of God as an abyss into which he must inevitably fall to nothingness. Like a gigantic black hole always before him, his forebodings vitiated any thought of happiness or accomplishment.

For a woman, wrong premises lead to pseudologic and deadening conclusions. A woman student complained to her husband—really reproaching him as she spoke—that she had too much to do. He said, lie down, make holes in the day, and all will go more quickly and be easier for you. But if I lie down, she retorted, who will finish my homework? The problem was in the premise that her ego must carry everything, with its false logic: If I do this, then there can be no time for that. She was stuck in insoluble either/or dichotomies that either rejected or denied her husband's concern. What he was suggesting, in fact, was starting from a different premise and then looking anew at the tasks before her. A change of premise here would amount to seeing the reality of the Self, which embraces every this and every that and offers the spaciousness of the both/and archetypal world to an ego confined in either/or dichotomizing.

From wrong premises come the anima and animus as negative voices. The anima slips a waspish humor, verging on the bitchy, into a man's speech that cuts off conversation, or a pompous pseudointellectual posture that abrogates meeting either people or life. Another anima ploy is the obstinate bass of destructive illusion, which underlies all a man says and does. He never has enough money; he always has too many responsibilities. Without any inner examination of what is happening to him, he goes through life under constant lashing from these animated negative premises.

The animus voice is more specifically and repetitiously verbal in its judgments than the anima, perhaps because it is so firmly reenforced by the misogyny of our culture. One woman calls her animus voices "the Wizards."[3] They act like vampires, sucking all the confidence out of her actions, regularly invalidating her intentions. "Oh, that doesn't amount to much," they say; or, "That's all in your imagination." A mystification occurs, as Laing puts it, where behavior is divorced from experience.[4] Another woman's animus chided her mercilessly; what she said or did was always "trivial, shallow, and obvious," especially when she talked about anything of the spirit. A deeply religious woman, she felt attacked at the heart of her most cherished beliefs. Her animus would say, "What is this? Women can't speak about the spirit or carry it the way men can. Men have the real spirit out there, up there, in the air. Women are earthbound. That's no good. For men it's like wind and traveling and knowing where it's all going." The woman was persuaded. All her diffuse certainty was in the gut. "If the spirit attends to me at all," she said, "it would be patronizing. What I think is inconsequential."

Women who know this attack on what they hold sacred feel done in by judgments that say "try harder," "do more," "not good enough," "amounts to nothing." Their convictions about the sacred become sacred convictions about their own inadequacy. Like the anima voice that insulates a man from the influence of reality, these fiercely critical animus judgments are themselves inaccessible to critical examination. They just are.

Sometimes the contrasexual killing voice is heard out loud, in meetings between persons. A man said a woman who told him all about himself, "no doubt accurately," just turned him off: "she killed my feeling." A woman said that as a girl she did not feel attacked by her father so much as "dismissed." He made her feel "negligible," "not worth taking seriously."

Judgment is the way in or the way out for the Self. When we fear it so much we cannot face any of its implications, we retreat from dialogue, we silence our inner conversation, we dismiss whatever we may know of our contrasexuality. The Self, or any part of it, small or large, that we may have possessed, collapses. That is the force of Albert Camus's pocket narrative, *The Fall.* The title in French, *La Chute,* conveys much of this—it means not only "fall" or "downfall," but "collapse" or "shoot." And that is what Camus's *récit* is about, the collapse of Jean-Baptiste Clamence, Paris lawyer turned, in his words, judge-penitent, and the shoot, the hunt, to restore his self-esteem. But how can one esteem a self that has collapsed?

In a new preface to *The Myth of Sisyphus,* written fifteen years after the first publication of the work, Camus says straightforwardly, "this book declares that even within the limits of nihilism it is possible to find the means to proceed beyond nihilism. In all the books I have written since, I have attempted to pursue this direction." The hunt for Self begins here, in this pursuit announced some two years before *The Fall* and followed in it, as promised. We find in works like this one and *The Plague,* expressed allegorically, that life has a value, even in a time of holocaust, of ritual slaughters of the innocent, of the making of humiliation into a social convention. We find it possible not only to forgive others, but to forgive ourselves—which is to say, to find the Self, the other within us through which forgiveness flows.

The allegorically named John-the-Baptist Clemency has much to forgive, if he can find the Self from which the mercy of forgiveness is to be extended. His assumption of the role of judge-penitent is what he must explain to the listener whose attention he has demanded, sitting in the grubby Amsterdam bar where the one-time successful Paris lawyer now pleads his case. His action, in oblique imitation of his illustrious scriptural namesake, is to make a way in the wilderness for clemency—for himself. He no longer wants to be the judge that his profession had made him into, and worse, "an irascible master who wanted, regardless of all laws, to strike down the offender and get him on his knees." In the past he would defend anyone guilty of anything as long as their guilt caused him no harm. That is no longer the case.

Jean-Baptiste's plea now has become: Judge not that I be not judged; let me be innocent, or at least seem to be. All of us naturally believe in our innocence, like the little Frenchman Clamence instances, who upon arrival at the concentration camp at Buchenwald demands that his complaint be heard. Laughter is the response from the guards: "Useless, old man. You don't lodge a complaint here." "But you see, sir," the little man insists, "my case is exceptional. I am innocent." Clamence's point is that all of us have exceptional cases to plead. And so he pleads his case, barely aware that his ironies have all but disposed of it.

He wants to win the laughers over to his side, the Buchenwald contingent and all others, beginning with whoever it was he heard laughing behind him one night when he was standing on the Pont des Arts, in Paris, looking down at the Seine, feeling the success of a courtroom performance that day and the warm response of some friends to an ad lib speech he delivered afterwards, denouncing "the hardheartedness of our governing class and the hypocrisy of our leaders." He is full of his power; he dominates the landscape. He is about to light his "cigarette of satisfaction" when suddenly, at his back, laughter breaks out, and continues for a while like sounds from a boat going downstream, though no boat is visible.

The laughter pursues him, to be joined as a nagging memory to the image of a young woman he had seen one November night on the Pont Royal, like a sudden incarnation of his anima self, staring at the river below the bridge, poised as if to jump. He hesitated for a moment, then moved on, perhaps fifty yards, when he heard the sound, appalling in the midnight quiet, of a body hitting the water. After that came a cry, which, like the terrible laughter, seemed to move downstream, followed by a silence that was "interminable." What to do? He could not move with the weakness he felt. Now, trying to recall this moment, which in his memory still mocks him, he speculates that he thought something like "Too late, too far. . . ."

Anonymous derision is the enemy. Women he had exploited, prostitutes included, who did not sufficiently pay their homage to him, or spread bad reports about his sexual performance, held him up to scorn, not only theirs and those around him, but his own. He could get back at them, however. Much worse, much more a part of the anonymous mockery that still haunts him, are those who simply found something of their own to claim, like the older of two whores he used to live with: "Unfortunately the prostitute had a most middle-class nature; she since consented to write her memoirs for a confessions magazine quite open to modern ideas." Like Clamence?

He is resentful of a German soldier coming out of a Metro station; a dog the lawyer had called over to him, instead of coming to him, followed the soldier, who had bent over and patted the animal. He achieves the recognition he seeks in an internment camp in Tripoli when, as "a joke," he confesses to having more failings than anyone else in his tent, and becomes "pope" of this segment of the damned. He knows that like all popes he needs forgiveness. But that is not his skill. What he does best is condemn himself, "indulging in public confession as often as possible." He points with pride to the painting in his cupboard, "The Just Judges," a panel of the van Eyck altarpiece in Ghent stolen years ago. Why doesn't he return it? He has a full-throated defense. It isn't really his; it was sold to the "ape" who is the proprietor of his barroom hangout, in return for a bottle of liquor. Those who look at the altar cannot tell the copy that replaced the stolen panel from the original, just as they cannot distinguish false judges from true ones— only he can do so. The judges in the altarpiece, "The Adoration of the Lamb," are about to see the Lamb, but there is no longer a lamb, or the innocence it symbolizes, in our world, and so he has followed the established harmony, the harmony of separation: Justice is on the cross, the innocence of the Lamb in his cupboard.

He used to dream of a wholeness of heart and body, "sensual enjoyment and mental excitement" joined in what passed in his fantasy for eternity, five years. After that, death would be acceptable. Not possessing that wholeness, he finds his dominating strength in self-accusation. Instead of the permanent embrace of Dante's Paolo and Francesca, he is separated forever, from others, from himself. The saving dream now is that the suicidal woman will jump into the river again and that this time he will rescue her—and himself. "Brr . . . !" the book ends. "The water's so cold! But let's not worry! It's too late now. It will always be too late. Fortunately!"

Clamence is Camus's Underground Man in this novel, which is, like so much of this writer's work, a set of variations on a Dostoyevskian theme. The lawyer's confession is meant, like his quickness to admit to more failings than anyone else, to draw us in, to exculpate him, or that failing, to elicit the forgiveness he has been pleading for by styling himself a judge-penitent. He can say with the diarist in Dostoyevsky's *Notes from the Underground,* "We are oppressed at being men—men with a real individual body and blood, we are ashamed of it, we think it a disgrace and try to contrive to be some sort of impossible generalized man." Dostoyevsky's figure insists, in these last of his notes from where he lives, between the floorboards, as the Russian title of the book suggests, that he is one of the "still-born . . . begotten, not by living fathers. That suits us better and better. We are developing a taste for it. Soon we shall contrive to be born somehow from an idea. But enough. . . ."[5]

Each, Jean-Baptiste and the Underground Man, may only be talking to himself, but that really is enough. As long as the dialogue of Self—even collapsed Self—and Other continues, it will be possible to proceed against nihilism and to say Yes to the invitation to live, even if only in faltering fashion. The young woman, the fleeing anima, may yet be rescued.

ARMOR AND THE MOTHER WOUND

When unlived energies of the Self amass behind an anima or animus bridge that has collapsed, the negative voices grow so strong they encase us like armor. At first the armor is not so firm or impenetrable, but rather more like the thorn hedge in the fairy tale *Sleeping Beauty.* When the thirteenth witch is excluded from the princess's baptismal party—for the good animus-reason that there were not enough place settings—she curses the infant girl. When she comes of age, says the curse, she will fall into a deathless sleep for a hundred years. Many suitors, as could be predicted, try to rescue her but are simply impaled on the hedge's thorns. When the time is up, a prince gets through to waken her with a kiss. A fine animus tale.[6]

A man complains in therapy of a woman interested in him that she wants to stuff him into herself to fill up some inward lack, and at the same time put him to endless tests. "It's like being stuck in a hedge!" he exclaims. A woman in treatment spots the thorn hedge around herself when she recognizes that she has been looking to men to confirm her shaky femininity rather than honoring it herself. The result? She has remained alone, without a man. To put it mythically, it was as if a goddess had said to her, If you will not honor me yourself, my revenge will be that you will find no mate. Sleeping Beauty sleeps again.

Our thorns thicken into an impenetrable armor when we need to be protected against the numbing pain of a wound we cannot heal. The so-called animus woman, whose opinions regularly step in front of her ego and surround her in protective coating, identifies with her masculinity, not to express empathy with the male but to flee the mother who hurt her, and the archetypal mother images that stand behind her. Armed with animus convictions, she can seal up the wound. But this is an animus hostile to women, which appears in their dreams as a berating or mocking voice and in their behavior as their own nagging voices attacking others.

If the animus woman's contrasexuality carries her inferior thinking function, the pseudoanimus puts on a show of pseudothinking that aims to dominate, not explore; to outlaw doubt, not inspire creativity.[7] Anima armor, in its turn, insulates a man against dependence on woman or women. He displays not self-reliance, but fear, even hatred, of the feminine. Or, he plays caring mother to himself in bouts of sentimental self-indulgence.

The wound underneath the afflicted woman or man stays neglected under the anima or animus armor. One woman put into a man's hands all the power to decide what mattered in her life and then felt herself victimized. In a rage she ripped the relationship to pieces. Digging down beneath her behavior in analysis, she remembered her mother's stinging words when she confided her love of a man: He won't see anything in you; he's just using you. The woman, whose voices judged anything she contributed as "trivial, shallow and obvious," reached far down for the insight—namely, that she disclaimed her own self-worth to keep from hurting her mother. "I would suffer if I did anything else," she said, "because I would lose my mother. She always went away from me to deal with her hurts, with her back to me, silent, angry, withdrawn. She left me in the frigidity of outer space and I was always unable to get her back. I had to wait until she chose to return." That wound was so lasting that, years later, this woman kept turning over her initiative to men, to teachers, never claiming any talent, any understanding, any impulse for herself. Uncovering this wound, she dreamed of a "bridge that stopped in the middle of a lake," like the animus bridge to the Self that collapses.

Another woman whose mother had never supported her growth into independence both feared losing her mother's support and felt imprisoned in permanent bonding with her parent. She carried this over into her relations with men, and inevitably found herself trapped with unsuitable partners. To be close was to be entrapped; to be distant, to be abandoned. Simple answer: choose men who are unavailable; have them and not have them both. All of which only bruised her the more. Sexual relations cannot be used to solve unmet dependency.[8]

A man describes the wound in his relations to the feminine. When he opens his front door and senses his wife's bad mood, any connection he has to the center of himself vaporizes. "I feel little and go numb." Any attempt to confront his wife just feels "too brutish." And so he remains stuck, embedded in his armor. Another man, who had suddenly left analysis to go to another city, wrote four years later to tell his female analyst that a major reason for his departure was feeling constrained by the choice he seemed to see between his mother and what his analyst represented. He remembered his dream at that time, in which the analyst had said, "I can't believe that silly woman is *your* mother." He felt overwhelmed by massive guilt for having abandoned his mother, and so ran back to her, he said. What followed was a year of depression and suicidal fantasy, which he emerged from with the help of another therapist in the distant city. A heterosexual affair and then a homosexual one followed. In the second he felt deeply moved to get what he needed from another man and had quite missed getting from his father and brothers. He wrote his analyst, now four years later, because of a dream in which an older woman harangues him for ignoring women because he was so preoccupied with himself. A young woman in the dream vigorously nods her head in agreement, but lets the older woman speak for her. That annoyed the dreamer. He wrote to affirm his work with his first analyst as providing "a jumping-off place" for what he now had to tackle—"to get the woman in him to speak"—that is, to get his own, not his mother's, contrasexual bridge to the unconscious.

A woman struggling to deal with her mother wound dreamed in very strong images about it. She encounters in her dream an animus figure who accompanies her but does not yet seem to want to help her much. She and the man go to a tag sale. A woman named Blank is selling her little girl, whose name is Barbiturate. The dreamer expresses horror that the child did not even have a name: she wants to rescue her. The man—the animus figure—says they can do nothing.

Anima/animus armor can lead to tragic results, as with that definitive animus woman, Ibsen's Hedda Gabler. When she could think of nothing to say to her suitor, she acted to cover up the blank space by pointing to a big house on a hill as the place she had always wanted to live. He, the least appropriate of men for Hedda, marries her and settles with her into that house, which becomes her prison. Her superabundant energies find no outlet. She sees everything—all the intricate connections among people around her, all the empty future unfolding before her—but no way to bring her great threatening energies into a living life. The negative animus that imprisons instead of connecting is in control of Hedda. It produces what Jung calls *Sol niger,* a black consciousness that burns much too brightly when a destructive animus moves to efface the ego.[9] It saps her femininity at the core. Contemptuous of her husband, jealous of the woman who had replaced her with her ex-lover, remembering that she had betrayed and deserted the lover and determined somehow to bring him back under her control, hating the smug, corrupt judge who seems to be succeeding in trapping her into an affair, detesting her pregnancy that will condemn her forever to the husband and marriage and house she loathes, she has only one acceptable way out. She takes it. She grabs one of her father's pistols, which have dominated the stage set from the beginning of the drama, and kills herself.

Hedda betrays her lover twice, in the first relationship by denying her feelings for him because he was poor, and then, in the second, by burning the manuscript of the splendid book that had rescued him from drunkenness. Losing it, he has no life to look forward to; his death apparently by accident, follows, as we expect it to. At each point Hedda turns from her wounded femininity. She abandons her love and the animus strength that stands behind it to gain material security. She denies who she is, a wounded animus woman, and acts out the role of mistress of the big house. In the emptiness of her denial and its corollary envy, she moves to destroy the good others create, most directly by killing her child-to-be. Her unlived animus connection to life through the Self doubles back on her, like the ouroboros snake, to eat itself and to bring an accommodating death all around her.[10]

The Devil's Pact and the Demon Lover

In *When We Dead Awaken,* Ibsen brings us another woman of un-
quenchable animus thirsts, like Hedda of heroic dimension. Irene von
Satow had stood naked, inside and out, to model for the sculptor Arnold Rubek. In her he had found the flesh of vision and produced a
masterful image in stone of woman awakening from the sleep of death
as an allegory of the day of Resurrection. When Rubek rejects the love
she brings him and with it his connection to a signifying art, his work
turns from beauty to the macabre. Irene runs off and becomes, like
Rubek, a caricature of her inner person as she displays herself in broth-
els. Rubek knows that she holds the key to the casket of his visions.
When she leaves, the casket snaps shut. He must get it open again to
free himself from the contemptuous, mocking animal faces that hide
just beneath the surface of his portraits of others in his sculpture. Meeting, as if by chance, many years later at a mountain health resort, sculptor and model awaken like Rubek's resurrectionary figure; but they can
only live now in a triumphant symbolic death to which Irene leads them,
falling from a snow-filled mountain top.

Irene and Rubek show how the collapse of the anima/animus bridge
can draw one, in a pact with the devil, to death. She has given herself
body and soul to Rubek, but has not claimed her own connection to the
Self center. She has given it entirely into his keeping, to be both connection and center, in the jargon, through projective identification. She
worships him—that is her pact with the devil; she loses herself in him—
that is her death warrant. Without an inner bridge to the Self, she cannot see his reality any more than her own. He will not use her sexually,
he says, and does not; but he is shameless in using her spiritually. He
takes all that she uncovers to him, the heart of his work, and then dis-
cards her as a mere episode in his career. That is his pact with the devil
to achieve worldly success. The price is the loss of access to his vision,
which he has projectively identified with Irene.[11]

In the devil's pact we always seek something for nothing. In anima/
animus struggles, the pact turns the other into a demon lover. We give
all to others in return for the happiness, the wealth, the fame they promise. We do not respond to the claims of our own ego work to integrate
what comes across the anima/animus bridge to us from the Self. We just

take what is on offer, all that promises ease and success, without thought as to whether we are really equipped to deal with what our past has thrust at us. Violence ensues. All our shadow qualities—everything in us which we would rather disown or blame on our neighbor—contaminate animus or anima.[12] We find ourselves in thrall to it, though it tortures us or looks to kill us. Animus and shadow, instead of enlarging and enlivening the ego world, gang up on the ego, leaving it helpless, without resource. A woman needing to do more work on her shadow constantly dreamed of her sister stealing her lover and running off with him.

When the anima or animus is inflated by its sense of the Self instead of being related to it, the ego feels hunted down as if by a killer. A man woke from a terrifying nightmare in which he was being stabbed to death by an unidentified woman. Working on the image in analysis, he uncovered what amounted to rage toward all women: "They can pierce your heart; they get you, and then they leave you." The anima of the dream helped him connect to his rage. He could say it now: "I have a hate in me." He saw how he had acted it out with two women he kept dangling before him at the same time, always withholding his love from them. He saw too how his hate attacked his body in bouts of colitis, almost the exact physical equivalent of the diabolically haunted psyche.

The demon lover pulls us into life-and-death situations. One woman insisted on holding onto her relationship with a man who made her feel she could never command either his respect or his ardor, for he also made her feel free of her family's tyrannies in his defiance of them. When he rejected her, she tried to kill herself. Fortunately, it was only an attempt. She survived to begin work in earnest on her sense of self and on differentiating herself from her family's confining strictures. "The best revenge," she concluded, "was to live well."[13]

Elizabeth Maddox Roberts describes a Kentucky mountain girl's awakening to the fact that the lover she had run off with, to get away from her ego world, could be her murderer: "I saw into the black of Langtry's mind. . . . I saw his eyes open and black. . . . Deep in there was a black nothing. . . . I said to myself, 'Would I marry a black demon with a cave of empty black inside?' And anger on him, enough to kill." In her mind she could not distinguish between his demonic power and her love: "All I want is to guard you and keep you." But she knew she carried the marks of both: "I hate his hand on my throat to make blue marks and his gun held against my left shoulder. . . . I can hate the one and want the other with my whole body and I can't cure myself."[14]

ADDICTION AND PERVERSION

We stuff everything into those holes in ourselves, the wounds left in us when the bridge to the Self collapses. We fill them with food, drink, drugs, or objects wrenched out of their proper use to do sexual service, a belt, a shoe, a stocking. We cram fantasy images into these holes, of being whipped or of whipping someone else, of being bound, beaten, and humiliated, or performing the same service for another. The bridge collapses, leaving a yawning gap that feels like a dead place. Intolerable, deeply frightening, it threatens to take us out of existence, "right down the bathtub drain," one woman put it. So we stuff our objects into the gap, trying to make a new bridge. All that happens, however, is that our wobbly ego merges with the addictive agent we have introduced, which in turn merges with the Self. The object, then, finds itself engorged with all the Self energies and acts as its substitute. Contact with it becomes vital to us. We feel compelled by it. We submit to it. We are the captives of a perverted scenario composed by a force far greater than ourselves.

We come to hate the Self because in its substitute form it bullies us. We have no place for the true Self to live in us, nor clearly are we serving it. Our addiction has worked a parody devotion in us. If the Self cannot live in us as creative energy, its distorted mirror image will hound us. Our bodies carry the unlived life of the Self in addictions that bring death.[15]

In his last book of poems, *The Burning Perch,* Louis MacNeice confronted the anguish of the unlived Self. There is nothing too violent, though there is an addiction to a past that was far more enriching than the present. The terrible uncreative sameness of the 1960s administers a systematic punishment. "Soap Suds" remind him of the smell of a big house he knew as an eight-year-old, of faded globes and a stuffed dog and the movement of croquet mallets; but they are all gone, and the hands experiencing the suds now are not a child's. What remains of this Irish-born poet's childhood that can be relied upon is the sea, with a content reaching back to observing Greeks like Xenophon, and to Columbus, and to the Bible. The past has more potential than the present. Now, a pet shop caters to those who "want something comfy," people contemplating a soft little animal that "will return affection /Like some neutered succubus," people offering in the diminishing returns of pet society, the successor to the ancient wild and the "tanks and cages" of the shop, "a home, a haven,/ That might prove worse."

MacNeice's language and forms are clear, the better to articulate the rictus gapings of people who have lost the spark of Self or, as with himself, have imagined too often that terrible possibility. He dredges up the past, as he has been doing since his first metered scratchings, but now with deadly intent. When he remembers a trip to Ravenna, he can dutifully tick off the Byzantine marvels ("The mosaics knocked me flat") and ask, as everybody does, how it was that Byzantium, following the example of Rome, went into slow decline and left us, after the grandeur of the sixth century, the bifurcated landscape of sugar refinery and church.

> What do I remember of Ravenna?
> A bad smell mixed with glory, and the cold
> Eyes that belie the tessellated gold.

Charon, ferryman to the dead, is a personage here, across the page from young people who meet in "a grave glade," a world of "Crawly crawly" twigs and a string quartet tuning up with the same "Crawly crawly" effect; the observing poet muses that they should have met long ago instead of now, with the string quartet, "in a green grave." Now, in this place, in this volume, "Greyness Is All":

> If black were truly black not grey
> It might provide some depth to pray
> Against and we could hope that white
> Would reach a corresponding height.

The lingering effect of these poems and their near neighbors is not depressing; it is summoning. MacNeice, near his end, speaking in the accents of a sibylline anima, is not without hope, even in the gray middens of his modernity. In a series of "Memoranda to Horace," he ruminates:

> Returned from my far-near country, my erstwhile,
> I wonder how much we are defined by negatives,

> Who have no more seen the Bandusian
> Spring than have you the unreadable Atlantic.

He will attempt, like Horace,"an appetitive decorum," go to his "tryst" against a "dirty" sky, settle for "blasphemous and bawdy exchanges" in the twilight, and even find the possibility of a senility filled with memories of childhood. That ". . . seems better than a blank posterity/One's life restricted to standing room only."

The past nags at one like scraps of pop tunes that will not go away when one fears the loss of Self, or worse, is sure of it. MacNeice is the master of melancholy, as he had almost always been. When he was five, his mother went off to a nursing home in Dublin and he and his sister and their mongoloid brother waved to her disappearing motor-car—and never saw her again. Father was a clergyman, later a bishop, courageous and trusting enough in his judgment to refuse to sign the Ulster covenant, but not persuasive to his son's agnostic interiority. The "Didymus" of the short poem of that name we can read not as Doubting Thomas but as Doubting Louis: "Refusing to fall in love with God, he gave/Himself to the love of created things."

We can see the God of these lines as Father MacNeice or the Christian deity or the abundant divinities of the Greeks the poet knew so well as a student, as assistant lecturer for six years under the distinguished professor of Greek at Birmingham University, E. R. Dodds, as translator of the *Agamemnon* of Aeschylus, as director of the British Institute in Athens. However we see his God, we are not likely to match MacNeice's hovering Uncertainty, the appropriate word to describe what he made of the figure with whom he fenced in the dreams of night, poked at in the poems of day, and met best perhaps in the persona of Didymus, who returned in a long poem named after him, to confess once again the poet's doubts:

> Oh but my doubt is a sea harsher than this that I see,
>   Oh but my hands tremble fumbling the night,
> To all of my questions I know the reply must be No;
>   To me those tongues of fire were fire, not light.

MacNeice's fiery Pentecosts, devoid of comforting light, came with his two wives, with the son who separated himself from him, with the multiple jugglings of his life as BBC producer and writer of an astonishingly large number of radio dramas, as poet, as critic, as translator, as doubter. Clytemnestra says in his splendidly made *Agamemnon,* "For while there is root, foliage comes to the house/Spreading a tent of shade against the Dog Star." But he could not remain in the tenting shade; he needed to test rougher earth. For his BBC play *Persons from Porlock,* he insisted on accompanying engineers recording sound effects underground. He caught a chill; a few weeks later he was dead of pneumonia.

"Of all the poets of his generation and mine," W. H. Auden said in a memorial address, "I would say without hesitation that Louis MacNeice had the least cause for self-reproach, and his example denies to the rest of us the excuse that in the historical circumstances under which we grew up, the temptations to fake feelings were unusually strong, true though this may be: Louis MacNeice's work is a proof they could be resisted." He did resist, and in the resisting found he had to admit to his true sensibility, that of a doubter. What steadies the doubter and keeps his agnostic interiority from turning into a querulous unbelief is the anima search that defined Self for him, for all the years from his mother's departure when he was five to his own when he was fifty-five.

In his translation of *Faust,* made with the aid of a German scholar, he is often brilliant, sometimes merely choosy, occasionally too much directed by a radio ear; but when he comes to the last lines of the *Chorus Mysticus,* the anima has her splendid way with him. The lines deepen here with a Self that Goethe knew and MacNeice had experienced, however infrequently. The reading of *das Ewig-Weibliche* as "Eternal Womanhead" adds a depth rarely glimpsed to words almost flattened of meaning by the usual translation, "Eternal Feminine."

> All that is past of us
> Was but reflected;
> All that was lost in us
> Here is corrected;
> All indescribables
> Here we descry;
> Eternal Womanhead.

"Womanhead" gives to Goethe's transforming feminine the force of the Godhead. Mary joins the Trinity, an understanding well within the reach of this poet, who could write to his woman, to his wife, to his love, of his love,

> With you, pray not without you, trapped on the edge of the world In the wind that troubles the galaxies, you my galactic Marvel of ivoried warmth. . . .

She is for him all the places he has been with her, from "blacked-out London" to Byzantium, and everywhere she has been without him. She is herself, in her "own right and light," for which he is grateful— "Without me yes, with me more yes." That is his hold on life, on being,

> For you are there, are here, and nothing
> Dare cancel that; you are my dear
> With whom, pray not without, I live,
> Incredibly ever-newly here

If in any way MacNeice lost that hold, in his poems of doubt, in his constant service to Uncertainty, in the fire of his burning perch, he could not, and he did not, efface the power of this tribute to his experience of the Womanhead. The last words of his "Coda," the last poem of the last book, are reassuring, even in their questioning textures. They read like lines he may have spoken to his love on that last trip, underground:

> But what is that clinking in the darkness?
> Maybe we shall know each other better
> When the tunnels meet beneath the mountain.[16]

One man, fearing the underground power of the female, was compelled to haunt porn shows, which allowed him masturbatory life but imprisoned him in infantile attitudes. Another man, as a little boy, hit on the device of a nylon stocking to bridge the gap left when the beginning of a bridge to the Self collapsed for him because of traumatic punishment by his parents. This fetish figured centrally in his erotic life, and it took him many years to unravel its meaning. The stocking replaced the anima bridge to the Self. His ego merged with the stocking, which merged with Self. With courage, he slowly separated them. His ego strengthened; his anima developed firm access to the Self. Another man, also as a little boy, developed a beating and cross-dressing ritual that focused on a tight belt, which in effect built an alternate route to the Self for him. This made it very powerful, dominant in him for over half a century. The Self will be lived, one way or the other. In this drama, the anima split into two hostile mythic figures characterized by white and black. Relief from his compulsion to enact what he called his perversion began when the two ladies exchanged belts, so that the white wore the black and the black the white. Repair comes from the anima as well as the ego.

A woman saw that she was always carrying the soul for other people, especially for men. She "fueled" them, she said, kept them in being, alive. She played the bridge to the Self for them. And they valued her, for in her they felt seen and supported. But she had no bridge of her own and feared she would "go dead" if she stopped fueling others. Then no one would see her. She worked for her supper and yet she was starving. All this compulsion to fuel others, as a way of keeping above the gap where her bridge to the Self had been, eventually fell onto food. Now, it fed her, soothed her, rewarded her. It made her more visible to herself as she grew heavy. Food became the Self she could not get hold of and feel supported by, her addictive shadow version of the Self.

In addictions and perversions, substitute objects or rituals become bridges to the Self. They replace the animus or anima bridge. But because our ego, in compulsion, cannot fully differentiate Self from substitute object, a fusion of ego, the addicting substance or perverted object, and the Self occurs, like a parody integration. Instead of ego joining Self in the anima/animus bridge, we get a false unity, a merger of undifferentiated, undeveloped parts that stick fast together, to defend against our fear of falling forever into nothingness.

CULTURE

Unfortunately, the compulsions that overtake us when the contrasexual bridge collapses on the Self side are not confined to individuals. Self energies amass, burgeon, and burst into the scene we share with others like a tidal wave. The energy remains dehumanized, impersonal. It crushes good and bad alike. When a bridge breaks, there is no way for the Self to get into our shared existence in a focused, felt, relatable way. We do not find access to any unified process of conducting energy into collective life, but experience the violence of fission. Mushroom clouds form. A rampant force pushes everything aside in ruthless disregard of consequences, for Self or others.

Without egos made strong by a slow, deliberate process of integration of masculine and feminine modes of being, we find no clear paths into a social life for Self-energies. Rough passages are carved out instead by violent eruptions. Not only do we suffer now a dried-up ego life, unsupported by the flow into life of the underground rivers of the Self, but we must confront the social epidemics that eruptions bring about. Some are flagrant and constitute the great traumas of history. Adolph Eichmann, for example, that obedient Nazi servant carrying out his extermination orders perfectly in order to kill more efficiently, was reported to have himself felt compulsive attraction to Jewish girls. That split-off disparaged anima image, which he had mirrored thousands of times over, would not leave him alone. Never let it be said that our individual psychic splits are not socially conscious.[17]

The epidemiology of the collapsed bridge is not always marked by eruption or even outward show. When the bridge collapses at the Self side, our contrasexuality may become simply a sad inner emptiness, in which the discourse of sexual elements barely exists and we make almost no contact within or without. We fall victim to literalism and fanaticism. Our sexual categories become stiff and intransigent. The male in the female becomes either crude or altogether inaccessible. The female in the male turns harpy or simply withdraws. We become intolerant of anyone, especially of the opposite sex, who does not altogether mirror our diminished sexual understanding. Conscious and unconscious split apart in us as our inner conversation comes to a halt.

Without the good functioning of the unconscious principle of identity—that we share the same kind of multifaceted mental life beneath all the conflicts of individuals and cultures—we fall into a "chaos of fragmentation." No center holds. We hang onto collectivities that blank out any great range of identity or affect, and especially to causes that offer loud, ringing rhetorical simplifications. But then we find ourselves bewildered, even there, by irresolvable conflict. The case for clean nuclear energy must, for example, face the concern for human safety, and we cannot find a view big enough to take in both. We expand bureaucracies as a way of quashing anxiety-making complexities. Everywhere we multiply rules in aid of reductive simplicity, making the cage tight after the tiger has jumped out.

Without the good functioning of the conscious principle of differentiation—which distinguishes variable identities and cultural and religious diversities in our basic unity as a human family—we fall into a "chaos of fragmentation."[18] We identify our brand with a whole class of products and oppress anyone who insists on the possibility of other brands. We refuse the indeterminacy of the archetype and prosecute adherence to stereotypes—if they are not ours. Literalism and fanaticism engage in a civil war to kill both tradition and originality. When a "new" spiritualism is proclaimed, promising to transcend conflict in its openness to all cultures, all points of view, it quickly shows the familiar bellicosity in prosecuting all other culturalisms, multiple or singular, that do not hold fast to the *letter* of its proclamation.

When the unlived feminine falls into the unconscious, it usually takes the body with it. A false materialism, as dogged as the new spiritualism, becomes manifest. In theology, where we need symbolic understanding, we get insistence on equating of cause or group with God. Oppression confers sanctity; victimization, real or assumed, makes one a Christ figure. We forget that God's mystery surpasses all words—and word games. We should remember how quickly word games turn into war games, in the academy, in countries like Ireland, in regions like the Middle East, in reawakened nationalisms from Yugoslavia through most of the disunited Soviet Union, in every area where "rights" can be contested.

When the unlived masculine falls into the unconscious, it takes with it any openness to differentiation. We armor ourselves with the truths of our causes. We fail to see just how tight-fitting and defensive our military dress has become. Our truths flatten into hard, inflexible shields behind which our egos disappear. We are open to no food of psyche or spirit. We have stopped learning. We see combat in defense of our truths as our duty. A great negativity accumulates in us, with a special unforgiving quality—because, in our armored encasement, we recognize as worthy neighbors only those who absolutely replicate us.

The Self that has no anima or animus bridge to cross stays unlived in us. It turns round and round in us, pushing us to find addiction-breeding substitutes and every pretext to pin the blame for its maladaptions and ill humors, for all the collective negativity that surrounds us, on others. Unlived Self energies, which are much like envy, are similarly hard to get at and to give healing outlet. For as with envy, the origin of our condition lies within ourselves, while its identifying swirling movement keeps pulling us outward and away from the interior dialogue we need to enter. The revenge of an unrecognized, unlived Self is persecutory feeling toward others, which finds its gleeful translation in scapegoating—racial, sexual, religious, economic, political, cultural, whatever or whoever lies at hand.[19] We miss a great deal if we do not see this component in Nazism, communism, and the other movements that have turned genocidal.

Collapse of the bridge to the Self forecloses our precious mediating space, that between total unconscious and total ego consciousness, the space that anima and animus create by bridging the two extremes. This grand middle space is where we engage in conversation with our deepest Self and the transcendent. It is where we find our creativity, both as persons and as peoples.

Out of it we concoct our dreams, and in it have our dream experiences.[20] How important it is to us is vividly illustrated when the space is invaded, and we feel driven in retaliation to act out our fantasies in the world outside. The examples proliferate among us, and each worse than the last, like the sniper who shoots schoolchildren thinking they are Vietnamese guerilla troops, or the woman who boils her child to save him from the devil, or the group of people who commit suicide because their spiritual leader, Jim Jones, gives the order to do so, or the grotesque, compulsive sexual couplings that turn persons into things.

Sexuality without the middle space quickly becomes compulsive or mechanical. The biology of desire is strong enough to sustain actings out in either mode, but the person disappears. In a parody of intense feeling, a consciousness that is all ego becomes possessed by its sexuality, insistent about its mastery of styles and techniques, and driven to conquer anything and everything in sexual sight. It has no alternative but to play the Don Juan numbers game, counting seductions, positions, orgasms. At the other extreme, in this world without Self, is an unconsciousness approaching the catatonic. There one falls into sexual performance as into anesthesia, physically present but with no other easily determinable participation.

At one extreme, sexuality has become a kind of guerilla warfare. At the other, it follows the Jonestown ritual—its troops stand up and come forward dutifully, in trance, to claim their sexual Kool-Aid. If pleasure exists in either practice, it is by the book, by the gland, by a predetermined specification. Spontaneous joy is the rarest of experiences. The delight that comes from meeting a person in sexual intimacy and finding one's own person defined and enlarged by the encounter depends upon what is altogether missing here, the middle space of Self.

Though we usually meet in such encounters under our real names, and perforce in our real bodies, we might just as well identify ourselves with algebraic symbols, like the late Malcolm X, and cover our bodies with shrouds cut away to expose the erogenous zones, like the brassieres open at the nipples and the panties with holes of the sex shops. The governing atmosphere is pornographic: surfaces are all that matter, and anything that enhances them is allowed, from breast implants to condoms studded, perfumed, or laminated with food. Nothing quite as masterful as the air brush of the porno magazines, to cover imperfections or swell body parts to heroic size, has as yet been discovered for the bedroom, but we can depend upon science to make up for this lapse.

Moral inversion is the prevailing tone. In that sense, "sexual revolution" might be the right term to describe the Self-less sexuality of the late twentieth century, except for the fact that the change in understanding moral propriety is not all that new. Two centuries ago, Friedrich Schiller, in a thoughtful essay, "Of the Cause of the Pleasure We Derive from Tragic Objects," took note of upside-down moral attitudes in the sexual arena. His example, the virtuoso endeavors of Robert Lovelace to seduce the heroine of Samuel Richardson's *Clarissa Harlowe,* could not be bettered today. What we may have gained in the instruments of prophylaxis to prolong the attack and accelerate the tempo, we have lost in our inattention to the heroics of shame, which cannot be matched as a means of heightening sexual tension. Schiller's reasoning, drawn from his own middle space, is impeccable:

It is not rare for intelligent perversity to secure our favour by being the means of procuring for us the pleasure of moral propriety. The triumph of moral propriety will be great in proportion as the snares set by Lovelace for the virtue of Clarissa are formidable, and as the trials of an innocent victim by a cruel tyrant are severe. It is a pleasure to see the craft of a seducer foiled by the omnipotence of the moral sense. On the other hand, we reckon as a sort of merit the victory of a malefactor over his moral sense, because it is the proof of a certain strength of mind and intellectual propriety.

Schiller's conclusion, that "this propriety in vice can never be the source of a perfect pleasure, except when it is humiliated by morality," would escape many today, all those for whom the words "No, no, a thousand times no!" can only be a signal for merriment, even if translated into a less-melodramatic contemporary idiom. On the other hand, rape, no matter how inventively described or fancifully excused, has come with its increasing incidence in our society to seem less and less a subject for jokes. Schiller, whose anima insights make the heroines of his plays engaging even when the drama around them creaks, understood the ancient principle associated with Thomas Aquinas and Richard Hooker, that we are all motivated by love, the worst of us as well as the best.

What is theological truth in Thomas and Hooker becomes psychological insight in the modern clinic. The language would not be the same, but the understanding would be close. Love moves the action, whether evil or good or on any characterizing level in between. It may be, as Thomas and Hooker would put it, love perverted, which is to say love of the wrong object, or love defective, too little love of the right object; or love excessive, too much love, even for a good; but it is always love that motivates our actions. If we understand this, we understand Schiller's insistence that even an inverted propriety in vice "is an essential part of our pleasure, because it brings moral sense into stronger relief." Sharing with him a middle space that surrenders its tension neither to total unconsciousness at one extreme nor to total ego consciousness at the other, we can see with him that in the moral drama of Richardson the "intellectual propriety in the plan of Lovelace is greatly surpassed by the rational propriety of Clarissa." We can, then, with Schiller, "feel in full the satisfaction caused by both."[21]

Thus it is that the Self creates its space and the life appropriate to it. It makes us sensitive to our many-layered past, and the lasting wisdom of the cultures of the middle space that have made it possible for us, with whatever awkwardnesses and imbalances, to survive. For out of this space we create the forms of culture that house us and feed us, creating them not by fiat but in the mysterious way cultures have always been formed, by the archetypes that give us our identities as men and women and as attendants upon the transcendent. When that space contracts, we get chauvinism and prejudice and feel a great spiritual hunger. Too often we receive only scraps when we go to our churches, mosques, and temples looking for food. We have lost our symbols. The space converted to dreaming, creating, symbolizing, feeding, and playing has become, for too many of us, the territory of the gap. Gaps, of course, exist to be filled. But with what?[22]

Part IV

Clinical Issues

Symptoms
and
Treatments

Transference, Countertransference, and Anima/Animus

PATTERNS

Liveliness and range identify the multiple guises the contrasexual archetype assumes in transference and countertransference. People find they can make use of that special sort of single person before them, the analyst. In that necessarily limited agent, they find ways to connect with their own unique contrasexual figures that the agent may never have dreamed of.[1] Beginning analytical work, two heterosexual men dreamed of their female analyst in related images, but with very different meanings. The first man reclined on the floor next to a bathtub where his analyst bathed. Although aware of her body, he was struck more forcibly by the ease he felt in being with her in such intimate terms. She *was* the unconscious to him. The second dreamed he was bathing a two-year-old child in a tub and the analyst joined in, as if she were the child's mother. He clothed the analyst in maternal robes, to be his helper.[2]

A homosexual man shunned anything to do with mother as "anathema!" He projected onto the analyst a daughterlike anima—young, enlivening, smaller than he, and thus never a threat to swallow him as a large mother would be. Another gay man happily found in his female analyst the holding mother he lacked in life but violently refused to see her "as woman," that is, as a sexual being. A man troubled all his life by a compulsive masochism found a way through it precisely when he experienced his analyst as a being who was sexual. He first cast her in the role of an anima that was all good, light, wise. When she took on very different aspects for him—dark, dominating, plotting evil—he fell violently in love with her. For once in his life, his split-anima image came together in one person, and he could glimpse the possibility of joining up in himself, after decades of separation, what he called his "life" and his "perversion." A female analyst in supervision reported that her female patient started a session with windy talk about the spirit. She, the analyst, found she wanted to do anything to puncture the inflated talk, which she did at last with a rude question: What did you have for breakfast? A woman analysand, wounded at the roots of her feminine self, found she had to begin her analysis working on what she called her "masculine parts," her doing and achieving, which rescued her from a smallness of life but also kept her from facing her wounded sense of herself as a woman.

The same question addresses all of us, no matter how different from each other, in our anima/animus adventures. What is the Self engineering? For anima and animus, one way or another, must fulfill their archetypal roles; they are *arche*, absolute beginnings, our starters, our originators. They make a wedge between self and other in us, and self and others outside us, by bringing in different ways of seeing, relating, and being. In what they give us, we discover an atemporality, an ahistoricity, primitive affect. Persistent, insistent, instinct-backed behavior explodes in great splashes of primary color into the more muted hues of consciousness. Our egos, protected by the structures of time, space, and causality that hold them in place, can delay the gratification our contrasexuality brings, can plan the best time and setting for us to see ourselves for ourselves separate from otherness. But they cannot hold anima and animus at bay forever.

Anima and animus demand entry. Their purpose is to open in us a space for interior conversation, where we can consult ourselves about the things we most deeply desire, and those we most dread. We can in this way identify what we have withheld, what we have buried in secret, and what we still yearn to bring into the world. We find ourselves positioned, with anima and animus, to encounter ultimates. We can ask ourselves what it is we really love, what makes us feel alive and real, what connections to others we have invested in most deeply, where we feel summoned. Being itself stands behind such scrutiny, such scourging of ourselves in inner conversation and in the exchanges with others that flow from it.

In Jung's terms, the Self uses the anima and animus to make us converse with it and with what transcends psychic reality. Inner conversation finally occurs between ego and Self and what surpasses Self. We learn the true wisdom of the psyche: Self is not God but that within us which knows about God.

We may not identify what the Self knows as God, but we are aware at this extraordinary level of experience that we have been in touch with something well beyond ourselves and the external world in which we find ourselves. With or without a disposition to accept philosophical categories, we start with something like Kant's variation on the *Cogito* of Descartes: "The *I think* expresses the act of determining my own existence. My existence is thus already given by the act of consciousness." But, the limits of my understanding are such that I have "no knowledge of myself as I am, but merely as I appear to myself." What we know for sure is that we exist in time, which is another way of saying that we are related, inseparably, to something outside ourselves, something that we accept as always there. We cannot go beyond this to isolate and face the Self in us with any assurance, because all we know is caught up in the act of knowing, all our awareness is in the awareness.

But something inside ourselves persists. Something joins us that is not in the outside world and yet seems to come from outside, even though we meet it inside ourselves. It is not part of the act of knowing; it is something that knows and that calls to us and that we feel urged to respond to. At the first level, it may be what Henri Bergson calls the "social ego"; we feel solidarity with the social group to which we belong and perhaps take pride in it—patriotic pride, ethnic pride, pride in our sexuality, pride in our church. At a higher level, it may be a response to the special call of those of moral stature: "The great moral figures that have made their mark on history join hands across the centuries, above our human cities; they unite into a divine city which they bid us enter. We may not hear their voices distinctly, the call has none the less gone forth, and something enters from the depth of our soul; from the real society in which we live we betake ourselves in thought to this ideal society; to this ideal society we bow down when we reverence the dignity of man within us, when we declare that we act from self-respect."

We can explain what we feel—or think we feel—as a logical extension of our social ego. Our group commands or demands this response; the ideal society that elicits our reverence is instinct in the group. But that does not always satisfy. We want something more certain and less political as an explanation, something that speaks more persuasively to that object of pride and humility that Hume calls the self, "that succession of related ideas and impressions, of which we have an intimate memory and consciousness."[3] We have made decisions, moral decisions some would call them, in which we take pride still. We have made others which shame us, and not necessarily because we have been exposed to public humiliation. The disgrace, like the pride, has been within. We have discussed our decisions, prideful or disgraceful, with ourselves. We have asked ourselves for explanations. We have pressed that curious, unidentified but persistent *other* inside ourselves for understanding. We have thought a good deal about how someone we respect might rate our behavior, often that person of the opposite sex in whose eyes we want most to be favorably reflected. And then we have, perhaps, looked to deepen the inner conversation, looked to find who it is that shapes the thinking and feeling of the person or persons we respect, asked ourselves where *their* values come from. This is our ideal society, well beyond the blueprints of social or economic or political thinkers, and we want to talk more about it and, as somehow we come to understand it, talk out of its wisdom.

For that conversation to develop in us, all our blocking defenses must loosen, split-off pieces return, dissociated parts mend. But above all else, anima or animus must emerge as our inner partner, one who makes interplay between conscious and unconscious mentation possible. Far from the obstructive animus that browbeats a woman into depression, or the ensnaring anima that mires a man in impossible assumptions about the fierce difficulties of his life, the functioning of these figures brings a positive calm, in which our inner space is enlarged, and our parts, even when ostensibly conflicted, can mix and match and build up an interior dialogue.

Anima and animus accomplish this in us more than other complexes do, because they touch all aspects of our identities in the most intimate ways. They charge our body reactions with sexual feeling. They enlist great bundles of emotion. They carry gladly our spiritual longing to reach other shores without leaving this one forever. Their embrace is large enough to encompass truth, justice, and beauty, and find meaning in them as in ourselves seeking experience of them.

When we analyze anima and animus complexes reductively, we usually uncover incestuous longings to regress to being child again to a parent, a little one dependent on a large, encompassing other. When we analyze the complex prospectively, asking where it leads, we often discover that our longing for "union on the biological level is a symbol of the *unio oppositorum* at its highest."[4] The conventional fairy-tale ending—where hero and heroine marry and live happily ever after—describes such a vision of unity. Oedipal resolutions touch the same vision at a younger age: a child navigates the direction of his or her sexual identity and finds, in renouncing a parental partner, a vision of a reparative wholeness in which mother and father come together to make up a whole world.

Children know at a very early age what it means to have an inner partner in dialogue or in nonverbal play. They speak to an object, within them or without, that nobody else sees or hears, an object that is very much a subject when endowed by the child with a name, that possesses physical qualities, psychological attitudes, and easy access.[5] The exchanges with inner partners often displace relationships with parents or siblings or friends. They offer a comfort and support that are often missing in the visible people around the child, and they have the conspicuous advantage of being available at any time of day or night, even when it is time to be alone, away from the world, and quiet. Furthermore, one can easily pursue audible speech with one's interior mates if that seems desirable; talking to oneself, as the world interprets this sort of encounter, is usually permitted if it is done away from company, and may even be considered charming or engaging, or worthy of that all-purpose encomium, cute.

Transference, a term that in the psychological profession is usually reserved for the analytical encounter or other meetings with a fixed program, as in the classroom, is an appropriate term to use for this experience. The child, displacing parents or older brother or older sister or other authority onto the inner object, has achieved its own commanding weight. What is not liked—whether rule or procedure or person—can be dismissed. Significance is the child's to define in people, things, or events. Long before a child has any real choice about the age or sex or behavior patterns of the people he or she would like to live with in intimacy, the child can elect or reject at will inner persons on whom he or she wants to confer authority.

Of course there are limitations here, as there are in all transference situations. But there are also conspicuous advantages, those that come with the absolute beginnings that characterize choices that are really free, choices that are not encumbered by declared, visible, and conscious restrictions. What makes the exchanges with inner partners seem so free, especially to the very young, is that they land so firmly within their own bodies. They are not abstractions. Here one meets Self and other in open exchange. Here one can fantasize at will about the mysteries of one's own identity and the identities of others, with particular pleasure when one turns over for inspection the puzzlements of the other sex, even when one's vision of the other sex is so uncertain or distorted that one can make no clear or satisfying distinction between male and female.

What counts is that the great dialogue has begun. Trust in another has been discovered, even though the other is a fictional being as the world rates the alter egos of these dialogues. The complexity of human interiority has been well entered. The question now is whether this will be built upon or allowed to go to waste in the way so much of the visionary experience of childhood has been permitted to lie fallow, or has simply been discarded, not to be reclaimed again except in the painful reconstructions of therapy or second childhood.

Transference and countertransference offer especially revealing instances of the way anima and animus work in us and the conversations they engender. Discourse abounds—between our selves and the one who carries our projected anima or animus, between their projection onto us and our egos, between us and our anima or animus, between smaller divisions of the archetypes. In analysis, the bits multiply because a patient may have to struggle, not only with her own animus, but her mother's as well. A daughter may have to untangle her feminine ego from her father's projected anima. A mad part of us may split off and then address us in the guise of the opposite sex to express our envy of another's goodness that we can never possess, symbolized by the sexual organs of the other sex.[6]

In general an analyst and analysand of the same sex gain the possibility for strong ego alliance in anima/animus issues, because they relate like to like. An analyst and analysand of opposite sexes find activated the separate ego and identity of the contrasexual archetype as they relate like and unlike. The problems that bring a person to analysis appear in both kinds of relationship, but packaged differently. In neither case do the rules apply more than generally, and they can be quickly changed and adapted for exceptions. Each analysis is its own adventure. Though many solutions to the presenting problems will offer themselves, only one will emerge as the right one for a particular person. Anima or animus fishes up what we specifically lack to find our path to the Self.

ANIMA AND ANIMUS IN SAME-SEX INTERACTIONS

A middle-aged woman screws up her courage and tells her female analyst she feels let down, disappointed, not really sympathized with or understood in the pain of her suffering in losing the affectionate company of a younger woman. The analyst agrees that that must be very hard and must bring with it anger as well. Yes on both counts, she says, but mostly feeling she has expected too much. She ventures that if she had had actual sexual relations with this woman, or if the woman had been a man, the analyst might have understood better. The loss would have been more apparent, and in any case she would have preferred a man, she goes on, claiming the preference as her own projection.

Previous conversations had touched on the same themes. Crucial bits had come to light. "Expecting too much" meant being seen as special, something woefully absent in this woman's childhood. As an adult, she always gave her untended-child part into others' hands, and invariably felt let down in the end. Now, her attraction to the young woman could not have fallen on a more unsuitable candidate to value her child part as special. The present disappointment repeated childhood trauma with her mother (reductive analysis), but also led (prospective analysis) to an insight: she could not rid herself of the child part by giving it into another's keeping, but must claim it herself, see it, welcome it, give it room at her inn. Another insight concerned the large age difference between this woman and her younger friend. She began to think of her as a daughter. Then, she felt, she could relinquish her possessiveness; she wanted, like a mother after all, a full life for a much-loved daughter. Thus she would disidentify the child part of herself from her friend. Thinking in mother-daughter terms, like a conversation between two parts of the feminine archetype, made her wonder about the young part awakened in her by her love and what future life it was leading toward.

Now she and her analyst could go further. The analyst, in her countertransference, felt an intrusive impatience that could easily communicate lack of sympathy. She sensed an animus dismissiveness, a wanting to cut into the bathos with clarifying questions and premature interpretations. She said she felt impatient with the woman's twisting of herself into a pretzel to appease her friend, suppressing her just anger at the friend's rude and mean-spirited behavior, fearful she might simply intensify the rejection. The analyst wondered out loud if her impatience was fueled by the analysand's unclaimed anger. The analyst felt she herself was carrying, in projective identification, the patient's animus, and that perhaps her own animus had gotten into the act as well. She let the patient's criticism sink in, not trusting any facile reply that came to mind.

The woman went on to other things and elaborated her suffering a bit more. After a while an image swam into the analyst's consciousness. Did connecting to her friend feel to the woman like life-giving water flowing out of her into her friend and back again, making her glad for life? Wasn't it for her like an exchange of energies? Looked at this way, her pretzel-twisting was an effort to get past a blockage on the friend's side. It did not matter much what the impediment was or who removed it, only that it be pushed aside so the water could find its natural course. Yes, exactly, the woman answered with excitement, and elaborated. After a period of quiet, the analyst asked if this coursing of waters, this exchange of energies, was not really like somehow entering the Trinity — the woman is a devout Christian — finding energy at its source? The woman gasped, and then confided, "That *is* God to me, how we experience God," and added that she had not dared to say it.

The analyst saw that in terms of contrasexuality, this woman's animus had penetrated her. She pinned her hurt and accusations on the analyst, though with care and delicacy. She did with the analyst what she had not yet done with her friend: she had used her aggression, instead of denying and projecting it, appeasing it. She had held her own, persisting in presenting her view in as related a way as she could muster. She had received her deep feelings, those of the child part, and taken care of them by sticking to them and speaking up for them. The analyst let her own impatience, her own animus dismissiveness, register and sink in. Slowly a deeper level of conversation emerged between patient and analyst that touched the woman's image of the ultimate center and made access to it easier. It is often the case with what looks like a negative animus, as in the excessive appeasing of the patient and the dismissive attitude of the analyst, that if we can submit to it without endorsing it, it will yield to the bigger view that stands behind its uncomfortable ministrations.[7]

A student analyst in supervision found this to be true when she considered her female supervisor's question: What might it mean about herself that so many of the cases she presented were of women reaching to a place of deep dependency in themselves past a defensive Amazon-like armor in their lesbian stances? The student responded. The question took her back to something unformed in her, a dependency and inertia she knew in herself. She felt again the depression and emotional starvation she had experienced in her childhood. Then to the next supervisory hour, she brought something startling that the work of the previous session had unearthed. She had been obsessed with her brother's failure to live his life. She knew she had been nagging him in true hectoring animus fashion. She could neither mobilize nor stop nagging him. She despaired. His life was going down the drain, and she was compelled to rush in even though he spurned her efforts. Connecting to her dependence and depression as a child, which her lesbian patients had brought back to her, made her vividly recognize that it had been her brother who had kept her alive. He, a brilliant, questioning, imaginative teenager, had received her adoring young sister's full animus projection on him as her hero. He encouraged her to be herself, and she had built a whole life for herself beyond the narrow bounds of her family horizon. She got out, but he, unhappily, gave up when he was sixteen. Now she was pleased to discover her own grateful love for him: "He saved my life," she said. She, loving him, wanted to do the same for him.

That was the root of the woman's nagging and obsessive concern, not a power motive or some righteous meddling, but a long-lasting, deep love. "I loved him," she said, "for being connected to what mattered, for wanting life. I feel he'll die now, unconnected, disconnected." She wrote him, expressing her girlhood love and her gratitude. Having done that, she could let him be. She had tried to bring the center to him but had not succeeded. In an unexpected way, her lesbian patients had reconnected her to a lost part of her girlhood and to her first passionately loved animus figure and had freed her from the animus obsession that had long besieged her.

PERSONA AND ANIMA

Jung remarks more than once that a man's anima compensates for his persona, showing him, if he attends to it, all the things his persona has excluded.[8] A homosexual man in his fifties sought analysis because he felt completely trapped in his persona. Working in a helping profession, he felt everyone took a piece of him with nothing left for himself but worthless scraps. The scraps were in fact really scraps, like the pieces, he said, left over after cookies had been cut out of dough. His job defined his shape. All he knew about himself other than his public face was unformed, without definition, and perhaps was only fit to be thrown out, like the pieces of dough. All things to all people, he lacked any bridge to himself. In analysis he reached the point where he could tolerate feeling all this and the discovery of a baby self that he felt his female analyst held in being. But then movement stopped. He said "We're not getting anywhere," and the analyst agreed, saying, "Round and round, nothing going in, nothing going in." That enraged him. He yelled, "You can't get into me! You can't!"

The analyst saw the two of them in their good trusting relationship, and another bristling couple present in the consulting room together. She suggested listening to the others. He yells, "You can't come in!" and she asks, "Who is this who says No?" He says he does not want her to be a woman, only a therapist or a mother. So there they are, the first pair, analyst-mother and patient-baby-self, and now the second, just emerging, a man and woman who are really ego and anima.

He discovers how much he really dislikes women; if he had a ten-inch penis, he would go around raping them. When she was a mother, he felt he loved the analyst. When he saw her as a woman, he wanted to hit her and walk out. She said they had reached a turning point. He answered: "I appreciate you holding me, but I'm not coming for solace only. I'm coming for renewal." But he is clear: he does not want to let her in as a woman. She asks if letting someone in is to become feminine, and he says, "Yes, that is the receiving posture, to be castrated." And if he were in any way to get into a woman, he knew he would be seen as inadequate. He knew, he said, there was "a big limit to my relation to God. If I don't open to you, I don't open to God."

Why would he feel castrated if the analyst—that is, his anima—were allowed to be a woman and get into him? He would feel controlled, he said. Reductive analysis traced the feeling back to his memories of his father being controlled by his mother and sister. They consistently made him feel put down too. He only felt a man when with other men. Still, his father told him it was the man's job to take care of women. But, said the patient, if he let his mother in, he would be running to her every call, even now. He would be upset when she was, would worry her worries, do all her chores, and totally forget or discount his own needs. To let her in was to identify with her, to live almost in full identity with her.

After his session, he dreams. His conflict with his analyst as mother and anima leads to an important moment of prospective analysis. He is in his analyst's office, as an adult. He lies on the floor near French doors, the analyst beside him. She says, "You won't break down, will you?" "No," he says. Then she brings over a baby and puts it in his arms as he stands up. He feels confident he can hold the baby, and so does the analyst.

What emerges in this dream is his anima beginning to hold him in being. At first, experienced as transference, it is all ego versus anima. He rapes her or she controls him; no other choice. Each can substitute for the other, but they can never cooperate. Risking the transference of this anima to the analyst, he could hate and fear her there and the anima could respond, in the figure of the analyst. That begins real conversation. Up until this time the analyst-as-mother had held the baby self, or it had been held between them. After he received the anger and fear coming across the anima bridge, he could hold the baby himself, having an inside of his own now and not just persona scraps.

THE HOMOSEXUAL ANIMUS

Some women find themselves greeted in dreams by a homosexual animus, or they project their animus onto gay men. The women vary in their dream-ego reactions. Sometimes they feel passionate sexual attraction to this figure. His inaccessibility to them may symbolize their need to involve themselves in their own sexuality. He may model for them the importance of the archetype of the double—as the one just like them—that they need to love. Other women come to understand their attraction to this gay man as giving them enough space to fully risk their own sexual desires with no fear that the man will move in on them. They can see too with such a dream figure that they are not being rejected; he is simply a lover of men. Sometimes a woman sees the figure as a weakened part of herself, something in her that is not at ease with the feminine or with women. She traces it back, in reductive analysis, to a father or brother with the same problems.

Sometimes a woman feels this figure shows hostility to her feminine sexuality, as he turns his back on it, and that she is somehow in collusion with him. One woman decided that she and her gay friend, onto whom she had projected her animus, both idealized the masculine and feared the chthonic feminine. They both went after the masculine where it was cut off from the feminine, toward a dazzling "sun-disc spirit severed from the earthly feminine." She recognized how deeply she had identified herself with this image of the masculine. It was the part of her that reached intense intellectual experience, "the best of me," she said. But beneath the intensity dwelt a rejected, disparaged feminine core where she did not feel at all like a woman. She looked down upon her body and her sexuality as disgusting, formless, lifeless, even mutilated—all the different ways, she said, to say "I lack."

The attraction to her homosexual friend felt numinous, as if they could merge and together find a new beginning. But because he forbade sexual contact, she had had to take him inside her to her feminine Self, as a symbol of the bridge she was looking for. She felt either cut off from the animus, mocked and degraded as feminine, or, with a man, she invariably projected her animus entirely onto him and as a consequence lost herself. The homosexual man seemed like a compromise solution, though a doubtful one. He did not want power over her but also symbolized rejection of her female sexuality. Both of them fled the dark, sensual, proud, powerful feminine. It would not work. Her feminine core felt broken, and she did not know how to repair it.

A startling dream-image led the way, giving her clues as to what the Self might be engineering in her strong attraction to a gay man. She dreamed that she was with him and encouraging his homosexuality. She gave him a pair of her underpants to take with him, "to go have a quick fuck in the men's room with a young boy who was with him." But a part of her felt sick and bad and as if she had the wrong attitude.

The underpants provided the clue. They were "a new pair, soft cotton with lace, covering the female part of me," she said, that is, where she differed from the man. "If he wears them, it's perverted." She saw that she was not accepting the fact that she was female, and he would have to relate to it. She felt wrong in using her femininity to service his male-to-male relationship.

This dream led her to the insight that she needed to call the masculine in her back to the feminine, not use it in an irrelevant servicing of male-to-male contact. This insight slowly translated into radical change for her. She renounced her animus identification. No longer was the bright masculine spirit the best part of her, though she did not altogether disclaim it. She struggled to set it within her feminine self where it belonged, as her contrasexuality. Whatever her body was—even if it seemed disgusting to her and broken—it was what it was and she would claim it. Thus she embarked with great courage on the hard work of alternate mourning and rage as she reclaimed the feminine ground out of which she lived and was content now to live. The animus shifted to support her feminine self instead of attacking it, to accept its primary task of making a bridge to her center.

Identifying the center in his life, discovering something about its nature and what lay behind it, and learning to live with the half-knowledge that seemed to be all he could acquire of it, preoccupies Marcel Proust in *A la recherche du temps perdu*. He is so earnest in his probing of the drama of sexual compulsion and so ingenious in his presentation of the theater in which it is acted out, that we can easily lose sight of the larger pursuits of the writer. He is meticulous in his detailing of the manners, the settings, the movements of the plays and the players, both the homosexuals, whose performances he knew so well, and the heterosexuals, whom he had observed with such care and whose practices he understood almost as well as he did those of his single-sex *confrères*. He is equally finicky about bringing alive the geography of the early-twentieth-century France in which his sexual revels took place. But still, though we are often enchanted by the travelogue and almost always moved by the logistics of sexual combat in Proust, the larger event, the one we do not quite see, the progress toward or regression from the center, is surely what accounts for our devotion to the book. For many of us, it possesses in our adult years the magic we felt in childhood in *Alice's Adventures in Wonderland*, which assures endless rereadings and a determination, like Proust's own, to remember things past, his and ours.

Proust's great complex novel is, whether by intention or not, a *paideia* of human sexuality. Everything Proust had learned about the subject, from childhood to his adult years, is crammed into the book. His description of his Aunt Léonie talking to herself captures Proust's own experience, lying in his cork-lined room, compiling his massive primer of the sexual life: "In the life of complete inertia which she led, she attached to the least of her sensations an extraordinary importance, endowed them with a Protean ubiquity which made it difficult for her to keep them secret, and, failing a confidant to whom she might communicate them, she used to promulgate them to herself in an unceasing monologue which was her sole form of activity." Marcel, too, cannot keep a secret; everything he knows is committed to paper. But what he knows is not enough. He must keep pushing, hoping to understand what it is that draws him and others to love; why jealousy, separation, and death hover over sexual life; why the making of a book, a painting, a piece of music is so imbued with sexual feeling; why that feeling can range in intensity from that of a trivial distraction to a profound *raison d'être*.

Proust's questions are not always asked in so many words, but they are omnipresent in the *Recherche*. We see this in the way he begins the central sexual narrative of his book, as Albertine turns up in the narrator's life. He picks her out from among a group of entrancing girls on the beach at Balbec, dark, smiling, pushing a bicycle, and sees her glance as "aimed from the centre of that inhuman world which enclosed the life of this little tribe, an inaccessible, unknown world to which the idea of what I was could never attain or find a place in it." We can dismiss Marcel's conviction that he is bound to be rejected by the tribe, and especially its most alluring figure, Albertine, as the normal timidity of adolescent sexuality. But there is more here as everywhere in the sexual epic: there is a push to the unknown that lingers in the eyes of Albertine, something far beyond their material beauty. He sees in them "the dark shadows of the ideas that the creature is conceiving," what she knows of the world, and "above all . . . her desires, her sympathies, her revulsions, her obscure and incessant will."

He does not find satisfying answers to his questions in his sexual encounters with Albertine or his thousand fussy intrusions into her life, in separation from her or in reconciliation, in any part of her life with him, or her death. His contemplation of her body as she sleeps brings some understanding. His attempt to run down and make sense of her widely attested lesbianism leads nowhere. He does at last reach a general sense of what she represents in his life in the great, long, elegantly crafted outpouring over Albertine's death—psychological, philosophical, prayerful—that makes up the first third of *The Fugitive*, the penultimate volume of the novel. He can say with conviction that he had, "in seeking to know Albertine, then to possess her altogether, obeyed merely the need to reduce by experiment to elements meanly similar to those of our own self the mystery of every other person." He knows now how mistaken he had been in thinking, in the low moments of this relationship, that her death would be his "deliverance." He is intent to discover, now that she has gone, what his whole recollective enterprise is about and therefore not to let anything of consequence escape his memory of the time he spent with her. That will, *in time*, free him to forget her and allow him in the perspective of a graced recollection to see finally "that my love was not so much a love for her as a love in myself." Then perhaps he can cast aside even that reflection on that day when, like all mental states, oblivion must overtake it and "everything that seemed to attach me so pleasantly, indissolubly, to the memory of Albertine would no longer exist for me." He would inevitably cease to treasure her memory or anything associated with her: "It is the tragedy of other people that they are to us merely showcases for the very perishable collections of our own mind."

How his book belies him! It makes the collections of his mind imperishable, especially as they touch the significant women in his life and their places and atmospheres—Albertine and the sea, Odette and the Bois de Boulogne, Gilberte and the trees at Tansonville, the Duchesse de Guermantes and the stained glass of the church of Saint-Hilaire. The impulses and strains and gatherings-in of the anima life have not often been so fully, so scrupulously narrated, puzzled over, dismissed, or accepted. The leading place of contrasexuality in the fashioning of an inner dialogue is presented here in remarkable detail. We could construct a guide to human interiority from Proust's epic. In doing so, we would learn how sexual circumstances, like all the other significant moments of our lives, can move us toward our centers.

Let us say, as surely we must, that Albertine is really Albert, that Gilberte is Gilbert, that for all the contempt that Proust heaps upon Baron de Charlus, his own identity and the *recherche* he conducts into it are focused upon the homosexual. Still, his contrasexuality remains fixedly anima-driven; his examination of sexual relations, his impulse to sexual identity, and his bias of sexual observation all point to the feminine as it operates in a man. If we turn to positive purpose his words about Charlus's homosexuality, we see the anima wisdom Marcel has accumulated upon the subject without ever denying his own predilections. For he, unlike the Baron, has not "refused to see that for the last nineteen hundred years ('a pious courtier under a pious prince would have been an atheist under an atheist prince,' as La Bruyère reminds us) all conventional homosexuality—that of Plato's young friends as well as that of Virgil's shepherds—has disappeared, that what survives and increases is only the involuntary, the neurotic kind, which we conceal from other people and disguise to ourselves."

Marcel describes his journey to save worthy homosexuals from perdition as a trip to hell without guidance or support: "The poet is to be pitied, who must, with no Virgil to guide him, pass through the circles of an inferno of sulphur and brimstone, to cast himself into the fire that falls from heaven, in order to rescue a few inhabitants of Sodom!" There is no saving grace in this work; it requires of one the same austerity as it does of "the unfrocked priests who follow the strictest rule of celibacy so that no one may be able to ascribe to anything but loss of faith their discarding of the cassock."[9]

It is a description Patrick White could subscribe to. The Australian novelist, who made no effort either to hide or to proclaim his homosexuality, was not at any greater ease in homosexual circles than he was in the heterosexual world. He saw pretensions and denials everywhere in human sexuality; he also saw, as his characters and plots make clear, opportunities for the compassion that comes with a deepening of sexual knowledge and a moral firmness. His brilliant performance as a novelist learned in the ways of the contrasexual archetypes invariably brings those who pay attention a large understanding of the contradictions and complexities of sexual identity. In his most considerable outing in this area, *The Twyborn Affair*, we see displayed the multiple pirouettings, the calculated separations, and the random reconciliations of the *complexio* and the *coniunctio oppositorum*.

Eddie Twyborn's *Affair* is with himself—and Creation. If at times they seem to be the same entity, put that down to the wit of Patrick White, who persists in his idiosyncratic way in seeing men as women and women as men and the twain constantly meeting. Eddie is an Australian soldier, and very much a he. He is Eudoxia, the "charming young woman (daughter, ward, wife, mistress—whatever)" who belongs in some doxyish way to an aged Greek, and as such is very much a she. Eddie also turns up in wartime London as a bawd, after his adventures as a male and as a female, now under the name and the proprietorial clothing of Eadith Trist, and rich with the wisdom gained from his several sexual lives. For once, "he/she," that barbarism of casuist rhetoric, might be appropriate, but fortunately for the sensitive reader, White indulges in no such false solemnities. Nor does he huff a hermaphrodite or puff an androgyne into place. No elaborate explanations mar his parable of contrasexuality. In trousers, skirts, or whatever item of apparel fits the occasion, Eddie's virtuoso sexuality is well equipped for all the matchings and mismatchings of a world better prepared for the disguises of sexuality than for its realities.

In skirts or trousers, Eddie is eager to learn. From Angelos, the elderly Greek, comes the confidence, imparted to Eudoxia, that "men are to women as apples to figs, the clean and the messy among fruits." She will not argue the point: "He disgusts me at times—this sensual Greek whose every hair rouses me." Working as a jackeroo, a hand on an Australian farm, Eddie pursues his sexual education with Marcia Lushington, the owner's wife. When he first sees her, she reminds him, like a parody of the Song of Songs, "somewhat of a raw scallop, or heap of them, the smudged ivory flesh, the lips of a pale coral." A poetics of food carries Eddie's dialogue with himself to pleasant thoughts of Marcia, who has made advances to him: "After eating a ration of cold mutton alone in the cottage, he began regretting his decision not to let himself enjoy Marcia's cooked meal, her down pillows, the warmth of her body."

Soon enough, Eddie is glad to extricate himself from all the farm cookery, from the homosexual thrustings of Don Prowse, the manager of the place, from the heavy graspings of its mistress, which inexorably couple gastronomy and sexuality. When he leaves Marcia for the last time, she is staring, in a caricature of Solomon's Song even more to the point than the earlier one, at a "breached cake, its yellow more unnatural, its pink more lurid in the evening light." His parting shot with the farm manager is a sexual exchange that starts out of a feeling of shared suffering, "to resuscitate two human beings from drowning," and ends nastily as Eddie's "feminine compassion" disappears, "shocked into what was less lust than a desire for male revenge."

Eddie finds he must accept the closeness of the two sexualities, Prowse's and Lushington's, and the male and the female, the anima and the animus, in himself. He discovers slowly, and we discover with him, in outer confrontation and in inner dialogue, how much he is like both his parents, his withdrawn, sometime lesbian mother, who really likes dogs more than people, and his father, Judge Twyborn, whose masculine authority is proclaimed by his mustache and whose feminine warmth embraced his young son when they traveled and slept together.

The book makes its way through bawdy house and blitz to a reconciliation of sorts with the conflicting sexualities that Eddie has known in himself almost from birth. But first, as he moves in the persona of Mrs. Eadie Trist into brothelkeeping, he must practice detachment. In an oddly fitting way, this last part of *The Twyborn Affair* imitates the movement of the soul in mental prayer to union, beginning with Eadie's purgation: "She was too disgusted with herself, and human beings in general, ever to want to dabble in sex again, let alone aspire to that great ambivalence, love. She could only contemplate it as an abstraction, an algebra." When she has her company of whores assembled, she decides that she "would expect them to obey what she saw as almost a conventual rule. If she had been artist or mystic enough, she would have inspired her troupe, or order, to chasten with boredom and self-examination those whose lust they indulged. As she was chastened by her own unrealisable desires."

Illumination comes with the recognition of her attachment to Lord Gravenor, the object of her unrealizable desires. He is a patron of the brothel, if not its patron saint. She will not altogether break through the clothing of her disguise for him, and so he must practice a brothel asceticism. He explains: "The reason I keep coming back is for you — not any of your boring whores. Risking every bone in my body with some thrashing negress, exposing my parts to an angular Midlands schoolteacher. If you won't let me fuck you, darling, what I enjoy is the supper, or best of all, breakfast when you cook it for me."

They do get away to his country place, splendidly named for this disquisition on sexual disguises — "Wardrobes." There Eadie returns in dream to being Eddie. As she must now accept the male beneath the madam's skirt, she comes to accept and to cherish qualities in Gravenor that recall the Judge's tenderness and bemustached authority. When she returns to London, for the union that completes her triple way, she makes her peace with the world of disguise the brothel signifies, which possesses its own kind of innocence, and with her mother, for whom innocence is not exactly the defining word. Sitting in church together, mother and child examine, open, and close each other's illusions. Mother asks: "Are you my son Eddie?" Child slashes her response on the flyleaf of a prayer book: "No, but I am your daughter Eadith." After a suitable pause, mother says, "I am so glad. I've always wanted a daughter."

Eddie tries, later, to make his way in the "brick no-man's-land" of London under German attack to keep an appointment with his mother in her hotel. The bombs fall. He loses his hand, which it takes him a moment to recognize as his own, and lives for another moment, just long enough to say to the imagined presence of the woman now in charge of the brothel, "Fetch me a bandaid, Ada." His mother, back at the hotel, insists upon waiting for her child. In a brief bright flow of her stream of consciousness, a lovely moment of inner dialogue, she completes the circle of the archetypes and asserts the blessedness to which even so tangled a sexuality as hers and her son's may be heir.

> Eadie said I must not fail Eadith now that I have found her Eadith Eddie no matter which this fragment of my self which I lost is now returned where it belongs.
> Sitting in the garden drying our hair together amongst the bulbuls and drizzle of taps we shall experience harmony at last.[10]

ANIMA AND ANIMUS AND MARRIAGE

Marriage therapy offers a special chance to see anima and animus in action, for there are always two couples in the room with any one couple that seeks counseling: the husband and wife and their contrasexual partners, or more often foes, at least to begin with.[11] Discerning the anima/animus couple provides a useful leverage to the analyst to pry open the work to be done. The contrasexual pair reflect the unconscious life of the marriage. Just as in any analytical situation, the analyst must look to see what the unconscious says in dreams, symptoms, and fantasies about therapy itself, so in marriage counseling, the anima/animus figures offer guidance to the progress of the work. They summon us to attention.

Inner marriage in a person, between ego and contrasexual archetype, or its inversion, inner strife, elicits the same anima or animus presence, reflected then in the outer manner. An obvious negative example is the man dominated by his anima who feels forced to exercise dominion over his wife, to keep from going under. The same choice is often made by the woman who controls her husband as a way of dealing with her own inner salvation, where prognosis turns on whether the husband is stronger than his wife's animus, not necessarily in any one quality—brains, brawn, or lung power—but the possession of his own individual identity and connection to the Self. Then he cannot successfully be bullied by her or she by the "him," the animus, in her. On the wife's side, her best freedom flows from knowing herself as distinct from her husband's anima, yet able to remain on friendly terms, in easy meetings with "her." This is especially important if her husband's anima is barely differentiated from his mother. For then, he will inexorably fit his wife into the maternal mode, which just as certainly will sabotage her sexual connection to him.

Perfect marriages can turn sour at any time. Balzac, who is a master at depicting obstacles to idyllic relationships, gathers almost all of them together in *Cousin Bette*, one of the last of the completed volumes of *La Comédie humaine*. The centerpiece is formed by a Napoleonic officer, Hector, Baron Hulot d'Ervy, a figure of some size in the government of Louis-Philippe, and his wife, Adeline, a woman of great beauty and decency, plucked from a peasant background to shine in her husband's glowing light. She satisfies her husband's anima predilections for earthy young women; he pleases her animus thrusts toward enhanced suffering. They manage twelve good years together before the Baron's gargantuan sexual appetites go on the attack. The marriage fades a little more with each of a series of mistresses, and goes to pieces with his liaison with Mme. Marneffe, the genius of the species. All of his family—children, brothers, in-laws—suffer, as Hulot grabs anything in sight to support his appetites, which prove more demanding in his sixties and seventies than they were in his youth. His rivalries with other adventurers seeking young Parisian flesh that is only too eager to be found demand more and more money. He borrows, he bribes, he steals, he forces his honorable brother-in-law into a situation in Algeria, in which all the poor man can do to uphold his honor is to kill himself. His own brother, a Marshal of France, does what he can do to extricate the Baron from the abyss of his appetites before dying, broken by the ordeal.

Adeline Hulot is appalled by the overtures of the Baron's chief rival, Célestin Crevel, who looks at her not-so-young flesh with quickened appetite, both for the flesh and to take revenge on her husband for having stolen a mistress from him. But well before the last scene, she will offer herself to Crevel, awkwardly, touchingly, in a frenzy to save her husband, her children, the world of appearances and whatever goodness might still be alive in them. She is a rank failure as a courtesan, but her willingness to do anything to support her husband does move Crevel. The one she cannot reach is her husband, for all his tributes to her sanctity, a fulsome flow of words available at the prick of an emotion. He is off, with Crevel and his son-in-law and a Brazilian nobleman, in the race for Madame Marneffe. But the race is fixed. No one can win, not even the master of manipulations, Valérie Marneffe herself.

Valérie plays sexual *doppelgänger* to Adeline's Cousin Bette, who is angry that she was not chosen as a wife by the Baron or somebody of similar rank and fortune, who feels demeaned by having to live on the charity of the Hulots, and is determined to bring their noble house down. Bette's collaboration with Valérie, who is as alluring as Bette is repellent, is grounded, the two women think, in Machiavellian principle; the great Florentine name is invoked several times as they plan their assaults. In fact, their maneuvers are closer to the *Psychopathia Sexualis* than to *The Prince*. Each of the two women knows how to tempt and whom to tempt. Each, the ugly and the beautiful, is abundantly supplied with animus weaponry. Valérie uses her contrasexual fullness to lure men into her cave; Lisbeth, to give Cousin Bette her baptismal name, uses her "masculine qualities" to good effect with both men and women. Her "feminine energy" easily forms an "alliance," we are told, with "masculine weakness." Bette may hate her cousin for having achieved so large a place in the world, but she can say of Adeline with a conviction that we feel as much as does Crevel, to whom the words are addressed, "Yes, my cousin is still beautiful enough to inspire passion. I should fall in love with her myself, if I were a man." But the warmest words she addresses to woman, about woman, are reserved for Valérie, as she puts her arms about her waist and kisses her forehead: "I share in the enjoyment of all your pleasures, your good fortune, your dresses. . . . I didn't know what it was to live until the day when we became sisters."

Such outbursts of feeling, normal to the Valéries and Bettes of this world, do not come easily to those who live by the conventions of schooled behavior. Adeline is voluble and all but sanctimonious in expressing forgiveness for her husband's malefactions, but she rarely has words of any sort for her own feelings, let alone the claim they might have on the Baron. Just once, disturbed enough to be open for a moment to herself and all that has happened to her, she lets herself ask Hulot, "Tell me how those women contrive to make themselves so attractive." She would like to do what would please him, she says, if he will just tell her: "Why have you not taught me to be what you want? Is it because I am not clever? There are still men who think me beautiful enough to pay court to."

Balzac records no response by the Baron. He offers instead his own conclusions about the twofold love that elicits joy: "The virile, austere pleasure of the most noble faculties of the soul, and sex, the vulgar commodity sold in the market, are two aspects of the same thing." We should admire women who can appease both hungers: they are "geniuses in their own kind" and uncommon, as rare in fact as "the great writers, artists, and inventors of a nation." Clearly Adeline Hulot is not such a woman. While hers is better than a copybook virtue, and she does spend some years before the end of her life helping women who have fallen on desperate times, she is ill equipped for the complexities of marriage. Her tolerance of her husband's sexual adventures approaches collusion in them. The ease with which she falls victim to Bette, and to Valérie behind her, looks at times like a restless masochism seeking a place to land.

Inversion is the rule in *Cousin Bette*. There is often more of love and marriage in the affairs of the courtesans than in those who think they are observing the sacraments. These are women true to their sexual profession, if not exactly honest brokers. They have taken the measure of their time, in a France bourgeois and bureaucratic as never before, and have created a virtual *nomenklatura* of bawdry. The stars of the profession know and learn from each other, frequent the same places and the same men, and are determined to be high sexual achievers. They are capable of disinterested sacrifice, and positively sentimental at times, as the most considerable of the baron's mistresses before Valérie, an opera star as well as a courtesan, demonstrates in finding a hideout and supporting life for the Baron at the point where he has lost all resource.

The studied devotion of these women to their affairs, each one for as long as it may last, is what one might expect of thoughtful married women; it makes the marriages of their Paris appear extramarital by comparison. Mme. Marneffe seems for a while to be the most skillful of the *Cousin Bette* troupe, but she is an overachiever; she has lost touch with her contrasexual self in her eagerness to organize and dominate the lives of five men. She cannot distinguish well enough among her men any longer; her plottings become too dense and elaborate. As the bureau chiefs of the KGB came to know, disinformation can only be allowed so much tether, so much complication, before secrets leak and control falls apart. There is, furthermore, an eagerness to be admired that almost always accompanies the sense of one's indomitability, and that simply destroys secrecy and the plots that depend upon it.

Valérie suffers from all the limitations of the species. She is more than found out; she is defeated by her fiery Brazilian admirer, a negative animus figure who becomes even more inflamed in his determination to bring her down. He will give "the most deadly of animal poisons" to a young girl who will infect him in the course of their coupling; then in the same way he will infect Valérie, who will pass the poison on to Crevel, now her husband. And so it is done. The cure for the poison exists only in Brazil; they are in Paris; mission accomplished, and with a fine application of the Dantean doctrine of *contrapasso*—you get just what you asked for, in greater abundance and with more intensity than you might have thought possible. Valérie wanted to live and die in sexual embrace; she does just that.

In a kind of ceremonial madness, Montes, the Brazilian, smashes everything that he can put his hands on in the room where he is making his plans. One of the courtesans comments: "*Orlando Furioso* sounds very well in a poem; but in a flat he's just Roland in a rage, plain prose— and plain expensive!" She's right about the cost, but not the style. Montes's fury exacts, as it is destined to do, a poetic animus justice. The insane imbalance to which Valérie's sexuality has brought her requires a matching madness. The poison eats her body up; she shrinks to nothing. But in her last moments, it is her soul that worries her—"There are worms for the body, and what is there for the soul?" She warns Bette, as if her inner conversation has just come alive at the point of death: "Do not trifle with sacred things, Lisbeth! If you love me, repent!"

The Baron is incapable of more than the rhetoric of repentance. Reconciled to his wife, the "reformed prodigal father gave the greatest possible pleasure to his family. He was quite finished with life and worn out, of course, but full of sensibility, retaining only enough of his old vice to make a social virtue." In a short time, everyone feels "completely reassured." Then his daughter hires as a kitchen maid a girl from Normandy, "short, thick-set, with stout red arms and a common face . . . as well-furnished with fat as a wet nurse, bursting out of the cotton cloth that she wore swathed round her bodice." One night, Adeline awakes to find that Hector is not in his bed. She is afraid. She discovers murmurings and sees light coming from the girl's room. She hears her husband say, "My wife has not long to live, and if you like you can be Baroness."

Adeline cries out, drops her candle, and moves quickly to support her husband's prophecy. Three days later, as she is dying, she grasps the Baron's hand and whispers to him, "My dear, I had nothing left but my life to give you. In a moment you'll be free, and you will be able to make a Baroness Hulot." And then, we are told, "a phenomenon that must be rare, tears were seen to fall from a dead woman's eyes. The fierce persistence of vice had triumphed over the patience of the angel, who on the edge of eternity had spoken the first word of reproach of her life."[12]

The ironies are bitter. Reproach is reduced to a statement of fact; now the Baron can once again reach down to the peasantry for his Baroness, which is exactly what he does, anticipating in his pursuit of a coarse-skinned, rawboned young anima figure, as he has several times in the tale, the nymphet predilections of Nabokov's Humbert Humbert. The patience of Adeline, somewhat acidly saluted here, has been that of a fallen angel, a parody of noble forbearance. No devil could have succored better the vice around her. Love, as Scripture reminds us, is as cold as death, but not dull-witted, not always fearful to speak its mind or open its heart. There can be very little love in a marriage that suffers anything rather than admit reality. That way lies only an abuse of fine feeling and a desertion of identity. The result is not marriage but a denial of it.

If either one of a married couple is completely divorced from the other's anima or animus, they are apt to find life together fearfully humdrum, without any zest, passionless. The question must be asked why each gives the other such wide berth. Have they settled into Mom and Pop roles, or Hansel and Gretel as married siblings? They can be sure something will swoop in to disrupt this childish idyll—either a witchlike force or a smashing affair. It happens not only to well-placed figures in the *ancien régime*, but to very ordinary people in very ordinary times.

Anima and animus figure decisively in typical sexual problems every couple faces. A man ready to make love precedes his wife upstairs, lights a fire in the fireplace and jumps into bed far under the covers, naked. It is cold. Wife enters, demands to know what is he doing in bed. Why not before the fire? Why does he never aggressively make love to her? For all the heat, his desire turns cold, feeling supoenaed for a court appearance. And he is angry.

What is happening here? She panics before her own wish to make love, and before this only too palpable other. She does not connect to her desires and fears, but her animus throws up the thickest possible smoke screen. Like a princess imprisoned by a dragon, she cannot free herself, but depends on her prince not to fall for her defenses, somehow to be stronger than her animus scoldings, to feel her desires hiding behind them. For this she would be passionately grateful. But he does not want to try to seduce a woman unless certain of success. With the easy compliance of his anima, he turns woman into permission-giver, as if he had no right to any sexuality unless she allowed it. This, in turn, nullifies her sexual response. Instead of melting, she must be vigilant to maintain the atmosphere of constant reassurance he requires. This soon enough turns into a clucking mothering of him. The result is zero sexual contact. In each of such persons, the anima or animus acts to insulate them against connection rather than offering a bridge to the feelings rising from the center. If a husband could see this in his wife, he would be enboldened sexually. If a wife could see this in her husband, her sexual panic would be calmed and she could happily begin melting.

The husband in another couple in similar straits dreamed of a huge barricaded castle with a woman locked inside, his anima. Suddenly he saw that there was the tiniest possible opening in the castle through which his dream lady was letting out a little piece of string that might show the way in to her. When his wife bombards him with You should's, and Why didn't you's? and You must's, he feels the castle walls grow thick enough to resist any invasion on his part. That his wife is usually correct in her judgments only makes it worse.

The wife in this couple is caught up in obsessive-compulsive reasoning about what should be the case. That she is often right makes it harder for her too. She cannot differentiate herself from the animus complex dominating her. She is only too much like a woman trapped in a castle surrounded by a dragon of opinionated certainty.

The two, husband and wife, work hard to rescue each other. But glimpsing the unconscious contrasexual part, each in the other, helps more. Bright and quick, she sees immediately how her approach, correct judgment by correct judgment, only walls up the little place his anima has to let down its string. Her own dreams tell her much. There is a starving woman who feeds everyone but herself, a baby who hangs itself, her own husband collapsing just before a long-anticipated planning session in which they expect to lay out the rest of their lives together, and then quietly recovers when he gets away from her. All communicate the hunger and despair in herself and make clear that her deliberate way of going at her husband simply will not work. "What happens to you," the analyst asks, "when he goes away?" She knows the answer: terrible fears, no nourishment, no future, a feeling of great loss. That releases her compulsion. Her nagging of her husband is not because she wants always to be right or in charge, but to defend against all that she fears. When he sees this, he is emboldened to follow his own way and to tell his wife more about it, to help her with her fears.

This couple, like others committed to long-term relationship, profit immeasurably from seeing the unconscious anima or animus, each in the other, and the battles each seems condemned to fight with their own complexes. That just is: it is psychic fact, not rejection. Often they can help each other out. This man remembers that what he complains of now is what most attracted to him to his wife originally, her keen intelligence, her wild imagination and passion to see things through to conclusion, no matter what. That is the enlivening side of her nagging. She recalls the man she looked up to way back then, his mind, his different easygoing rhythms, his sly hints to her, like the little string showing the way into the castle. Letting anima and animus into the dance drama makes it come alive, reach to happy climax.

Some couples reach to the farthest castle of all. They discover enjoyment in a reversal of roles while simultaneously keeping their own. They do not substitute the new for the old role. They enlarge to fulfill the demands of both. They know a lot of fun in approaching the other in terms of the opposite in themselves. The woman turns out to be the Beast, fierce, hairy, marauding, the man, the delicate Beauty; the man, the lovely flower, the woman, the rake who plucks it. Man and woman, anima and animus, together transfer and countertransfer the different parts of themselves, not to substitute or replace them but always to add, to increase, to enlarge. The many levels of conversation they enjoy, each of them, within themselves and with the other, fill the space of their relationship with play. The eternal element central to love enters. The doors of the anima/animus castle are wide open.

Acting Out Animus/Anima
and Its Alternatives

SEXUAL ACTING-OUT in analysis, as in so much of our lives, poses one of the gravest dangers to analysand, analyst, and the work itself. People know this, worry about it, try to ward it off when they can. Why, then, does it happen? And happen it does, often and to many, not just to sociopaths who exist in all professions, but to decent persons who make every effort to do their work with care and integrity.

ANALYSTS AND ANIMUS/ANIMA

Most analysts know the experience of feeling inhabited by some bit of anima or animus a patient has projected onto them. They know, too, the countervailing move of falling into identification with their own contrasexual parts. A male analyst in supervision describes taking on his female patient's positive animus: "I began to feel brilliant!" he said. "And to say too much about myself." Doing good work, he caught himself. He was in good relation with his patient, but still her next dream caught him again. In it, she came into his office and saw too many of his private things openly displayed. A female analyst in supervision says she can tell when her animus takes over: "I fizzle up with excess energy and start babbling, lecturing." Another male analyst brought into supervision the fear that he was falling in love with a female analysand, who fit his own anima image perfectly. Working on his own fantasies enabled him to find where the patient had touched wounds in him. That also gave him information about the patient's wounds.[1]

A female colleague confided that she fell in love with her male patient because he was "dead" as a person. That touched the dead place in herself. What should she do? She answered for herself, "Nothing. Just go on analyzing." Such were her standards that, when pressed, she believed there was no possibility ever to find herself in relation to this man except analytically. Even if he should stop treatment, she would never see him. Her role in his life was as analyst. Who knows—her projections may have made the first live contact in years for this man. Through her countertransference to him, libido came across the contrasexual bridge to both of them. For her, it was a rescuing mission to the dead spot in herself. Anima and animus projections tell us how our libido is engaged and where the Self is luring it; they encourage us to venture across the ego-Self bridge.

THE MIDDLE SPACE

These examples are routine, easy to handle. Flammable situations that threaten to go out of control occur when complete projections of the contrasexual archetype fly onto the analyst, or from analyst to analysand. Such an intensity of emotion, sexual desire, and spiritual longing builds up that it must ignite. What is going on here?

A bridge is being built to the center, through rough material, sometimes torturing detail. The center of a person's woundedness, in Balint's language, is the "basic fault." Culver Barker calls it the "critical hurt"; Robert Stein, the "incest wound"; Heinz Kohut, the "narcissistic wound." In Jung's language, the ego feels weak, vulnerable, not at all intact. We are dangerously exposed there, bruised, perhaps still bleeding.[2] There the powerful Self with all its images of unity, wholeness, healing, and kinship with others rushes in. But instead of our ego relating to this inrush, it merges with it. Rather than developing flexibility to regulate its intake, digestion, and response to this energy, the ego glues itself to the Self energy, inflates with it, feels driven, puffed, and intoxicated with it. Then, when some event or person penetrates and punctures our inflated state, or a lapse occurs in the analyst's attunement to us, we feel our wounds are beyond repair. Everything presents our vulnerability to us. We feel gaps in ourselves, great holes, an abyss in which we see nothing but chaos, meaninglessness, death in life. No wonder some patients want to stuff their analysts into that abyss! Anything to staunch the flow of pain, the agony.

Jung talks about this place, magnetic to all things good and bad, in terms of incest, filling out Freud's Oedipal theory with his own thinking about what incest symbolizes.[3] Desire pulls us in two directions at once: backward to the womb, to the supporting enclosure we knew as children in our parents, that pre-ego unity, which, if we can find it again, will relieve us of life's struggles; and forward, to union with our own inner being, with others, with the world. Numinosity then makes a full arc from our earliest beginnings as seedling child to our most advanced fullness as a whole being. It reaches past our wounds to our core sense of the Self.

It is a demanding and often disheartening process. No matter how developed we are, we still know a nagging anxiety, a depression that seeps into our bones, a failure of nerve, the shame that comes when we think of risks unlived and petty treacheries committed. To feel in analysis some other person touch those places, see into our suffering, abide with us in the face of our shame, evokes awe and gratitude in us—and more. To know that another sees that somewhere in us we dare and we love, that somebody recognizes our small acts of kindness, and understands that in us flames of originality can be kindled, engenders excitement about being alive, the thrill of Being itself.

The drive toward wholehearted participation in life, we see, does not just turn on ourselves. In the middle of it, boldly facing us, is connection to other people. The move toward wholeness is away from ego toward Self. An analyst carrying us onto our anima or animus bridge represents the entire world of otherness, those we love, those we barely know, society itself. Jung underscores the experience: "That mysterious something in which the inner union takes place is nothing personal, has nothing to do with the ego, is in fact superior to the ego because, as the self, it is the synthesis of the ego and the supra-personal unconscious. The inner consolidation of the individual is not just the hardness of collective man on a higher plane, in the form of spiritual aloofness and inaccessibility: it emphatically includes our fellow man."[4] In sum, as Jung says tersely, "the soul cannot exist without its other side, which is always found in 'You.' "[5]

This middle space is the place where we sort out the crucial meetings of our lives. We do not simply dwell on our wounds, however painful, or our nostalgia for home and parents, our kinship with others, our reach into the universe. In that space, we conduct our conversation with our own soul, rooted in our own body. The body takes on new importance as a limiting set of boundaries, our finite container. Our inner conversation is not with something general or abstract, something vaguely out there beyond us. We know ourselves, in such interior dialogue, as fixed in the here-and-now, in this life, in this particular biography, in this place, in this time. We cannot indulge ourselves in soothing maxims, in high-sounding but essentially hollow platitudes. We must face the concrete facts of our physical existence, of our psyches where they live, for it is there that the infinite touches us. Our body brings us consciousness of the extraordinary *thisness* of life.[6]

It is the force of the body they inhabit that makes the projections of anima and animus in an analytical relationship flame into passion. The body insists on having its say about the soul's wounds and putative unions. These must not come in abstract terms, the body insists on telling us, but with the inner feeling, the outer texture, the full panoply of physical and psychic facts of sexuality and contrasexuality in us. When a female analyst dreams of wanting to embrace her male patient's suffering, she must look to her own vulnerability that her patient's wounds symbolize. For her wounds too need her embrace. Her psyche has borrowed his suffering to make that point in her. The danger is that she may fall into identifying her inner figure with her outer patient and think that that is what he needs and act out her inner desire in the analytical relationship. Even if that is what he needs from someone, her dream reminds her by its rearrangement of office furniture so that the scene no longer resembles her actual place of work, that it is symbolic, not literal, in its details. She must, as every analyst must, work and work on her own complexes and projections, her own wounds and longings of soul. That is the very basis of analysts' work, as rudimentary and as toughening as dancers' daily exercises.

If a male patient, stammering out his feelings for a female analyst, also has the guts to say that at that moment he feels his genitals lubricating, we get an immediate sense of how hot this place can become. Similarly, in a negative response at least obliquely related to the first, a patient can say he or she feels "fucked" by an interpretation the analyst makes, or "raped" or "sexually poisoned," to quote just a few. All this is felt in the body, in the wound, in the expanding place of inner conversation that the body shelters. In this space we conduct conversation with our selves, with the Self, with our soul as the immortal dwelling within our bodies.

The Self is an archetypal lure in these conversations. It calls us out of ourselves by pulling us more deeply into ourselves. If we feel received in this talk, it is because we are simultaneously honest with ourselves and with God or whoever it is we think might be listening to us, anima, animus, Self, phantom friend, or lover. We conjure up Being in some form to address, but we never forget that we are also talking to ourselves. We know how inexact our words are to convey all we feel, but we are driven into this conversation and will not quit it simply because we are ineloquent or at a loss for the precise locution, and recognize as we frame our words and listen to ourselves saying them that, in the memorable excuse of stumbling politicians, we have "misspoken" ourselves. If we are old hands at this interchange, we may achieve the sense of the transcendent coming to meet us that the Russian poet Marina Tsvetayeva expressed in a "Prayer" written when she was seventeen. She pleaded for a miracle from the very beginning of the day and then to be allowed to die when all of life was opening like a book for her.

She has her miracle. She feels she can ask for everything—the soul of gypsies, to be allowed to walk alongside songs, to be a robber, to ache for the world as an organ plays, to run off to war, to be an Amazon. With such fullness, and having been graced with her youth, she is ready to die. Thus speaks not a girl, but a young woman, gifted with the courage of her animus convictions. Fifteen years later, drawing on the same contrasexual strengths, with a keener ear and a more secure grasp of her poetic skills, she writes a poetic manifesto that is also a prayer in verse. Three monosyllables say it all for her—"*Och!*" for difficult things, "*Ach!*" for the wonderful, "*Ech!*" for things that cannot be accomplished. "Confess it, poets," she says, this is the way it is. How does the great king respond to the Shulamite's fiery display in the Song of Songs? *Achnuvshii Solomon*—"Ahhhing Solomon"—thus the monarch speaks the all-purpose sound, *Ach*, for joy, astonishment, wonder, hope. With *Ach*, an ecstatic heart bursts; with *Och*, a drayman yokes his cart (in the Russian alphabet, the word is written *Ox*). *Ech*! is Tsvetayeva's response to an unstopped faucet of words. She longs for the *Ach*-ing of Polovetsian herds; she intones a warm *Ach* thinking of a gypsy camp. Finally, she invokes primordial times, and a raw, unformed flesh that cries out *Och*! *Ech*! *Ach*![7]

Sound was the informing element, not only of her poetry, but of the inner dialogue from which it sprang. In "A New Year's," a poem written to Rainer Maria Rilke two months after his death in December 1926, as poet to poet, she cries out to him where she knows he is, in Eden, his new dwelling place: "Here's to new sound, Echo!/Sound, to echo new!" She wants to know what the place is like, how he feels, in this "Positively, absolutely first/Eye encounter of the universe." She has all sorts of questions—Is Eden hilly? Terraced? How does it feel to write at his "new spa"? She signs off: "Here's till we meet! . . . Let's not miss each other—drop a card," and fervently salutes his new attention to resonances in the afterlife, one poet to another, "Here's to your new sound-recording art!"

Tsvetayeva knew Rilke only through his poems and her friend Boris Pasternak's warm talk about him and the letters she exchanged with him in the spring and summer of 1926, after Pasternak put them in touch with each other. She never met him in the flesh, but she knew his person, his inspiration, the sound and spirit and sense of his poetry. She knew that Rilke had been besotted with the literature and art and people of Russia ever since his two trips to the country with Lou Andreas-Salomé, in 1899 and 1900. He had met many writers in those journeys, including Tolstoy; had quickly learned the language, had translated from it, even written poems in Russian. He had thought for a while of moving to Russia, perhaps "for good," he wrote the publisher Suvorin: "I love your country, love its people, its suffering, and its greatness; love is the power and ally of God." But Rilke's name apparently meant nothing to Suvorin, who never replied to the poet's letter.

When Rilke wrote Tsvetayeva, however, a reply was in the mail within days. "You, poetry incarnate, must know, after all," she wrote, "that your very name—is a poem." Her German was fluent; she had lived with her family in Germany as a child. She could be eloquent in the language, in which she had read much, and importunate in her own imaginative way: "What do I want from you, Rainer? Nothing. Everything. That you should allow me to spend every moment of my life looking up at you—as at a mountain that protects me (one of those guardian angels of stone!)." He was Germany for her, and "Listen, so you'll know," she wrote him, "In Rainerland I alone represent Russia." He could take that and more from her, at least to begin with; he found her deeply moving: "You, poet, do you sense how you have overwhelmed me . . . I'm writing like you, and I descend like you the few steps down from the sentence into the mezzanine of parentheses, where the ceilings are so low and where it smells of roses past that never cease. Marina: *how* I have inhabited your letter."

The words were rapturous, from her to him always, from him to her until the last of their exchanges in August 1926. Then he was made uneasy by her insistence on being his "only Russia" and on banishing Pasternak from their confabulations. "I object to any exclusions," he wrote. But whatever silence he kept—and the leukemia which was soon to kill him made writing increasingly difficult—he was with her to stay, an archetypal incarnation, "a miracle," as she wrote him, "after all: you—Russia—I." She pursued in him that love of hers, drenched in feeling, endless in imaginative extension, that required no physical expression or even meeting: "Love lives on exceptions, segregations, exclusiveness," she wrote him in her last letter; "Love lives on words and dies of deeds." She had been clinging to the hope of coming to see him with Pasternak; she did end the last letter with the words "I take you in my arms." But she was not reaching out to him; he was already with her. She was holding onto him where he was so much alive and full of spritely energies for her, inside her, inhabiting her, as he had said he was in her letters. He was not her phantom lover; he was a real presence within her, a numinous masculinity; he was her animus connection.[8]

Anima and animus connections make us feel, in the flesh, here and now, that we converse out of our doubled sexuality. Another voice enters, different from ours, beginning from a different departure point. The conversation occurs on many levels at once. We know a rhythmic interchange between lavish identification with the All and a discrete separating into a sharply defined *this.* Our attention enlarges and intensifies to embrace wholes; it contracts, when necessary, into sharply delineated parts. We bring our attention to little things, so that we can link them to big ones. We focus with a new precision that can pierce to the heart. Whether we call them that or not, we are experiencing male and female ways of being.[9] We receive; we penetrate. We make our mark and feel marked by the interchange. A lively imagination thrives here in a personal self dwelling with others, fed by tradition, eager to add to it original flavorings. This is the space where wholeness achieves the shine of the new that comes with the putting of parts together. It is a level of creative living out of a self that transcends psychic structure, as Masud Khan says, that goes beyond the id-ego-superego model of the psyche. It is the space, as Hans Loewald says, where primary-process unity and secondary-process differentiation find their balances; the space Winnicott calls "transitional," the one Jung points to between ego and archetype, the space from which prayer originates.[10]

All this—the danger and the delight, the wounds and the urge to wholeness, the body's insistent presence and the move far beyond— goes on in this flammable space of transferring and countertransfering anima and animus. No wonder we are warned so strongly against acting out.

ACTING OUT

Acting out, like so much in the life of the psyche, moves in self-canceling ways. Its first move is to translate analytical intimacy into a sexual intimacy. Fantasy becomes reality—and loses its own reality. The conversation a patient conducts within herself or himself, which the analyst is privileged to listen in on, is broken in upon, disrupted, scattered to the winds by the sexual action.

Except for the very small minority of cases where the two persons, analyst and patient, stop analysis to begin a relationship well outside its boundaries, this sexual action leads nowhere. Sexual acting-out by analyst and analysand brings neither deeper analysis nor actual intimacy. It usually flares up and dies out. The analytical work must be lost unless the patient can somehow retrace, with this analyst or another one, the steps back to the point where analysis left off and sexual interaction began.

Retracing of this kind is almost unbearably arduous work, requiring endless time and patience to work through the turbulent emotions.[11] Very often, and with good cause, the patient feels betrayed, enraged.

Analysts involved in such sorry dramas must reckon with their own angry and remorseful reactions to their failures or to those of their colleagues. Temptations to judge against self and other, to rant and to rave, to condemn, abound. Sometimes a way back cannot be found. Not only is the original analysis lost forever, but analysis itself, as a therapeutic resource, may be irretrievable. For instead of entering into the patient's inner conversation, lending not just an ear but the full range of his or her own responses where they meet the patient's work, the analyst has interrupted that conversation or substituted one of his or her own.

When we remember that the analysis of transference must go on reductively, tracing the childhood wounds that are being transferred onto the analyst, we see that acting out the sexual dynamics inherent in the process amounts to a kind of child molestation.

We must remember that analysis also proceeds prospectively. Alongside its retrospective retracings, it asks where a transference is leading and what purpose it serves. Sexual acting-out can steal from a patient future wholeness with Self and others. Analysts who insert themselves as substitutes for appropriate partners in intimacy can promise nothing. They are not available for future life outside the consulting room. The issue goes beyond ethics to the basic terms of the profession. Analysts, like writers, must train themselves to work with elements in the psyche that are often simultaneously grubby and alluring, or even alluring in their very grubbiness, without surrendering to them.

Analysts, like writers with their characters, must allow their patients full freedom with their qualities, grubby or alluring or whatever. Nothing should be allowed to interfere with patients' conversations, either with their analysts or with themselves. The analyst must accompany a patient's psyche wherever it leads, no matter where, observing, understanding, feeling, but neither joining in nor standing aside from the disagreeable.

Analysts must recognize what a range of human nature they must deal with, just as writers must. As Chekhov explained to a critic affronted by a coarseness he saw in one of his stories, a professional who has to deal with human reality cannot be overly fastidious or judgmental. Chekhov associated himself with "Homer, Shakespeare, Lope de Vega, the ancients generally who did not fear to grub in the 'dung-hill,'" the critic's word for the world of Chekhov's story, "Mire." A writer is "not a confectioner," Chekhov explained, "not a dealer in cosmetics, not an entertainer; he is a man bound, under compulsion, by the realization of his duty, and by his conscience; having put his hand to the plow he must not plead weakness; and no matter how painful it is to him, he is constrained to overcome his aversion, and soil his imagination with the sordidness of life." Nor should a writer look down from his superior perch—social, moral, whatever—at his subjects: "To be condescending toward humble people because of their humbleness does not do honor to the human heart."

And so it is with the analyst, who must face every divagation and deviation of the human that presents itself in the consulting room with something that at least resembles equanimity. That does not mean to collaborate in dubious behavior or to condone it; it does mean, some of the time at least, a suspension of judgment, and all the time a sense of moral proportion, which is another way of saying a sense of humor. Chekhov again offers instructive example, in the notebook he kept in the last twelve years of his life.

What he recorded, really, was himself talking to himself, often to his contrasexual self. "That sudden and ill-timed-love-affair," he tells himself, "may be compared to this: you take boys somewhere for a walk; the walk is jolly and interesting—and suddenly one of them gorges himself with oil paint." Then there is the man with two wives, each in a different town. Arguments and threats follow him; telegrams are sent. He feels suicidal, which brings him to a solution: "He settles them both in the same house. They are perplexed, petrified; they grow silent and quiet down."

Chekhov's notations of human behavior encase a strong morality, but one that is strong enough to make its judgments simply in the form of what he chooses to record, with only such conclusions as the facts themselves proclaim. For example: "An officer and his wife went to the baths together, and both were bathed by the orderly, whom they evidently did not consider a man." About another military man, it is enough to say, "A certain captain taught his daughter the art of fortification." As sexual principle, he offers an epigram: "Women deprived of the company of men pine, men deprived of the company of women become stupid."

His sexual observations are as entertaining and as enlivened by anima perception as the dialogue in his plays, where he shows such fullness of understanding of sexual identity and the range of behavior that springs from it. "A man who cannot win a woman by a kiss will not win her with a blow," says Dr. Chekhov, who even in an abbreviated medical practice had seen his share of sexual abuse. In the same order of observation, softening his dyspepsia with humor, he defines "an unfaithful wife [as] a large cold cutlet which one does not want to touch, because someone else has had it in his hands." But, we remember, there are many sides to this sort of marital situation. There is for example, N., who has "learned of his wife's adultery. He is indignant, distressed, but hesitates and keeps silent. He keeps silence and ends by borrowing money from Z., the lover, and continues to consider himself an honest man."

Chekhov can offer, in good temper, "a plump, appetizing woman: 'It is not a woman, it is a full moon.'" He can describe another woman as not having "sufficient skin on her face; in order to open her eyes she had to shut her mouth, and vice versa." Of the other sex: "When Y. spoke or ate, his beard moved as if he had no teeth in his mouth." There is the man who imagined his wife to be, not the person she really was, "but always, for some reason, a stout woman with a large bosom, covered with Venetian lace." And there is his own related mad dream: "When I become rich, I shall have a harem in which I shall keep fat naked women, with their buttocks painted green."

Though he would have been the last to claim the achievement for himself, there is wisdom in Chekhov's insistence on scrupulously honest and open observation of the world outside himself and inside, opening everything up, as much as he could, with the senses of the soul as well as those of the body. There is no technical language in his writing, no talk, say, of "sexual dynamics," though jargon had begun to impede serious discussion in the medical circles of his time almost as much as later it was to do in the psychoanalytic profession. This is what he has seen, he tells himself—and us. He gives us two whole lives in a brief exchange, without comment. We can find the etiology of a dozen possible sexual dysfunctions in the dialogue, but it is up to us to find it; he is content to let the people speak for themselves.

SON:	"Today I believe is Thursday."
MOTHER:	*(not having heard)* "What?"
SON:	*(angrily)* "Thursday!" *(quietly)* "I ought to take a bath."

MOTHER: "What?"

SON: *(angry and offended)* "Bath!"[12]

Sometimes the analyst becomes the patient's victim. A patient may have in him or her a need to defeat the other utterly. Seduction is the means. Arduous sexual efforts really mask a determination, out of an insistent inner demand for power on the patient's part, to bring professional ruin upon the analyst. The analyst will need, then, Chekhovian fullness of observation and scrupulosity of behavior to defuse the situation and escape victimization.

Denial is one of the great resources of an analyst who does not or will not understand anima/animus intrusion when sexual tensions arise in analysis. Sometimes the denial takes the form of pretending that the tensions do not exist, are not really there. More often the sexual feeling is dealt with by trying to talk it to death, often in high-toned spiritual language. The pretending will break down, sometimes explosively when a patient lunges at an analyst, generally more quietly, as the patient simply leaves treatment. Nattering on about "the sexual dynamics" of the situation is a surefire way for an analyst to smother a patient's inner conversation.

These anima or animus contents are alive and kicking, however, and neither analyst or patient, nor both in collusion, can altogether gather them into words. This will be apparent when sessions run over, or phone calls between sessions become necessary when the patient "must talk" to the analyst. The body has been denied and only words are left to carry this enormous load. It will not work. And it must damage the analysand, who can be bound just as securely to the analyst by a lofty verbal spiritualizing as by a physical exchange.

What remains is acting out, whether the anima-animus interaction is physicalized or spiritualized. Both are false to the psyche. Both deny the fullness of fact. In the acting out which takes the form of pretentious verbalizing, the analyst's uncared-for needs creep in to control and bind the patient by what, for all the flood of words, remains unvoiced. One woman, seeking a woman analyst after her work with a male analyst had run aground at an anima-animus impasse, said she felt that all her psyche was working at was feeding his needs.[13] She felt that her dashing ways delighted him and even found herself fantasizing becoming a better partner to him than his own wife. Another woman analysand complained that her confiding to her analyst the full range of image, body feeling, wound, soul longing, myth, and symbol in her psyche seemed to animate his being, not hers. It did not return to her in any way or find itself held between them so that she could look into it and find the bigger Self mirroring her there. It was as if he were "eating it excitedly," she said. She felt "mentally fucked." That offended her as a woman, not really made love to, and as an analysand, not honored as a patient. It killed in her for quite a while the possibility of trusting in anything that resembled sacred moments of communication.

Another woman gave herself and her problem of enacting the role of a man's anima into her male analyst's keeping, while all the time doing exactly what she always did, playing the part of his anima. She saw in retrospect that instead of analyzing it, he fell for it. Once again, she got away with avoiding the construction of an inner bridge for herself by synthesizing one for the man.

A patient's need to revenge himself or herself on a former analyst with the next one can turn ugly. To analyze the dodges, the tricks, the denials of a patient means to uncover where his or her ego fell into identification with a contrasexual figure. That inquiry inevitably disrupts the tone of harmony and excitement between analyst and analysand. A female analyst found that out when she asked her male patient, who was bringing her flowers every session, for the other foot too—his negative feelings. She got his anger all right! And no more flowers. But also no more denial.

Acting out is always a form of denial. Psychoanalysis attests to it; modern drama confirms it. From Ibsen and Strindberg to the theater of the absurd, playwrights delight in showing the follies of those who act out their difficulties without ever inspecting them in detail. What is more, they seem to tell us, a course of therapy would not do them much good; they are too committed to the drama of their lives and too determined to act it out without interference, as Pirandello demonstrates with crackling irony in *Six Characters in Search of an Author*. In the last moments of the play, the son of the family that provides the six characters rails at his father: "Have you no decency, that you insist on showing everyone our shame? I won't do it! I won't! And I stand for the will of our author in this. He didn't want to put us on the stage, after all!" The manager of the acting company protests—"You came here. . . ." The son insists it was the father who wanted to come. There are cries, a great sobbing; the son describes the little boy of the family, who is "watching his little drowned sister, in the fountain!" A shot is heard from behind the trees where the boy is hiding. The terrified mother screams, "My son! My son!" and yells for help. The boy is carried off by some of the actors. One group of actors says that he is dead; another, that "it's only make believe, it's only pretence!" The father answers with a "terrible cry" in his voice: "Pretence? Reality, sir, reality!" Then the manager brings the curtain down by repeating the father's words, adding bitterly, "Never in my life has such a thing happened to me. I've lost a whole day over these people, a whole day!"[14]

But the six characters—and all others who insist on acting out without reflection—may have lost their whole lives. That is the terror that hangs in the flies over the stage of this "Comedy in the Making," as Pirandello calls it. That is the equal tension, without visible relief, that accompanies Gregers Werle's relentless pursuit of "the claim of the ideal" in Ibsen's *The Wild Duck*, a pursuit that drives a young girl to suicide and leaves those who remain as walking dead. Reformers who act out, like Werle, are the worst in the long list of Ibsen's villains, the real enemies of society, for they encourage quick, confident, thoughtless pushes ahead in the name of their rhetoric-infested causes.

The spokesman for a recollected sanity in the play, Dr. Relling, is given its last wise words. He is speaking of the hapless father who in his constant acting-out has everywhere followed Gregers Werle's lead. When "the first grass" appears on his daughter's grave, says Relling about the father, "you'll hear him delivering himself of fine phrases about 'the child torn untimely from her father's heart,' and see him wallowing in emotion and self-pity." Werle objects: "If you are right and I am wrong, then life is not worth living." Relling's answer is concise in its wisdom: "Oh, life would be tolerable enough, even so, if we could only be rid of these infernal duns who come to us poor people's doors with their claim of the ideal."

The duns, the debt collectors, and their easy marks are almost always, in the dramas of acting out, people of ill-defined sexual identity or without comfortable access to their inner selves. They cannot keep their own counsel and so must search out others for advice, usually the wrong ones, or if they are the right ones, when it is too late. Hedda Gabler, the very model of a woman pursued by her animus, turns to all the wrong people, having married the least fitting of men for her, leaving herself finally with no recourse except that splendid symbol of her military father's virility, one of his two matched pistols. John Gabriel Borkman, in the play named after him, has not known how to choose between two sisters or where to find balance in his Napoleonic approach to finance. When, after a term in prison for embezzlement, he tries to make peace with his wife, the particular sister he chose in marriage, the other sister's appeal remains to remind him, though only in fitful thrusts of his unconscious, of his failure to deal with the lure of the feminine within him, what we would call his anima. He dies *in* the cold *of* the cold.[15]

The examples multiply; the identities become more muddled. When they shriek to emerge, as they do in Strindberg's domestic dramas, the best they can hope for in the way of disentanglement is a last moment of decent sentiment—saying "Look after my children!" or "Forgive them, for they know not what they do"—before the final silence of a stroke, like the Captain in *The Dance of Death*, or the parallel event in the life of his progenitor, the Father in the play of the same name, who at the end of his misery falls with a cry into the lap of his old nurse, just after explaining to her that he's not praying to God but to her, to send him to sleep: "I'm so tired. Good night, Margaret. Blessed art thou amongst women—"

It is the woman outside or the woman within who must bring ease to such men, who alone can send them comfortably off to sleep. They are arrested, in their relations with women, at the stage of nurse or mother. Their lovers, married to them or not, ask too much, often by asking too little. Not enough is out in the open. When truths are exposed to clear view between lovers, as in Strindberg's trilogy *To Damascus*, so are their nasty edges. The Stranger, who is the plays' central figure, is challenged by the Lady, his love object in the Expressionist drama. At midpoint in the middle play, he asks her if she has called him. "No," she says. "I only drew you. I didn't want you." The wounds continue. He reproves her for talking to him as if she were sure he would fail in his undertakings as a writer. "I am sure," she replies. "Torment me in some other way, dear Fury," he tells her: "Try to say something cruel that the other one didn't say." She understands: "You mean your wife. Charming of you to remind me of her." His response is crucial to the drama: "Everything that lives and moves, everything that is dead and stiff, recalls the past."

All that is alive and all that is dead bring us inexorably back to the past, Strindberg's magnum opus testifies. With some such certainty, we can go forward; without it, we merely act out, thoughtlessly, senselessly. So the very structure of the trilogy proclaims, moving from deconversion from belief to reconversion to deconversion to reconversion, until the Stranger in the last scene of the third play cries, "Enough! Or we shall never end." In fact, Strindberg is saying, as he does in all his mature plays, we shall never end, we must not, we cannot, it is not ours to choose to do. The Student says as much at the end of *The Ghost Sonata*, to speed the dying Daughter, his contrasexual other half, on her way: "Unhappy child, born into this world of delusion, guilt, suffering, this world that is for ever changing, for ever erring, for ever in pain! The Lord of Heaven be merciful to you on your journey."

We are deluded, we err, we suffer, but mercy may yet be ours. Heaven and earth are an opposition awaiting reconciliation, a union expecting dissolution. In the last scene of his last play, *The Great Highway*, Strindberg moves more tersely than before over the same territory. His last testament is given to a final incarnation of the chase after beatitude, a figure named the Hunter. As always in Strindberg's dramaturgy of combat against the content of denial and its complementary form, acting out, the sexes meet in contrasexual parallel. The Hunter hears the voice of the Woman, to whom half of this scene in the Dark Wood is given over, asking, "Is it dark?" He repeats the question, which cannot make sense to him, for clearly it is dark in the Dark Wood. She enters and explains: "I ask, because I cannot see. I am blind." The Hunter wants to know whether she has always been blind. "No," she answers. "When the tears ceased to flow, my eyes could no longer see."[16]

There is much more to come in the scene, but nothing that significantly deepens or enlarges these words. We must observe very carefully, this exchange tells us, or we are liable to draw quick, foolish conclusions, another kind of acting out. If we judge this particular woman's question about the dark as foolish, we are blinder than she is. If we deny the pain and suffering of this world and our tears cease to flow, still another way of acting out, we must indeed be blind, whatever an eye test may say. Of course, there always remains the alternative wisdom of Lucky in *Waiting for Godot*, which, if it is not the ultimate acting-out, is the acting out of the ultimate: "Given the existence as uttered forth in the public works of Puncher and Wattmann of a personal God quaquaquaqua with white beard quaquaquaqua outside time without extension who from the heights of divine apathia divine athambia divine aphasia love us dearly with some exceptions for reasons unknown but time will tell. . . ."[17]

The theoretical question of countertransference turns on how much an analyst will act the gratifier in response to a patient's deprivations. This bears as well on how central a role an analyst's countertransference plays in treatment. If countertransference is at center stage, chances are the analytical couple has also moved to center stage, seeming to put the analyst on offer as a better object than any in the patient's life. But it is a sham offer, for the analyst is not available in this way. The patient too may confuse the interchange by wanting to talk as if the analyst-analysand relationship is a "real" one, but resenting it when the analyst makes real-life responses.

In general, countertransference works best when it is allowed to work its own way silently into a patient's life.[18] The patient in all his or her settings, personal, social, political, religious, is what matters. In the anima/animus situation in particular, it is dangerous to call too much attention to transference or countertransference actions and reactions. Caught up in their responses to each other, both patient and analyst can lose sight of who they are and what they are meeting to do. The analytical couple then may replace the ego-Self couple, the process of analysis substitute for the process of living, and the Self and all the larger aspects of life simply disappear into an inaccessible latency.

ALTERNATIVES

How can we become conscious of anima/animus interactions without becoming fixated on them? How can we use them instead of being used by them? How find connection through them to the imagination, the spirit, and a fullness of body life? Here, of all places, we should not look for blueprints. We must accept the special qualities that define the intimacy of the analytical relationship, in which anything can be admitted to discussion and nothing to acting out. The river that may bubble up from their work must be allowed to flow into the patient's life and the analyst's separately and in very different ways, but not into a life lived together in the world. The aim of analysis is to enable life, not to substitute for it.

Still, the meetings must elicit genuine participation on both sides. Patients find it intolerable to have their love reductively reduced to a phase in treatment. As Jung puts it, "A doctor must go to the limits of his subjective possibilities, otherwise the patient will be unable to follow suit. Arbitrary limits are of no use, only real ones." What, then, are the real limits? Jung offers a clue: "No longer the earlier ego with its make-believes and artificial contrivances, but another 'objective' ego, which . . . is better called the 'self.' No longer a mere selection of suitable fictions, but a string of hard facts, which together make up the cross we all have to carry or the fate we ourselves are."[19]

The hard facts of analysis are the strong, deep reactions, of intense friendship or love, feelings which may some of the time include a sexual excitement that the Self initiates to bring about change in the analysand. Facing such feelings, consenting to them in the odd but real way of analysis, despite their irrationality and decided inconvenience, will take patients back into the wounds that brought them to analysis in the first place. Surprisingly, that place of suffering and illness often turns out to be the shortest route to a patient's analytical destination, to coming home to small self and large Self.

When an analysand touches that center, or some place close to it, the analyst touches it too, feeling the rawness of old wounds and remembering experiences of the Self. The patient may feel for some short while that the analyst is himself or herself the bridge to the Self, embodying, as he or she does for the moment, anima or animus. All the numinosity of the contrasexual figure and its possible connection to the center fills the consulting room; if only for the briefest moment, each of the persons there is touched and changed.

The changes must be allowed to flow into two separate lives. The analytical relationship possesses its own history and place in each life, but its purpose is to go beyond itself, to support the patient's life now and in the future and to enlarge the analyst's life as well. Both must avoid that sickening dodge that the relationship is unreal because it cannot be acted out. Each must find the toughness of mind and generosity of spirit to use its intensity and protect its warmth without abusing its privileges.

A male analyst reports in supervision that an Indian woman in treatment is accusing him of denying that he loves her as she does him. He says he knew he did not in fact love her, in the sense she intended, but then he wondered if he did, and felt almost hypnotized by the effect. What, he is asked, struck him so strongly? "The feminine courage I saw in her, the fact that she did not hide her vulnerability and would not meekly accept what I said without challenging it." What moved him so deeply was that this woman, notable for fragility, could speak so boldly out of her center, was willing to expose her feelings and challenge him upon whom she was dependent in treatment. Here was a woman with her own phallic strength, held firmly within her, so that she could both show her vulnerability and penetrate him in her questioning.

That touched his own fragility, a wounded place left by his mother, who could never exert anything like a centered or centering boldness. In moments of stress, she always collapsed and wept, especially in tense moments with his father. The analyst's fear that his woman patient might hypnotize him came from reacting to her for the moment as if she were his mother, but a newly repaired mother, strong, able to claim what she thought belonged to her. Recognizing, then, what lay behind his urge to believe that perhaps he was in love with his patient after all, he could respond in his own way, a much more related one. He allied himself with her ego, the wholeness in the woman that allowed her to speak out of what she felt as she got hold of the penetrating strength in herself. Now he could join in as analyst and help her aim it where it belonged. The woman's urge to union was transferred to uniting with this animus part of herself that she had projected onto him. His reconstruction of his feelings for her was transferred too, to work at healing the hole in himself that was his internalized mother. The Self works its wonders in one person and always evokes an equal and opposite response in others, exposing what is hidden, strengthening what is weak, providing the sustenance for sexual and contrasexual identity.

That shrewd keeper of a thirty-year notebook on *The Human Province*, Elias Canetti, knows the difference that the Self can make in an analyst's—or anybody else's—wavering attention: "The most embarrassing illusion of psychoanalytical treatment is listening eternally to the patient." For too many, "only that is heard which is already known before [the patient] even opens his mouth. He could just sit mutely through every session." But really listening "brings one to completely new thoughts." Resist, Canetti says, that "pose of listening" which is "arrogance, nothing more. The changes and schisms in the doctrine are due to the few moments in which someone forgets himself enough to listen."

Observation, honesty, attention, and steadfastness are what are called for: "The trick is not to fool oneself about certain things: small rocky islands in the sea of self-deception. Clutching them and not drowning is the utmost that a human being achieves." If one's attention strays, maybe wanders over and over again, there is still a kind of rude comfort available: "All the things one has forgotten scream for help in dreams." As for the more conventional way of remembering called memory, it is "good because it increases the measure of the knowable. But we especially have to make sure that it never excludes the dreadful." Something we hold onto in memory may be softened in the remembering or may be no better than it actually was; all we can be sure of is that "nothing is ever past." And that, says Canetti, is the point: "The actual value of memory lies in this insight that nothing is past."

The interior confabulation is not negligible, nor to be tossed aside lightly: "It still is something to have lived, thought, and fought with oneself, even if no one else ever finds out about it." Canetti supports putting things down on paper in much the same way, though he does it in the third person: "Every word he writes down gives him strength. No matter what it may be; it may be nothing; but writing it down gives him strength." The respect he has for what the Self may communicate, not only in words, but in ways that go beyond them, is tersely summed up: "Everyone ought to watch himself eating."[20]

In a long, successful analysis, the Self inevitably enters and makes itself known in anima/animus interactions that sometimes break out into speech, or playful moments in which it is fitting for a male patient to talk of sending his female analyst a valentine. Patients often complain about the one-sidedness of the analytical conversation. Only they are burdened with uncovering all their fantasies and embarrassing secrets. Only they have the courage to bare their sexual feelings for the other, the analyst. Altogether too much one-way, they complain. Here they are, vulnerable and exposed, while the analyst remains unknown, with stories untold, feelings unvoiced. Hard-working patients who are also hardheaded ones can feel justly pleased that in this odd asymmetrical relationship with the analyst, they bravely took the risks involved in uncovering so much. For their efforts will yield at least as much again in the revelation of where their reality lies and how to claim it and live it.

On the other side, a matching if not identical vulnerability exists in the analyst. The analyst too is opened, even exposed, in the meetings with patients and needs courage to admit vulnerability on his or her side, and to deal with it. What is more, that openness and its accompanying vulnerabilities must enter an analyst's life as thoroughly, as willingly, as hopefully as a patient's.

Analysts, too, may feel left behind, burdened, holding a roomful of accumulating transference. If the treatment goes well, all that has burgeoned in the consulting room is picked up, tended to, gathered into the patient's life to be lived, no more to be analyzed. Then the analyst who has served as the patient's bridge to reality is likely to be dismissed, and rightly so. The bridge has worked its purpose. It can be dissolved. The patient is free to live a life, to find or extend a love that can be acted upon.

Analysts can often tell how thoroughly they have been involved—or have not—in work with a patient if the patient suddenly breaks off treatment. The analyst now has much to work through to bring the analysis to closure. In the more usual treatment that reaches its own natural conclusion, the analyst relinquishes the bridge function, not feeling left behind, recognizing with joy the patient's renewed life. If any analyst feels deserted, robbed of something when a patient terminates, then it is clear that the analyst has neglected his or her own life.

To live one's own life as an analyst is to feel daily, year after year, decade after decade, service to the Self. This may sound grandiose, but it is the grace of the analytical vocation. The sense of enlistment in a large service emerges from ordinary moments of analytical sessions, in the choice at one point to keep silent, at another to speak out, to interpret, to keep covered, or to reveal something personal that is unmistakably apposite. All these are little moves, guided by a central question: What does the Self want? What is it moving us to do? A kind of loving exists in the work of analysis, which finds its outlet in the service of the Self. Where lovers love each other in the Self, analysts and analysands love the Self in the other.[21]

The best defense analysts have against either acting out or feeling deserted is to live their own lives with the utmost passion and daring. The best defense against being conscripted into a patient's fantasy is one's own reality, secure in one's own body, one's own history, one's own experience of the Self. Even when that is less than a patient's capacities, it is still enough; it fits one's own psyche. That is all one needs. In this fidelity on the part of analysts to their own being, patients find their best protection; it communicates a loving kindness that is in itself a healing process.

Borderlines, Bluebeard, and Death

THE ANIMA and animus are themselves liminal figures and thus particularly helpful in dealing with the difficult issues of the borderline condition. There we often meet an animus so discontented it turns into a Bluebeard figure eager to cross the ultimate border, death, with its victim. The very nature of anima and animus positions them on the borderline between personal and collective life. The composition of the particular contrasexual figure that is ours will show the influence of our parents and the images of masculine and feminine dominant in our culture. The function of these archetypes, to make a bridge for us to the Self, can be defined in general terms, but the way they do so is not only directed to us as individuals, but to us in our most idiosyncratic behavior.

The contrasexual archetypes in effect hop from foot to foot, with one foot as the personal unconscious, one as the objective psyche we share with others. Thus animus may reflect the cruel interventions of a molesting stepfather, and then, precisely because of that trauma, an impersonal, larger-than-life mythic Bluebeard figure may invade our psyche. Our struggle to deal with animus or anima gives us in such ways connection to what lies beyond their personification. They leave us a legacy that may become our best preparation to face death.

BORDERLINES

Anima and animus often manifest the harsh negativity of the borderline condition in such destructive ways that one may feel split at the center, assailed by competing views that will not suffer reconciliation. Life threatens to fall apart. We despair at ever putting the pieces together into some kind of workable whole. Yet the same anima and animus, as bridge, may also facilitate the constructing of a whole and give us our surest way to see that what is special to us will end the confusion and heal the split.

There is nothing abstract about the borderline condition, though it is almost as difficult to describe as to experience. A person living and suffering in this territory stands on the borderline between neurosis and psychosis. There are no precise categories here. A person may use psychotic mechanisms but not behave in a way that can be classified as psychotic. Clinical observation refutes the neat arrangement of diagnostic categories in this condition where persons may at any time move back and forth between phenomena long isolated as neurotic or psychotic, and thus appear to be both or neither.

Otto Kernberg describes the borderline personality as a stable pathological fixation, at a weak level of ego organization in which identification, idealization, denial, splitting, and projective identification—no less—predominate. Pregenital strivings for emotional food to provide the nutrition of security and cohesion conflict with a child's Oedipal strivings for pleasure and power. Because of the sense of deprivation at the root of this suffering, these conflicts occur under "the overriding influence of aggressive needs."[1] As adults, such people present special problems, sometimes agonizing ones, in analysis, because their ego-weakness and inclination toward transference psychosis make what might counteract all this, regression in treatment, intolerable to them. In transference, they act out their instinctual conflicts and aggression. What might appear a working through of conflicts may be no more than repetitive gratification that will accomplish nothing except keeping the pathology intact. Using Jungian terms, Schwartz-Salant points out that the Self in these patients appears dead or absent because the borderline person cannot house the Self in daily living. Instead it is overridden "by power drives and compulsive states."[2]

It seems to us that a moral problem may also play a significant part in this network of conflicts and indistinct categories. In cases where good, sustained work has been accomplished, analysands may still resist taking up as inner structure the conversation they have so ably and for so long carried on with their analysts. The conversation with the Self, at the patient's end, has been given over to the transference relationship. One woman said outright she did not want to carry on this inner conversation or to use her analyst symbolically. She preferred the analyst to do it all. This was not a matter of any lack of ability on her part; this was pure choice. It raises the interesting question of our freedom at any time and in any circumstance to say No as well as Yes to the Self.

Because anima or animus functions first to open up and then bridge the space between ego and Self, it makes their conversation possible. But the archetypes can also slip across the borders at any point. It is as if borderline persons had no bridge available to them to span the distance to another side. The bridges just seem to start and go nowhere. They collapse, go into the sea, run aground on the mud, disintegrate. The animus, for example, may appear more split than usual, in mutually excluding roles. One woman contended with all these animus personifications: bad father, good sex partner, sadistic men, homosexual animus. Utter confusion and despair afflict such patients.

One woman reached to her despair in a dream landscape. Before her stretched endless miles of ash-gray, bombed-out land, littered with dead trees, fallen animals, corpses, and battered refugees wandering like ghouls in the broken landscape. The sky was dark; nothing was growing, nothing existed as far as the eye could see. The dreamer fell into identification with the despair pictured in her dream and felt herself one of the living dead. Finding a set of images for her forlorn feelings opened the possibility to her of relating to this state instead of drowning in it.

Another woman, plagued with feelings of insecurity, dreamt repeatedly of houses without walls, ceilings, or floors. That aptly depicted her state of being to her. Over a prolonged period, she took heart from dreams that gradually added walls and floors and roofs to her houses, undergirding her sense of sustained conversation with herself. The dialogue and the person were, finally, housed.[3]

The animus figures for persons experiencing such suffering frequently turn up as murderers; their anima opposite numbers, as diseased or deranged. All these figures are elusive, slipping in and just as quickly out of consciousness, in and out of dreams, or appearing as partners in one's life.

The borderline condition is exacerbated if patient or analyst seeks to ameliorate it by adhering to the defined behavior of a functional, earthbound ego, which can be expected to develop in stages from the foundation of a reasonably good mother relationship. One sets standards, then, which deny the gap over which borderline people must fashion their lives. They have never had a holding, grounding parent to woo them into being and lovingly assist the successive developmental stages. Even should the analysis fill in that hole, it will not be the same as having had it knit into one's bones and blood. Such persons know a chasm as a central part of their personal history, built into their foundation. To deny that is to drive them crazy. To think it can easily be repaired is at best a folly, and at worst a cruelty. There is another approach, we think, that is not only constructive and healing but also makes accessible the quite wonderful gifts such people often bring to the world.

The borderline ego can be imaged as an archipelago, reflecting the splitting off of opposing states of emotion into little islands that is typical of people suffering this condition. In one session they succeed in a tremendous breakthrough; in the next they cannot recall that it ever happened; the other islands do not exist for them any longer. But all the islands of the psyche are in fact connected to each other under water. They are not so split up as they appear; connections exist well beneath the surface, where everything is mixed in with everything else. That is the condition in which such a person lives—islands on top, merged below. The borderline ego, then, is not the cohesive, grounded one of most people, with clean separation from the waters of the unconscious. This ego is a string of islands that arise from, rest in, and stay connected in their home territory, under the waters of the unconscious.

In illness, such a person appears to hop from island to island, split up into severe separations and discontinuities. In a typical experience of working with persons suffering the condition, they will say No to every Yes and Yes to every No. No substantive ground to build on exists. Another pattern of borderline behavior is to totally identify with one view at a time, discounting all others; there is only one island and they are on it—there are no others. The ego remains univocal in such cases, utterly inflexible, without any perspective from which to see the archipelago of the whole.

Projective identification of the anima or animus can assume psychotic proportions. The analyst becomes for the patient the animus who brings the Self into the analysis. The analyst does not symbolize Self functions or realities but is equated with them.[4] That leaves the patient's ego impoverished, for everything, including any capacity to connect to goodness or wholeness, is seen as entirely belonging to someone else, never to oneself. One woman suffered such a love for her male psychiatrist, in what amounted to delusional transference. Many, many months of ensuing work with a female analyst were taken up with separating everything that had been merged together—her ego and animus, her animus with the male analyst, and he and her animus with Self. Another woman reaching to differentiate the sadistic part of her animus projectively identified it with her female analyst. Her analyst, overestimating the strength of the woman's ego in the face of this animus attack, went on operating out of their long-standing and patently good ego alliance, failing to catch at first that interpretations now felt to her patient like sadistic attacks, amounting, in the intensity of invasion she felt, to rape. A chart of the ways in which the animus is handed back and forth offers a reliable map of this difficult terrain. We learn, too, to watch for the transfer of the animus function from one woman to another, to see how useful it may be or even zestful. For the animus within a woman's feminine identity connects to a deep feminine sense of Self, which can be illuminating, empowering, and supportive all at once, coming now from the analysand, now from the analyst.

To see the borderline ego as an archipelago means that, restored to health, we may be graced with a vision large enough to embrace all the islands and all the unconscious connections among them. This ego is porous, open to the inrush of the unconscious at any time, and, like the tides, observes a rhythmic cycle. What is a detriment in illness is an asset in health.

In illness, the separate islands, though joined under water, seem simply split, fragmentary, without links, and connected only in a submerged, undifferentiated way. That accounts for the tendency of a patient in this borderline state easily to project the bridges among the islands onto someone else, anyone else, and then to feel both merged with such persons and defiantly split apart. This splitting and merger foreshorten the inner conversation usually facilitated by animus or anima. The different parts of us and of others stay sequential and sharply separated, rather than united into persons, complex but also complete unto themselves, operating out of their own centers.

In borderline states one does not achieve participation and interaction with others but rather substitutes experiences—one part for another, the analyst in place of one's own bridge function. Instead of flexible defenses, a borderline person, constantly under threat of being entirely submerged when the tide of affect or rage rolls in, mounts massive defenses. What feels at stake is one's very existence, one's own self, and *the* Self—any sense one may have had of a center dwelling no matter where, but within reach.[5]

The animus that defends a wobbly borderline ego mounts big-time opinions, massive attacks, eviscerating depression, and the anima, in counterattack, mounts matching trumpetings of the argument from reason. A man subject to such a counterattack feels reduced to pulp. He learns that he is nothing but an emotional cripple, and as for her, she is nothing but a bitch. Together they are really nothing but social fascists. Generalizations, scapegoating, intellectually armored defense are the order of the day—or of the years.

In health, however, the archipelago-like ego of persons who suffer from the borderline condition offers something very different. Because of the gaps in their psychic makeup, more than most, they remain open to the transcendent. Just because of the underwater flow of the unconscious among the parts of their ego, the transcendent can swim into place at any time. Such people, at peace with their changing borders, make unusual partners, analytical or any other kind. They possess true originality. Precisely because their ego is without clear borders and because they have the multiple view from many islands, they can, as the rest of us cannot, stand outside any boundaries—of family, culture, social class, or religious tradition. They speak from beyond, bringing fresh insights, images, observations to whatever may be at hand. They see traditions in new ways, not dismissive, but thought-provoking ways. They lack the strong observing shift of the typical cohesive ego that can simultaneously suffer conflict and stand aside and judge it calmly. But their archipelago ego affords them a greater simultaneity of viewpoints, none of them identified with an earthbound ego. They see the relativity of all ego positions, as if they were speaking in the voice of the transcendent itself, reminding us all that our positions float in untrustworthy waters because we are finite.

The French poet René Char gives elegant voice to the disparate worlds of borderline creativity. In a long prose poem, "The Library Is on Fire," he speaks for those whose wholeness depends on a constant awareness of parts, connected parts, disconnected parts, parts struggling with each other, parts seeking and finding reconciliation with each other. The poem is dedicated to Georges Braque, and for good reason—it evokes images from his paintings, especially of his strong, serene birds in flight and the assured earth that stands beneath them.

There is, as always in Char's work, a surrealist edge to the poem, but not a doctrinaire adherence to a school. A strong, complex position, both philosophical and psychological, holds everything in its own place, wearing its own colors, sounding its own tones, bearing its own identifying touch. When snow falls at the beginning of the poem, it does so from "this cannon," stressing the odd particularity of the event, at once bellicose and irenic. "There was hell in our head," the poet tells us, but only as prelude to the happy announcement that spring has come back and we can go out into the world again, "the earth in love, the grasses exuberant." Everything trembles, including the spirit. A great visionary bird, the eagle, is "for the future."

The poet's psyche makes its stand in the next few short, terse, arousing paragraphs. The defining one is the first: "Every act that absorbs the whole self, even though the self may not be aware of it, will have as its epilogue either contrition or chagrin. It must be accepted." Penitent or deeply disappointed, we must believe, like an act of faith, in the way little and big things, all the parts of our lives, come together in the wholeness of self. Char's writing comes to him this way, like the rubbing of a bird's down against a winter windowpane, which immediately rouses the embers in his hearth to a battle that never stops. The "silk towns" of our "everyday gaze" at the world, "squeezed in among other towns, with streets marked out by us alone," summon the Braque bird-image: they respond to us "under the wing of lightning flashes."

We should celebrate with joy, we are advised, the things of our world whenever something unpredictable occurs, something about which we know nothing, but which will find its own way to "speak to our heart." Char records his own hold on the wholeness of parts through epigram and assertion, image and speculation. "With me," he says, "lightning lasts." He triumphs over the "border-lines of the old desert" only when he is released from the torpor of his days by his *semblables*, his companions, female and male. Poetry, he says firmly, will "rob" him of his death, because what the poet discovers and transcribes he soon loses — for in the very process of writing his poetry are to be found "his originality, his infinity, and his peril."

The characterizations of his vocation and his hopes and convictions blaze in his burning library. He points — his craft, he has announced, is a craft of pointings — to books that do not move but insert themselves into our days in order to complain and to begin a festive dance. He brings his reader ageless night and slender birds whom we resemble, as in the cold they trust their uneasy sleep to beds of reed. The examples mount. The gathering of flammables comes to fire — or falls into ash — in our response. Char speaks for both kinds of response, of those whose fiery natures can match the conflagrations he has set before us, and of the unmoved, those who see only the residue left by the fires. He offers himself to us as everybody's guide, rising and shutting himself up, pursuing and being pursued, facing the concreteness of the poet's world in sharply outlined waters, in flowers that burst into aroma where "the Hours marry gods."[6]

There is, in such a jumping back and forth over boundaries as René Char's, a creativity that will either inspire or bewilder the reader. It is the way a poet whose psyche and inner dialogue are filled with sensations must come to us. Yves Bonnefoy, a somewhat younger French poet, with an equally penetrating gaze and his own finely tutored philosophical gift, defines much of what is contained in such borderline creativity in his explanation of what he means by poetry. It is not to give structured meaning to an object, either to produce "moments of revery" or to convey a sense of oneself.

> This object exists, of course, but it is the castoff skin of the poem and not its soul or intention. To attach oneself only to it is to remain in the world of dissociation, the world of objects — of the object that I, too, am, and do not wish to remain. The more one seeks to study the subtleties and expressive ambiguities of the object, the more one risks overlooking an intention of salvation, which is the poem's only concern. Indeed, the poem aspires only to interiorize the real. It seeks the ties that *in me* unite things. It must allow me to live my life in justice,

and sometimes its finest moments are notations of pure evidence, where the visible seems to be on the verge of being consumed in a face; where the part, devoid even of a metaphor, has spoken in the name of the whole; where what has been silent in the distance rustles once again and breathes within the open, the whiteness, of being.

The passage concludes with a sentence that speaks directly to his definition of poetry, to Char's example of it, and to what we mean by what certain borderline people bring to or inspire in others: "The invisible—it needs to be said again from this perspective of the word—is not the disappearance but the liberation of the visible: space and time dropping away in order for the flame to arise where the tree and the wind become destiny."[7]

They engender creativity, these borderline people, in those around them. One woman often seemed to her female analyst like a beautiful wild animal in analytical session, whom one had to learn to approach with a tutored care. The uncanny connection such persons feel with the unconscious of others, because of their underwater linkings, can pull an analyst into remarkably different ways of relating, greatly expanding the analyst's capacity to hear and to look and to respond. The wild-animal patient reminded her analyst how often wild animals inhabited her own dreams. The primeval lizards, giant sloths, and lions of her patient's psyche joined forces with the analyst's hippos, rhinos, bears, and panthers. The analysis came closer and closer to the Self layer of the psyche in its underwater linkings of patient and analyst.[8]

A difficult, demanding work schedule and a defensive fragmentation combined in one woman so that she often forgot the hours and sometimes the days of her sessions, even several years into analysis. Instead of reducing this to resistance, the analyst enlarged the analytical work to embrace all the islands of the patient's archipelago, allowing for lapses of contact between them. Instead of falling into the usual impatience and annoyance over such repeated disruption, the analyst looked at her own schedule now from a new angle, as if from another island in the great interlocking group. To see these interruptions as simply the patient's splitting yielded, as one might expect, a picture of a split between a dense, plodding analyst, fixed on routine, and a fragmenting patient flying into pieces. To see the interruptions from the perspective of the archipelago ego and its underground linkings afforded a view of the splitting as multiple entries in a psychic ledger. There was not a single animus bridge, but many, between the work of analysis they were doing and the life that might lie beyond it. For the patient, the work moved to identify and find ease in an identity connected to the center: the flyings-off, looked at this way, revealed a pattern of large arcs, formed around a defined center. For the analyst the work engendered a new capacity to enter into the flying patterns, to be quickly present, whether in transatlantic calls, or, after missed hours, in long continuous stretches of face-to-face sessions. Together analysand and analyst found a greater-than-normal ease in moving into and out of in-between spaces, liminal areas of subtle experience where ego and Self meet and converse. Sometimes the patient, carrying her own animus, made the bridge, sometimes the analyst did so, so that together they could look at the woman's ego positions from the point of view of Self. The archipelago ego makes that possible with the multiple entries to the transcendent that its islands provide.

Because of their own originality and zest for living, even in the midst of vexatious problems, these patients enliven everything around them. One woman sought analysis because she was either going to commit murder or kill herself. She had projectively identified all her intelligence, all her plans for the future, all her money, onto a man she had loved since her youth. The relationship had finally run out of energy. She wanted to get free of him, but felt trapped. What would happen to him if she left him? How could she manage her business? And then there was her fear of his ranting and raving when she talked about separating. He had functioned as her animus; now she wanted it back. Her murderous feeling arose from the way he had wielded power over her through the money; the suicidal, from her failure to get free.

It is hard to convey the size of her struggle to claim her own animus and its bridge to the center. A dream dramatizes her plight and the beginning of breakthrough. In it, she comes up from under water in a place this man controls. She thinks she has been saved from drowning, but then, as far as the eye can see stretching before her, there is nothing but water under what looks like an impenetrable ceiling that leaves her a bare eight inches in which to breathe and the prospect of a lifetime of treading water. She asks herself, Is this a movie set? With all her might she makes a fist and pushes herself up to strike the ceiling—and she gets through to the outside world! As she broke through in the dream, she broke through in her life. She went to the man and told him she wanted out—and right now. It so moved her that she could live apart from this outer man with her own inner man, and separate herself without violence to him or to herself, that she declared celebration was in order, starting with great bunches of spring flowers. The office bloomed. She said it would set an example to other patients to bring flowers when they got their souls back.

BLUEBEARD

Seeing the animus as bridge between ego and Self helps us understand one of the most discontented and dangerous of its negative figures, Bluebeard, who, as some women know all too well, is not a blithe fairy-tale character, but a killer animus, an archetype with a long history.[9] This primordial figure blots out women's egos, cuts off their participation in life, drains their life's blood. Women suffering from the highly negative animus complex we identify with Bluebeard describe the annihilation he works in different ways, but the end effect is always the same—life-killing. One victim acted out of her anger internally, becoming abysmally confused, never clear about anything, even her own feelings, and unable to act on what little she could make out that she wanted to do. She fell into nearly unceasing panic. Another was so buried under guilt she could not acknowledge that all she could say about herself was that she felt "zapped with confusion, taken right out of life." Others talk about similar convictions, of being "wiped out, paralyzed," under a barrage of negative self-judgment, consumed by murderous rage, burned up. One gifted woman felt a total blighting of even the germs of creative impulse. She dreamt of beautiful blue birds frozen in a pond's ice, unable to move, much less take wing.

The Bluebeard animus manifests itself in dreams as rapist, sadist, "wolf-robber," as one woman put it, gangster, assassin, thug. All embody a crazy, death-bringing aggression toward women. All show fear and hatred of the feminine and of women. Women under the spell of this animus obsession inevitably fall prey to the misogynist strains in their culture, either as their victim or coconspirator. Like the fairy-tale character, the animus Bluebeard figure that turns up in a woman's dreams lives far away from the familiar precincts of the dreamer's life or society. He can only connect to her ego world by breaking into it from outside, always with violence. He knows little more than persona identification with the ego world and its values. His contacts are all on the surface; as in the tale, he parades his wealth and puts a big castle and much money at his bride's disposal.

We can best understand this violent Bluebeard aggression as the result of the breakdown of the animus bridge at both ends. The animus lives in the gap between Self and ego, in the waters of the unconscious. He has neither access to release his energies into the channels of social or ego action nor any lens through which to see the Self. He feels overwhelmed by all that comes from ego and Self with no bridge to connect them and falls heavily into the gap between them, drawing their energies into a whirlpool with him, giving nothing of value back in return. The animus figure, like his fairy-tale prototype, is devoid of concern or of remorse, even of motivation for his murderous aggression. That is because he lacks humanizing contact with the ego world. His only access to it is through his aggression, by breaking in ruthlessly.

The fairy tale gives clues. The bride's household lacks a father and Bluebeard lacks, to begin with, any feminine presence in his castle. The two modes of being are far apart, split off from each other. He needs a wife, and she takes him, odd and unknown as he is, because of his astonishing wealth and apparent position, as a sort of father substitute, offering material substance and security. This curious animus figure will, she reasons, just plug her into the riches of the Self. She does not have to develop anything for herself. Of course, he is ugly, with blue hair sprouting all around his mouth. The color suggests spirit and mind, the hair, a self-propagating animal force. But Spirit does not properly manifest itself as a beard; it is not growing where it should, within.[10] So it is with patients suffering the effects of this destructive animus. These women could not use even the considerable thinking resources they already possessed, much less grow in them. They went blank, and their thoughts autonomously burst from them, usually directed to hurt someone, or to maim a newly forming attitude in themselves.

The hair surrounding a mouth suggests in the Bluebeard fashion a mixing up of the intellectual and spiritual energy coming from the Self with a hungry ego, what Guntrip calls the ego mouth.[11] Sucking, eating, devouring—all go to fill ego needs, but the blank in the ego remains unsupported by the animus. The identification proceeds to the wives

Bluebeard has murdered and hidden in a secret room. His omnipresent mouth and the blood of the murdered women suggest early oral attacks on the fertile female, a primitive envy that lays waste her life-giving flow of blood. One of the patients dreamed of fighting a man who repeatedly wanted to suck the blood out of her into himself. As Jung puts it, "When the animus succeeds in killing the creative impulse, there is no rest for him because then the creative impulse goes into him."[12]

We see this impulse become a compulsion in Bluebeard. He must insistently point out the room forbidden to his wife. He is obsessed to reveal that he has a secret, one he wants his bride to know and hold in confidence. She must keep the secret of his hidden room free from exposure. He needs her to mirror the central fact, that he is holding something back. But when she pries, as she is driven to do, the mirror breaks, and he must kill her. No reasoning, pity, or affection will stay his aggressive compulsion or the killing that goes with it. If the ego cannot gain the energies of the Self by its holding of the confidence of the animus, these energies will run through the animus and strike the ego dead by beheading.

Bluebeard's bride shows just where the ego goes wrong. She succumbs to curiosity rather than to sustained, serious interest. She is eager to know what the forbidden room hides but makes no provision for coping with what she may discover, no plan for her own safety, no respect for the monumental aggression that surrounds Bluebeard's secrecy.

Bluebeard's loud, persistent prohibitions can be seen as animus appeals for help from the ego in holding in consciousness his need for a mirror. He, as allegorical figure or as animus, needs a conscious container where he can safely deposit his secret. It cannot be tolerated on its own; it is too ill, too ugly, and must lead immediately, when exposed, to a pathological acting-out against the female who failed either to obey him or to contain him. The animus here is a mad, envious, split-off piece, mixed in with anxiety fantasies about the destructive or painful aspects of sexuality that may accompany defloration or menstruation.[13]

Once the bride knows her husband's murderous secret, she cannot go back again to an unknowing girlhood. But she remains unprepared to absorb and deal with her discovery. She just wants to deny it, by slamming the door to the secret room, anything not to be responsible for what she has found out. She remains at the trivializing level of curiosity and will not inspect what it is in her that drives her to know and how then she may carry its consequences. Compulsive denial works no better than compulsive curiosity. In both, an ego like the bride's remains blank, and in both a destructive animus invades the vacuum.

The tale sets the terms clearly before us but offers us little help in dealing with the force of the Bluebeard animus. In the end, the bride's brothers ride to her rescue and kill Bluebeard. They could be taken as friendly animus figures, not at all sexual, that support and defend the ego. Women patients often take the cure much beyond this surface suc-coring. They see that it turns on their egos becoming strong enough to stand up for themselves, for their worth as women, and harnessing the animus energy for their own positive use.

Two dreams detail the healing process. In the first, a woman dreams of Ted Bundy, the serial killer of women, jumping on her back while she is lying down. Has he broken it? she wonders fearfully. He is going to kill her too, she is sure. "But if," she tells herself, "I can compose myself deep down in myself, I can explain things to him and save us both," because, she thinks, in some way he really cares for her. He is violent with women, hates them because they are so weak, but he sym-bolizes to her a great source of energy. If she could only harness it, "big creation could happen."

The second dream is that of a woman who had worked hard to face her own murderous aggression, long repressed, which clustered around a childhood molestation. She dreamed of tracking a man in a foreign country, one who rapes and kills women. When she asks the help of a policeman, a farcical interchange ensues. It mirrors Peter Sellers in one of the Clouseau films, receiving a decoration from a French government official and getting the medal mixed up with the official's tie, so that both are pinned onto Clouseau's chest. They laugh in the dream as Sellers and the bureaucrat do in the film, and then discover that dreamer and policeman are hunting the same murderer who had attacked the policeman's wife and daughter. They team up. She felt after this dream that she had acquired some of the aggression to hunt for the missing parts of herself. Like the brothers in the fairy tale, the policeman—who is skilled, after all, in hunting criminals—allies with her ego. They will succeed. The lethal aggression will be captured, dealt with, even rehabil-itated.

There is another way to deal with the murderous aggression of the

Bluebeard contrasexuality in its animus form, as a woman might know it, and in its anima manifestations as a man might experience it. It is to transform it into something positive and in so doing to make it even more powerful than it is in its negative form. This way of transformation is suggested to us neither by fairy tale nor depth psychology, but by a piece of music. It is to be found in the measured thought and contemplative underpinnings of the most considerable of the attempts to turn *Bluebeard* into an opera, Béla Bartók's *Duke Bluebeard's Castle.* Bartók's librettist, Béla Balazs, begins the transformation with his reworking of Maurice Maeterlinck's libretto for Paul Dukas's *Ariane et Barbe-Bleue, ou la déliverance inutile.* We are far from Maeterlinck and even farther from the tale as Perrault tells it in his 1697 *Mother Goose.* We are in the world that was before fairy tales had become a literary genre and in a time long before confections like Maeterlinck's were made from fairy tales. We are, in the Bluebeard story told this way, in a primordial time, when stories begin with warnings such as that of the bard whose spoken ballad opens the Bartók-Balazs opera.

These ancient tales, the bard says, pass judgment on us. Their terms are clear: in such tales we are either guilty or innocent, no happy middle ground. To fit this tough, condensed sort of thinking, the story is streamlined. For the purposes of the one-act opera, all the wives become one in the person of the last of them, Judith, who faces only one other character on stage, Bluebeard. In a great circular Gothic hall that "is empty, dark and forbidding like a cave hewn in the heart of solid rock," she and Bluebeard emerge from a small iron door at the top of stairs. Their figures are black against a "dazzling white opening." Sharply distinguished contrasts, approaching diametrical opposition, define the scene, the drama, and its two characters. The orchestral setting is charged with the textures of opposition—it is noisy, stirring, determinedly rhythmic. The keys assigned to the characters—F to Bluebeard, F-sharp to Judith—carry the opposition beyond violence. They emphasize both closeness, in the half step from F to F-sharp, and distance, in their almost opposed tonalities.

The opera is about keys, musical keys and keys that open doors. There are seven doors and seven keys. Judith persuades Bluebeard to give her first one key, then another, then three more, then the last two, but now just one at a time. The tension is finely tuned this way; the drama, like each of the doors, turns on the keys. Every door, when it opens, reveals something different—a torture chamber, an armory, jewels, a lovely garden, Bluebeard's kingdom drenched in power, a lake filled with Bluebeard's tears, finally a beam of pale blue light in which three of Bluebeard's former wives can be seen. "Now you see the other women," the monster says. Do we actually see them, we are bound to ask ourselves, or are they dream figures? The answer is not the opera's to give—it lies in our own interior drama.

Bluebeard falls to his knees, opening his arms to the women for a moment, identifying the charms of each of them to Judith before they disappear. Each time, she rejects as vain any attempt to compare a former wife to her. Her mood changes when he is about to describe a fourth wife—that is to say, Judith. "No more!" Judith begs; "I am still here." Bluebeard pronounces: "Yours is every nightfall now," and moves to the third doorway to gather up a diamond crown, a heavy cloak, and jewels with which to festoon Judith. Again she pleads, "No more! In mercy, Bluebeard!" She wants neither diamond crown nor jewels for her body. The implacable Bluebeard speaks on. He hails the beauty of Judith, the best of his wives, he says, and the one he has loved the most. There is a pause. They stop briefly, to stand looking fixedly into each other's eyes. Then Judith makes off for the seventh doorway, her step labored under the weight of the ponderous mantle draped over her by Bluebeard and his aggression. She goes off, as the other wives had done before her, and the door shuts. "Now," Bluebeard intones, "night has fallen forever . . . night . . . night. . . ." The stage, Bluebeard, and all that his fearsome contrasexuality represents fall into darkness.[14]

A dark interiority is surely the content of the opera composed by the thirty-year-old Bartók. The combat revealed in it is mortal—between running toward and running away from what seems both a highly desirable and an intolerable contrasexuality. The allurements of each of Bluebeard's anima figures are unmistakable; he feels them, he must have them, he comes to possess them. But with possession there also comes a terrible transformation: their power possesses him. He will not have it; they must, each of them, die in a way that will demonstrate his power.

George Steiner, in the 1971 Eliot lectures he called *In Bluebeard's Castle*, examines with at least faintly jaundiced eye the textures of modern Western culture, against a backdrop of what he calls the "myth of the nineteenth century" or the "imagined garden of liberal culture." His subtitle, playing on Eliot's 1948 *Notes towards the Definition of*

Culture, is "Some Notes towards the Redefinition of Culture." For him Eliot's book is "not attractive." It is "gray with the shock of recent barbarism, but a barbarism whose actual sources and forms the argument leaves fastidiously vague." He is good enough to grant that the mind behind the book is one "of exceptional acuteness" and promises that he "will be returning to issues posed in Eliot's plea for order."

We think it might be said that Eliot's emphasis on religious verities comes closer to explaining the barbarism that troubles both men than anything in Steiner's "Notes." What gives Steiner's book, in which neither Bartók nor his opera appears at any length, its moments of persuasiveness is the strength of the composer's notes. They go some way to define, or redefine, leading textures in our mixed nineteenth- and twentieth-century culture. There is today, as Steiner says, in the absence of ceremony and ritual, "a thirst for magical and 'transrational' forms." Readers of Jung will not be surprised to read this. But Steiner adds a fresh note, deepening Matthew Arnold's prediction that religion's "facts" would come to be superseded by poetry. However hard it may be "to demonstrate," we would have to agree that in our time music has replaced the "poetry of religious emotion" for many, who find it not only "as exalting and consoling" as religion may once have been, but actually indispensable. Steiner shares with them "the feeling . . . that there is music one cannot do without for long, that certain pieces of music rather than, say, books are the talisman of order and trust inside oneself. In the absence or recession of religious belief, close-linked as it was to the classic primacy of language, music seems to gather, to harvest us to ourselves."

There must be many, too, who would agree with Steiner in placing such emphasis on the talismanic powers of music, knowing the easy accessibility of that magic in recordings. The medium in this case may not be the magic, but it delivers it to us, and often does so in that solitude where it can "harvest us to ourselves." There are intimacies of understanding of such a work as *Duke Bluebeard's Castle* that can come to us in repeated listenings to recordings that even a first-rate mounting on the operatic stage cannot equal. Steiner recognizes that fact when he suggests that the technology of the recording, as it represents its "culture outside the word," rivals the development of modern printing. Thus it is that he uses a figure from the rhetoric of music to indicate the "motion," at the least, of his lectures: "a tentative upward arc and descent in the orchestra—it holds one's breath—towards the close of Bartók's *Bluebeard's Castle*. We seem to stand, in regard to a theory of culture, where Bartók's Judith stands when she asks to open the last door on the night."[15]

We stand, at that point and many others in the opera, where Judith stands, facing the murderous aggression of the Bluebeard contrasexuality, or where she fumbles her way toward it, or kneels before it in appeasement, kissing Bluebeard's hands. She walks cautiously, she walks boldly; she is dazzled, awed, fearful, drooping; she recoils; she is tremulous, anxious, overwhelmed. This is a work of art, not a case history, which makes its representation of the power of the contrasexual archetypes all the more persuasive.

DEATH AND ANIMUS AND ANIMA

The struggles we engage in all our life long meet their limit in death. Death is our final border. Insofar as we have much experience with anima or animus linking us to the beyond-ego world, we may find our dying eased for us. We know about feeling linked to a terrain beyond what we can grasp with our senses or understand in our minds. Our panic about death is thus calmed. Insofar as we have grown accustomed to anima or animus appearing now in a personal guise borrowed from our particular history, now in archetypal guise, we have built up experience of the collision of the collective with the individual, which we face again in the predestined end of all of us in death. Our encounters with anima or animus slipping across the borders of health into neurosis, or even into moments of psychotic intensity, prepare us for what death might bring—images of terror and of nothingness, and then of something being there where there was only a terrifying void, and of someone greeting us. Two examples of people finding a bridge across death to something beyond make the point.

The first is of a man in early middle age who had worked hard in analysis with a tough split-anima situation, caught as he was between wife and other woman. Prominently employed in a helping profession, and constantly having to deal with a split-off and aggressive shadow life, he wanted to guard at all costs against his secret sexual life splashing into public view. He felt the split in himself so strongly and feared its consequences so greatly that when he began analysis, he was assailed with suicidal temptations. His analysis succeeded in making the split bearable—though it did not altogether disappear—and in strengthening his ego by integrating some shadow aggression so that he could carry his life in the face of feared public opinion. The persons he worked with at his job felt the great change. He was tougher now, more of the splendid person he was meant to be, as he grew up to the Self.

A dream best conveys this man's split-anima desperation: he is trapped between two rooms, in each of which stands a woman with a gun, threatening to shoot him or the other woman or both. Each holds back because the other woman is in a position to take aim and shoot first.[16] The dream portrays the menacing split between two images of his anima fascination. He was able to use his female analyst as a bridge between the two sides of the split anima and to ask with her the explicit question: Where is this frightening stalemate leading? He ended his analysis with a satisfactory but incomplete resolution.

Several years later, this remarkable man called his analyst to announce he had been diagnosed as having a rare, swift-moving brain disease that had always threatened its victims with psychosis before death. He had, as it turned out, three months to live, much of the time in terror that if he went psychotic all his secrets would spill out, hurting his children and his friends, undermining all his good work. The initial suicidal temptation leaped up again; it seemed a good way out. But simultaneously he felt himself crowded with all the grand questions such a death brings—about meaning, about why this particular disease, and where there might be purpose hiding there in it and in him.

He found some relief through the resumption of reductive analysis, seeing the way he projected onto the terminal illness his old shadow fears of being discovered and the anima split that still held him somewhat suspended. Then, by asking the prospective questions again— what the anima stalemate intended, what the disease intended, what this particular path to death indicated—a new understanding arose.

It is fair to say that he solved in dying the split he could not heal in living. In the midst of the encroachments of gross physical debility, his ego marched all the way across the anima bridge to find the necessary strength at the Self side to do what it was heretofore incapable of doing. He voluntarily and completely gathered up his fears, splits, remaining sanity, and incipient insanity, and gave full attention to the escape suicide offered. And then he offered it up, to God. All he feared and wished for, all he could do and could not do, he presented as an intensely personal offering back to the source of life. In dying, he reached beneath the splits between his public and his secret life to deliver himself over utterly to Being. Of the recorded cases of this illness, he was the only one who did not become psychotic before death. The disease gave him the chance to heal all of himself, and he corresponded willingly, openly with the grace given him. Accepting and offering what he feared, he did not suffer what he had expected. He triumphed in death.

An example of at least matching quality is that of a woman who died at forty from a malignant brain tumor. She was just completing analysis when the tumor was diagnosed, and the analysis continued all through the remaining year and a half of her life. The placement of the tumor gradually robbed her of language. The theft of speech took with it her ability to use her dreams. She could not gather them into words to communicate. They simply scattered into the night.

She had suffered for some time from a chorus of negative animus voices whom she named "the Wizards."[17] They were killing the life in her by their steady attacks on her hopes, her imagination, her plans, saying over and over that they did not amount to much, that they were silly, and hadn't she just made all that up? In her analytical work, she had finally reached the point at which she could stand up to these poisonous voices and walk away from them. With her illness, however, all those attacks and questions, those accusations of meaninglessness, of amounting to nothing, of going nowhere, came back. But the analysis held—and so did she. She faced down all those momentary reawakenings of old personal problems. She stood up aggressively, when she had to, against invasive, impersonal treatment procedures and made hard decisions about where she would die. She shed any inhibitions she had felt about expressing her deep emotions to her husband. She took courage in her hands and faced the dark.

She had lost the animus bridge that her dreams had provided to the large country of the Self. She felt near despair, but would not give up. She devised a new bridge, painting pictures of what she saw—alternately frightening and peaceful—coming toward her from the side of death. The pictures allowed her to differentiate her reactions into two clearly opposed types, one of angry and outraged terror, the other of resolute acceptance. The pictures, to her wonder, also brought her to spy some Other out there, beyond, waiting for her. Sometimes that Being seemed implacable, cold; at other times, forgiving, kind.

This woman is exemplary in her courage and what she accomplished in living her last days toward death, in showing us how the animus bridge can do its great supporting work, first in her dreams, then in her pictures. Her animus showed the same range, the same moving back and forth in transference. Her female analyst felt that sometimes she herself had been entrusted with the bridge and could at least for the moment direct the focus of the animus right onto the Self.

Most remarkably of all, this gallant woman demonstrated beyond cavil the way the animus bridge dissolves after its goal is firmly achieved in the meeting with transcendence, only to reappear when necessary to keep one connected to the task of facing death. Something of this connection wordlessly communicated itself to the analyst. A month before her patient died, the analyst hit upon the procedure that was to fill the remaining sessions, reading to the woman the notes of all their work since the diagnosis of the tumor. The reading recapitulated everything she had undergone: her terror, her fierce struggle to live, using surgery, chemotherapy, experimental drugs; her outrage that her life should be snatched from her just as she had started fully to live; her grief for herself and perhaps greater grief in her husband's suffering; her lost language, and the frustration and loneliness it brought; her painting of the richly communicative pictures.

The session notes concerned with the pictures showed a gradual emergence of a Self figure in the midst of the woman's ego fears. Finally, they came to where she had crossed the bridge. The analyst reached the end of the notes at the last session they had. The woman died early the next morning.

We should perhaps be prepared to face in death what we have known so well in life, as the last of that familiar series where we know things by their opposites, the tall by the short, the dark by the light, day by night, what is by what is not. But, as we remind ourselves very quickly when we come to contemplate death, this is an event all by itself. If it has any resemblance to the process of understanding by opposition, it is to states of being rather than to measurable quantities or qualities. We cannot precisely define joy by its apparent opposite, sorrow, or happiness by misery, or, in an even more shadowy area, explain intelligence by stupidity or wisdom by poor judgment.

Death is in one sense the opposite of life, or more exactly an absence of life, at least in the body where a person was once present. But death is a great deal more than this—and much less. It is beyond question a vacating, a giving up of the ghost, by which we mean the departure of a signifying presence. That does not mean, however, that the spirit of a person has left the world of which it was a part. The spirit remains, often enough, in those who survive and in their environments. What we miss is its physical nearness, its readiness to our senses. Still, sometimes it is more present after death in what Shakespeare called its ghostly influence than it was before. For in certain cases, when the body of someone especially dear to us goes from our midst, we work with a zeal we have never quite known before to account for precious timbres of being, to summon them up with clarity, to keep them with us.

This is where the contrasexual archetypes offer an incomparable tutoring, as the two deaths we have been discussing show so well. To philosophize is to learn to die, said Cicero and Montaigne again after him, with notable strength of argument and illustration. To live constructively with one's anima or animus, to build and to move comfortably across the bridge from ego to Self, is to do the same. It is to be so much a part of life, one's own life and the life of others, and so open to its productive complexities, that the terminus that death brings can be given its place without undue fear or discontent or psychological disturbance.[18]

When we have drawn our contrasexual Self into the comradeship of interiority, we can face anything, at least as a subject for meditation or inner conversation. We can prepare ourselves, as the wise of all ages and cultures have insisted we should, for what must come. Best of all, perhaps, we can conceive of someone, to whom our anima or animus may lead us, to extend the conversation, to deepen the discourse, to join the Self in mediating the suffering, even if it is only the pain we know others will feel in our final bodily absence.

We do not cozy up to death this way or make it into a jolly social event. Rather, we hold on all the more firmly to our connections to everything that being alive means to us. We look with awe, in our contemplations, at the marks of humanity in our universe, at what of consequence to human relationship remains in a culture, at what passes away. We look ahead in our interior dialogue, as we have looked back, to find and as far as possible penetrate the mystery of being and having and doing that life and death share. We understand what the philosopher Theodor Haecker meant, in the journal he kept in the dark hours of the Hitler regime, speaking to himself of the "dread" with which he looked toward eternal life, vowing not to turn away from it, but rather to move into it with fitting respect for its unfathomable dimensions:

> If *eternal* life were not free from "dread," I should not desire it. But supposing for a moment there was a man in this life who was entirely without "dread" (and at the present time there are many in high places who pride themselves upon the fact), then I should not want to be that man. I should indeed "dread" him.[19]

Haecker is thinking of the Nazis who had no "dread," in his sense of the word, no eternal standards of value to guide them, for whom the death of a human being or a whole country was as trivial as the squashing of an insect, except for the skills and technologies they had to develop to accomplish it. A half-century later, in a time when senseless killing has become a commonplace, we would have no difficulty in extending the list of the dreadless. Our care, in our interior converse, has to be to move as directly as possible to develop our own contemplative "dread." We must make ourselves ready for death, as Jeremy Taylor argues so winningly in his *Holy Dying*, and to remain ready always:

> Some are not willing to submit to God's sentence and arrest of death till they have finished such a design, or made an end of the last paragraph of their book, or raised such portions for their children, or preached so many sermons, or built their house, or planted their orchard, or ordered their estate with such advantages. It is well for the modesty of these men that the excuse is ready; but if it were not, it is certain they would search one out: for an idle man is never ready to die, and is glad of any excuse; and a busied man hath always something unfinished, and he is ready for every thing but death. . . . We must know God's times are not to be measured by our circumstances; and what I value, God regards not: or if it be valuable in the accounts of men, yet God will supply it with other contingencies of His providence. . . . Say no more; but when God calls, lay aside thy papers; and first dress thy soul, and then dress thy hearse.[20]

We dress our souls, in Taylor's sense, by the mirrorings of interiority. We know, from the experience of our contrasexuality in inner conversation, that the mysteries of human identity are reflected in the language and images in which we take up and mull over our sexuality and the sexuality of others. In that dialogue with ourselves, as in our dreams and fantasies, we meet the truths of our sexual being, however disguised or obliquely presented. We begin with some degree of conviction to declare, in this intimacy of inner being, what really matters to us, what kind of relationship we seek. In the ease of access to anima or animus that we find in the contrasexual meeting, and the honesty and directness of understanding that are in it, we prepare ourselves for that being-with-another, that loving companionship, for which our identity has been forged. We can see why some, in an experience of such fulfillment as persons, have been reconciled to death.

Part V

Repairing
the Bridge

14

Repair from the Ego Side

EACH OF us, out of the things that mark us as different, reaches to individual solutions to our anima/animus dilemmas. But we share certain fundamental moves in the ritual of repairing our broken bridges to the Self. The crucial reparative move for the ego arises out of a secondary psychic position, the passive one, where we do not receive the contents the anima/animus bridge conveys and often do not respond at all. We do not house them, we do not engage them in conversation. As a result, the anima or animus fills the vacuum. The ego leaves its moorings and rushes into the world with all the impersonal instinctual dynamism of the archetype.

When we can make our move, we find that it works its repairs both backward and forward, thus paralleling the healing in analysis through both reductive and prospective interpretation. The causes of our dilemmas are addressed when our ego responds directly and without reluctance to what animus or anima brings. As in reductive analytical interpretation that traces present sufferings to past origins, our repair work soothes old hurts and softens past deprivations with warm feeling. As in a prospective interpretation that asks of present suffering where it is leading and for what purpose, our repair work enables us to open up to the meanings hiding within us. Retrospectively, we heal and fill out the ego so that it gets bigger. Prospectively, as a result of acquiring more

Self, we see more in others and see them more clearly, as objectively there in their own subjectivity.

Like the alchemists, we must engage in the lengthy process of *albedo*—the repeated washing, purifying, and separating of our psyches from the thickening meshes of our anima or animus complexes in order clearly to establish an ego position and relate to the contrasexual archetype.[1] We integrate as much as we can the personal aspects that belong to us and treat with respect the parts that stand over against us, that connect us to the objective psyche. How do we do this? By undoing what snared us in the first place.

CLAIMING THE EGO

To repair the broken bridge to the Self from the ego's side means a full claiming of our ego responses. We stand up to anima or animus. We move out of the secondary position where we feel blank, unsuitably armored, identified negatively with our contrasexuality, or ready to deliver our power to someone else through projection. We no longer hang back passively, no longer allow anima or animus to take over as a substitute, as pseudoego. Our major healing movement is to turn toward what comes across the bridge and admit and claim for ourselves all our different reactions. We may then withstand those contents, suffer or challenge or house them. But a *we* or an *I* exists now to respond, reject, receive, sort out, channel. *We* engage our life and take up with vigor inner conversation with the one who addresses us, or tries to thwart or attack us. We hold up our end of the dialogue. We look to clarify our goals and values, claim our needs and wishes, discover our talents and faults.

The specific ways the contrasexual bridge to the Self collapses show us the means to its repair. If we live in states of identity or identification with the parental container, and have not yet even discovered our own anima or animus, we must disidentify with it and inquire into our actual reactions. Take the man who plopped his dream down for the women who were in group therapy with him to work on—he must register what he feels when they poke, tease, and challenge him to find his own attitude to his dream. In response to the women he feels angry, embarrassed; he says so. When he turns toward his dream, he discovers he feels awed by its numinosity, afraid almost. He discovers that he has been using the women as buffers between it and him, scared that the power of the dream will take him apart. He goes on to uncover the same moves in his relationship to his wife. When gripped by deep feeling, he fears it too much to give it to whom it belongs, to his wife, maneuvering her instead to help him somehow. He establishes her as permission giver: she will say when to take two giant steps, when to share his feelings, when to do his chores. He has been using her too as buffer between himself and awesome emotion.

Carry your own emotion; use your aggression to figure out when to speak, when to stay silent, the women in the group urge him. To be manly in that way feels almost too heady to him, almost "balloonish," he says—and suddenly remembers his strong feeling for one of the women there. This heady, manly feeling is just the way he feels when his attraction to this woman overcomes him. She attracts him by her power to stay close to the truth, even if it makes her suffer. This is the way the anima emerges in him, as personification of another standpoint, another way of experiencing awe. She shows him how to stand loyal to truth, even if it brings suffering. With understanding and experience inside him, he can cease hiding in his wife, letting her carry his feelings as if she were his mother. By claiming this anima bridge in himself, he can disidentify from the wife-mother container.

This process of turning to accept his own reactions must be repeated many times. He must take note of the fears bred in him by emotions of awe and still claim them. He must stop using women as buffers and encourage the emergence of an anima that loves truth more than it fears suffering. That is the *albedo* process, an endless washing equivalent to repairing the bridge to the Self. A stronger ego builds up; a second perspective moves onto the scene, personified as anima.

If we project anima or animus functions onto others and ourselves act out the bridge for them, like men afflicted with the Don Juan complex who feel compelled to animate women but remain unable to come alive themselves, the repair indicated is an active turning toward the projected content. We need to isolate exactly what we have allowed to fly onto the other. For the Don Juan men, it is the willingness to effect animated connection to being, to engage in lively inner conversation, to awaken awareness to Self process.[2]

The women whom the Don Juan men woo are often helped to claim their own split-off sexuality, to discover what they believe in, to dare aim at a vocation for themselves. But too often their men remain empty, half-dead, and have to be made to turn sharply toward that deadness within them, sometimes a fearful task. It means renouncing the Don Juan behavior that had so long defended them against the despair aroused by an inner emptiness, an absence of conversation within. Now their egos must go slowly, turn to and wait upon the deadness, brood over it, imitate the Spirit moving over the waters of the deep at the beginning of time in the first chapter of Genesis. In one man's case, it meant discovering the courage to begin serious engagement with a gift for poetry. He waited for the images to well up in him, what Bachelard calls the first articulations of being.[3] For another man, it meant transferring the animating conversation he carried on with women into his work as performing artist, to get into his work the play, toughness, and ingenuity he could count on in his meetings with women.

If projection becomes projective identification, so that another person does not just carry a good part of ourselves but becomes equated with our animus or anima, becomes our threshold to the Self, we must persevere all the more, but not change tactics. With intensified feeling, we turn toward what the other carries for us, owns, embodies. We make lists of the other's qualities, keep it before our eye, ask where these capacities take root in us, where they belong to us. How, we must ask ourselves, do we make our animating conversation arise within ourselves?

For animating conversation we must, all of us, ultimately go back to the Self, where conversation originates. We must find our resources where they begin, as the ego moves toward the Self. We do this in solitary reflection, in reverie, in dream. Bachelard tells us that in the dreams of a philosophical solitude, when we "truly" contemplate it, the "humblest object . . . isolates and multiplies us," and we become aware of our "multiplicity." We fall into primary meditation, which is "at the same time total receptivity and cosmologizing productivity." That is the best way to begin our days.

In the morning, primary meditation brings us to such an experience of its "naive dynamism" as we find in a story Bachelard instances from Oscar Wilde to demonstrate its ways. A saint, we are told, had the habit of arising well before dawn and each day praying that God would make the sun rise as it always had before. When the sun dutifully rose, he would thank God on his knees for granting his prayer. One day, the saint slept past dawn; when he awoke, the sun had long risen. He was bewildered and uncertain, but only briefly. Quickly he fell to his knees and thanked God that despite "His servant's culpable negligence, He had made the sun rise all the same."

In the evening meditation of Bachelard's kind of philosophical solitude, we turn from denial and from the fruitless task of attempting to snuff out unpleasant memories: "Trying to forget is the bitterest kind of remembering. One little pain cast off like a faded leaf—does that really prove that the heart is soothed?" Rather than the suffocation of the past, we take the pain with us into the night. In the repose and tranquillity of the night's darkness, we accept our smallness in the universe. That may not altogether quiet our troubled being. We may find ourselves moving back and forth in our mind across pains and doubts and rebellious feelings. That is the moment for the ego to be gold. We turn an unhappy reflection into a happy one. "Unhappiness has meaning," we realize; "it possesses a function and a certain nobility." We carry this reflection to where it leads, to the wise conclusion Bachelard offers: "Doubt, so widely studied by philosophers, remains a great deal more foreign to our time than the feeling of solitude, loneliness, the terror of abandonment."

Like the unhappiness we have transformed into happiness, the pains of solitude and the terrors of abandonment must be turned around. "We need solitude," Bachelard reminds us, "to detach us from occasional rhythms," that is, from the topsy-turvy alternation of pleasing and displeasing states of being, the constant movement from serenity to anxiety, from irritation to delight, round and round the feelings that keep poking at us and make us want to rush away from ourselves as from a bad dream. "By placing us face to face with ourselves, solitude leads us to talk to ourselves and so experience an undulatory meditation which reflects everywhere its own contradictions and is perpetually attempting an inner dialectical synthesis."[4]

That synthesis is what the ego hunts in its anima or animus dialogues. It seeks a coming together with the functions of interiority in willing awareness that what we call contradictions are the defining rhythms of being, the systole and diastole of thought and feeling that keep us alive. For every moment of anxiety or despair, these dialogues reveal, there is an answering restorative. It resides in our willingness to accept the up-and-down nature of our complex being, placed as it is in an often unfriendly world that will not become any more welcoming just because we so obviously deserve a better reception. We have some small control of the world around us, but not enough to ward off affliction, cataclysm, automobile accidents, and lethal bacteria. And as we have surely more reason to know than our ancestors, blueprints of human perfectibility and utopian schemes for society bring only disaster. Our great resource is inside ourselves; there we have some control. But we cannot exercise that control without accepting, to begin with, the complexity of the contrasexual dialectic of our interiority, and making every attempt, as we go on, to see that the very pains and terrors manifested to us in our solitude are the guarantors of our freedom. They constantly turn us back upon ourselves and ask us to embolden our egos to the point where we can provide our own welcoming environment in the exercises of self-examination and its mate, self-discovery.

The Asian woman caught in a marital quadrangle with a man she had overendowed found the renunciation of him fearfully hard, but the discovery of corresponding talents in herself freeingly rich. She was able to sacrifice the comfort of her well-paying job to take premedical courses merely with the hope of acceptance by a medical school. Her capacity to sustain risk and hope had been well schooled in her unhappy multilayered romance! Her passion to live close to the center, which she had earlier attributed to this man, she discovered was her own necessity, her own talent; and she channeled it into her medical career, which she did indeed succeed in achieving for herself.

When we project and identify so much of our center in another, it is important to remember that what we will find in ourselves is not identical qualities but analogous ones. This woman's way of living at the center took root in an ambition to serve as a doctor. The man was not a doctor, but she saw in him a like persistence to live from the inside out. Repair came from the contents she had projected into him and her willingness now to claim them for herself.

When animus or anima steps in front of the ego that has become like dead air space in its blankness, repair comes from tuning into the blank space, our inner void. We allow its emptiness to reach the senses of our body and the senses of our soul. We no longer let anima or animus cover it up by sheer force of presence. Something strong hurt us there; we fled, hid from our interior deadness, allowed that place to remain unseen, blank, unfilled. Now we can turn to it and fill it with warm feeling. We can engage in open loving of an unconscious suffering become conscious. The man who berated his sweetheart for her past romances jumped over his void, would not acknowledge it, for there lay hurt from his difficult past. He protected himself by denying it, refusing to see it. But it remained unchanged, unseen as it was, hurtful. He needed to turn, look, let the hurt to his self-esteem be seen, gathered up, admitted to full participation in his being.

The woman who sought analysis specifically to look into the trauma of child molestation found a link between that painful past and a curious blanking out that was happening at work. Presenting something in a meeting, her mind goes blank. Where she should be broadcasting information, dead air space takes over. Dimly she discerns a connection to the place in her still hurting from her brother's molestations. She had not been able to look into the pain before, so that it had been transformed into this curious symptom of blankness. Around the problem an animus layer wrapped itself, judging her inadequate on the job, a guilty participant in the ancient sex games.

In analysis, instead of heeding the animus judgments, she listens now to the dead air space. Slowly, the void is filled as her ego reclaims bits and pieces of what actually happened with her brother. She mourns what she lost as a child, the sexual damage she sustained. She rages at her brother, at herself, at family behavior that allowed and even encouraged this encounter between its children. The analyst aids her by allying, not with the wound in the void, but with her ego, now tending to the hurt and filling in with the experience of it.[5]

Spontaneously, she connects the blank space to her loss of function on the job. "I was afraid I would say too much," she recognizes, and hears in those words the little girl who, out of love for her brother, did not give away their secret. Once she registers that fact consciously, the job symptoms abate. If they return, as occasionally they do, she knows to listen to what is there under the blankness, to recover another piece of unspoken trauma. Turning to the hurt, and having compassion for it, repairs it. The blank space gives over to fine, warm human feeling.

The split anima or animus yields and finds healing in similar ego efforts. We reach beyond the split to the place as it was before the hurtful event. Something intolerable happened to us that we have protected ourselves against by splitting in two. We have been receiving only one tolerable part of what anima or animus brings and split off the intolerable remainder, and with it allowed our ego to split also. Repair will come when our ego can turn toward the intolerable moment and address it directly, claiming all, intolerable and tolerable, that comes across the bridge, and knitting it all into our lives.

The woman who found herself constantly enamored of unsuitable partners, who regularly made her feel abandoned and without worth as a female, gradually turned to face just exactly what came across this animus bridge. She had been projecting her connection to well-being onto these men and giving them power that way to invalidate her as a person. What came across the bridge was a dreadful experience of abandonment that had indeed left her desolate and enraged, but in the past, not the present. Her mother had abandoned her to her grandmother's care until she was three. When the grandmother suddenly died, she returned to her mother, but with no explanation of what had happened to the grandmother. Her trauma doubled—loss of grandmother added to loss of mother. Her desolation reached suicidal proportions.

Unconsciously she chose men who made her feel negligible and in a sense worthy of abandonment. They made her experience the feelings she needed to feel, but in tolerable doses. She saw in unsuitable partners exterior dangers less threatening than the interior persecution she knew in her feelings of abandonment and rage.[6] When she turned to receive those emotions into her ego, slowly, carefully, piece by piece, she closed the split both in animus and ego. When she could integrate the intolerable losses she had suffered, she found she need no longer reproduce them in diminished form, in supposedly tolerable doses, with partners who hurt her.

The woman who married a man because he spelled security, and then turned against him because he was so unexciting, faced the same split in her image of men as a whole. She turned toward these images of separation coming across her animus bridge to her ego, and discovered there something that astonished. As a little girl she had loved her mother lavishly, all out; her mother was the sun to her. She could never cross her mother, in any way differ with her, for the sun would then go out, disappear, leaving her with nothing. Her sense of joy changed abruptly to a feeling of sorrowful isolation. She remembered now how utterly she felt in her mother's emotional power and the vow she had sometimes made never to love anyone like that again. It was much too dangerous. Her animus-split, between a safe but dull husband and an exciting but dangerous fantasy lover, she now saw, protected her against the utter dependence she feared when all her loving went to one person.

When her ego could take this in, she dreamed about her beloved daughter, who also symbolized the woman's own younger, unsplit self. In the dream, the daughter is engaged to two men simultaneously, one secure but dull, the other exciting but also frightening, a tribesman. Her younger self was thus trying to heal the split in her animus. In another dream a check for a small fortune is written out in the daughter's name. The mother fears someone will forge her daughter's signature and steal the money. But that is impossible, for to claim the money the daughter must identify herself with her Social Security card. The dream says that the tremendous influx of energy, the great sum of money, can be received only with security in hand. She can have one only if she has both. The split begins to mend.

Another woman, suicidally depressed about not finding a good mate and berating herself with harsh animus judgments, repeatedly dreams a harrowing dream. People pretend to be one thing but are in fact another, forcing her to remain vigilant lest she be tricked, humiliated, treated sadistically. In one, for example, an attractive actor keeps flopping out his penis, exposing himself to her. In real life he has been reported to be vicious in his treatment of women. She traces her fear of being tricked, in reductive analysis, to a childhood of sadistically tinged teasing at the hands of her father and her brothers. But what stops her cold now is what comes when she asks in prospective analysis what the dream is leading to, with its exhibitionistic actor figure. Suddenly, she sees her own behavior in his exposing himself. She behaves just like that when she blurts out at the wrong time and in the wrong place her "honest" feeling that she wants a husband and a baby. It is not her honesty that is the problem, nor the dream man's penis; it is her utter unrelatedness to the situation. Her blurtings out are like flopping out a private and strong part of herself in a way that embarrasses others and even seems perversely aimed to put them off. The animus brings her understanding of where she goes off. She flops out her dearest female wish and aim like the handsome actor showing himself, in the wrong place, at the wrong time, in the wrong way. That is for private communing, not public display. She too needs to commune privately and deeply with her genital longings for a loving partner and a full womb, but even then only at the right moment and with a trusted partner. Exhibitionism aims for self-validation, but the dream shows her she cannot get this from others, any more than the exhibitionist actor can.[7] She needs to receive herself, for herself, in herself.

Another woman's dreams show that what has caused a split is injury to the animus itself. She dreams of men wounded both physically and emotionally. Working in analysis on receiving into her ego the hurts done to her image of the masculine, she often dreamed of overpowering sexual attraction to men who had been injured. The dream was leading her to integrate her wounds by sexualizing her attraction to them. She wanted to embrace them, to tell them they really were good, validate their deepest selves by opening to them sexually. One dream even employed a lavish devotion of the kind attributed to the saints who think of kissing the wounds of Christ. She wanted in her dream to kiss the lips of an animus figure afflicted with canker sores. A man, slowly turning toward injuries done him by his anima, knows the same motif, though with more ambivalence. He sees his anima as injured, and in a dream his heart goes out to her to heal her, to love her—but he also fears she may make him sick.

The man who found his split anima had landed him in a marriage triangle had to make almost exactly the same ego move to repair the split: to turn toward what the split portended. Through love for two different women, he had tried to put together what had fallen apart or had never grown together in the first place. He did not know how to hold in one place in himself the excitement of his instinctual life and his need for a secure continuum. He lived one part with each woman. Unable to give up either, his ego was forced to look inward to the source of the division. In reductive analysis, this task took him far back to his relation to his mother, where what Winnicott calls the "environment mother," who holds us in being, never fused with the "instinct mother" who excites us. In prospective analysis, the task of integrating both sides of himself made his ego enlarge enough to knit spirit with flesh, passion with permanence.[8]

Jay Gatsby, *The Great Gatsby*, that woman-driven man, opened himself as far as he could to bring spirit and flesh together. His passion was wonderfully certain, but his understanding of it and those who stood in the way of it was woefully uncertain. Out of Gatsby's struggle to make a life for himself worthy of his passion for Daisy Buchanan, F. Scott Fitzgerald constructed a parable of American life which, both in the character of Gatsby and the book that celebrates him, is worthy of the adjectival crown: there is greatness here.

The melodrama is absorbing, even in the umpteenth reading, and not so contrived, as it makes its way to its final violences, that we find it difficult to suspend disbelief. The deaths of Gatsby and Myrtle Wilson, the garage-owner's wife with whom Daisy's husband has been dallying, take on the tones of *verismo* opera, and we return to them with the sort of feeling that we have—if we have any—for *Cavalleria rusticana* and *I pagliacci*. They serve their noisy purpose as the narrator, Nick Carraway, serves his quieter one: we need a mixture of newspaper styles, tabloid and op-ed, in which to locate a figure who gathers up in himself so much that made the 1920s luminous in our history. There is more than pathos in the schedule the boy Gatsby had written out for himself on the flyleaf of a copy of *Hopalong Cassidy*:

Rise from bed	6:00	AM
Dumbbell exercise and wall-scaling	6:15–6:30	"
Study electricity, etc.	7:15–8:15	"
Work	8:30–4:30	PM
Baseball and sports	4:30–5:00	"
Practise elocution, poise and how to attain it	5:00–6:00	"
Study needed inventions	7:00–9:00	"

The list, dating back some two decades before the events of the book, is Gatsby's father's contribution to his son's funeral rites. It is followed by a number of GENERAL RESOLVES—not to waste time at specified venues, to give up "smokeing" and chewing, to take baths every other day and read one "improving" book or magazine a week, to save $3 a week (he had originally planned on $5), to "Be better to parents." His father points to the lists with pride: "Do you notice what he's got about improving his mind? He was always great for that."

Gatsby clearly had spent much of his life talking to himself in the quest for self-improvement, making lists, elocuting, learning poise, putting together a facade more mysterious than plausible, behind which to hide his life as a bootlegger. He knew interior dialogues. He knew something about how to make inner aim into outer achievement. He knew after his meeting with Daisy during the war that the real point of everything for him was somehow to hold onto her: "He had committed himself to the following of a grail. He knew that Daisy was extraordinary, but he didn't realize just how extraordinary a 'nice' girl could be. She vanished into her rich house, into her rich, full life, leaving Gatsby— nothing. He felt married to her, that was all." To make himself worthy of her "nice"-ness, of her rich house and rich, full life, he contrived an "old sport" Oxford manner, a fine display of wealth, a knightly pursuit of her worthy of a Lancelot.

Fitzgerald did not himself know how much he had achieved. His own talking to himself was always best in a fictional setting, as we can see in the notes and outlines that are all we have for a conclusion to the unfinished novel he left at his death, *The Last Tycoon*. He was much too quick to agree with John Peale Bishop that the character of Gatsby was "blurred and patchy," and to say in extenuation, "I never at any one time saw him clear myself—for he started as one man I knew and then changed into myself—the amalgam was never complete in my mind." His closeness to Gatsby is no limitation, though it does explain his fawning letter to H. L. Mencken, in which he admits to "a tremendous fault in the book—the lack of an emotional presentment of Daisy's attitude toward Gatsby after their reunion (and the consequent lack of logic or importance in her throwing him over)."[9]

Gatsby-cum-Fitzgerald is only as blurred or patchy as a man would be whose boyhood "resolves" had never left him, who had attained poise, who had improved himself, but who had not yet learned in his self-inquiry that just as he could not forever be satisfied with a life of crime, he would not always be content with boyhood improvements. That is exactly right for Gatsby, improved but incomplete, as it is for his mid-1920s America and for much of the country's achievement after World War I: it was still making boyhood—and girlhood— improvements and finding the strengths of its extended pubescence. Equally, Daisy is right. No "emotional presentment" of her later feelings about Gatsby would have been possible; they were not accessible to her, except in the most superficial way. She is an anima fixation, a contrasexual incarnation met in the Midwest in the midst of war preparations, as Fitzgerald-cum-Gatsby prepares to become a figure to be taken seriously, and therefore grabs at anything that looks finished—they did, after all, "finish" nice rich girls, didn't they? Scott Fitzgerald learned some unpleasant answers to that question in his life with Zelda Fitzgerald, never perhaps realizing that there were good answers to that question and even better questions accessible to him in his Gatsby persona. Ego after anima—Scott never gave up the pursuit. Anima after ego— Zelda lasted longer than Daisy, but did not stay the race; it is much harder to be the hunted than the hunter, though she did try from time to time to reverse the field.

EGO-ENLARGEMENT

When we move out of a secondary position and turn inward, toward what anima or animus brings our ego, we enlarge. We have found a conscious identity. We can use the spacemaking capacities of our ego to respond to what comes across the contrasexual bridge, to integrate its disparate contents. This produces in us an astonishing vitality and the presence of our own person. Our predominant sexual stance is heightened, made more flexible and individual, as it wrestles with its opposite. We differentiate from our family's images and society's stereotypes of woman or man. We find an ease in improvising within the large boundaries of a complex identity. We no longer try to fit standard forms and sizes. We show ourselves more as a woman, more as a man, because we are more particularly our own woman or man. We are less defensive because more secure. We reach down through our contrasexual parts to anchor ourselves in the Self. We can afford to entertain the new and the strange and are not embarrassed to embrace anything that really fits us.

This is our experience of what some have called androgyny, in space and time: We are not an undifferentiated blur of two sexes, but each of us a particular person with our own combinations of the masculine and feminine. An increase of Being flows into us because two avenues of approach open up: our ego's on one side, our anima's or animus's on the other.

Some of the difference is visible to the eye in the work of those two great anima painters of this century, Matisse and Bonnard. The one, Matisse, is the master of the ego-centered line. In a rigorous economy of drawing, he indicates everything that a line can convey, all that it carries which, though clearly marked on the surface, makes a mockery of those who write off surface appearances as trivial. When in his paintings he fills in between the lines, he does as much for color, showing us how much human value can be gathered from the spectrum and how thoroughly a woman can impregnate a chair, a curtain, a window, a bowl of fruit, with her womanliness. In such paintings, we discover anima furniture, as in the bare outline of the Stations of the Cross and the figures of Virgin and Child and Saint Dominic in the Vence Chapel of the Rosary of Matisse. The sacred finds a fitting, self-enclosed space.

The other, Bonnard, goes behind the line, and even behind the colors, pointing to, suggesting, asking questions about anima life, but never clearly identifying it. His mastery is of events and people and places as prosaic as those of Matisse—food on a table, people talking as they eat, women defining themselves in a flutter of light and color that never settles into permanent place in spite of the spatial limits of the paper or the canvas and the boundaries of the frame. Everything, even as it proclaims a fullness of Being, takes us away from precise definition. We pause in contemplation of the contrasexual feminine and find ourselves drawn to something even larger. The shimmering light and hazy outline evoke a presence: Being itself seems to find its waves and particles in Bonnard's light.[10]

By not letting the archetype of the opposite sex rule us, but rather converting it in such contemplation into its prime function, as connection to the Self, we discern the spirituality that underlies our instincts. Biologically, it seeks sex drives toward the goal of reproduction of the species. Psychologically, it drives us toward the center of the psyche, Self. Instead of identifying with either process, by projection or by splitting, we regain access to the contents of anima or animus. Their energy flows into consciousness, free to be shaped for use in everyday life.

The missing pieces of the ego that had earlier fallen under the dominance of anima or animus return to the ego. We know now where we are pained and how; we can all but diagram our weak spots where the fabric will never be strong. But we know too about mending and caring for wounds, how, in turning toward them, to fill in the blank spaces. Anima and animus put at our disposal our unclaimed shadow life, which our egos are now strong enough to identify and accept as their own.

One of our Don Juan men found, when he stopped playing at being the bridge for his women, that his dreams were dishing up for his delectation one thug after another—foreign-born toughs, city-bred ruffians, then one produced from his own work as an actor. Only after this series of hoodlums had appeared did an anima figure come up from her underground kitchen, to best a chic French chef in a culinary competition with her delicious plain food. The dreamer was stopped by her because he could not seduce her. She responded from her own center, not simply in reaction to him.

When the ego moves with confidence to receive what the Self is offering through anima or animus, the chthonic element in our sexuality springs back to life. The masochistic man found himself, in response to this primordial sexuality, filling up with irritability, aggressive moods, dreams of shooting, beating, sometimes using people sadistically, and all when he was consciously working to mend the split between black and white anima figures.

The ego can enlarge to meet even such complexities of opposing elements in us by developing double vision.[11] Not only can we experience then the startling differences between our ego views and the opposing ones of our anima or animus, but we can actually descry the Self at the other end of the bridge. We take possession of the full span as we move to own our whole psyche. We acknowledge unconscious motivational forces in us. We accept what life has dealt us. We look to have a future that is our own, personal to us, not a mere reflection of our social or economic class, not a lock-step adherence to cause or movement, not a series of compliances with one or another establishment.

The past we work so hard to uncover in reductive analysis joins with the future that perseverance in prospective analysis reveals, asking always where something is leading, to what end its symptom is taking us. The psyche keeps telling us that the past is here in our present, in the appropriations of our unconscious life.[12] The passageway between it and our ego must be kept open.

Self ceases to be a thing or goal and becomes a mode of mentation, a complex instrumentation of psyche and spirit. It acts as the base of our continuum, the enlivening source of the individual ego and of a collective ego life that everywhere seeks to humanize, and to articulate its differentiations.

Unconscious archetypal energies circulate through these grown-up ego containers. Archetypes become ours to the extent that we house them and integrate them into the conscious modes of our experiencing. A mutual shaping between ego and archetype and the processes of communicating occurs. It is like simultaneous translation into different languages. It is all a matter of tuning in. The more languages, the more levels of interplay, the richer our life.

The ego itself is complex; the orienting archetype we find at its center is the Self.[13] When anima or animus functions as threshold to the Self, we experience its great boisterous centering energies circulating into all we do, think, feel. It backs us up and makes us secure in our finitude.

When the ego is claimed with absolute assurance, it is because its energies are the energies of the Self. The end in view becomes absolute. We become unshakable in our determination to carry through to our announced destination. Almost any means will do to enable us to reach it; we have no qualms, or if we do, we suppress them; we feel blessed in our certitude. The figure of Judith, in the book of the so-called scriptural Apocrypha devoted to her, shares that certitude with us; some might say it blesses us with it.

Judith is one of the startling animus women of the Hebrew Scriptures, reminiscent of Tamar and Rahab in her virility, mindful of Esther and Ruth in her unwavering belief in Yahweh. She is an icon in many faiths, reaching from the Judeo-Christian to the feminist—the woman who cut off the head of a tyrant and with it his tyranny. She stands in bronze iconographic coolness, poised to behead Holofernes, in Donatello's statue in the Piazza della Signoria in Florence. She lets the tyrant's head fall into a sack held by her maid, looking far away from the doleful sight, fixed in some awesome awareness of her act, in Mantegna's painting of the scene. In Michelangelo's Sistine Chapel painting, she and her maid move in their space with the captured head, both turned firmly away from any close inspection.

Judith will, in fact, stand up to any scrutiny, as she does to the elders of her town, Bethuliah, under siege by Holofernes. She is a wealthy widow, rigorous in her piety, but beautiful, too, in her widow's weeds. She is appalled by the decision of the elders to wait out Holofernes for another five days in the hope of rescue by the Lord, with their promise of surrender then should deliverance not come, as it has not for thirty-four days. "Who are you to test God?" taunts Judith. "If you cannot plumb the depths of a person's heart or understand the thoughts of his mind, then how can you fathom God, who made all these things, or read his mind, or understand his reasoning?" She is going to do something, she says, that "will go down among the children of our people for endless generations," but she will not say what it is. The leaders agree to let her do it, whatever *it* turns out to be.

What she does, after arraying herself in finery worthy of a Renaissance painting, is to go under large escort to the enemy camp. There she persuades Holofernes that she is desolate in the knowledge that her people have broken the laws of God in eating food reserved for their priests, so ashamed of them, in fact, that she will become his spy, promising to return to him each day with news of Bethuliah and its behavior.

Three days at the camp are enough for her, followed each night by ritual bathing to cleanse herself. On the fourth, dressed for seduction, she leads Holofernes to drink more, we are told, than he had ever done in any one day "since he was born." She achieves her purpose. He is left unconscious by the day's drinking, stretched across his bed in an alcoholic sprawl that painters of the scene have reveled in. Her barbering can begin. She grabs his hair, asks for help from the God of Israel, and then after striking at his head twice "with all her might," chops it off. To complete the task, she rolls Holofernes' headless body off his bed, pulls the canopy from its poles, and makes off with her servant, to whom she has given the head to put in her food sack.

The Israelites bless Judith. Achior the Ammonite, a king who has been honest and temperate in his advice to Holofernes, is moved by Judith's act to change his faith, to be circumcised, and to become an Israelite. The Assyrians, seeing the head of their leader hanging on the wall of Bethuliah, fall apart as an army, shamed, as one of them cries, by a "single Hebrew woman." Soldiers, heartened by Judith's act, come from all over Israel, and Israel's enemy is destroyed. There the book of Judith ends, with a pointed song of praise sung by Judith and a brief epilogue like a last chapter in Dickens, dispatching Judith to the rest of her hundred and five years, still a widow, accepting no man into her bed, in marriage or otherwise.

Judith's hymn recounts the story briskly, in seventeen verses. The accomplishment is clear:

The Omnipotent Lord has foiled them
By the hand of a female.
For their champion did not fall at the hands of young men;
Nor did the sons of Titans strike him down,
Nor did towering giants set upon him;

But Judith daughter of Merari
Undid him by the beauty of her face.

We hear again that she removed her widow's sackcloth, "anointed her face with perfume," donned tiara, gown, and sandal to bewitch Holofernes, to ravish his eyes. "Her beauty captivated his mind./And the sword slashed through his neck!" She is full of her tribute to her Lord, to the might of his spirit—"The rocks will melt before you like wax." God's mercy will be great to those who fear him; sacrifice that is made "for its pleasant smell," or burnt offering, holds no significance. It is enough to fear the Lord; he who does so "is always great."[14]

The Judith of Jean Giraudoux's play of the same name is a more worldly woman than her biblical progenitor. She wears Holofernes' cape when she returns from the killing. She has little taste for those who spurred her on to do the deed or were her rivals for the assignment. "You killed him," says one of the women. "Kill? Assassins kill," Judith replies. The woman counters, "Even God knows no other word for what you've done." "Then," Judith rejoins, "God has a very limited vocabulary." Judith insists that her story did not end in hatred: "The truth is that what died in that chamber was a man and woman in love."

Giraudoux's Judith wants everyone to know that the bed on which she met Holofernes was a real one, "with real pillows and real sheets, and down feathers that blew through the air, mixing memories of home and childhood with every excess of passion." She sought pleasure in it and found pleasure in it. A guard, who persists in confronting Judith with all that her deed represented, speaks as one of the heavenly host "reduced" to making himself "vulgarly visible, in the heavy, sweaty vestments of a drunken guardsman."

"If you are God talking to me at last, it is too late," Judith tells him. "Do you really think that God is ever going to talk to you?" the guard asks. "Do you think that God is ever going to talk to any man? No, Judith," he explains, "it is not in words that God is articulate. Those chosen by Him are anointed with thistle oil, their ears ring with the silence of the night, they stumble across the battlefields and where they pass even the dying cease to cry. . . . Can you truthfully say you felt none of this presence along your path last night?"

She wants to hear more, and she does. The guard knows her tenderness and understands her passion. Why must her "night of blasphemy,"

Judith asks, be made to look "like something holy?" That, says the guard, is God's worry: "From where He sits, a thousand years away, God reserves the right to project saintliness on sacrilege and purity on self-indulgence. It's all a question of knowing how to light the stage." He tells her this, "God's most hidden secret," at the cost of his place in heaven. He knows the truth; he speaks it. In the last moments of the play, he mimes her kiss and in doing so proclaims himself "Judith the whore." Judith and the Grand Rabbi agree that he had better be killed. "Then," says Judith, after a last glance at the truthful guard, "let the world make way for Judith-the-saint!"[15]

Giraudoux is not so far from Scripture in the ironies of his play, which he calls a tragedy. Both sacred and secular text insist on the revelation of ego strengths through animus transformation. Judith's tenderness in the play may issue from human entanglement rather than devotion to the supernatural; her song of praise in the biblical narrative may spring from a practiced asceticism; both proclaim her sexuality; both find their conviction after an act dictated by her contrasexuality. Both, in their ironies, point to the tragedy of a world in which a woman's manliness so far exceeds that of men. In each telling of Judith's tale, her potency thrusts itself forward at least as much before and after the deed as during it. In each case she receives as much as she gives and receives all the more persuasively as a woman after the display of her manly strengths. In the play, on her way to the deed, she says of the men pressing her to it, "If I object to the way they're pushing me into this adventure, it's only because I've been dreaming, in my bed at night, of doing something like this on my own." In the biblical narrative, from her first appearance we know she has been long prepared for this, to do it in her own womanly-manly way, to claim and to proclaim her ego, infused with the energies of the Self on whose threshold she stands.

ANIMA AND ANIMUS SERVE THE EGO

The great reversal that comes about when we move our egos out of secondary position is that anima and animus take their proper places, serving the ego instead of mechanically armoring it, or substituting for it, or stepping rudely in front of it. Anima and animus connect now to the ego side of the bridge and deal with what comes over on it. This connection, this service that has replaced competition with the ego, works dramatic changes.

A divorced woman who suffered acutely when her fourteen-year-old daughter refused to see her and stuck to her resolve for four years suffered a cancer of the breast that necessitated its removal. In a sense, she felt bitten through the breast by her daughter and poisoned. After her mastectomy, she found it urgent to her psychic health to undergo an operation to reconstruct the breast, using her own muscles and skin. The operation succeeded extremely well. Through these years of surgery, the woman had worked hard on the meaning of the rejection by her daughter and on differentiation from her daughter. Healing came slowly, but powerfully. It was best expressed by her statement after the dual success of operation and differentiation: "With my breast restored, I have got my manhood back!" Her maleness now supported her femaleness. Her femaleness, now restored to physical wholeness, after poisoning and mutilating, recovered her maleness for her.[16]

A woman in treatment felt the impact of the serving animus when she dreamt of a commando soldier coming into her house from his fighting, carrying a newly born baby in his hand. He was trying to feed the baby at his side, but in his rough, brusque movements dropped it. She heard its head thunk on the floor. Picking the infant up, she saw that it needed to be held, wrapped in a soft blanket, and given milk. The baby responded urgently to her ministrations, clutching her arm, saying fiercely, "MORE MILK!" The dreamer felt her animus had had to care for her baby self and now was turning it over to her to be cared for in a feminine way. She saw that her doing in the world, her commando activities in a successful career, had had to carry her small feminine self. Now she was able to make space for it and care for it in what she called a "being way."[17] Being with the child, holding it, nursing it, was what her femininity cried for. Some women, who have been bruised at the core of their womanliness, must start analytical work out of the animus and stay with it until they can build up their feminine capacity to receive, to be. Then analysis can proceed from that deeper place. As this dream shows, the animus often facilitates that passage.

Sometimes the service of anima or animus to ego occurs in the life of a couple. A wife and mother of three children, who had long functioned to nurture her family, had also over the years quietly painted. The first gallery owner to whom she brought her work snapped it up. She had her first show. Success all around. Her husband was pleased for her. But one night in bed, in the dark, he said to her, "Now that you're getting famous, and all these people are crowding in to see your work, look and see this little guy in the back of the room [he is shorter than his wife]. Will you have time for him?" She let a pause go by and then said, "We'll see." She would not let him make her once again the emotional support of the family and turn himself into a charity case needing sustenance from her to feel himself a man. For the moment she played anima bridge to a bigger view. Her answer kept him on his toes, injecting more spiritual and sexual zest into their connection. She claimed the complexity and excitement that were in their coupling and did not allow any of this to settle into a Mom and Pop operation.

Sometimes the service of anima or animus speaks to our solitude, not to another person. It asks us to make sure our solitude is positive, large, complex, and sees to it that we do not foreshorten our inner conversation. A fantasy that substitutes for our ego takes us out of life. A fantasy that our ego receives enlarges our conversation. Thus a sexual fantasy may direct us to what moves within us. We can awaken to it, come alive in it.[18] This is true of the poetry that most moves us. When we read a poem that touches us, we neither repress our response nor substitute it for our ego. We do not become the poem. We receive something living and moving in it and in us. It opens us to meditation, like Mary pondering the things of Christ in her heart, receiving, not usurping Being. So it is with the love of God. We can take religious experience to replace the ego, or open the ego to allow a religious moment to course through it. When we replace our ego with the love of God, we seal up, armored in fact against faith or love. When religious vision serves the ego, it runs through us like a great river pulling us into the current of love which is Being itself.

Whether we live singly or with another is not the point. What is centering here, in any state of life, is anima or animus feeding ego with things brought from the Self. We must decide then whether we will allow it or not. If we do, we will know quickly what it feels like to house something other than ourselves.

The man or woman who integrates anima or animus looks different, for everyone has become different and in odd and wonderful ways peculiarly themselves. The person is marked by an unmistakable vitality of presence. There is a "there" there, or, better, a "who" there, to paraphrase Gertrude Stein. One woman in analysis spoke of her husband's vital presence. "Something cooks in him all the time," she said. "It makes for excitement, because new ideas or projects or feeling gestures keep popping out of him. He originates." This is the freedom, the absolute beginnings, of the *arche*.

Absolute beginnings—that is an excellent way to describe the mixture of spirituality and sexuality, traced in exalted verse to its source, which is the Song of Songs of the Hebrew Scriptures. The Hebrew title, *Shir hashirim*, simply puts together the singular and the plural of the noun— The Song the Songs. That is a way, better than most, somehow to make the ineffable "effable," to say that of all songs this one is the most sublime, that it reaches to the very essence of its content, or at least tries very hard to do so. We understand, when we get to know it well, why one of its sturdiest and most far-seeing defenders two millennia ago, Rabbi Akiba, said of it that if the Bible is the Holy Book, then the Song is "the holy of holies."

No work has better served mystics seeking a rhetoric to accommodate an experience that seems beyond words. Unspeakable it may be, but they have felt urged to say something about the analogy of love—the human for the divine, the divine for the human—that they have known not as a scholastic thesis but as something alive in themselves, in their flesh, in their souls. They have been there, insofar as finite human beings can be, where beginnings are absolute, where Being seems for the first time to be taking on shape and purpose, even though it may be the tenth or twentieth or hundredth time in this person's experience it has seemed to do so. Identity, there, in such moments, is in Being itself. One is all one can be, for the first time, for ever; male *or* female on the outside, male *and* female within. This is where anima and animus pronounce their archetypal vows. This is where the inner dialogue that springs so naturally from the contrasexual economy discovers its supernatural roots.

We do not have to be mystics to understand this. We have the Song of Songs, with its endless interweaving of masculine elements in descriptions of the female and of the feminine in descriptions of the male, to take us there, to the experience some have had of ultimate freedom. There, each of us in our own way can discover what portion of that freedom might be ours, can see how, without any compunction, we might claim our ego, our definitive I-ness.[19] A splendid illustration of the process lies ready to hand in Jean Giraudoux's one-act play *Cantique des Cantiques*, the Song of Songs.

The substance of the play is contained in a conversation between a Statesman—very much with a capital *S*—and his mistress, Florence, who has come to tell him why she must leave him. She has met Jerome. Who is he? Someone who is always getting hurt, burned, bruised, lacerated. "He bumps into things, he gets caught in doors, he jabs his eyes out with umbrellas." Florence has become an expert in first aid with Jerome: "If he were condemned to be eternally bitten by a snake, I couldn't be kept busier. He's the God of Little Troubles."

What does he look like? Well, not handsome like the Statesman, not with his "pitiless forehead" or "imperious mouth," not with his "fine bearing, serenity, poise and straight, well-shaped legs." If Jerome "isn't knock-kneed, he just misses being so." He doesn't sing as the Statesman would, if such "a great man" could ever condescend to sing for her. She has some sense of what he would sound like from the way he closed his eyes during parts of *Don Giovanni* and *Othello*. As for Jerome, "Well, *he* whistles. At least, he did whistle, but since 12:45 today he has had a fever-sore on his lip."

She met Jerome by bumping into him on the Boulevard. "He was running as fast as he could," and he hurt her. Is he intelligent? Well, he does have intelligent eyes? says the Statesman, who has seen him from a distance. What does he do? "Nothing. He's just there. . . . He uses the furniture for all it's worth. Watching him, you can easily see why men created things like hooks, knobs, dresser-drawers. . . . He gets involved with window hasps or bed casters for hours at a time and sometimes stays up till midnight trying to cope with them. . . . He constantly and meticulously studies the weather: looks out the window, examines the barometer, peers at the thermometer. But he never goes out, never disappears. He is like an aviator before airplanes existed."

This is the man Florence is going to marry. They understand each other, she says; they will be happy. "Quite possibly," is the Statesman's statesmanlike response. She is captivated, and she will explain why. He entered her life like a bullet in her flesh when he banged into her on the Boulevard: "And he's remained embedded." There is no need for surgery. She knows of cavalry officers who have "lived like that for years, with a bullet in their hearts." They just have to "remember not to bend over to open a cask of wine, for instance, and they're capable of living a hundred years. I promise you I'll be careful." She pauses. "Not to mention that Jerome is charming." But there is something more.

She returns to the Statesman's question, What does he do with his life? He manages; he will always do so. "He's clever, ingenious, industrious. He solves the problem of existence as if it were a Chinese puzzle—with his hands." And there is "a future" for him in mechanics or electricity: "I may be ignorant of such things," Florence says, "but I feel there are certain flashes of light, certain short-circuits and fusings which need people like him. He is a nobody. But he is one of those people who might have invented fire."[20]

We can see some such affinity with ultimate fire in Teresa of Avila. She talks to the Self directly. She knows through her own unshakable images for God, such as "His Majesty," direct intimacy with Being.[21] What separates her from a Jim Jones, who also claimed to be on intimate terms with the Almighty, is her obedience and delegation of power. That is what engendered action and service in her nuns. Like the husband in whom something was always cooking, she demonstrates stamina for the boundless freedom the *arche* brings, as it begins things anew and charges our enthusiasm as it has never been charged before.

A husband in treatment speaks of a quality in his wife that we would say has emerged from her inner meeting with her animus, and then, through it, Self. He says that she really receives herself, and as a result he always feels her coming out to meet him. He is speaking of his wife's sexuality. She is a deeply sexual woman because she tunes into her deep belly responses; when he touches her, he feels her rise to greet and grasp him. But he is talking about the way she rises to meet herself too. He contrasts her with other women he has known. They were always available when it was not necessary and never there when they were needed. They were like a train that you must catch at seven to get to work at nine that does not come on time. It sidles into place at ten o'clock, just when you no longer need it. The husband says he has learned that to be really receiving of the other, a woman has to receive herself.

A woman patient speaks of a moment of animus fullness, watching a bright yellow bird. What would it be like, she asks herself, to be like that, mostly bright yellow, with a swathe of black wing? Would it feel as if one were noisy? Like playing a big trumpet? Would one feel like a ray of the sun, landing on earth, hopping and bobbing there? Would it feel like beaming gold, pealing gratitude for being? Yes, like that, she says.

Vitality, presence, originality, stamina, service, receiving, gratitude— these are the glad ways we experience inner meeting with anima or animus en route to Self. And then something more is added—fierceness. A woman spoke in analysis of her astonishment in discovering the radical power of loving. "It rearranges everything into a different order," she says; she feels "both freer and more precarious." What matters most is the relation to what we love—the person, the god, whatever. Holding to the central focus comes first, whether or not we get enough sleep, think ourselves too fat, do not have enough money, are beset with heavy tasks and insoluble problems at work, with a child, from wartime or peacetime distress, or physical pain, or want. Those issues, from the most trivial to the most important, fall into perspective; they have relative significance in our lives, not ultimate importance. They exist and we do not deny them. But they are not central.

What is central is the connection to the other, or actively pursuing that connection, fighting to clear away the rubble from our lives made by the bombs that fall within us. We risk exposure in new ways of making love, new foolishness in our devotion, faults, wounds, fears, as we share secrets kept from everyone till now. Now history is being made, the narrative that really matters as we see ourselves connect with the other. The woman patient who has discovered the power of love says she feels "entirely rearranged."

This same radical determination to keep the route to the center unblocked shows up whenever love achieves its heights in our egos. Etty Hillesum, the Dutch woman sent in her twenties to death in a Nazi gas chamber, writes of her growing discovery in her imprisonment as a Jew in a deportation camp: "There really is a deep well inside me. And in it dwells God. Sometimes I am there too. But more often stones and grit block the well, and God is buried beneath. Then He must be dug out again."[22] The letters and journals Etty Hillesum left behind are a record of her digging and the triumph of her ego's meeting with animus and Self and the Being that informs them. Though more dramatic than most enactings of it, it is the essential scenario when ego and contrasexuality and Self talk to each other.

Ego and Other

OTHERNESS

A repaired ego is an enlarged ego. With an anima or animus that serves it, it now recognizes others as other. Open to the anima/animus bridge on the ego side, we can risk otherness. Housing the contrasexual archetype, we can dare a life of complexity. For what the archetype brings us is the absolute beginnings of the *arche,* and the indeterminacy of the *apeiron.*[1] Within us and in our dealings with others, we know true freedom and its endless variations on the theme of choice. Anima and animus offer solutions, offer puzzles, and always, with either, a vast increase in the consciousness of complexity.

As an anima or animus fills out the ego, it digs up missing shadow pieces and articulates to the ego many planes of unconscious activity, coming as it does as ambassador of the Self. Images rise and tumble into awareness, ideas form, possible new attitudes, fresh thoughts and projects. The advantage of this theory, which Jung deprecates as "clumsy" at the same time as he speaks for it, is that anima and animus as images do not diagnose us with any finality, do not scold us for not having reached a more advanced stage.[2] Images present themselves instead, without value judgments, to begin conversation and ask for response. They surprise us with their vitality. Their energies animate our connection to being. Archetypal images always bring with them lines leading somewhere, beyond themselves. They do not bring finality or an end to things. They keep fishing up for our inspection contents from the collective unconscious, the miracle being that among them is always precisely the fish our particular ego needs to fry.

A well-functioning animus in a woman points her both up and down. The male archetype penetrates her ideas to make her own explicitly what she has implied but has not been willing to put into words. He connects her to what, deeply inside herself, she lives by, to make her step forward to utter her own original word. When we connect to our sacred convictions and our own living inner mystery, we can risk otherness.

Rainer Maria Rilke risked otherness at every turn of his imagination and constantly confessed as much in his poetry. After his first trip to Russia with Lou-Andreas Salomé, he dared to wear the persona of a Russian monk in his *Book of Hours.* In the first of its three parts, "The Book of the Monastic Life," he makes bold assertions as much out of his own *Innerlichkeit* as the monk's:

> I believe in all that's unuttered still.
> My devoutest feelings shall have their way.
> What no one yet has dared to will,
> I shall involuntarily one day.

He was writing, he explained some years later, from an "inner dictation." If what reached paper were creativity and invention of such freedom and boldness that they contained an "admixture of unbelief," it was not as "the result of doubt but . . . of not-knowing and beginnership." Thus Rilke in his monk's robes seems to be boasting when he says to the Lord,

> You see my will's wide extent.
> Maybe it embraces all:
> the darkness of every limitless fall,
> the tremulous light-play of every ascent.

But in fact he is simply claiming with a poet's ego the full range of otherness that is now his.

He speaks to God of painting Him, of feeling Him, of *being* Him, for the poet who dares to assume the Creator's mantle can be said to achieve a kind of divinity: "When you're the dreamer, what you dream is me." If you awaken, he says to God, "then I'm your will, assuming dominion over all sublime." But he remembers often enough that the voice he has taken is a monk's, that the hours he is celebrating are those of the monastic discipline, and that what he has undertaken is a strenuous process: "I dig for you, you treasure, in deep night," he confesses to God. "And my two hands, all bloody and unskinned with digging, I uplift into the wind."

The digging is no less bloodying when his apostolate to otherness moves from sacred precincts to secular. The besetting images are of women now, or of the artist's wars, violent conflicts between sexual desire and poetic yearning, struggles that disfigure and strip and tear him loose from the comforts of tidy creation. The closer he came to the giant works of his last years, the *Duino Elegies* and *The Sonnets to Orpheus,* the more he felt the contradiction between the bloody digging and the treasure that made him exult. On the night before he began the *Orpheus* sonnets, he wrote: ". . . When will, when will, when will it have reached saturation, this praising and lamentation?" Would that he could be content, he muses, with the wisdom of the "master-magicians" of the past:

> O vanity
> of further experimentation! Is not humanity
> battered by books as though by continual bells?

But he could not satisfy himself by just listening to the "old and oldest fathers . . . speaking."[3] Even such wisdom was not enough. He was a speaker, not a hearer. He had something to say in his own voice now about his grasp of otherness, something that others had tried to say or had lived for or died for, but that had been too long forgotten. He had archetypal longings. He knew with absolute certainty what the links between the living and the dead were, and in his elegiacal modality he would describe them clearly, elegantly, persuasively.

In the first of the *Duino Elegies,* he contrasts the Hero—one even whose "fall was a pretext for further existence, an ultimate birth"—with the legendary lovers of unbroken fidelity to their love. They are the true lovers, those who stay on after they have been deserted or repudiated.

But instead of being saluted, they are simply taken back by an "exhausted Nature into herself, as though such creative force could never be re-exerted." He is undoubtedly thinking of the sixteenth-century poet Louise Labé, whose sonnet sequence he had translated, with its mixture of exaltation and pain in her memory of a faithless lover. He instances the case of her Italian contemporary, Gaspara Stampa. Does any girl, deserted by her lover, ever ask herself whether she could become like Gaspara? Should we not, all of us, take more, learn more, from the sufferings of the masters and mistresses of suffering of the past, the great lovers whose desire intensified rather than fell away with desertion? Enough, he is saying, of the marvels of "the loved one"; let us herald now a heroism that links us, the living, to our distinguished dead.

Who are "these travellers" who have gone before us? They are children who possess forever the childhood in which they died. They are all those lovers whose earthly wooings have ceased, with their special icon, the fig tree, which "almost entirely omit[s] to flower"—made barren, the poet must have remembered, by Jesus when he thirsted and longed for the juicy fruit of the fig and found it hopelessly out of season. That tree has long been "full of meaning" for Rilke, as are those girls who "out of their unwithholding graves . . . come and gather" for him, Labé, Stampa, and all the rest. These, finally, are the anima images he has been looking for, girls and women who held their passion to white heat and then stilled their demands, without losing their desire. This is the permanent peace that, he thinks, earth itself has always sought, the serenity of the invisible, of love caught at its peak and held there forever. The poet addresses the earth:

> Is it not your dream
> to be one day invisible? Earth! invisible!
> What is your urgent command, if not transformation?

He makes quick assent to this, the greatest change that earth can work, into death; he will accept earth's bidding. *Erde, du liebe, ich will,* he says: "Earth, you darling, I will!" The wonder of that eternal holding transfixes him, though he is still alive:

> Look, I am living. On what? Neither childhood nor future
> are growing less. . . . Supernumerous existence
> wells up in my heart.[4]

The German translated into bureaucratic English as "supernumerous existence," *Überzähliges Dasein,* conveys a more celebratory sound, but its meaning is the same—surplus Being, something well beyond the usual, an existence that reaches into the beyond, a link between life and death.

That is what Rilke offered time and again to his anima incarnations. One can read what was on offer in his letters to Merline, the name he gave to the artist Baladine Klossowska, separated wife of an art historian. In three years of communications that become more and more burdensome, the poet changes his salutations to Merline from Dear Madame, to Dear Friend, to My Love, to My Dearest, and back again to My dear Friend. Soon enough, he is asking, "Am I going to hurt you?" assuring Merline that he has hurt himself first in their enforced separation. Enforced by whom? By Rilke himself, who is the "servant" of his work, who embraces her (though from a distance) and reassures her, as if to place her in the company of Labé and Stampa: "Nothing mean, nothing degrading has happened to us, to you, Beloved, but only something too *great.*" Finally, in this beautifully crafted set of obsequies for a love that must find its permanence in elegiac memories alone, he sounds the note of *great*ness again, reminding Merline of their time at the Chateau at Muzot where he returned after many years to the *Duino* sequence, beginning with "that adorable Sunday morning when we camped on the bank opposite Muzot, and couldn't get in. . . . Do you remember how long and sweet and light and all permeated with tender benediction that morning was?"[5]

It is to the angels of otherness that Rilke brings his archetypal longings in the *Elegies,* creatures of the coolness and unfazability of acrobats of the high wire, like Picasso's *Saltimbanques.* These transforming spirits of Rilke's late theology earn his "jubilant praise" for their guidance away from "pseudo-silence" and "bursting memorial" in the "City of Pain." The connection he knows now, and has almost made permanent for himself, is to the "Primal Pain," to where the symbols he lives upon are awakened in him by "the endlessly dead."[6] The world of the living is too small, too confined, too noisy, too much given to beginnings and endings for him. His tender benedictions now can no longer be held to specifications of time and place and person. He is altogether one with the "silent friend of many distances" of the last of *The Sonnets to Or-*

pheus. That figure, whom he himself identified as a friend of Vera Knoop, the young dancer whose death the sonnets memorialize, could be Rilke himself, or more particularly his contrasexual self, his anima. Perhaps even more to the point is to see in the concluding lines of the poem a meeting of the poet with the Self of his ultimate destiny:

And if what is earthly has forgotten you,
say to the silent earth: I flow.
Say to the roiling water: I am.

"It can hardly be said," Rilke wrote in explanation of such writing, "to what degree a human being can carry himself over into an artistic concentration as dense as that of the Elegies and of certain Sonnets; often it is uncanny for the person who brought them forth to feel beside him, on the thinner days of life (the many!), *such* an essence of his own being, in its indescribable ultimate weight." His archetypal longings had brought him to the far edge of otherness.[7]

PROJECTION AND RESURRECTION

Anima and animus are notorious in their negative formulations for masking the other. Like Magritte's painting "The Lovers," where two heads completely wrapped by bags kiss each other, we know how we disguise the reality of the other with the images we have projected onto them of what we want them to be or fear they will become. We often forget, in this knowledge, that anima or animus can also act as the lens through which we perceive the presence of the Self in the other.[8] Our projections fly off from us onto all others who offer us a hook in themselves for easy hanging of the projections, things that belong to us that we refuse to acknowledge as our own. When we work hard, in consciousness, to withdraw our projections and to integrate into ourselves the good and bad qualities we have ascribed to others, we may also discern how much information about others our projections give us. Why, we ask ourselves, does the animus fly to this one, and not to another? Why do we project onto this woman, and not another? Why, in the life of the spirit, do we gravitate to this image of the divine over all others?

The unconscious choice of the projective other tells us that this he or she shares something with us, not an identical psychic content perhaps, but certainly an analogous one. The woman whose wooing animus keeps falling on men for whom, in fact, she has no use pulls those men into her dreams just because she does not like them. The animus personifies for her a missing piece or pieces she has repressed in sexual trauma. The contrasexual archetype arrives in the guise of a man she would usually reject, one who arouses her sexually in the dream, precisely to communicate that she must open herself to the sexual responses in herself that she has rejected.

Anima and animus are not confined to personal enactments. They also turn up in impersonal archetypal images that represent the other in us. Who is closer to us and yet farther apart than that one in the other kind of body? The archetypal reach of anima and animus is then to embody otherness itself, not just another sexual anatomy, a particular incarnation of oppositeness or difference. What, it asks us, is this alterity that comes into our most intimate places and occasions our most passionate responses? We learn, in responding to the question, that when we move toward the impersonal aspects of anima or animus, the archetype will bring us to contemplate the rooted otherness in others—their capacity to live in the Self.

This can be dangerous territory, for much confusion and abuse of our own sense of self may arise from forcing others to live their best selves for us. But if we have worked hard to identify and claim our projections, and are familiar with our shadow weaknesses, then our anima or animus can make easy and safe our perception of a centered otherness in others. We can hear the hum of their inner conversation, if not the actual words, unless we have been invited to participate. But even missing details can be descried in the other—generosity, humor, originality, talent— qualities often enough that the other has neglected or disparaged. We find ourselves, in this reach into large impersonal images, temporarily acting for the other as bridge to the riches of otherness.

Teachers of quality do this for their students. Students learn when they are the objects of their teachers' projections in the impersonal range.[9] Teachers see how students' minds work and elicit the development of students' gifts. They make room, through the animus/anima bridge, for their development beyond the school years. The anima or animus can penetrate, in this dazzling mixture of the personal and the impersonal, right into soul space. The learning process approaches here the writing of a poetry of intimacy.

How many of us have been lucky enough to find ourselves suddenly writing poetry out of a sense of connection, through love, to the soul, our own or the other's? Because anima and animus involve sexuality, body, spirit, emotion, imagination, their power to galvanize the other into living in the Self is incomparable. This does not necessarily mean a fleshification of anima or animus in a living person. Some of us find our poetry in outer exchange with another, some of us inwardly. All of us, sooner or later, must have both.

Single or mated, celibate or sexually active, when we come to clearer relation with our own anima or animus, we possess that lens through which we can glimpse the Self of another. One female analyst dreamed many times of meeting with a famous analyst whom she did not actually know, in an office whose French doors opened onto the sea. There she spoke with him about her deep-seated problems of child molestation and the split in her that resulted from it. He, and all that she associated to him, became the animus lens to her Self. She, with this image now living in her, used him as a lens to help her see the Self in others.

Another woman, on the departure for college of her last child, a beloved son, dreamed with a full set of images and sounds a scene that conveyed that his Self, as part of her dream, symbolized the Self in her. In the dream, the boy creates a poem. It is first rate. That is clear, and so is the way the poem ends, with a humming, hissing sound. The sound she hears in the poem is like that of leaves rustling. It is the sound of his moving out.

In remarking the dream, she says he is living so creatively that his poem must issue forth in sound, to bring its hearers into its poetic life. Leaves rustling in the wind, soft but distinct, mark her son's leaving, sounds as of a god passing by, just what is involved in her son's leavetaking: what she hears is his passing into manhood. Seeing his Self, she is given the lens to see the Self living in her. Her projections upon him as her son fade and die; he is resurrected as the man he is becoming.

When our anima and animus projections die to permit us to define the otherness of others, the others resurrect as the Self's version of them. We glimpse that otherness, may even hear it and come to its aid. Our anima/animus projections may function then in any of three different ways: one, defending ourselves by putting onto others what we need to claim as our own; two, noticing who or what is there, as altogether other than our projections, as we withdraw them; or three, trying to glimpse the Self living in the other.[10]

The first function of projection we know well. We connect with the other sex by throwing our nets over this alien territory of the other. Without such projection, we know no interest, feel no love. Libido flows from us to others, but others mean nothing to us; it is an empty process. If, however, we persist and park on another our own contrasexual archetype, then we are forced to deal with ourselves and to recognize that our projections, far from bringing connection, have blocked them. We must then spend great time and arduous effort sorting out what belongs to whom before we can claim responsibility for all of ourselves, sexual and contrasexual, conscious and unconscious, anima or animus.

In the second mode of projection, what we notice is the free-standing existence of the others who have survived the destruction of our projections upon them. When we withdraw our projections, or the others' reality so contradicts our version of them that our image of the otherness there is demolished, what we want others to be for us dies.[11] It is really dead, destroyed. And yet there the other is, standing before us—alive! The fact is that the other exists, as an objective subject, not dependent on our projections for existence. Others come back to us, resurrected, not because we have effected a miracle, but because of the life flowing in them. This can be a central event in our lives that frees us of our fear of our anima or animus aggression. We know now that the archetype is not omnipotent. The existence of others and our feelings for others do not depend on our endowing them with our psychic contents. We do not have to do it all. In truth, we cannot do it all.

This second mode of anima/animus projection makes us notice who really is there, outside us and inside us. We see the other person as other and we see the otherness of our anima or animus psychic content in itself. Where before there was one, now there are two, and both are other than our ego identity. Persons stand in their own right, pronounce who they are out of themselves. Anima or animus stands on its own in contents that represent otherness to the ego. The world begins to get crowded, as well it should, for contrasexual images live in us, between us and others, and, as more and more we are permitted to see in others, as their own anima or animus.

The third mode of anima or animus projection provides the instrumentation through which we meet the Self living in others. Only contra-sexual projection can reach to the threshold of the Self in the other, give access to the utter intimacy Self demands. Here finally are answers to the question we always ask about the grand messes and heart-stopping experiences wrought by anima or animus projection: What is the Self engineering? The Self engineers its being seen, by us, by others, by everyone. To see the Self is to know it and to want others to see it and know it, and thus to live out of it.

Out of nowhere, in the most ordinary of encounters, in the most prosaic of settings, we may be brought to cross the threshold to the Self. A man moves to a new town in Soviet Russia. He loiters in the rooms of his new house, some not yet finished. He is bored; he is a writer in a room with windows that look out to all four directions of the compass. It is the best of places to write in, but he does not feel like writing. Suddenly, the weather changes, a squall makes its noisy entrance. This is Andrei Bitov's "Life in Windy Weather," title piece of a book of stories that find their shape as their central character, Alexei Monakh, finds his.

For all their surface of normality, these are not simply stories about ordinary people doing ordinary things. Nor are they those airless vignettes, forgotten as soon as they have been read, that too often pass for serious writing in the genre. They are movements in and around a man's mind, heart, and spirit, a man set apart, as his name, which means "Monk," suggests. He is not an allegorical figure, but neither is he a study in realistic portraiture, socialist or any other. He is a large-scale human being in the making, a master of projections, a victim of projections, but, in gentle or windy weather, one who will not allow himself to be long oppressed by the pressures of the ordinary in the familiar.

In the squalls of ordinariness, which make up much of the "Windy Weather" episode, he finds substance where Baudelaire looked for it, in asking himself about the things that really matter as he recognizes the "joy and pleasure" his one-year-old son gives him: "How did he get to be like that? He's alive and already has everything? Hands, and eyes, and even ears? And he looks like his father?" He talks to the newspaper he holds in his hands about formalism and academicism, subjects familiar to readers of the Soviet press. He argues with his wife, talks aimlessly, quarrelsomely, driving in a car with his father. Trips to town, target shooting, tea drinking on Saturday, a walk around his village on Sunday with his son in his stroller—the fundamental terms of being in a Russian backwater are defined by example, amiably, movingly, with a touch of Franciscan spirituality, of all things, when Alexei introduces his son to a flowerbed. "It's your flowerbed, these are your flowers," he tells the child. "Here's a little flower, it's just like you, it's your brother." But might it be rather his sister? And then, suddenly again, everything changes. Nothing much happens. Everything happens.

A friend he had forgotten he had invited for the day turns up with a girl. She is, he realizes, an old acquaintance, and at first a confirmation, in word and gesture, of the pleasure he takes in his new study. Then she shows more, "a sense of acceptance of the whole place, Alexei included, that made her presence here seem to him at once natural and eternal, as if she should stay and his friend should leave." Old places and new float through his consciousness, evoked by her presence: "A kind of agreement, some kind of thread stretched between them, and both felt it, he knew it and she did too." Talk leads to song, and she sings, unpretentiously, making the best of "no voice," touching Alexei, who is sure that she is singing for him.

He feels a kind of adolescent hopelessness every time he looks at her and sees her quickly turn away. What shall he do? He finds a piece of dandelion fluff that had stuck to his trouser knee; he plays with it to his son's squealing delight and with a kind of bemused participation by the others. The day is getting on. They come back to their adult senses, all of them, and Alexei accompanies his friend and the girl to the station. The train comes; they shake hands, the friend first and then the girl. She squeezes his hand and looks at him as if he were still playing foolishly with fluff, "but there had been something, there would be something, and he felt a pang and tried to restrain himself, but couldn't—his eyes clouded over and he saw only dimly, and was afraid he might blink out a tear." There is wind on the tracks as the train goes off. They wave. She waves. The train moves off with the wind.

The wind whips up as Alexei moves back to his house, mounts to his study, feels a chill, and shivers. But the house is whole. He feels happy. Evenings in it with his wife, drinking tea, listening to the radio, bringing a toy to his son—"to Alexei it seemed that he would remember this peace and quiet all his life—after all, who knows what direction life might still take."[12]

Thus is anima projection served, very much in the Russian manner—

though not many others, Russians or otherwise, have been so eloquent in their understanding of the grandeur of such moments when our inner life is so directly served, by nothing more, perhaps, than the exchange of some strong glances, a song simply sung, a squeeze of the hand and a wave from a train, moments when, suddenly, anything is possible. Boris Pasternak felt the same enabling force in the women he remembered looking back over sixty or more years to his childhood. The women who lived in his dark lane gave it a "mysterious air." They caught his childhood attention, more than the "fragrance of fresh musk-cherry" that sweetened the windows of the girl next door. He remembered the "grownup quarrelsome women" who "Stood cross in the doorways, like trees/That border municipal rosebeds." He endured in a sulking silence their "lashing tongues and twitter": "To love them became, like science,/An act of devotion and wonder." That is what he remembers of these women of his childhood, and remembers with the appropriate reverence for a projection so long-lasting and filled with so much love: "I say to them truly, 'I thank you,'/Convinced I am still in their debt."[13]

CULTURE

Repairing the contrasexual bridge from the ego-side brings not only more ego life and more perception of others. It changes culture, as clearly writers like Pasternak and Bitov do sooner or later. Here again we see the social aspects of anima and animus. For when we see that what the Self engineers is that it be lived by us and in us, we see that as we draw near to the Self it brings us closer to others. Dorotheus of Gaza had a vision of this: from God, the center of being, all of us radiate out like so many spokes of a wheel. The closer we come in our living to the center, the closer we come to each of the other spokes and thus to each other.[14]

When we disidentify from our parental containers, and anima or animus emerges in us, we open channels in society for the *arche,* the absolute beginnings of infinitely variable, new ways of living as men and women. Our personal emergence combats the deadening effect of society's stereotypes of the masculine and feminine. When we project our anima and animus onto others, we enable their energy to circulate back and forth among us, connecting us each with the other in astonishing ways. This is community in the making. Community—indeed, something close to communion—is achieved when we then withdraw our projections to take the care of these psychic contents into ourselves. For then we perceive others instead of burdening them with our unlived life. This widens the circulation, not just of psychic energy, but of that particular kind of contrasexual energy that seeks intimacy and quickens our hope to live all-out, to be filled with loving.

When we turn and send our loving kindness to the hurt places in our unconscious, and fill those blank spaces with compassion, we build fellow feeling in the world where, at best, pity reigned before. We intercede on behalf of the suffering that made us go dead and blank. We bring the pain home to consciousness and learn to tend it. We are less likely, now, to pollute others with our undigested pain, more skilled in introducing loving kindness into a shared atmosphere.

If we can feel our way into our blank space, we can redeem it from its deadly existence as a vacuum into which rushed animus and anima opinions, low moods, negative judgments, prejudices. We learn to hold our own against the forces of collective impersonal unconscious energy. No better discipline exists for holding our own against the fearful negations of society than the inward exercises of ego clarification and consolidation.[15] We can build an ego strong enough to relate to and offer channels to the unconscious. Thus we eclipse the diminutions of narcissism as we build an ego attitude of sufficient breadth to go beyond our personal ego needs or those of our small group.

We accept now animus or anima attacks of self-judgment as signals to think more intensely and over wider areas, to let our feeling go to deeper realms, to gather all the fragments of reaction in us, to construct a personal viewpoint which is really our own. We dig down beneath the layers of family, group, and social stricture to a spirit deep in our unconscious wells that inhabits us as wordless beliefs and acts of faith. This becomes a skill, a practice; we let the spirit touch us and do not feel we must arm ourselves with conclusions before the fact, though we know there are great risks here. We open not just to others or to the otherness view of the anima or animus, but to the otherness of the spirit; we touch the still point from which life moves into us and through us into our culture.

When we face the splits in ourselves by receiving the suffering that originally occasioned them, we show a formidable social consciousness: we are moving to heal and bind up the divisions in our world. Becoming more sensitive to the pain the splits reflect, we put back into the world around us our capacity to mend and to reconcile. A willed activity replaces the wishful longing characteristic of the split-anima or split-animus condition. Claiming in our ego its residue of the split archetype permits us to use its aggression for a clean blow, where necessary, without the old dragging, demanding undertow of reproach to others. We can sustain action, can submit to the disciplines and routines of productive work.

To take in now, in full consciousness, the abandonment we earlier felt intolerable, the sorrow that came with it, the fear, opens us to our own feeling. We may really give ourselves up to love for another—person, attitude, aim, faith—not as child to parent, but as vital sexual adult, capable of surrendering ourselves in our devotions. We have become venturesome. We are not frozen in customary functions; we fulfill no typology. The introvert follower runs for public office. The extravert leader resists inflation and withdraws to a cell to reconnoiter the paths to the center. In matters of mind or soul, we can give and take criticism without fearing the after-kick of inferiority.

Above all, an interdependence builds among us. We relate to our collectives differently. A woman relies on other women to live out the ways of being a woman that she cannot or will not find in herself. A man discovers conjunction where he has known only competition with other men. Mutual dependence beckons, opens, supports, where earlier it threatened. We do not have to do everything ourselves. The ragged nerves of the fateful omnipotence dream quieten and die. We find a fitting dimension in the complex repair work we have done on the archetypal bridge to the Self, moving from the ego's side; it is the size of human fulfillment.

We have discovered that the bridgework we have been doing is a work of love, a going-out, a going-toward, even when it is a going-in. When we meet ourselves in the inward journeys of contrasexuality, we are still going out and toward otherness. We have been tutored in our understanding of what it means to be by the presence of all *others* we have met. The very notion of "meeting" points to otherness; we cannot meet even ourselves without knowing that others exist, and more than knowing, wanting to know that they exist, if only to confirm that we do too. But it is not a mere assent to Being that such a meeting brings about; the confirmation is larger than that in this work of love. We come to something like the "ethical subjectivity" that Emmanuel Levinas celebrates in the philosophy he has constructed on the edge of theology.

Levinas is clear about this: "Ethical subjectivity dispenses with the idealizing subjectivity of ontology, which reduces everything to itself. The ethical 'I' is subjectivity precisely insofar as it kneels before the other, sacrificing its own liberty to the primordial call of the other." The other always comes first, as "the richest and poorest of beings: the richest, at an ethical level, in that it always comes before me, its right-to-be preceding mine; the poorest, at an ontological or political level, in that without me it can do nothing—it is utterly vulnerable and exposed." Levinas illustrates his argument with an arresting image: "The other haunts our ontological existence and keeps the psyche awake, in a state of vigilant insomnia."[16]

This set of insights is not contradicted but simply enlarged and deepened, if it is understood in terms of the other we meet in our response to the contrasexual presence in us. There, acknowledging the enlargement of the person that anima or animus brings us and affirming the claims of the ego in the presence of the Self, we experience the right-to-be of something infinitely larger than ego and that always comes before it, the wealth of Self. There, too, we do not merely come to understand, but actually experience at some level of consciousness, the truth that without the intervention of Self, the "me" in us must be unspeakably poor, the poor that we always have with us. *If* we reach out to others— *when* we reach out to others—we do so from this mixture of wealth and poverty that is our enabling, empowering, ethical being.

The Russian theologian S. L. Frank makes the same point in his exposition of a reach to otherness that extends from us to the transcendent. It starts with any and every response to the world around us, to ideas, to things, to persons, wherever and however it is that in the modes of cognition, in our acts of consciousness, we discover ourselves: "If the subject's cognitive activity is to be directed upon an external object at all, it is necessary that prior to and independently of such cognitive contact we should already 'have' the object in an *immediate* way; otherwise, the very idea of it—the idea of something existing outside us— would be impossible. We 'have' the object, because we and it are from the first indissolubly interconnected in the all-embracing and all-pervading unity of reality; this is why we 'have' that which cognitively is *not given* us, and are aware of the object's existence when we are not perceiving it. The very conception of *transcendent* being is based upon this unity."[17]

That is the unity which the contrasexual Self looks to effect and make clear to us in the abiding language and symbolism of male and female. Here we find the mystery of our identity, rooted in otherness. In the contemplation of that mystery, we are brought inexorably to face death, our own death and the deaths of others, in the place that death occupies in what Frank calls "the all-embracing and all-pervading unity of reality." What will we choose, then, as the organizing center of our reflections? The ego alone, which is tantamount to a death wish? Or the ego in the light of Self, a life wish, *the* life wish?

Repair from the Self's Side

THE REPAIRED anima/animus bridge, with our ego stronger, stands open to the otherness of other people and eager to move toward the otherness of the Self. When that eagerness yields to repair from the Self side of the bridge, union with the Self becomes possible. Large-scale purpose enters our lives.

As the repair begins, the bridge itself becomes more personally ours. Our anima or animus shows its own special face to us. Yet at the same time, paradoxically, it emerges as less subjective. It is intent on assuming its role as a psychic function. Thus, trying to repair the bridge from the Self side, we enter modes of thinking and experiencing typical of the Self, textured with self-contradictions, apparent absurdities, which ultimately we will see make good sense. So it is that our anima or animus becomes at once more precisely ours and more unmistakably an impersonal psychic function.

ANIMA AND ANIMUS DIFFERENTIATION

When we identify ourselves with our ego's views, as most of us do most of the time, we see the unconscious only as it directly affects us. We forget that we also affect the unconscious. It can change at any time as a result of our conscious interaction with it.[1] We not only sublimate the unconscious but participate in its transformation. Anima and animus provide some of the best examples of this blessed process.

When we make honest efforts to engage the contrasexual archetype, with full ego-responsiveness to meet whatever comes across its bridge from the Self, the roles anima and animus play constantly change. They may grow positively or negatively in response to the attitudes affected by our consciousness. At best, we are so utterly open to them that their role-playing personifications cease and they operate in our psyches as connecting bridges. But their transformation depends on more than our attitudes. Other factors, such as illness in our bodies, upheavals in our culture, the behavior of others around us, are major carriers of change.

The best way to track such change in ourselves is to observe our dreams over months—even, if necessary, years.[2] One woman's animus figure patterned itself on a man with whom she was intimately involved. Even after she brought the relationship to an end, she went on dreaming about him, indeed in remarkable ways. The dreams, after the breakup, did not match his actual personality any more, but used him instead to make their own points about the animus that remained there in her.

Her first dreams configured her old lover as a bum—absolutely down and out, unemployed, bedraggled, smelly. After several months he appeared cleaned up in the dreams, with better clothes, and a job. Still later he appeared well dressed, well engaged in a professional career, with his own office. At the end of two years, in the last dream in which he appeared, he telephoned her to say, "You are a dear woman. I will always love you." She felt healed. A weak side of her was strengthened.

To the dreamer's surprise, more than ten years later she dreamed of this man twice again. In the first dream, he appeared before her with a male lover. To this she associated the wounded side of the man's masculinity. In reality, he was not homosexual, but did lack erotic connection to the depths of his own identity as a man—and spent much time defending it. She feels his taking a male lover symbolized a filling out of the animus in herself, underscoring the greater range of emotional life now open to her. Several months later, in the second dream, she and he "discover a deep love" between them, in their enduring friendship. To this she associated the difference between the inner animus and the real man, who had refused ever to see her again once their relationship had ended. She felt her animus had grown much stronger. Because, in the dream, he loved and claimed his maleness, he could now afford to love her femaleness, too—though, in the dream as in life, they were no longer lovers.

Another woman, a celibate religious of middle age, worked hard in analysis to recover her blighted masculine side. Her relationship with her father had been marred by his drinking and her mother's rage over his extramarital affair, which she had confided to her daughter. He was "a loser" in the daughter's eyes. Her early entry into convent life removed her from any contact with men that might have modified this negative image of the masculine and its compensatory counterpart, her idealized version of what a "real man" would be. She rose rapidly in her religious order, so that when she did meet men again, it was in her formidable persona as Sister, or, assuming the badge of office, as Mother. At the time of a significant dream series, she had reached the point where consciously she felt positive about men and even considered a change of life in which a relationship with a man would be possible.

The dreams occurred over the span of a year. They showed that her unconscious fear of men remained, which surprised her; they also revealed a gradual growth in her animus figure, which changed from a threatening invader to become a possible partner. The series begins with a young boy breaking into her room. She grabs his leg, acting to threaten him so that he will not return. The next dream presents her brother, telling her that she is so controlled that even the pleats in her skirt stay firmly in place at all times. A month later, she dreamed of awakening at night to find a man sitting on her bed, apparently meaning no harm to her. But she is fearful nonetheless, and she tells him to go, which he does.

The dreams progressed in a kind of benevolent melodrama, showing the way the unconscious tries one way, then its opposite, bringing out our worst fears, then our fondest hopes. She dreamed she was holding a boy captive, and that an androgynous figure, boy-cum-girl, kissed her. She dreamed that she was in bed with a man, about to begin something sexual, but just then he was called away. A mess dominated another dream, junk all over, which a man promptly cleaned up. Again a girlish boy kissed her, and she feared being caught. She dreamed that a man was waiting for her; that a man left her money; that a man was protective of her. She fled a man who looked as if he might rape her. A man told her mother that her father was dead—that is, that the father image that had captured her was no longer alive in her. She dreamed herself very much upset because her brother was about to move in with her. She goes on dreaming of possible mates. Her life, in and out of dream, is greatly enlarged.

Serial dreams work that way, revealing change, effecting change. A case in point is that of a man who underwent a remarkable transformation of his anima. The change occurred through more than four years of hard work in analysis. The dreams of the early years featured a crazed anima, a diseased one, one that was dying. A turning point came when his female analyst appeared in his dreams, identifiable as herself, but with a crazy quality in her, and again in an episode of physical illness. Finally, in the last dreams of the series, the anima presented herself to the dreamer asking for his help. He responded and took her under his protection. Acting in parallel to the anima's changes were changes in the dream ego. At first fascinated and frightened by the crazy anima, then concerned and moved by the analyst's suffering, then willing and eager to help this woman with her troubles, the dreams showed the patient his potential to be transformed in reality in ways that matched the transformations in his dream anima.

The Self is remarkably accommodating to the progress from dream to reality in the contrasexual life. A wise as well as engaging example is presented in the central plot of Anthony Trollope's *Ayala's Angel* and its subsidiary stories, which bring everything in the novel to happy conclusion in a rash of marriages and promise the possibility of union even to those who seem most recalcitrant to the sacrament. The book, published in 1881, the year before Trollope's death, is one of astonishing psychological depth, probing, witty, tied to the genre of social comedy. But Trollope's mature view of people and events here is closer to happy endings as Dante understood them in his *Commedia* than to the minor pleasantries that usually conclude tales like this one, cast in the Cinderella mode.

Twice in the novel Ayala is likened to the fairy-tale character. Her constant dream is of being brought to experience "the beauty of love" by a hero of "almost celestial,—or at least, aethereal" qualities, who "should think it well to spend his whole time in adoring her and making her more blessed than had ever yet been a woman upon the earth." He is her Angel of Light, surrounded by an aura that seems like an early forecasting of the orgone-box effect, "a tinge of bright azure." The greatest deepening of the animus figure that she can manage is something, the narrator tells us, like a "Sallow, sublime, sort of Wertherfaced man"; although, lacking direct acquaintance with "that beautiful description," she must make do with her own private version of the configurations of Romanticism.

The Werther association arises in her early ruminations about the man who, in spite of every contrary indication, eventually turns out to be her Angel. He is Colonel Jonathan Stubbs, who is, she thinks when she first gives him serious thought, "very, very ugly. She was almost disposed to think that he was the ugliest man she had ever seen." But for all that, she likes dancing with him, "unangelic" though he is. She is clear soon enough that he is more attractive to her than her cousin Tom Tringle, whose manic determination to marry her makes for some entertainingly tumultuous scenes, including an attempt to storm the Colonel as if he were an enemy bastion. It takes some hundreds of pages before she can see how good he is, "this red-haired ugly Stubbs. How well had he behaved to Tom! How kind he had been to herself! How thoughtful of her he was!" Given her age and the terms of her life, she is not quickly prepared to see that Stubbs, the Genius of Comedy, as the narrator describes him, can fulfill a role that for her must have something of the tragic in it.

Ayala and Lucy, the Dormer sisters, have just the right family name, left to their apparent fate as nineteen- and twenty-one-year-old orphans, thrust for living accommodation upon the mercy of relations—another pair of sisters, one married into poverty, one into wealth. The madly importunate Tom is the son of the wealthy sister. The impoverished one can provide as largesse only a merciless flow of cautionary platitudes. The complications of unruly and overly ruly family feeling, of manifestly ill-sorted visions of the good life and the place of sexual desire in it, and of a range of fools and follies of Erasmian proportions produce an absorbing series of plottings and counterplottings, of wooings and counterwooings. In a set piece, splendidly put together around a hunt, Ayala and Stubbs trade such complexities and fatuities and move wooing and counterwooing into plotful place.

Stubbs asks for her hand: "Ayala, may I still hope?" "No," is all she can say. He is simply not her Angel of Light. Is it because he is ugly, he asks her, because of his name? Yes, she says, to both. Is it because she has imagined something more grand in her imagination than he? Another nod. "Then, Ayala, I must strive to soar till I can approach your dreams." The chief comfort she takes from this exchange is that the Colonel had admitted "that the something grander might exist."

Indeed it does; it exists, as things turn out, in her. She comes to understand that she must merge dream and reality in a kind of parallax effect, achieved by changing her point of observation. "Her dreams," she concludes, "had been to her a barrier against love rather than an encouragement. But now he that she had in truth dreamed of had come for her." All of which is a way of saying what cannot quite be said, that the dreams were right and wrong. To have infused her animus figure, her angel of azure light, with elements of pure spirit that no earthly creature could possess, was mad. But to dream of a man of heroic proportions who might come for her, and to begin to see those proportions fleshed out, as clearly they were in red-haired Colonel Jonathan Stubbs—that is the essence of the sanity of Self, and with even a touch of its sanctity. For insofar as this newfound angel of earthly light is the Genius of Comedy, he is proportion itself, which he demonstrates in one entertaining exchange after another, with Ayala and all the many players in this beautifully turned comedy.

The sense of proportion of the novelist is handsomely displayed in the many trips to the altar that make up the book's happy ending and the gathering of related bits and pieces. There are characters of a wisdom becoming in age, and others of a foolishness that spares neither the old nor the young; there are characters of such a mixture of drollery and substance, and in such number, as to make them candidates for an addendum to La Bruyère or the characters in John Aubrey's set of very brief *Lives*. It is not unexpected that among these Trollopians should be one who sacrifices dreams of wealth for what the sententious Victorian would have called "true love." Less expected, and a true measure of *Ayala's Angel* and its animus endowments, is the fate of Tom Tringle, "who," says the narrator in a somewhat taunting phrase, "if the matter is looked at aright, should be regarded as the hero of this little history." That is not to make Ayala less than its heroine, but to confer upon Tom, for all his follies, the high credit he deserves for his "persistent passion." Rilke would understand such a longing as Tom's for his angel, that anima figure "he had been able very clearly to pick out . . . for himself." He had "failed in his attempts to take the angel home with him," but he had been constant in his attempts as long as success seemed possible. Like Goethe's Faust at the gates of heaven, his striving will pull him through.

There are faint ironies in the long paragraph of praise of Tom Tringle, which ends as Trollope commends Tom to his readers as the hero of his narrative for having "fought his battle out to the gasp." But there is also something well beyond irony, a conviction based upon understanding. Tom may even reach beyond the Colonel in his heroic despair, for "it may be doubted whether the Colonel ever really despaired," Trollope muses. "The merit," he concludes, "is to despair and yet to be constant." And so in the annals of anima/animus travail, Tom Tringle rates a place beside Louise Labé and Gaspara Stampa—and Ayala and her angelic Colonel must surely agree.[3]

HEALING

Trying to repair the bridge of anima or animus from the Self's side brings healing to the specific wounds we suffer there and large possibilities of happiness in such gaudy terms as Trollope proposes, in which failure so often leads to success. The negative animus or anima that always gets us off on the wrong foot yields its secret when we add to the reductive analysis, where we seek to find the source of the negative judgment we have internalized; and to the prospective one, where we ask what that judgment might lead to. We are insistent, reductively and prospectively; where, we demand to know, does this voice belong?

One of the most discouraging things in analysis is to realize some understanding of our symptoms and its causes without being able to do much about them. We may analyze origins and development in very fine detail, see all the complex interweavings of all the variables, and still suffer. The answer to our dilemma is in the question, Where does this voice, this negative voice, belong? Different solutions quickly propose themselves, but even more important is that we know now we cannot just rid ourselves of the judgment, but must listen to it and include it in our treatment.

The woman patient who suffered from constant animus hectoring, pronouncing everything said or thought "trivial, shallow, obvious," found this question went right to the center of her soul's quest. She had not herself accepted what this was, had not found her way into her own way of working, thinking, praying, which everything in her proclaimed she should have. She had always identified instead with those scolding masculine voices, the judges who looked at her from on high, pointing to the standards of her church or her profession or her own self-imposed sexual canon. Where her stern inner judges were right, she saw, was in indicating that she had remained too much on the surface, and seemed, as a result, shallow, trivial. She stayed too easily with what she knew, what others knew, as collective and conventional. In that sense, what she did was "obvious," inadequate, not fair to herself. She saw now that she needed to go down into the midst of her false safety and the confusion that came with it, and claim there what really moved her body and her soul.

She discovered, as other women today have been discovering, the place of the Self in the body, in her own female body. This gave an entirely different entrée to truth in her life. Her struggle to define and assert her own spirituality met her struggles with her sexuality and the sense she always had in both areas of being alone. Though shared, at least on the surface, with friends and colleagues, her life was a lonely one, and more than once she had felt compelled to pick up and move to some other part of the country.

These three strands—of sex, spirit, and loneliness—came together in an unexpected way in her body. She slipped on winter ice and broke her back. A tiny fracture of three vertebrae at her waist—the precise point where the upper body of spirit joins the lower pelvic body of womanly sexuality—called loud attention to her drama. The physical split mirrored her psychic split.

She remembered, then, a vital dream of a few years before. In it a woman of authority sat before her, asking, Where does the Spirit come into you? The same woman answered: For me it comes through my back.[4] She felt this dream now was coming true. For she was forced to remain in bed many weeks and find her own rhythms of work and rest for each day. She waited now on her body, and a good thing she did, for its trauma provided the place of breakthrough for her. Her body forced a major change in her: no longer was her ego in combat with its animus judges; the body-Self was guiding her now. It was not lost on her, either, how much she had resisted, and for how long, submitting to her most commanding strengths. Inside her inferiority lurked a steely determination to run her own life. She saw now the folly of resisting the promptings of spirit in her body, now that she had no choice but to submit. Pain forced her to bed—where she met her Self.

Breaking her back, she said, was to break away from that mercilessly competent one who had managed everything for her. From her sickbed, she both told off her judges and began at last to take their counsel seriously, asking where it might make sense in her life. To her surprise, she found connection this way to others in big things and to the transcendent in little ones. She found the spiritual in the daily round of her life. Her body kept her fixed on her own path. When she wavered, her body hurt; she knew she had strayed. She felt she was apologizing to her body for years of disregarding it. This was confession and atonement.

The body was the vehicle for her bigger Self. Before, she had felt the spirit was its only vehicle. Now she found a new feminine mode in the incarnation of the spirit in her body, and she found herself listening to the messages the combined forces brought her from the center. Summing it up, she said, "My injury is about transformation from a masculine to a feminine base, from holding myself above life to moving in the midst of life; from a thought-centered life to a fullness of life in the flesh." She had happily been brought down to foundation truths—all her analytic sessions necessarily conducted on the floor, she flat on her back, her analyst sitting beside her.

We can always ask, and should really demand of the infamous negative animus or anima, Where do you apply here? What is your place in my life? The answer will not come by the negative voices stealing silently away. They have demands too; they insist by their defining archetypal character on being knitted into us. They can even say with Lady Julian of Norwich that it is God's work, after all, to knit us whole.[5] The man, for example, who is always weeping because he feels homeless, despite the many women who would like to make a home for him and his relentless courting, is expressing his anima's feelings. She is the one who is homeless and bereft, because all his flirting goes outward; he never turns toward her warm, holding strengths. Identified with her instead of relating to her, he weeps now, bereft.

That is the exact situation at the beginning of Boethius's *Consolation of Philosophy,* that seminal work of the Middle Ages. The writer, he who used to pen his verses, "with youthful heat," sits weeping now in his prison cell, his work dictated to him by bruised and roughened muses. Fortune has turned against him. He lives drowned in sorrow. As he prepares himself to compose a work full of his woes and complaints, he looks up to find a woman standing above him. She shows a grave mien, a clear eye, ruddy color that bespeaks a strong and confident sensibility, and an oddly changing stature—now of average height, now seeming to touch the "very heavens." Her clothing is handsomely made, though darkened as if by long use. At the lower end of her skirt are fixed two Greek letters, *pi* and *theta,* separated by "certain degrees" that indicate an ascent from the first, which we learn soon enough stands for philosophy, to the second, which stands for theology. There are pieces missing from her garments, as if ripped away by people anxious to have some part of them, but she herself seems undisturbed, holding books in her right hand and a scepter in her left.

There is no more arresting anima incarnation in literature than this noble lady, drawn at the lowest point of his life from Boethius's inner dialogue to bring him consolation. She is Philosophy personified, come with strong remedies, "Mistress of all virtues," as he calls her. He has been thrown into prison, falsely accused of plotting the restoration of "Roman liberty" and the practice of astrology in the Roman Empire, and condemned unheard by the Ostrogothic King Theodoric, whom he had served well enough to rise to the rank of consul. The great lady who stands there with him cannot free him from death; his execution may come at any time. She can lead him to discover the course of his affliction, the offending wound in him, and from that discovery begins the cure of his despondent soul.

The five hundred miles from home he has been taken to reach his prison is the merest suggestion of the distance he has gone in banishment from his inner Self. His journey in the five books of the *Consolation* is over a series of vexed questions back to Self. He must accept that the world is not governed haphazardly, by chance; he must see the role of Providence in human affairs. But before restoration of faith in the nature of things, he must recognize, says his beneficent anima, "the greatest cause" of his illness, that he has forgotten who he is. What follows this solemn conclusion of the first book is an elegant allegory of being and time, in which the villainous role is assigned to the blind goddess, Fortune, and Boethius's plentiful calumniations of human destiny are arrested at the source—his misreading of his condition and everybody else's. In alternating passages in prose and verse, in fitful dialogue and thoughtful cadence, we confront with Boethius the perils of misplaced faith in Fortune's wheel, the pitiful spoils of fame in a universe that measures its time in ten-thousand-year bites, the emptiness of self-evidently short-lived pleasures, the quickness of beauty to decay. We must put our trust only in those things that are intrinsically good. We must everywhere distrust what comes to us openly proclaiming its frailty and easy mortality. We must move toward sources, to our own beginnings. The argument concludes in Book III as Philosophy sings a series of swiftly negotiated lines, beginning with a defining aphorism — *Felix qui potuit boni/Fontem visere lucidum* — "Happy is he who can behold the fount from which all good arises."

It is the warm, steadying presence of Boethius's philosophical anima that makes the *Consolation* the rich allegorical work it is. Without her, we would still have a theological treatise of some stature, but not one that makes us so eager to be compassionate with Boethius in his misery. We might well understand how effectively he translates Augustine's definition of evil as a *privatio boni,* a deficiency of being, into his own idiom, but we would lack that sense of the living power of the doctrine that comes from its unfolding in dialogue. There is conviction in Philosophy's pronouncement that "others' wickedness does not deprive virtuous minds of their proper glory." But what makes us accept this as more than doctrinal definition is what we have been privileged to see of Boethius's inner life in his anguish over what seems to him the unmitigated reign of evil in this world. If we accept Philosophy's argument, we must do so with more than intellectual assent: Boethius has demonstrated in his person that he has the will and power that those who follow evil ways altogether lack. His anima, brought by him into theological combat, has made persuasive by her person (which is, after all, part of his own person), as much as by her rhetorical skill, the assertion that "evil men leave to be that which they were . . . by embracing wickedness they have lost the nature of men."

Boethius's rhetoric in the *Consolation* serves him and us splendidly. It makes possible some ease with the mysteries of a Providence that give so much latitude to the ungodly and such travail to those, like himself, of sturdy faith. But clearly he is doing more in his last days on earth than persuading himself that there is a trustworthy governance in the universe and that contingencies such as his serve some purpose beyond a tortured martyrdom. It is not to make his logical case and stop there, though few have ever been better equipped than he to do so, as we know from the technical works of logic of his own, from his translation into Latin of all of Aristotle's *Organon,* and from his commentaries on the *Categories* and *De Interpretatione* of the same philosopher.

The underlying purpose of the *Consolation,* which becomes clearer with each reading of the work, is to make all of us who read it aware that we share his situation. We may not have been moved five hundred miles to await our death far from home, and we may none of us have been the victim of equal injustice. We may not know so firmly the day of our departure from this life or the means. But all of us are under sentence of death, and all of us have known some gross intrusion in our lives, some indecency that has made us question the whole fabric of our existence. What is more, so secure are the terms of his allegory that even the notion of being conveyed a long distance away from home to await death may be said to fit us all: when we die, we are banished from our familiar surroundings; we leave what we thought was home. What we have to give sense and dignity to our lives, if we follow Boethius where he leads, is the assurance that we are seen by the "beholder of all things," in whom we do not put our trust or turn to in vain. If, says Boethius's gracious lady, "we do this well and as we ought, we shall not lose our labour or be without effect." How do we know this? By the consoling presence of Self embodied in all of us as it was in Boethius, a philosophical voice, a calming one, whose remedies could not be more closely at hand, the very model of a Self-centered anima.[6]

Works like the *Consolation* teach us that we cannot simply rid ourselves of our vexing negative anima or animus problem. What we can do is to place ourselves in different relation to them, after having vowed to know as much as possible about them. Even the Bluebeard animus, with all its horrors, serves a major counseling purpose: some of us, the Bluebeard legend tells us, will be caught in the plots of the animus and be killed. We need to see it coming, to respect its monstrous powers, to be canny in dealing with it. Some parts, even of such a malevolent archetype, we can integrate; some we never can make use of; but we need not fall victim to any part of it.[7]

A deep mother-wound is a special case. We tend to armor all around it with our anima or animus assumptions. Repair comes only by penetrating that armor, discovering and filling in the wounded place. Then we can convert the anima or animus energy we have used to equip us with a new weapon to peel back the armor, to see and claim our wound. One woman had worked hard to absorb the pain she had known when her mother abandoned her to a servant to raise, out of preference for her sister. Then came a remarkable healing dream. In it, four women — she, her mother, her sister, and the servant — are all cleaning objects in her old childhood room. Preparing for her death, her mother wants to paint an abstract picture showing the experience of death. The dreamer hopes her mother will bequeath the picture to her, but feels it is also all right if she leaves it to her sister. All the parts of her feminine legacy — the two mothers, her ego, and her shadow sister — come together on the eve of the death of her wounding mother-complex. The mother imago initiates a summing up of her life knowledge and a passing over into the unknown. The dream ego hopes to inherit this knowledge, but accepts the shadow's right to it as well. Significantly, it takes place in her child-hood room, though the dreamer is in fact a middle-aged adult; thus it spans the womanly generations of her whole life, from birth to middle age.

Often healing a mother-wound expresses itself in a woman's dreams as a final acceptance of the mother for what she is or a fitting of her to the woman's own psychic dimensions. Three separate women exemplify this motif. All experienced their mothers as annihilating their younger femininity. All were caught in insistent defense against this threat. In analysis, all three learned to use the animus energy that had armored them so they could sustain the prickly, questioning penetration of the defenses they had erected against their wounds. Their animus energy changed from a repellent shield to a newly accessible power to take what they needed. The first woman dreamed that it was necessary to chop her mother into little pieces and then to eat them. The image graphically expressed her dismembering of her negative mother-com-plex and her coming to integrate it. The second woman dreamed that her mother gave her an elegant and very expensive red suit. She promptly cut it up, saying, "The suit doesn't suit me." She delighted in what she made out of her mother's suit for herself; it made her feel creative. She knew her mother would resent what she was doing to her beautiful suit, and she was dutifully sorry about that, but she did not feel guilty in any way. Here the dream ego received something of sub-stance from the wounding mother, but fashioned the gift to her own reality. The third woman dreamed that her mother's dresser was full of blouses, all of which she, the dreamer, could now wear.

Sometimes a female analyst constructs the anima bridge to fill in mother-wounds. The man who expressed his hate by withholding himself from two women, while simultaneously he played with their affections, dreamed of his female analyst as a combination of both women. The dream analyst says to him that she cannot quite fathom his commitment to her. In talking about the dream, the man says he knows that though he has gone in and out of therapy, the analyst will always be there, despite all his efforts to thwart her. "You have not let that happen," he says. "I am grateful." He had never in his life known a durable connection. He takes the anima energy he had used previously to protect himself and uses it now to look into his elaborate defenses. He risks new and different experiences with his analyst; he allows the full weight of his dependence to rest in her.

When the bridge to the Self is broken in the devil's pact or the demon lover obsession or prolonged bouts of addiction, repair becomes a fierce undertaking. The analyst must go into dreadful places, himself or herself temporarily acting the contrasexual bridge, in order to open a space where the patient's inner conversation can resume.

Addiction to a demon lover or to a substance usually effects merger with animus or anima. But that is only the beginning. The contrasexual bridge then merges with the Self, and the ego that should be the motivating force in the psyche is swallowed up in all the parts. The analyst must intervene, interrupt, somehow break up the gloom of fallen inner life to make space for an emergent anima or animus. Once that can be made to happen, a person's ego can prompt inner conversation again. One gains a standpoint outside the addicting substance, which may not make it disappear immediately but does give psyche and person elbow room, which is to say, living space.

Take the woman addicted to food who had known such success in her profession. Her idealistic animus always turned outward with its energies to engender and beget new work and new attitudes for others around her. When she herself needed some of that energy, her animus invariably disappeared from sight. Or, she said, she could see it, as if it were speaking in a public forum, with its back turned away from her, never deigning to acknowledge her and give her what she needed. Her ideals did not support personal inner conversation for her. She felt spiritually starved. And so once more she binged on food.

Her female analyst had to forge a new animus bridge, constructed in questions about what was going on in her own interiority, behind the public forum, when she languished, sick, in bed. The analysis was directed to probing, poking, bringing energy into her, fighting off and differentiating from the idealistic animus so eager to express its interest in the world's great problems. A space was opened. Conversation began—a startling one!

The conversation was wordless. Utter stillness filled the woman. Many times in her analytical sessions she and the analyst descended together into this silent place. Then the patient brought her stillness into group therapy. It was interesting to see the reactions of different group members to this silent communing, mirroring all her previous fears of it. She descended to her utter stillness, simply into being there, with no words, no expressed purpose, no project, no lines of development. She was suspended, as if in a womb, a being without doing. Her body was visibly still; in its negative form, pulled down into an immovable inertia. But arriving there, she found images came in some abundance, not to explain her silence, but to express it. No categorical tag can be assigned such stillness, no words can conceptualize it. Images express it, and do so spontaneously. It is like air or soil out of which things rise, grow, breathe, live. This state does not need to explain itself. It just is. And will be.

This is a state that wants to be shared. The silent woman induced a similar mood in other members of the group. One woman, who could accept it willingly, found her own anxieties draining away and pleasant images arising in her to restore to her her own sense of being. A man felt perplexed, not really understanding where this woman was. Another woman wanted to fix it, seeing the mood as passive, she said, infantile, compensatory to this woman's very active life. Another woman had an image of a plumb line hanging straight down, swinging until it stopped, pointing downward, absolutely centered. Another saw herself facing the quiet woman on a double porch swing, moving gently back and forth.

The quiet woman herself felt the mood as both positive and negative. This dark nonverbal stillness—would she ever emerge? Could she come back? Yet there she met Being itself, and she knew that it fed her hunger properly and gave her the room she needed to dispense with addicting foods. The silence lay beneath her compulsion to stuff herself; it stilled the addiction.

Analyzed reductively, the quietude led all the way back to the woman's premature birth and confinement in a hospital incubator for months without benefit of being held by her mother. Analyzed prospectively, the stillness opened her to the feminine strengths moving in her body, in a being that could sustain her once it was quietly accepted for what it was. It was like Heidegger's reaching toward *Dasein*—the state of being-there—but he needed thousands of words to arrive there. Words are of little value in trying to deal with this sense of being, either to speak for or against it.

The quiet woman borrowed her analyst's animus temporarily to uncover the place of nonbeing where she had been left alone in the hospital, unsupported emotionally in the first months of her life. When she could receive it back into consciousness, it filled her—with dread, with full silence. Consenting to it, she knew this state engendered Being. It was her core, the Self as feminine. It fed her all the food she needed.

Being arises out of such encounters, but its defining stillness makes it easy to reject it. We are in a place of meditation and prayer and waiting on God. It is what lies underneath Simone Weil's asceticism and willed illness, out of which she learned, she says, that we must get rid of ourselves in order to let God in.[8] This is a space whose silence proclaims its determination to be shared.

The sharing of that space is the determined end of the medieval writers whose insights Jung courted so assiduously. They looked back and forward to spiritual experiences of an intensity and fullness that deserve to be identified by that much-abused term *mystical*. Jung looked, as we might all do, regardless of the degree of our religious concerns, for some deeper penetration of psychic process.[9] That the penetration is there in these writings seems to us inarguable, for what their authors work and pray for is to be able to cast all of themselves far into the inmost depths of human interiority. What they accomplish with remarkable frequency is not only the experience itself, but a rhetoric appropriate to describe what they have experienced. Their aim is to share what they have shared of a space that they are certain is accessible to all of us who will go after it as determinedly as they have. Thus they set forth what has happened to them audaciously, in great detail, and as systematically as possible.

The rhetoric of these writers is bold. It does not scruple at issuing commands. The writer of *The Book of Privy Counsel,* the same anonymous master who wrote *The Cloud of Unknowing,* explains to the "spiritual brother" whom he is counseling that he is "not yet prepared to be exalted all at once to a spiritual feeling of God's being." Because you are just beginning, he says, and "your spiritual feeling is inept, I therefore first commanded you to chew on the naked, blind feeling of your own being, so that you could climb step by step to the point where you could be prepared, through spiritual perseverance in this secret exercise, for this exalted feeling of God."

The "secret exercise" is blunt and clear: it is to take "God as He is, as quickly and simply as you would take a plaster, and apply it to your sick self as you are." In other words, "try to touch by desire our good gracious God as He is, to touch Whom is endless health, as the woman in the Gospel witnesses: 'If I touch only the hem of His clothing I shall be saved.' " You are to do this "without any subtle or special regard" for the things that belong to your being or to God's, whether they are "pure or foul, of grace or of nature, divine or human. Nothing is now required of you except that your blind beholding of your naked being be lifted up joyfully in loving desire to be fastened and united in grace and in spirit to God's precious being, in Him only as He is, and nothing else."

The informing principle is that of the "perfect lover," who strips himself of himself "for the sake of the thing he loves, never allowing himself to be clothed except only in that thing which he loves." But we do not come easily or quickly to such exalted exercises, and so we must begin by chewing on the naked, blind feeling of our own being.[10] This is something we do of ourselves, within ourselves, displaying that holiness that Socrates works so hard in the *Euthypro* to establish as inherently human. When we have worked long enough at this gathering in of ourselves, this dedicated chewing, we will be motivated to move on. Karl Jaspers describes the feeling well as the end purpose of philosophizing:

> Although as finite temporal existence we remain veiled, and must uneasily make do from moment to moment with preliminaries, yet there is within us a hidden depth that we can feel in exalted moments, something that permeates all modes of the encompassing [being] and that becomes certain for us precisely through them. Schelling said that we

are "privy to creation" — as if in our ground we had been present at the origin of all things and then had lost this awareness in the confines of our world. In philosophizing, we are engaged in awakening the memory through which we will return to our ground.[11]

In the contrasexual experience, this awakening is the dividing point of the inner journey. This is the point where we leave the conveyance of knowledge behind and enter that of love. The twelfth-century narrator of the journey, Hugh of Saint-Victor, is clear that both modes are essential. In our knowing, we build "the structure of faith"; our love "embellishes the building by its virtue." Each requires the other, "for the building could not be glorious if it had never come to be, nor could it give delight were it not glorious."

Hugh's language is cast in the heightened rhetoric of medieval exegesis, seeking and finding in biblical texts a deposit not only of faith but of love. A well-honed scholarship is thus directed to make warm and alive symbols which, even in the serene religion of the twelfth century, had begun to calcify. So in this passage from his *De Arca Noe Morali,* his moralization of the story of Noah's Ark for knowing and loving purpose, he takes up "the two modes of God's indwelling in the heart of man" and leads us from his knowledge to the inner spaces of our love:

> Now, therefore, enter your own inmost heart and make a dwelling-place for God. Make Him a temple, make Him a house, make Him a pavilion. Make Him an ark of the covenant, make Him an ark of the flood; no matter what you call it, it is all one house of God. In the temple let the creature adore the Creator, in the house let the son revere the Father, in the pavilion let the knight adore the King. Under the covenant let the disciple listen to the Teacher. In the flood, let him that is shipwrecked beseech Him who guides the helm.[12]

And so we are provided, as we are so often in our inner dialogues, with images and interpretations out of primordial text, out of dream and fantasy, out of every kind of human experience. This is moralization with a humble as well as an exalted purpose. It is to lead us in prayer and meditation to our point of origin, but just as surely to give us support in the shipwreck, as Jaspers and his existentialist confrères never tire of reminding us, that life so often becomes.

A moral element also belongs to our addictions and our obsessions with a demon lover. In the devil's pact we want something for nothing. We want to use another person to short-circuit the long, arduous work of building our own identity. If X will be mine, my life will be secured. Ecstasy, money, a high place in the world, health, peace—whatever I wish will come to me. No one makes me feel the way X does. With X, my soul blooms, new insights pour into me.

We substitute X for our own life, and work especially hard at the arduous task of differentiating ourselves from our shadow. For what identifies X as a demon is the fact that in X we are persecuted by all the qualities we have steadily refused to grapple with in ourselves. But X is more than a destructive presence. In X we are given glimpses of what living toward and from the Self might be like. We must not then just bewail our fascination with the demon. We need to use the contrasexual energy it brings to seize that glimpse of a life well lived, to pay it close attention, to free it of its shadow contamination.

Addictions always possess elements of moral choice. To recognize this fact is to be returned to our own power to make choices. We can refuse the next drink, or joint, or bout of cookies. But now we make the choice out of an acknowledged dependence on something that is really there outside ourselves, not inside us. We choose now not out of ego, but out of ego-related-to-Self. This is the higher power of the Twelve Step programs used so successfully to combat alcoholism and the like. What our addictions short-circuit is exactly this obedience to something beyond ourselves. We betray Self, as sign and symbol of Being, by denying its existence and persistent presence in our lives. Then we need to gorge on it in substitute form, because our absence from it leaves such a gaping hole in us. We fear we will fall in, and forever. Better, we think, a drug, a drink, a stuffing with food.

What rests on the side of addictions and of demon lovers is creative energy. Sometimes our addictions arise from fear of that energy; we fear that it will galvanize us to an unsupportable pitch of awareness. We are sure we will burn up in its fires. Again, we have short-circuited the work we need to do with our ego to withstand the intensity of such a presence by housing it. The man who suffered from masochism, and saw his anima split into opposing light and dark female figures, found in the bridge of unity built in analysis a religious dimension that broke wide open in him. Symbols of precious meaning arose to confront him in himself, in his own inner reality. His anima appeared as a tiny infant girl whom it was his task to nurture into life. Even his forgetting her, por-trayed in dreams as his leaving her on the street or in the subway, brought him home to the Being there in himself. Instead of staying passively in thrall to dominating anima figures, he accepted his little ego work, to care for the little girl. He saw that hidden in this small task of his psyche was a majestic ritual: to house the great religious themes that were moving through him. He renounced, as we do all such diminutions of being when we cross over to Self, his death-dealing fetish and mas-ochistic drama, to serve what lives deep down inside all of us and far, far outside.

Self and Other

WHEN WE confront the Self on the repaired animus/anima bridge, we confront ourselves as persons. We can face the negative energies of anima or animus, see where they belong, deal with them. Healing begins. And suddenly we recognize operating in us an impersonal anima or animus. It is an odd experience. We stand well within our contrasexual complex and well outside it at the same time. Just to be able to see it functioning in us brings a certain detachment, even as it goes on functioning. What we are seeing is, in fact, nothing less than our habitual orientation to Being.

THE IMPERSONAL ANIMA OR ANIMUS

Perhaps now we can gather the strengths of what at first seems a dualism of anima or animus.[1] On one side, the personal, the contrasexual archetype operates in us as it is shaped in its personifications by its meetings with the significant persons of the other sex in our lives and by the dominant images of masculine and feminine in our culture. On the other side, rooted in the objective psyche, we find those impersonal elements of the archetypal masculine and feminine that somehow have been constellated in conjunction with our particularity of person. The qualities here are large; their reach extends back to the primordium. For one woman it might be the animus as hero; for another, the animus as weak and humble; for a third, the animus as sexual ignition.

In the reconstructed anima/animus bridge to the Self, the archetypes are less subjective than they have been, more concerned to connect us to our center. We can perceive then what kind of bridging they offer, which is our particular way to the center, what is its dominant quality.[2] Healing finds a deep level in us. The plates of our psychological foundation shift. It is not that we must change our orientation to Being under anima/animus pressures. Rather, they change us when we see what that orientation really is. We see through it to Being-as-such; and we are not so easily trapped in our negative contrasexual problems any more. We can walk swiftly now across this bridge into Self-living; we are not constantly stopped along the way by anima or animus pot-holes and icy pavements. The bridge works now.

Our struggle to house and humanize archetypal energies breaks the hymen of our understanding: wisdom can enter. We see, finally, the struggle of the sexes as an interior one. We are open where once we were impenetrable to these mysteries. We go directly to interior inquiry, that ongoing conversation with ourselves that underlies any true communication with others.

For example, the woman much wooed to sexual intimacy in dreams by an importunate animus began to break open this recurrent plot and all its variations.[3] Either the dream man was one she would utterly reject in real life, but felt strong attraction to in dreams, or he was drawn strongly to her, or the two of them were strongly drawn to each other. The repeated point seemed to be a wooing of her into ecstatic surrender to her own feelings. She was being courted by a different way of being, where her own feelings dominated events. In reductive analysis, she uncovered the roots of this motif in the childhood molestations by her brother that had split off a piece of her own sexual responsiveness from her. She saw the wooing motif as her own attempt to recover the missing part of her feelings and sexual responses, and through the objectionable animus figure, to recover connection to her love for her brother.

In prospective analysis, she discovered, in the wooing mode, her own automatic orientation as the one who wooed others as she wooed meaning in her life and Being-as-such. She saw that she always, in a kind of automatic reflex, unconsciously positioned herself to woo others for their approval and thus to draw interest and connection to herself. But then there was something more in the orienting principle: the wooing that came to her in dreams, and her courting of others also reflected Being-as-such wooing her.

In wooing others, she really was trying to woo them to Being—to get them to see, feel, hear the center of life. She did not trust Being-as-such to woo either her or others for itself. Her ego as a result often felt overburdened and anxious. She needed others to mirror her to feel at ease. But, as the analysis of the dreams revealed, what she wanted was to make them feel at ease as they recognized that Being itself mirrored them. The fact was that Being-as-such was wooing her. Through the animus complex, now, she had found and could respond to the transcendent's wooing—directed, of all persons, at her.

What space this brought! In its efforts to win others, her ego could see reflected the efforts of the center to win her, to win others, to win all. She relaxed. Being could be allowed to work through her. She did not have to do it all. The Self was using her problems, her wounds, anything it could find in her that would open to Self and permit it to woo and to enter and win her back to wholeness.

Two numinous dreams a few days apart confirmed this insight. In the first, she dreamed she was dreaming in an afternoon nap. In this very deep place, the dream within a dream, she played with many straight stalks of grain, gathered them into a bundle, and then dropped them. They were transformed into hundreds of small beads of dark blue, crystal-clear, shining light, blinking on and off like sequins, like stars. She associated the dream experience with a throwing of the *I Ching,* a casting about for predictions—which she rarely did, thinking one should resort to it only after using all one's ego. Here, however, she gave over to a wisdom beyond her ego or any other.[4] Here the stalks, thrown into random configuration, became scintillas of light, all reflecting possibilities of Being, all beautiful to the sight.

Several days later, in dramatic contrast, she dreamed that she had utterly collapsed, in a significant public forum. She was to speak or read something to an audience, and suddenly found she could not. She had lost her place; all her papers had tumbled down around her. She simply could not do the job. She said it felt like a total breakdown of her ego. She was helpless. Then one of the wooing animus figures appeared to lead her to the top of a mountain, in the night, to see the wind and the stars. Working out her associations to the dream, she said it seemed to be telling her she could no longer manage her life from an ego point of view. It was not at all like a nervous breakdown. She functioned very well. But there it was—her orientation was still too much ego connected and ego conducted. The dream told her that was over, done with, finished. None of her usual self-bolstering, self-gathering techniques would work any more; they lay around her in disarray.

Then the wooing animus arrived, and she knew immediately the great size of the attraction between them. He gathered her up to the wind and the stars, where the spirit shines in the dark. She linked that dream event to the dream of the hundreds of scintillating points, shining like stars in a dark night sky. Her wooing animus was directing her to look beyond her ego, to see in the vast night the guiding light she had found in throwing the stalks. The split-off part of her that was personified by the animus figure—the outcast she had rejected along with its problems—provided a point of access where the transcendent could reach and infuse her. In response to all her work on this motif and its accompanying dreams, her analyst said simply: "The wooing god."

The wooing god can speak to us without words and can fix images of the transcendent in our minds even without light—that is the point beautifully made by two poems called "Tenebrae." One is by the German-speaking Romanian poet Paul Celan, perhaps the most arresting writer in his language after the Second World War, a master of terse, tense, gnomic lines. The other is by the English poet Geoffrey Hill, a writer slightly more loquacious than Celan, but equally a master of teasing oblique verse. The darkness of *tenebrae,* the ancient ceremony that fulfills the functions of Matins and Lauds on the last three days of Holy Week, is splendidly suited to the temperaments of both poets. It also serves the wooing god superbly.

In the *tenebrae* ritual, sung in church as a vigil service on each of the nights before the concluding days of Passion Week, the lights are put out one by one, reducing everything to darkness, except for fifteen candles fixed on a triangular frame called a hearse. They in turn are extinguished one by one at the end of the Psalms that make up the liturgy of *tenebrae,* right up to the last candle, which is not snuffed out until after the *Benedictus,* the song of thanksgiving customary at this service as it is at Lauds. Finally, in full darkness, the solemn words of Psalm 51, *Miserere mei, Deus,* "Have mercy upon me, O God," are recited.

Celan's poem addresses the crucified Lord as one among many fellow victims. *Gegriffen schon, Herr,* "Already held, Lord," he says, we have been clawed and have clutched and clawed ourselves, "as if the body of each one of us were your body, Lord." And so he says, simply, *Bete, Herr, bete zu uns,* "Pray, Lord, pray to us," and then repeats what is the central physical fact announced by the poem, "We are near," which he will reprise once more as the last line of his ceremonial address to the holy darkness, *Wir sind nah.*

We came to you to find water, Celan tells Christ on the cross, and discovered that you had shed blood: "It glittered." The effect of that shining blood was to "cast your image into our eyes, Lord," the poet explains. He pictures us, we of his time, we of this time, standing with our mouths and eyes open and empty of expression to drink the blood and with it the image of the crucified Lord that is stamped in it. Our nearness to the crucifixion has become identification with it, so thorough has this wooing of God been. Celan speaks these words from experience: his parents were victims of a Nazi concentration camp and he himself spent time in a Romanian labor camp in the time of the German occupation. He has every reason to feel at one with the God of the cross and to ask for his prayers.[5]

Hill's ceremonial darkness resounds with similar images, etched in ironic outline. We perform our responses to the divine wooing under the supervisory ministrations of a strange creature in motley—at once an angel with a "flushed and thirsting face," an "Eros of grief who pities no one," and "Lazarus with his sores." We are identified in some way with all this mosaic of misery, but especially with the figure of Lazarus, for we too will be brought back, if not from the dead, then from a "desolation . . . where sins rejoice," from "false ecstasies," from preoccupation with self-celebration: "Our love is what we love to have;/our faith is in our festivals." If we have any "rectitude," it is one "that mimics its own fall/reeling with sensual abstinence and woe."

Hill's ceremony recalls us to go beyond the "true marriage of the self-in-self," beyond "a raging solitude of desire" and the voice we eagerly contribute to "the chorus of obscene consent." We confront in the Good Friday that follows upon *tenebrae* the drifting cold of a world that sees only a figure of folly on the cross, a mere fulfillment of "auguries." And yet so powerful are the poet's lines and so telling the wooing of the crucified Lord that we are left, as in Celan, with the image of the cross stamped on our blood. We know now, having rehearsed with Geoffrey Hill the fearful event and the flatulent responses to it, something of what he meant early in the poem by the phrase "the darkness of your choice." We can read again, but with larger sympathy now, the lines at the midway point in the poem that speak so memorably to the redemptive power of a lasting Passion:

Stupefying images of grief-in-dream,
succubae to my natural grief of heart,
cling to me, then; you who will not desert
your love nor lose him in some blank of time.[6]

The persuasiveness of such poetry resides in its evocation of the contrasexual dialogue. The Christ of Celan and of Hill is certainly more than an animus figure, but nonetheless exerts some of the same claims on our attention. He is the Christ of the liturgy, of history, of faith; he is also the incarnation of passion that haunts our inner conversation, not only of the suffering and exaltation of the redemptive god, but of every experience in fact or in anticipation that we may have of such intense mixtures of grief and desire, of ecstasy and desolation. Reaching for some understanding in our own flesh and blood of Being-as-such, of Being at its source, we conduct ourselves into our own signifying darkness, a *tenebrae* service, even if only of stammered words and truncated images, in which we pledge ourselves not to desert our love or lose it or him or her "in some blank of time."

Some of the most moving examples of an animus figure revealing our orientation to Being come to us from woman writers separated, by choice or otherwise, from companions. They eloquently show us that this sort of revelation comes in an inner process, working with a partner within us, not necessarily with an outer person. Gertrude Kolmar, Irina Ratushinskaya, and Emily Brontë are such women, the first two alone in prison, the last alone in her introversion on a lonely heath.[7] The first pair suffered deprivation and degradation, Kolmar at the hands of the Nazis, Ratushinskaya at the hands of the Soviet state. Even in the midst of enforced labor in a Nazi factory and later in a concentration camp, and a Soviet maximum-punishment prison for political undesirables, these poets show the begetting powers of truth, of life creating life. Kolmar writes about experiences she never was to enjoy with another—

of desire, of lust, of bearing a child. She digs down into the lives of other castoffs, in the world of reptiles, to carry her poetic energy. She likens herself to the whole Jewish people, and her body to a continent on earth.

Ratushinskaya writes of being abandoned, of feeling betrayed, lost, having to create out of nothing. That was what she was forced to do, given no paper, unable to allow her politically incorrect sentiments any other outlet. She carved the words of her poems on soap with a matchstick, standing in the shower where no one could see her. Then she would memorize her poems and wash them away, off the soap. They must not be found. She knew that her dossier defined her crime finally, simply, as "poet."

Emily Brontë conceived new visions about the interactions of good and evil in *Wuthering Heights* and demonstrated out of her lonely musings a remarkable insight into the power of the Self to overcome a negative contrasexuality. These women, in their transformation of unpromising personal situations, entered new life into the world, new vision, new mixtures of old and new, feminine and masculine, personal and impersonal.[8]

A woman's dream shows how an inner reunion with an animus figure may connect her to the objective psyche, and connect her in her own odd idiosyncratic fullness of being. She dreams of an important animus figure, a public man of recognized wisdom and standing in her profession. She has never met him but has read his books. In her dream she holds a long conversation with him, first where he works, then over tea at his mother's house by the sea. The doors of the living room open right onto the sea. He reaches over to take her hands in both of his, in a warm and friendly manner, looking right into her eyes. He is alert, interested, admiring; they are colleagues. She feels it possible to talk with him about her wounds. Both dream openings make sense, that they might be colleagues and that she should show him where she is wounded. His mother is absent, but the dreamer feels her presence in the background, like the sea. In her associations to the dream, the woman says she feels something healing coming from deep inside her. This man really sees her, recognizes her as one who matters in his world. Behind him, mother and sea also seem to receive her. Her woundedness is recognized too, but it is not the center of attention; like the wise man, the wound is her colleague, no more, no less.

In a male patient's orientation to Being, an abyss that can swallow one up and devour hope becomes a dominating dream image. His ego works hard to fight back, but like a Sisyphus figure is always defeated by the rock of depression rolling down on him again just as he reaches the top of his energies and is about to free himself from his burden. To compensate for this burdensome ego-orientation, his anima—or at least a part of it—beckons to him seductively. He feels in this mood great attraction to a woman, a drive in him to expand and exceed his known boundaries, to unite with being. He falls into a bliss that is Dionysian in its intensity of feeling. But that frightens him all over again, and he comes to see this anima figure as threatening. It is just another way life is organized to "get you," he says. After the stress of such a mood, he feels ashamed and infantile and does so each time the mood assails him. It is as if he had plunged into some kind of fusion of being with another person, as if he were striving to return to the womb. "It is not manly," he says to his analyst. But the anima part of him dislikes his overdetermined ego attitudes, his unremitting hard work, which dooms her to feed on meager scraps. He begins to suffer depressions.

A shift of emphasis and eventual recovery comes from two directions: his ego listens to his anima and ceases to be so singular in its goals. Then his ego responds in still larger measure: it makes space for the expansive feelings of the anima. Contrasexual space arises, in which he can begin to receive his experiences instead of always scrutinizing, distrusting, and emending them. His anima relinquishes the manner and behavior of a frightening, crazy temptress in order to show him another side or archetypal reality. Being shows itself now as a *plenum,* not as an abyss, but as a resolving fullness. Here his expansive feelings and drive to union with another person find a life of belonging. The tyranny of "too little" gives way to the freedom of "much more."

This major shift in the foundation of his life gives the man ways to see through his depression, to take it as signifying that there is more in him, much more, that wants to be lived and deserves to be claimed. His depression, he understands finally, rose from the fusion of anima and ego in a negative conjunction of opposite pulls—one side pushed him to work ever harder; the other, to play, to expand, to see the muchness, the abundance. When he could grasp and accept the plenty that was rightly his, he discovered in himself something that amounted almost to religious vision.

Another anima-orientation to Being was uncovered by a man who always positioned himself to "take care" of women. That was his "position"; in an actual relationship, he neither asked nor gave enough of himself. Inexorably, he felt cheated, unsupported, not backed up. He was stuck in a plodding sense of responsibility, in overburdened attitudes. His blood pressure zoomed. He knew from his work in reductive analysis that his anima position stemmed from childhood, where he did in fact take care of his mother. Caught in the toils of narcissistic need, she evinced little interest in him or his needs, his wishes, or his hopes.

He felt caught in the toils of the mother-feminine. He longed to reach a woman who would have a transforming, enlivening, exhilarating effect on him. He idealized such an image of the feminine and looked worshipfully from afar at anyone who might produce the desired effect. And there he seemed destined to stay, between the two opposites, the depleting mother anima and the fulfilling but much too distant transforming anima.

With much work and the development of creative dialogue with his anima figures, profound change entered the arrested life. It can best be summed up by his saying that he had discovered the feminine "in-between." He meant exactly what he said. From his conversations with the opposed anima figures and by painting elaborate pictures of them, he came to experience the feminine as a palpable presence, in between himself and imaginary figures wrested from his anima struggles, in between himself and others he knew at work, in between himself and cultural objects, in the theater and films, in music. "This in-between feminine comes from a different place," he said, "out of feeling and body presence. Reaching the right feeling-tone makes such transformation possible. It really does exist there between us."

INNER CONVERSATION IN THE PLACE IN BETWEEN

When we see the impersonal side of our anima or animus, we can begin to understand how we position ourselves toward Being, whatever the position, whoever we are. We conduct conversation with ourself from a range of departure points: now from the ego point of view, now from an animus or anima perspective; now from the Being that comes through that perspective, now from the Being that exceeds it. We no longer need to remain identified with any one standpoint. Hence great movement arises in us, amounting in rhythmic vitality and range of imagination to a whole new set of dance steps. It is almost as if our animus or anima had disappeared and this lively inner space had arisen to replace the archetypes.

Here room for all opposing viewpoints exists. The impersonal archaic energy of the archetypes meets with the humanizing adapted standpoint of the ego and the culture of which it is a part.[9] Everything mixes and meshes. Each element changes the others. Tradition and originality coinhabit. An instance is a woman theologian, puzzling over the meanings of the Trinity in her work. She feels the reality of the dogma take root in her own experience, teaching her students. There, in brisk interchanges over the difficult but also energizing materials, arousing the fullest use her expertise and a fine range of questions and insights, Being accumulates in her students. Being circulates in a rich conversation that goes far beyond the normal parameters of discussion. The students teach as much as they learn. The teacher learns as much as she displays expertise. The material is as much added to as opened up. All inhere in each other, yet each brings distinct gifts. The questioning—Who is Father? Who is Son?—ranges around and around, less clear to these discussants than the place of the Spirit in the three-personed deity. Spirit acts as the agent of interchange, supporting the lively conversation among the persons and the material between them in pairs, in threes, and within each of them in reaching out, part by part, to all the parts of a Being so fully formed that it has no parts but can only be understood in terms of part-objects by creatures who are all parts. The material acts like a fertile father; the teacher and students, like an articulating son.

The enduring strength of trinitarian symbolism is in its emphasis on relationship. However we configure the three persons of the Trinity, as an article of faith, or an "interesting" survival of the beliefs of a distant time and culture, or simply as part of the typology of the visual arts, they bespeak relation—close, familiar, mysterious. The mystery is not solved, but rather supported by the great theologians of the Trinity, for in the relations of the persons of the Trinity we confront Being itself, and with or without the graces of faith can only speculate about the complex metaphysics that a seamless Godhead, altogether without parts, can spawn. With Augustine's majestic work, the *De Trinitate,* the complexity and the seamlessness find the most productive of human mirrorings.

Conceived in the image and after the likeness of God (Genesis 1:26), we must bear in our soul the marks of the Trinity, Augustine reasons. These are most clearly seen in our seekings after self-knowledge. There, the way we understand the Self, and what we understand of it, and the will with which we bring the means and the end of understanding of the Self together, become a trinity at the center of our own being. This is the trinity of *memoria, voluntas,* and *intelligentia,* of memory, will, and understanding.

For Augustine, *memoria* is the record of ourselves, of all that we have been and are and have stored away, not simply a set of facts or impressions that we can summon up to fill out forms or to answer examination questions or to satisfy interrogators of any kind who are in search of simple, one-level responses. Our *memoria* is where we go for the knowledge that *intelligentia,* understanding, seeks. In the quest for self-knowledge, *voluntas* becomes *amor,* a more powerful form of the will. Now our trinity of memory, love, and understanding can demonstrate that sense of Self, as Augustine says, where "the mind remembers itself, knows itself, loves itself." We do not "as yet" see God this way, the theologian admits, but we do see the image of God, and we see it in ourselves.

The identifying "predicate" of the Spirit in Augustine is *munus* or gift, corresponding to the fatherhood and sonship of the other persons of the Trinity; it is that gift, that giving of the Spirit, that informs every significant penetration of the mystery of the Self. The motivating force in our exchanges with anima or animus, in our inner conversation, comes from such a giving or givenness. There, in those exchanges, we find our identity—that most precious core of self-knowledge—and do so in relationships quite within ourselves, however much they may owe to the life we have lived with others or the shaping forces of family, friends, and lovers from which our inner archetypal presence draws its informing energies.[10]

Our understanding of language, and thus of speech and thought, rests upon some such conscious construction of relationship, along trinitarian lines. Historically, the doctrine of the Trinity, "the most important element in christian thought," according to Gadamer, "is all the more important for us because in christian thought the incarnation is also closely connected with the problem of the word." In the development of Augustinian ideas in the Middle Ages and the Renaissance, the relationship between human speech and thought was freed from any kind of mystagogy of the logos, and the fleshification of the Word in Jesus accomplished not a distancing of language from natural understanding, but exactly the opposite: "The uniqueness of the redemptive event introduces the historical object into Western thought, brings the phenomenon of language out of its immersion in the ideality of meaning, and offers it to philosophical reflection. For, in contrast to the Greek logos, the word is pure event."

The astonishing fact is the power of the Word—not, as Gadamer says, "that the Word becomes flesh and emerges in external being, but that that which emerges and expresses itself in utterance is still a word." It is not simply a word, but an entity that reveals. By itself it is nothing "and does not seek to be anything. . . . It has its being in its revealing." Appearance does not matter for the word in human use any more than it does for the Word at the source: what is important is not what Christ looked like on earth, "but rather his complete divinity, his consubstantiality with God." Theology's "task" is to "grasp the independent personal existence of Christ within the sameness of being." The Word performs its revealing function again, here the "mental word": "This is more than a mere image, for the human relationship between thought and speech corresponds, despite its imperfections, to the divine relationship of the Trinity. The inner mental word is as consubstantial with thought as is God the Son with God the Father."[11]

In the consubstantiality of word and thought, our inner conversation defines the nature of relationship for us, not as a general rule or by the use of abstract terms of any kind, but in the most concrete ways. We prepare ourselves to meet particular persons with the particularity of inner contrasexual dialogues. We do setting-up exercises, so to speak, with anima or animus, with word and image connected to specific moments and to specific feelings, or to something that would like to become such a feeling, with its own clear identity, in a particular moment in our lives. We do so in the middle of the night, in the morning, during a meal, while washing up, getting dressed, riding in an elevator. We may not, even for a moment, translate the experience into such terms as "consubstantiality"; we would think ourselves grandiose to do so. But even so, the experience does have such grand dimensions. We are addressing or being addressed by our reality. It is a reality in which our inner conversations prepare us for outer relationships—in which, if we respond to the archetypal promptings with a sufficient consciousness, we make ourselves ready for the most significant experiences of our lives, not the least of which is to be able to recognize them when they appear and to dare to take them on.

Our inner conversation is not confined to our interior space; it can address the soul of another, too. Our contrasexual faculty permits us to see Self potential in any bearer of otherness that springs into our meditations. We may or may not hover over another's soul in the life we share with others. Something important may come of this, or nothing may ever arise in outer relationships. In either case, we hold on to the power of loving within us, because we are so concentrated, dwelling as we do upon the center as it is manifested in others. This is the way we come to know the profound work of intercession for others.[12] Silent, hidden, as an intrinsic part of our interior dialogue, we offer something of ourselves for them, or even in place of them, so that they in their turn may risk reaching far down into themselves, to identify the center in them and to grow from it.

Our periods of grief find a receiving place, a nesting place, in the center we have uncovered in our inner conversation. Images, sorrows, affects pile up here. We can sort them through, give them their appointed place. We can see what we want to keep. We can feel free to discard some of what is in the large piles.

This in-between place builds into a realm of great resilient toughness in our lives, nestling there between ego life with others in the world and our purely unconscious instinctive life, where the archetypes command. Anima and animus make their bridges most comfortably here. On them, the in-between realm finds its place, or even sometimes becomes so large and authoritative that it replaces the bridge. It becomes our precious middle kingdom, our trustworthy one, our center of reality.

Here we do not have to repress murderous impulses and envious slashings, but neither do we have to act upon them. They can circulate. We can examine them from our ego vantage point, from anima or animus, from Self, from within them.[13] Multiple perspectives allow multiple reactions, endless combinations. We mediate. We meditate. We hover over life as it is given to us and to others.

Here is where things get conceived. We improvise our world of possibles. We put things together and knock them apart, trying every which way. We meander mentally; we try on emotions. Almost anything will do, even archetypes, and so in our imagination we become the dread witch, the slimy toad. No conclusions have to be reached. Without immediate purpose, this in-between space ultimately gives rise to the deepest purposes of our lives, those that we end up devoting ourselves to.

In psychological terms, we build up a capacity here for the dialogue of active imagination, which may speak through painting, or dancing, or playing an instrument, or keeping a journal. We find ourselves in touch with all the different parts of our lives—our moods, our eagerly joined feelings, our unwanted shadow parts; our animus or anima, the public face we adopt as persona, our real center.[14] Our skill in conducting this conversation grows as the figures emerge with whom we can converse.

What Jung calls the transcendent function builds up, the ability to transcend the bitterness of conflict and to hear two or more sides speak back and forth until a new view—a third, or even a fourth—emerges that combines opposites but cannot be reduced to them.[15] It arrives as new. Its destiny is reconciliation where once opposition set the tone. Symbols begin in this work, and contemplation becomes almost instantly accessible, as we move to root ourselves in body, instinct, and archetype.

In this space, civilized ego and the underground river of unconscious Being meet. From the meeting, society receives its revivifying water. Without the meeting, we either dry up in an aridity of ego or are flooded by unconscious torrents; our whole social existence heaves and buckles in psychic illness. As Jung puts it: "The needful thing is not to *know* the truth but to *experience* it. Not to have an intellectual conception of things, but to find our way to the inner, and perhaps wordless, irrational experience—that is the great problem. Nothing is more fruitless than talking of how things must or should be, and nothing is more important than finding the way to these far-off goals."[16]

UNION

In repair from the Self side, we find orientation to Being; we open conversation in the in-between space, we risk union. The deeper we go to engage all the parts of ourselves in inner conversation, the stronger our ego becomes. The stronger our ego, the deeper we can go.

We have entered the world of the collective unconscious, the objective psyche that stands against our subjective ego consciousness. As we saw in the last chapter, that means consciously seeking relationship with the collective, deliberately joining ourselves to the collective anima or animus. Thus a woman suddenly feels indissolubly at one with other women, feels them as her sisters. Interdependence replaces competition and its tensions. A man feels part of an enormous gathering of his sex, men different from him and the same, feels indebted to his brothers for a new awareness of enduring aspects of masculinity and their being made available to him in the large dimensions of the collective that he alone could never encompass. So it is too with persons who carry psychological functions that have been recessive in their lives, what Jungians call their inferior functions. Thinker welcomes feeler, glad to receive what he or she makes available in a form developed beyond what one could achieve on one's own; intuition type yields to sensation, for new perception, enlarged experience.

Interdependence replaces an earlier fearsome dependence. We share, we trade, we make things available to each other that we never thought to possess or even, perhaps, to understand. We discover that not only have we all as fellow sufferers been trying to put the parts of ourselves together into some kind of workable whole identity, but that each of us is a working part in a whole of astonishing complexity. Urges to intercession and compassion arise in us. We can carry others' projections now, at least temporarily; and with tact, we can return psychic contents to those to whom they belong.

Our appetite for risk is extraordinary. Our ego unites with anima or animus; images of Self are born in us. This may be an entirely inner experience, or it may emerge in relation to a partner when we clearly feel the distinctiveness of another person's otherness interwoven with the distinctiveness of our own contrasexuality. This is union, not merger. This is the joy of conjunction in which, believers like to think, God directly participates.

Sometimes the marriage is an inner one only, altogether without an outside partner. But that is not so different from our conjoinings with actual living other persons, for they too, to survive, must always include just such an inner marriage. A woman's dreams show how inner matches outer for passion and intensity. She comes, in dream, into ownership of an underground clay factory, where the earth is turned into something of high value. A man who works there joins her. We are on a deadline, she says to him. Can we get it done? Her hands are full of dirt and clay. She puts her lips to his and kisses him warmly. It is hot, she says. Yes, he responds; he will do it for her; she is his. She has three orgasms in the dream.

The woman had strong associations to this dream. She loves clay pots—"They hold Being," she says. This factory is a place that belongs to her, yet it is also beneath the ground, in her unconscious. The man is a worker, a peasant, an earthy chthonic man. She works hard too in joining her dream man, getting her hands dirty. Animus and ego cooperate. To the deadline that the dream asserts, she associates her work life as a writer. That is the large significance of the joinings of her dream, woman with man; her orgasms signal the ecstasy of union.

Next night, in her dreams, she finds herself seated at a square table, across from another man, one she does not know, but whom she quickly comes to esteem highly for his work. She learns much from him. Still another man with whom she works and his woman sit opposite each other in the other two places that the table offers. Water flows near them, but they sit comfortably; they are on firm ground—very near the unconscious, but not awash in it.

This dream feels like an image of Self to the woman. The two couples sort themselves out. First she and the man she admires—he seems whole, simple, original, wise. They make a pair, ego and animus. Then, in the second couple, the man is like the workman of the previous dream, the woman explains, more primitive, perhaps, but now fully known to her, closer to her actual life. His woman she does not know, but she can accept her as part of the man's life. They make another ego-and-anima pair. But she can see the pairs in another way also. The first couple unites ego to ego; the second presents their animus and anima. As a foursome, facing each other at the square table, seated near water, the men and women felt complete yet brought the dreamer images of a life that was also open-ended and at peace with its open-endedness.

The Self, even when it brings adumbrations of completeness, is never a sealed, finished affair. It is process as much as content, relation of parts as much as their unity. The indeterminacy of the archetypal *apeiron* flows into us. The ego experiences it as the abundance of Being revealing itself as a greatness of possibility, a widening of personality. Liveliness comes from a sense of living inventively, and thus the ego feels fulfilled, but not an end of anything. Living this way means feeling the preciousness of each moment into which we bring our own specially marked participation in the All and recognition of the vastness of what it contains, the mark of the eternal.

Uniting with the other, inside and outside ourselves, brings us to the life of Self, which is itself a union of female and male parts. Union here transcends sexual polarity. Its urge is to give witness to Being itself. Sexuality, we understand in Self, is not an ultimate principle, but it does play a decisive role in our reaching to the ultimate and our first experiences of it, here and now. We taste it, feel it, know it, deepened for us as a woman in feminine terms, as a man in masculine terms, by the intensification of our sexual identity that comes through our contra-sexual dialogue. Anima and animus can be, we realize in the heightened presence they now assume in us, the graced threshold to the Self.

With wonder we greet the other—an animal of the same stripe and fur—and in that joining we feel held by a greater power. Jung calls this the Self. It was, he says, "always there and yet appears only at the end. This thing is the Self, the indescribable totality, which though it is inconceivable and 'irrepresentable' is none the less necessary as an intuitive concept."[17]

Our efforts at union, at meeting, receiving and giving between ego and anima or animus, give birth to specific images of the Self that are our very own. They come from the Self as we know it and live it and experience it living in us. This fullness of living returns to our ego identity a depth, a breadth, a support that otherwise we should lack. In taking us beyond the ego, it itself is filled out.

Instances are rife, especially where one willingly gives oneself over to the ministrations of the Self. One man, over a number of years, dreamed a series of dreams about his love for his wife, about coming to his anima and to an ever-greater fullness of Being. One dream gives startling advice: a strong presence commands him—"Instead of all those crossword puzzles, draw or paint your wife, and especially her orgasms!" A dream a few years later presents him being pulled into an embrace by a young woman, barely past pubescence. She has a "cunt," he says, but one that is "unenterable, not yet finished." An older woman makes the same approach and is more approachable physically, but still incomplete, not there. The final woman, clearly related to his wife, is authoritative, he says, smaller than the others "except in cuntry matters—firm, smooth, open, welcoming. She has the authority and the equipment."

A dream a month later takes up the same themes. Here a triptych is displayed. A problem the dream poses is to try to see the middle part clearly. A figure gathered from an Italian Renaissance painting stands at the triptych's right side, pointing to the center; an abstract painting on the left side makes an arc toward the center. The center tryptich slowly comes into view as "a womanly center." The whole dream, the man says, "concerns going beyond the painting, to the real thing. It will not become clear until you make the playfulness lead somewhere. The pointers point. You have to plug in." A dream of a year later responds to the man's quest. The dream states: "A new fragment is found in Jerusalem. It reads: 'The answer to all your questions is Yes.' The thought is that things will survive if the 'is' survives." In association to the dream, the man says, "The 'is' is a copula and is what Yahweh is; the one who says 'I am who am, and who is, is with you.' " These images speak of a man's experience of living in the Self.

The Self, as we understand it, is not God, but is that within us that knows about God and that in us that God knows. Our images for the Self picture the transcendent where it "is," beyond our psyche, and our meetings with it. To the extent that we risk union with anima or animus, we experience this transcendent Other coming to us in images of the center that, paradoxically, we ourselves inhabit.

Images of the Self vary among us, and yet invariably reflect our very different personal histories and impersonal cultures. One woman, for example, knew the Self as a wonderful house party in a place near the ocean, with plentiful food, flowers of great beauty, with everybody present joined in lively, spirited exchanges about what really matters. Another woman saw the center as one ever-fruitful flower, its multitude of petals opening to reveal its center, *the* center. Another woman dreamed of a Buddha, made up of all the ordinary things of life—cars, roads, trees, houses, people, rivers, animals. Another woman dreamed simply and movingly: "The Grail cup sings!"[18] Two men, unknown to each other, but patients of the same analyst, both referred to a particular place at the ocean as their dream vision of the center. Both dreamed of it as a numinous space, a place where Being was gathered in. Others draw upon images out of their own religious traditions, of a God who knocks at the door, of God as a dinner party host or a seamstress or a woman searching for the lost mite, of God as rock or citadel, of One with giant wings under which we crawl to join the divine.[19]

When we work with the images our psyche gives us and with those our religious traditions bequeath us, we experience the willingness of the transcendent to take up residence within the psyche. We know it then as center of the psyche, as our center, durable and hard like a diamond, much greater than the ego and beyond its territory. We see the world in very different terms now, for this center is not significantly conditioned by the here-and-now of our society, our family, our own history. Nor does it obey the laws of rationality or conventional morality. It lives in the order of eternity.

One woman experienced it pouring into her like "golden" energy. "It never went out," she said, and she feared utter exhaustion, because "it does not have to sleep. Only I have to sleep." Her daily experience—the very order of her life—changed radically. "All the time this energy buzzes on," she said, "while I go about my business. I am preoccupied with how to accommodate it, how to house it. It is always there, pouring in, being with me, *being.*"

It is not too much to say, we think, that the transcendent living in us as our center, communicating to us through images that know about the transcendent, is what the Self finally engineers in us. This Other becomes for us an immortal objective subject, right there, in us, in our days and nights, every day and night, receiving us, mirroring us, living through us. This, surely, is what anima and animus, we finally understand, have all along meant to bring us: direct experience of the immortal Self-Object.

The Self as we know it resident in ourselves is not perfect. Rather, it is a way of living large enough to house all the parts of us, and of our world. Thus there is room alongside the adumbrations of eternity for anima or animus images that do not transform, but stay split, wounded, bleeding. Some princes always remain toads. There is room in Self-living for them too. That is a necessary part of our human mixture, our all-too-human mixture. We provide shelter, even in the life graced by a strong Self presence, for finite parts of us that are not fixable; some wounds we carry go on bleeding unto death. But these wounds are set for us now in a different order, a larger context. They may not heal, but our flesh grows around them more firmly. We can carry them, and through them can join ourselves to the suffering of others, avoiding all the scoldings and narrowings of the fix-it ego mentality. Such wounds are another set of unlockable doors through which the transcendent can put its paw upon us at any time. They serve the function of keeping us connected through Self to the beyond; they prevent us from being sealed up against life. Religious traditions recognize this fact in their images of the wounded Christ, the wailing wall in the middle of the holy city, the compassionate Buddha.

Sometimes we give witness to the presence of the transcendent in our Self-images through failure rather than successes. They too pull us across ego boundaries to make us transcend the limits of our ego values. We may not, for example, achieve intimacy with others, but the big soul among us will still rejoice that others find such intimacy. We, any of us, may become such a big soul in the fullness of a love that we must, one way or another, share the good news with our friends. Big souls greet all happiness with gladness, all celebration of Being, even though it is not their own happiness or celebration. In their greeting, they celebrate Being, they know happiness. Other friends may carp, pick at faults, point out limits. Out of Self, in an enlargement of soul, we can instead give witness to Being, even in our incompleteness, and to our longing for and opening to the love that we do not yet possess but see and celebrate in others.

The astonishing experience that is ours when we come upon images of the Self that know about God, and that God knows, is the sudden sharp awareness that the images have come of their own accord and work in us with their own momentum. We do not cause transformation, nor do we have to initiate a process in which it will occur. We need only not block it. It does; it is; transformation was not and now is. The woman graced with energy discovered, after many weeks of meditating on how to house the light pouring in upon her, that she did not have to figure this out for herself. The energy would supply its own masters. "*It* did it," she said; "it does it. It's like a compost heap that transforms all the debris of leaves, grass, and dead plants into dark, springy, nourishing matter that makes everything grow."

Living into Self images that know about God changes us, changes all who know us. Others sense something different abroad, something that they may or may not connect to us. It does not matter; what matters is that they gravitate toward this difference that is suddenly clearly there.

Whatever form this living from the center takes, it must share itself. It goes out of people into their neighbors, to catch fire there too. On good days, it seems to all of us enough pie exists to go around. As with the loaves and fishes, all our broken, incomplete bits, when blessed by the center and offered up, turn out to be more than enough for all who would eat. On bad days, when we resist the tug of the Self, it continues to pursue us, hound us, drive us, so we can even fear it will close in on us. We resist it, we flee, hide, turn away. For the coming of the Self, we know at some level of consciousness, means a rearranging of our whole being to set things in new order, with first things first. Extraneous matter is pushed aside, given only backseat accommodation.

We often feel the approach of Self like a prison closing in on us. Or, in this same negative experience, if we spy its presence in our neighbors, we attack it there, accusing our neighbor of acting superior, as seeing himself or herself as better than anyone else. But of course the Self *is* better. When we act to hurt our neighbor, we are denying or lessening Self in ourselves. Sometimes our resistance to the Self becomes so twisted, our defection from its presence so great, we end by killing the neighbor who carries it.

If we do not consent to house the Self, it will push into us anyway, and we will suffer it in our crass denials as merely negative. Thus it is that images of God turn ugly in us and, in our resistance and defensiveness, we house evil where good should be. The energy that pours into the woman as grace might, when denied or even combatted, actually kill her, quickly or in such lingering suffering as that of a stroke. The diamond-hard stone of the Self, ungreeted, unassimilated, fenced off, can itself assimilate a person's ego so that the person petrifies, in a stony defensiveness that may take the dysfunctional form of anything from catatonia to rigid neurosis. Instead of the crystalline realization of Self to which the diamond metaphor points, a resisting person may, out of the negative version of Self, cripple up with arthritis, or lose the blood rhythms of life in a heart attack.

A positive ego attitude toward the presence of Self is, as Jung emphasized, a religious one. We pay careful and close attention to a presence and power well beyond our own small existence, and we find that even in that smallness we are linked deep down inside ourselves to the power and the presence. All our parts, knowing Self, known by Self, achieve a unity that, we now perceive, others may also have discovered in themselves—witnesses, unity by unity, to the transcendent power whose presence unites.[20] When unity joins unity, in whatever number, we know the mystery of community in the flesh. We have come to the end purpose of the anima and animus archetypes.[21] Their rule in our lives is properly to serve the ego, so that the ego may properly serve the Self and the transcendent that the Self knows and that knows the Self.

Once we experience the immortal presence mirroring us within us, we are joined for life. We can no longer survive without consulting its opinions, even about the least little facts and doings of everyday life. We are pledged to it and it to us. We see the others who are similarly pledged and share kinship with them, wherever they are. We know that this Other we have sought for so long, wanting it to find us and to mirror us, does indeed want us to mirror it, wants to flow into life, our life, and needs a loving partner in us. That is the instruction by example we receive from the anima or animus wooing of the ego: it is our preparation for the center wooing us right there in us.

No matter how "clumsy" the theory, to use Jung's self-deprecating word again, or how uncertain our understanding of anima and animus, they remain a tutoring experience in all of us, a towering one, that can give the most positive direction to our lives. It takes some resolve to accept the direction anima and animus bring into our lives, for we will be changed persons as a result, living toward the Self, in the Self, and for the Self. We will quickly enough recognize that the changes worked in us are serious, enlarging, and deepening. We will also know relationship as we have never known it before, if we allow the processes and effects of change to move, as they clamor to do, into full consciousness. We have seen this confirmed in clinical experience and over and over again in that record of human interiority that religion, literature, and the arts provide.

The literary imagination was particularly alive to the contrasexual impulse in the writers who followed Dante and the troubadours in what has been called the religion of beauty in women. There, in what Dante defined as the *dolce stil nuovo,* the sweet new style, poets of consequence found their analogues for his Beatrice, the intercessor and guide who replaces Virgil in the *Commedia* to conduct Dante from Purgatory to Paradise. Similarly, Petrarch's Laura and all the rhetoric associated with her made conquests for centuries in the literature of the European Renaissance. Poets froze and burned at the same time in response to

their "ladies" as Petrarch did in his response to Laura, sometimes reacting with honest emotion to an unmistakable anima presence, sometimes
simply following literary fashion. When we confront the real thing, as
we do in Petrarch's great admirer Boccaccio or in that universal man of
the late fifteenth century Lorenzo de' Medici, we know almost immediately that this is no mere modishness or meretricious imitation of an
august model.

Lorenzo casts two women in the role of mediatrix, to inspire him to
high literary performance and the experience of a passion of lasting
consequence in their time on earth, and then to go before him into the
next life and become his sanctified intercessors. So far, so good; the
Dantesque and Petrarchan models have been scrupulously observed,
and, we might be pardoned for thinking, the prosaic nature of the enterprise suggested by the title of the work in which the women are presented, *A Commentary on Some of His Sonnets,* has been fulfilled. But
Lorenzo, good Dantean that he is, has something more than literary
procedure in mind in his *Comento.*

This is, after all, Lorenzo *il magnifico,* the presiding officer of the
great *quattrocento* city-state, Florence. He is aware that he is subject to
criticism, not simply because of his inadequacies as a poet—for which,
following convention, he must apologize—but for being seduced from
his duties by a passion that some would call, he tells us, "reprehensible."
He is aware that he may also be criticized for using the commentary
form usually reserved for theological and philosophical discourse and
for having written in the vernacular, which, even so long after Dante's
plea for using the language of the people for serious literary and philosophical purpose, will lose him both respect and understanding. But his
is a serious task and he jumps to it, defining love in terms of beauty,
endurance, and loftiness of person.

The good really needs no excuse, Lorenzo says—nor, we might add,
does the vernacular tongue—but Lorenzo does what he can to justify
what he is doing, to give the sonnet *cachet* equal to such longer forms
of high literary standing as the *canzone.* This looks at first like another
exercise of literary convention, but Lorenzo's work everywhere bears
the marks of that feeling heart which is its subject matter and which
quite transcends convention.

Lorenzo himself defines death as the beginning of his work. He supports his statement with evidence from the journeys to the worlds of the

dead in Homer, Virgil, and Dante and then embarks on his own trip, using the form of Dante's *La Vita Nuova*. Sonnets celebrate the death and virtuous life of his two women; commentary then follows, sonnet by sonnet, to elucidate, to defend, to assert principle. Convention is served, outwardly at least, but as quickly becomes apparent, Lorenzo is speaking out of a profoundly personal experience of his own interiority. He is not merely a disconsolate lover, reporting, in what is by now a long-honored fashion, the death of a blessed lady. He is telling us that the dialogue goes on. He understands now from his own inner experience that the *gentilezza* of the lady, necessary for her election as her lover's intercessor, has a purging power that works toward the perfection of the lover, that is to say, Lorenzo. The *gentilezza* and the love that builds upon it combat the "natural pettiness and diffidence" of most of us, from which spring the despair and sloth in which even an attempt to find a joyful love such as Lorenzo's will not and perhaps cannot be made.

Life, in Lorenzo's reading, "consists of opposition, contrariety, and multiple evils"; it is "conserved" as long as its humors possess equal strength and they remain at war with each other. Satisfy one appetite, let one conquer another, and death must follow. Thus pain, privation, and the anticipation of death lead to life; all our fears of death, our tearful compassion, our fitful struggles, act to sustain it. In our restlessness, our sinfulness, in all the infelicities of our mortality, we prepare ourselves for the graces of love.

Lorenzo's inner conversation has prepared him well for the experience of love, and his well-filled narrative, like Boethius's and Dante's, alternating prose and verse, prepares us, too, to understand why that second love, when it comes, takes him over so completely. Opposition and contrariety remain the hallmarks. Transcendence is experienced, but in the most concrete, fleshly way. When, at a moment of intense feeling, Lorenzo looks at his lady both "fixedly" and with what seems a contrite conscience, she moves to comfort him. She approaches him, as we might expect with *gentilezza*, then puts her hand on the left side of his breast. He asks why. She is waiting, she replies, to feel the beating of her own heart in him. He understands. Her heart, he says, and everything else that lives in him, is hers. Then she announces, with equal conviction, that he speaks the truth, "for the heart that was living in me now lives in you, and the one that was yours I hold in my breast."[22]

Notes

Chapter 1: The Anima and Animus

1. C. G. Jung, *Letters,* ed. Gerhart Adler and Aniela Jaffé, trans. R. F. C. Hull (Princeton: Princeton University Press, 1975), 2:192.

2. For Jung, "logos" represents order at the source; its archetypal stature is suggested by the opening words of the Gospel of John, *In principium erat verbum,* "In the beginning was the word." "Eros" represents the principle of psychic relatedness.

3. All case examples are from the psychoanalytic practice of Ann Ulanov and are used with permission of the persons involved, for which the authors are grateful.

4. See A. B. Ulanov, "For Better *and* for Worse," *Psychoanalytic Review* 76 (Winter 1986).

5. See D. W. Winnicott, "The Meaning of the Word 'Democracy,' " in *Home Is Where We Start From* (New York: Norton, 1986), 252–253.

6. C. G. Jung, *The Structure and Dynamics of the Psyche,* vol. 8 of *The Collected Works of C. G. Jung,* trans. R. F. C. Hull (New York: Pantheon, 1960), 406, para. 798 (hereafter cited as *CW*).

7. Karl Barth makes a similar point, though with a typology of the sexes that contradicts his own strong arguments against rigid typologies. *Church Dogmatics: A Selection* (Edinburgh: T. & T. Clark, 1961), 194–204.

8. C. G. Jung, *Mysterium Coniunctionis, CW* 14, trans. R. F. C. Hull (New York: Pantheon, 1963), 180, para. 226.

9. Lecturing on this subject in Chapel Hill, North Carolina, some years ago, we were asked by a member of the audience what distinguished these

Self contents from, say, shadow materials. Self contents, we explained, have to do with matters of life and death. The bridge analogy may also be used, however, in relation to the shadow or other major psychic complexes such as the persona, but there is an unmistakably different feel to the way the contents address us in these cases. Self contents coming across the anima/animus bridge do not confront us with the bad in ourselves (or, for those of us who think of ourselves as bad, with the good); Self contents question our very existence. For further elaboration, see A. B. Ulanov, "Disguises of the Anima," *Gender and Soul in Psychotherapy,* ed. Nathan Schwartz-Salant and Murray Stein (Wilmette, Ill.: Chiron, 1992), 49, n. 2.

10. C. G. Jung, *Two Essays in Analytical Psychology, CW* 7, trans. R. F. C. Hull (Princeton: Princeton Univ. Press, 1953), 181, para. 399. See also Jung's "Concerning Rebirth" in *The Archetype and the Collective Unconscious, CW* 9:1, 124, trans. R. F. C. Hull (New York: Pantheon, 1959) para. 223: "They serve as bridges to the unconscious"; and *Dream Analysis: A Seminar of C. G. Jung 1928–1930,* ed. William McGuire (Princeton: Princeton Univ. Press, 1984), 337, 486.

11. Jung, *Two Essays, CW* 7, 224, para. 370. See also "The Secret of the Golden Flower," in *Alchemical Studies, CW* 13, trans. R. F. C. Hull (Princeton: Princeton University Press, 1967), 42, para. 62.

12. See A. B. Ulanov, *The Feminine in Jungian Psychology and in Christian Theology* (Evanston, Ill.: Northwestern University Press, 1971), 256–257.

13. See Sigmund Freud, *The Ego and the Id,* trans. Joan Riviere and James Strachey (New York: Norton, 1960), 21, 23. See also Freud's *Three Essays on the Theory of Sexuality,* Standard Edition, vol. 7, trans. James Strachey (London: Hogarth Press, 1974), 220n; Melanie Klein, *Envy and Gratitude and Other Works, 1946–1963* (New York: Delacorte, 1975), 82, 135, 169, 306, 307; D. W. Winnicott, *Playing and Reality* (London: Tavistock, 1971), 72–75, 80–84; Harry Guntrip, *Schizoid Phenomena, Object Relations and the Self* (New York: International Universities Press, 1969), 250ff., 257ff.; and Janine Chasseguet-Smirgel, *Sexuality and Mind: The Role of the Father and the Mother in the Psyche* (New York: New York Univ. Press, 1986), 42–43.

14. D. W. Winnicott, "On the Kleinian Contribution," in *The Maturational Processes and the Facilitating Environment* (New York: International Universities Press, 1965), 177.

15. See, for example, Jeffrey Seinfeld, *The Bad Object: Healing the Negative Therapeutic Reaction in Psychotherapy* (Northvale, N.J.: Jason Aronson, 1990).

16. See A. B. Ulanov, *The Wisdom of the Psyche* (Cambridge: Cowley, 1987), 21.

17. Jung, *Letters* 1:490.

18. See A. B. Ulanov, *The Feminine,* 36; see also B. K. Fowles, "Thoughts About the Tomgirl," *Journal of Analytical Psychology* 23, no. 2 (1978):161–175; Andrew Samuels, "Beyond the Pleasure Principle: A Post-Jungian Viewpoint," *Harvest* 34 (1988–89).

19. One should read *La Vita Nuova* both before and after the *Divine Comedy* to gather some sense of the mixture of the natural and the super-natural with which Dante has endowed his anima figure and to see con-firmed in that grandest of literary-theological structures the majestic psy-chological reality of Beatrice Portinari.

20. See Ann Ulanov and Barry Ulanov, *The Witch and the Clown: Two Archetypes of Human Sexuality* (Wilmette, Ill.: Chiron, 1987), 250–254.

21. See, for example, Naomi Goldenberg, "A Feminist Critique of Jung," *Signs: A Journal of Women in Culture and Society* 2, no. 2 (1976); Jean Baker Miller, *Toward a New Psychology of Women* (Boston: Beacon, 1976); R. R. Reuther, *Sexism and God-Talk: Toward a Feminist Theology* (Boston: Beacon, 1983).

22. Jung, *Letters* 2:490. See also Jung's discussion of archetypes in *CW* 8:136–138, 201, 213, paras. 277–282, 398, 417.

23. See Gaston Bachelard, *The Poetics of Reverie,* trans. Daniel Russell (New York: Orion, 1969), chap. 2. See also James Hillman, "On Psycholog-ical Femininity," in *The Myth of Analysis* (San Francisco: Harper, 1972); and Verena Kast, *The Nature of Loving: Patterns of Human Relationship,* trans. Boris Matthews (Wilmette, Ill.: Chiron, 1986), chap. 8.

24. "Each case is a unique process surrounding an individual and the individual way is always different," says Marie-Louise von Franz of Jung in her book *The Psychological Meaning of Redemption Motifs in Fairy Tales* (Toronto: Inner City Books, 1980), 8.

25. See C. G. Jung, *Memories, Dreams, Reflections,* ed. Aniela Jaffé, trans. Richard Winston and Clara Winston (New York: Pantheon, 1963), 19–20, 33, 45. See also Claire Douglas, *The Woman in the Mirror: Analyti-cal Psychology and the Feminine* (Boston: Sigo, 1990), 148–149, 176, 199; and June Singer, *Androgyny: Toward a New Theory of Sexuality* (Boston: Sigo, 1989), 257–258. Winnicott interprets Jung's Number 1 and Number 2 personalities to mean that he suffered and recovered from infantile schizophrenia; see his review of *Memories, Dreams, Reflections* in *Interna-tional Journal of Psychoanalysis* 45 (1964):2–3.

Chapter 2: Anima/Animus as Complex

1. See C. G. Jung, *Psychology and Religion: West and East,* *CW* 11, trans. R. F. C. Hull (New York: Pantheon, 1958), 8–9, paras. 8–10.

2. See Elie Humbert, *C. G. Jung,* trans. R. G. Jalbert (Wilmette, Ill.: Chiron, 19), chap. 2. See also A. B. Ulanov, *The Feminine,* chap. 2.

3. C. G. Jung, "A Review of Complex Theory," in *CW* 8; see also Jung's Tavistock lectures, "On the Theory and Practice of Analytical Psychology," in *Analytical Psychology,* in *The Symbolic Life, CW* 18, trans. R. F. C. Hull (Princeton: Princeton University Press, 1976), 71–85, paras. 148–175.

4. See C. G. Jung, "General Aspects of Dream Psychology," in *CW* 8, 253ff., paras. 489ff.

5. In *Psychological Types,* Jung compares complexes to demons that harass us and all but disclaims the usage in which we speak of having a complex in favor of complexes having us, that is to say, acting as motivating life forces within us. See *CW* 6.

6. See Jung's "Symbols and Interpretations of Dreams," in *CW* 18, 189, para. 429. See also Jung's *Two Essays, CW* 7, 188–192, paras. 296–303; Jung's *Aion: Researches into the Phenomenology of the Self, CW* 9:2, trans. R. F. C. Hull (New York: Pantheon, 1959), 11–23, paras. 20–42; M. Esther Harding, *The "I" and the "Not-I"* (New York: Pantheon, 1965), chap. 5; and Katherine Bradway, "Gender Identity and Gender Roles: Their Place in Analytical Practice," in *Jungian Analysis,* ed. Murray Stein (LaSalle, Ill.: Open Court, 1982).

7. See Paul Tillich's "Remarks" in *Carl Gustav Jung, 1875–1961: A Memorial Meeting* (New York: The Analytical Psychology Club, 1961).

8. A diagram may make easier our understanding of the structure of a complex:

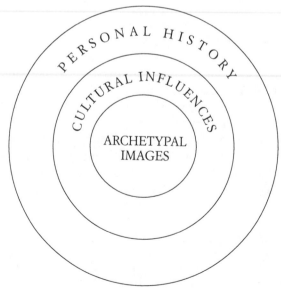

PERSONAL HISTORY

CULTURAL INFLUENCES

ARCHETYPAL IMAGES

9. The women's movements of the late twentieth century may be understood as attempts to investigate images of women in our collective cultures that have seriously hampered or exploited women, often leading to wholesale repudiation of these images and their surrounding rhetoric, especially where they appear to have restricted women's free development and use of their gifts and skills.

10. This dream is presented at some length in A. B. Ulanov, *Receiving Woman: Studies in the Psychology and Theology of the Feminine* (Louisville, Ky.: Westminster, 1981), 122–123.

11. See Bachelard, *Poetics of Reverie,* 124.

12. Cited in Matthew Fox, *Meditations with Meister Eckhart* (Sante Fe, N.M.: Bear & Co., 1983), 60.

13. For a discussion of the question of who is in charge of the psyche, ego or Self, see A. B. Ulanov, "Fatness and the Female," *Psychological Perspectives* 10 (Fall, 1979).

14. See Barbara Hannah's discussion of this point in her pamphlet "The Problem of Contact with the Animus" (London: Guild of Pastoral Psychology, 1962).

15. Interview by Glen Collins, *New York Times,* 3 March 1990.

16. See Jung's examination of these two principles of mental functioning in his "Two Kinds of Thinking," in *Symbols of Transformation, CW* 5, trans. R. F. C. Hull (New York: Pantheon, 1956), 7–34, paras. 4–46. See also Ann Ulanov and Barry Ulanov, *Religion and the Unconscious* (Louisville, Ky.: Westminster, 1975), 28–32; Michael Fordham, "The Androgyne: Some Inconclusive Reflections on Sexual Perversions," and J. O. Wisdom, "The Perversions: A Philosopher Reflects," both in *Journal of Analytical Psychology* 33, no. 3 (1988).

17. For further elaboration of this point, see A. B. Ulanov, *The Feminine,* 296–302.

18. For the place of anima and animus in relation to the particular figures of the witch and the clown, see A. and B. Ulanov, *Witch and the Clown,* chap. 1.

19. See C. G. Jung, *The Integration of the Personality,* trans. Stanley Dell (New York: Farrar & Rinehart, 1939), 25; see also in the same volume 19–23, 24, 38, and Jung's *Dream Analysis,* 57.

20. A readable translation, with a useful "Afterword," is Harry Steinhauer's *Sufferings of Young Werther* (New York: Norton, 1970).

21. See Anne Sexton, *Love Poems* (Boston: Houghton Mifflin, 1969), 31, 30, 4, 33–34.

22. See Sylvia Plath, *Winter Trees* (New York: Harper & Row, 1972), 47–51, 59–62.

23. See Robert Lowell, *Life Studies* (New York: Farrar, Straus & Cu-

dahy, 1959), 85–86, 68, 76, 87; and *Notebook* (New York: Farrar, Straus & Giroux, 1970), 262.

24. John Berryman's *Dream Songs,* which appeared originally in two volumes, as *77 Dream Songs* (1964) and *His Toy, His Dream, His Rest* (1968), consist of 385 eighteen-line poems, alternately sweet and bitter, charming, exasperated and exasperating, lively and tedious, and very much worth the respectful attention they demand, for all their invocation of case-study mechanics and melodrama.

25. See Von Franz, *Redemption Motifs,* 72.

26. See Karl Popper, *Unended Quest: An Intellectual Autobiography* (La Salle, Ill.: Open Court, 1976), 180–196; and Ernst Cassirer, *Language and Myth,* trans. Suzanne Langer (New York: Dover, 1946), 7–11.

27. Elvis Presley's gyrations often recalled the sinuous maneuverings of the black masters of the art of bodily twist and twirl to a jazz beat, Snake Hips Tucker and Rubber Legs Williams, but by comparison to those dancers, who worked with the best of the jazz musicians of the Swing era, Presley's body motions in support of his singing seemed clumsy and untutored. Michael Jackson's epicene appearance, sounds, and gestures, on the other hand, are unmistakably calculated, or perhaps more precisely, calibrated to the last decimal point of surgical conversion.

28. See Jung's *Two Essays,* 80–90, paras. 121–140.

Chapter 3: Identity

1. Rosemary Gordon examines this notion of creativity in "The Symbolic Experience as Bridge between the Personal and the Collective," *Journal of Analytical Psychology* 22, no. 4 (1977).

2. Charles Taylor argues with a persuasive fullness of example for "the essential link between identity" and orientation to value: "To know who you are is to be oriented in moral space, a space in which questions arise about what is good or bad, what is worth doing and what not, what has meaning and importance for you and what is trivial and secondary." This statement appears early (p. 28) in his *Sources of the Self: The Making of the Modern Identity* (Cambridge, Mass: Harvard Univ. Press, 1989), but the whole of his large, well-reasoned book is informed by this conviction.

3. See François Truffaut, *The Films in My Life,* trans. Leonard Mayhew (London: Allen Lane, 1980), 75.

4. C. G. Jung, *The Vision Seminars: Two Books* (Zurich: Spring, 1976), Book 2, 370.

5. See Paul Tillich, "You Are Accepted," in *The Shaking of the Foundations* (New York: Scribner, 1948), 153–164.

6. See Charles Baudelaire, *The Intimate Journals,* trans. Christopher

Isherwood (Boston: Beacon, 1959), 28–29, 3, 20, 56, 32; and *Paris Spleen,* trans. Louise Varèse (Norfolk, Conn.: New Directions, 1970), 70.

7. From the preface to *Les Fleurs du Mal;* see M. A. Ruff, *Baudelaire,* trans. Agnes Kertesz (New York: New York Univ. Press, 1966), 66.

8. See Ludwig Wittgenstein, *Culture and Value,* trans. Peter Winch (Oxford: Blackwell, 1989), 28, 35, 37–38; *On Certainty,* trans. Denis Paul and G. E. M. Anscombe (New York: Harper, 1972), 44, 25, 83–90; and Ray Monk, *Ludwig Wittgenstein: The Duty of Genius* (New York: Free Press, 1990), 579. The questions Wittgenstein put to himself that begin "Are *all* men great?" appear on p. 47 of *Culture and Value.*

9. See Selma Lagerlöf, *The Story of Gösta Berling,* trans. Robert Bly (New York: Signet, 1967), 63.

10. This dream is discussed by A. B. Ulanov in "Transference/Countertransference: A Jungian Perspective," in Stein, *Jungian Analysis,* 79.

11. Though Pascal's clear intention was to compose an apologia for his Christian faith in carefully organized discursive form, what we have instead, in the notes, outlines, and passing thoughts of the unfinished *Pensées,* is an incomparable record of a man talking to himself about the things that really matter.

12. Tinguély's machines do not necessarily produce significant works of art, but they almost always signify something of value to their operators. Like anyone's handwriting magnified to a great size, the pictures made out of the dots and dashes and colors that the machines make available reflect more than the random impressions of a working psyche.

13. Jung insists, "In this struggle the individual is never a spectator only; he takes part in it more or less 'voluntarily.' " He speaks of "a determining power which comes upon man from outside, like providence or fate, though the ethical decision is left to man. He must know, however, what he is deciding about and what he is doing. Then, if he obeys he is following not just his own opinion, and if he rejects he is destroying not just his own invention." See *Aion, CW* 9:2, 26–27, paras. 94, 51. Jung, like a gifted poet, intuitively grasped the positive and negative aspects of lunar consciousness. He describes it as belonging to woman: "Her consciousness has a lunar rather than a solar character. Its light is the 'mild' light of the moon, which merges things together rather than separates them. It does not show up objects in all their pitiless discreteness and separateness . . . but blends in a deceptive shimmer the near and the far, magically transforming little things into big things, high into low, softening all colour into a bluish haze, and blending the nocturnal landscape into an unsuspected unity." See *Mysterium Coniunctionis, CW* 14, 179, para. 233.

Chapter 4: Anima and Animus and Other People

1. See Michael Polanyi, *Personal Knowledge: Towards a Post-Critical Philosophy* (Chicago: Univ. of Chicago Press, 1962), 112–113, 266–267.

Christopher Bollas offers some germane reflections on the idiom of the psyche in *The Shadow of the Object: Psychoanalysis and the Unthought Known* (London: Free Association Books, 1987), 238, 280ff., endnote 6.

2. See Jung's *Psychological Types, CW* 6, 457, para. 783; see also Marie-Louise von Franz, *Alchemy: An Introduction to the Symbolism and the Psychology* (Toronto: Inner City Books, 1980), 117–118, and her *Projection and Re-Collection in Jungian Psychology,* trans. W. H. Kennedy (La Salle, Ill.: Open Court, 1980), chap. 1.

3. See Melanie Klein, "On Identification," in *Envy and Gratitude,* chap. 9; Rosemary Gordon, "The Concept of Projective Identification," *Journal of Analytical Psychology* 10, no. 2 (1965):127–149; and M. Esther Harding, "The Anima and the Animus: A Curtain Lecture" (New York: Kristine Mann Library of the Jung Foundation, 1951).

4. See Charles Williams, *Descent into Hell* (London: Faber, 1937).

5. See Rodney Needham, *Circumstantial Deliveries* (Berkeley: Univ. of California Press, 1981), 51–52.

6. See D. W. Winnicott, *The Child, the Family, and the Outside World* (Harmondsworth, Middlesex: Penguin, 1975), chaps. 15 and 16, and especially p. 102; see also his *Playing and Reality,* chap. 10; and "This Feminism," in *Home Is Where We Start From,* 189–190.

7. See Jung, *Memories, Dreams, Reflections,* chap. 6; from his "Confrontation with the Unconscious," reported there, came his *Septem Sermones ad Mortuos,* trans. H. G. Baynes (London: Watkins, 1963).

8. D. L. Kay, "The Paternal Psyche and the Emerging Ego," *Journal of Analytical Psychology* 26, no. 3 (1981). See also A. B. Ulanov, "The Search for Paternal Roots: Jungian Perspectives on Fathering," in *Fathering, Fact or Fable,* ed. E. V. Stein (Nashville, Tenn.: Abingdon, 1977).

9. Robert Stein discusses the instinctive side of eros in a woman's psyche in his *Incest and Human Love: The Betrayal of the Soul in Psychotherapy* (New York: Third Press, 1973).

10. For a discussion of the effects of a mother's negative animus on a boy's anima, see Marie-Louise von Franz, *Puer Aeternus* (New York: Spring, 1970), viii, 17; see also her *Apuleius' Golden Ass* (New York: Spring, 1970), p. XIII:13.

11. Helene Deutsch observes that a daughter may identify with her father and thus endanger her core of feminine identity; she may assume an overly passive or overly masculine character, and her feminine ego, as a result, may not be strong enough in relation to other drives. See her *Psychology of Women* (New York: Grune & Stratton, 1944), 1:287–289; see also 275, 279, 281.

12. For full treatment of the witch figure, see A. Ulanov and B. Ulanov, *Witch and the Clown,* chap. 2.

13. See Jung's *Dream Analysis,* 52–55.

14. See Michael Polanyi, *Knowing and Being* (Chicago: Univ. of Chicago Press, 1969), 148–149.

15. See Maurice Merleau-Ponty, *Phenomenology of Perception,* trans. Colin Smith (London: Routledge & Kegan Paul, 1962), 166–167.

16. See Augustine, *Selected Letters,* trans. J. H. Baxter (London: Loeb Classical Library, 1953), 443, 445.

17. See Michael Rosenthal, "Notes on Envy and the Contrasexual Archetype," *Journal of Analytical Psychology* 8, no. 1 (1963).

18. See Klein, *Envy and Gratitude,* 192, 193, 216.

19. For a pertinent example, see A. Ulanov and B. Ulanov, *Cinderella and Her Sisters: The Envied and the Envying* (Louisville, Ky.: Westminster, 1983), 28–31.

20. See A. Ulanov and B. Ulanov, *Cinderella,* 31–36, and chap. 3. See also B. Proner, "Envy of Oneself: Adhesive Identification and Pseudo-Adult States," *Journal of Analytical Psychology* 33, no. 2 (1988); and D. S. Jaffe, "The Masculine Envy of Woman's Procreative Function," in *Female Psychology,* ed. H. P. Blum (New York: International Universities Press, 1977).

21. Much more useful to an understanding of children's attachment to books of the order of *Gulliver's Travels* or *Don Quixote* than anthropological jargon, or any other vocabulary or concepts borrowed from the social sciences, is the kind of analysis to which the phenomenological philosopher Roman Ingarden subjects the literary work of art. In one significant response of reader to literature that Ingarden notes, "The aesthetic observer, in apprehending the artist's work, attains to a sort of creative cooperation with him. By this I mean that the observer must also develop a certain creative attitude in order to arrive at the aesthetic concretization of the work and thus to an aesthetic object." Children, we suggest, know such closeness amounting to a feeling almost of coauthorship with the books central to their early years of reading. Their interior conversation often finds its grammar, rhetoric, and dialectic here, as they move to meet their contrasexuality in the dramas of the books that first seize them. See Roman Ingarden, *The Cognition of the Literary Work of Art,* trans. R. A. Crowley and K. R. Olson (Evanston, Ill.: Northwestern Univ. Press, 1973), 198, n.26.

22. See A. and B. Ulanov, *Cinderella,* chap. 5.

23. For an illustrative example, see A. Ulanov and B. Ulanov, *Witch and the Clown,* chap. 3.

Chapter 5: The Ways We Educate Each Other

1. The presence of Adeodatus in Augustine's *De Ordine,* his dialogue on providential order in things large and small, from a cockfight to the

disposition of the universe, seconds all the arguments advanced by his father: his name, "God-given," proclaims the point of everything and supports the possibility of positive movement even when the only visible signs are of deficiency of being, Augustine's definition of evil.

2. See A. B. Ulanov, "The Birth of Otherness: The Feminine Elements of Being and the Religious Life," in *Receiving Woman*.

3. See Winnicott, *Playing and Reality,* chap. 9.

4. For further discussion of this point, see Winnicott, *Child, the Family and the Outside World,* chap. 17. See also Vera Von der Heydt, "On the Father," in *Fathers and Mothers,* ed. H. A. Wilmer (Wilmette, Ill.: Chiron, 1990); Harry Wilmer, "Jung: Father and Son," in the same volume; Amy Allenby, "The Father Archetype in Feminine Psychology," *Journal of Analytical Psychology* 1, no. 1 (1955); and *The Father: Contemporary Jungian Perspectives,* ed. Andrew Samuels (New York: New York Univ. Press, 1986).

5. See *The Poems and Letters of Andrew Marvell,* ed. H. M. Margoliouth (Oxford: Clarendon Press, 1952), 37.

6. See Plato, *The Symposium,* 189c–193d.

7. See Philo, "On the Contemplative Life," in the Loeb Classical Library edition of Philo (London: Heinemann, 1960), vol. 9, 151.

8. For a discussion of this subject, see Vera Heisler, "Individuation Through Marriage," in *Psychological Perspectives* 1 (Fall 1970); and Adolf Guggenbühl-Craig, *Marriage—Dead or Alive,* trans. Murray Stein (Zurich: Spring, 1977).

9. See Florida Scott-Maxwell, *The Measure of My Days* (New York: Knopf, 1968).

10. The resurrection motif in both *The Winter's Tale*—which, though based on a play by Robert Greene, is very much Shakespeare's own—and *Pericles,* in which several other hands may be perceived, takes shape around male protagonists coming to peace with the feminine textures of their interiorities as well as the actual women in their lives. They must strip from themselves—or have stripped from them by events—their contemptuous open dismissal of the feminine or more covert banishing of it, by sentimentality. Jane Austen's chief figures, male and female, experience less violent confrontation with self or other, and almost always come gracefully to terms with the fullness of sexual identity of which they are capable in ways that make the attentive reader understand, as in late Shakespeare, a kind of birth or rebirth of being, as we see, for example, in the case of Emma Woodhouse (*Emma*) or Captain Wentworth (*Persuasion*). Hugh of St. Victor's conversation with his soul, apposite in many ways to the experiences of Shakespeare's and Austen's protagonists, is discussed by Barbara Hannah in *Encounters with the Soul: Active Imagination, as Developed by C. G. Jung* (Santa Monica, Calif.: Sigo, 1981), chap. 6.

11. See C. G. Jung, *Dream Analysis: Notes of the Seminars in Analytical Psychology, 1928–29 and 1929–30,* (Zurich: 1958), 2 vols., vol. 2, 151.

12. See C. G. Jung, "On the Psychology of the Trickster-Figure," in *CW* 9:1, 271, para. 485.

13. See Hermann Broch, *The Spell,* trans. H. F. Broch de Rothermann (New York: Farrar, Straus & Giroux, 1987), 171.

14. See M. Esther Harding's discussion of the "anima woman" in *The Way of All Women* (New York: Putnam, 1970), chap. 1. See also A. B. Ulanov, *The Feminine,* 252–255.

15. See A. Ulanov and B. Ulanov, *Religion and the Unconscious,* chap. 11, and Von Franz, *Projection and Re-Collection in Jungian Psychology.*

16. See Robert Musil, *The Man without Qualities,* trans. Eithne Wilkins and Ernst Kaiser (London: Secker & Warburg, 1960), vol. 3, 275–277, 280–282, 286.

17. See Eve Metman, "Woman and the Anima," *The Guild of Pastoral Psychology,* 71, 1951. See also A. B. Ulanov, *Receiving Woman,* 125–126, 129–131.

18. See D. W. Winnicott, "Freedom" and "Some Thoughts of the Meaning of the Word 'Democracy,' " in *Home Is Where We Start From,* 237, 252. See also C. G. Jung, *The Undiscovered Self,* in *Civilization in Transition, CW* 10, trans. R. F. C. Hull (New York: Pantheon, 1964), 258, 276, 278, paras. 511, 537, 540; and A. Ulanov and B. Ulanov, *Witch and the Clown,* 87–88, 146, 200.

19. For a treatment of the healing powers and the destructive threats of the demonic, see A. B. Ulanov, "The Psychological Reality of the Demonic," in *Picturing God* (Cambridge, Mass.: Cowley Publications, 1986).

20. See John Dourley on celibacy, in his *Love, Celibacy and the Inner Marriage* (Toronto: Inner City Books, 1987).

21. See Josef Pieper, *About Love,* trans. Richard Winston and Clara Winston (Chicago: Franciscan Herald Press, 1974), 69–70. The Augustinian text is from the *Confessions* 13.9.

22. See St. Bernard, *On the Song of Songs,* trans. by a Religious of C.S.M.V. (London: Mowbray, 1952), 23.

23. For an elucidation of the *albedo* stage of alchemy, see Jung's *Mysterium Coniunctionis, CW* 14, 177, 197, 220–21, 238, 314, paras. 220, 253, 319, 334, 434. See also Jung's *Alchemical Studies, CW* 13, 68, para. 89; von Franz, *Alchemy: An Introduction,* 220–223; E. F. Edinger, *Anatomy of the Psyche: Alchemical Symbolism in Psychotherapy* (La Salle, Ill.: Open Court, 1985), 40, 156; and Barry Ulanov, "Mysticism and Negative Presence," in *The Gaster Festschrift, The Journal of the Ancient Near Eastern Society of Columbia University,* vol. 5, 1973.

Chapter 6: The Transformative Animus and Anima

1. See Erich Neumann, *The Great Mother: An Analysis of the Archetype,* trans. Ralph Manheim (Princeton: Princeton Univ. Press, 1955), chaps. 3, 10, 11, 12, 13. See also Winnicott, *Playing and Reality,* 10, 47, 71, 81, 89, 111–112.

2. See Vyacheslav Ivanov, *Freedom and the Tragic Life: A Study in Dostoevsky,* trans. Norman Cameron (New York: Noonday, 1952), 57–58, 74, 76.

3. See *The Penguin Book of Russian Verse,* ed. Dimitri Obolensky (Harmondsworth, Middlesex: Penguin, 1965), 237–238. The Penguin books of verse in the major European languages are all bilingual, with generally accurate and unpretentious translations printed as prose.

4. For an extended discussion of this space—*liminal space* in the jargon—and its appearance in clinical work, see *Liminality and Transitional Phenomena,* ed. Nathan Schwartz-Salant and Murray Stein (Wilmette, Ill.: Chiron, 1991).

5. See Louise Labé, *Sonnets,* trans. G. D. Martin (Austin: Univ. of Texas, 1972), 20–21. The Ulysses sonnet, the first of the twenty-four, is also the only one written in Italian, as one can quickly see in this bilingual edition.

6. See *The Penguin Book of Italian Verse,* ed. G. R. Kay (Harmondsworth, Middlesex: Penguin, 1950), 181–182.

7. For examples of such transformations involving the anima or animus, see Linda Fierz-David, *The Dream of Poliphilo: The Soul in Love* (Dallas: Spring, 1987), and her *Women's Dionysian Initiation: The Villa Mysteries in Pompeii* (Dallas: Spring, 1988). See also A. B. Ulanov, "Stages of Anima Development" and "Stages of Animus Development," in *The Feminine,* chaps. 11, 12. See also, A. B. Ulanov, "The Perverse and the Transcendent," in *The Transcendent Function: Individual and Collective Aspects,* ed. Mary Ann Mattoon (Einsiedeln, Switzerland: Daimon Verlag, 1993), 212–233.

8. Jung calls this transformation "assimilation of the ego by the unconscious." See *Two Essays,* 151–155, 160–171, paras. 239–242, 250–265.

9. M. Esther Harding, *Psychic Energy: Its Source and Its Transformation* (New York: Pantheon, 1963), 124ff., 174ff. See also C. G. Jung, "The Transformation Symbolism of the Mass," in *CW* 11.

10. See *The Penguin Book of Italian Verse,* 89–95. The translations here are by Barry Ulanov.

11. See Stein, *Incest and Human Love,* 93–95.

12. For a large number of examples, see Marie-Louise von Franz, *Interpretation of Fairy Tales* (New York: Spring, 1970) and *The Feminine in Fairy Tales* (New York: Spring, 1972).

13. From an unpublished paper by A. B. Ulanov, "The Ego as Spacemaker."

14. Jung uses the images of Sol and Luna to contrast symbolic levels of the masculine and feminine; see *Mysterium Coniunctionis, CW* 14, 26–37, 92–110, 129–146, 154, 180–183, paras. 20–30, 110–133, 154–173, 181, 226–233.

15. See C. G. Jung, "Psychology of the Transference," in *The Practice of Psychotherapy, CW* 16, trans. R. F. C. Hull (New York: Pantheon, 1954), 240–242, paras. 453–454. See also von Franz, *Redemption Motifs in Fairy Tales,* 21–31.

16. For an extended discussion of the "head" and "heart" egos (Erich Neumann's terms), see A. B. Ulanov, *The Feminine,* 169–172, 175–179, 183–184, 269–270, 325–326.

17. See Basil Bunting, *Collected Poems* (Mt. Kisco, N.Y.: Moyer Bell, 1985), 60, 61, 95, 149, 127, 67.

18. See Winnicott, *Playing and Reality,* chap. 5; see also "The Feminine" in his *Home Is Where We Start From,* 183–184, and "The Split-Off Male and Female Elements to Be Found in Men and Women," in his *Psychoanalytic Explorations* (London: Karnac, 1989), 168–192. See also Guntrip, *Schizoid Phenomena,* chap. 9.

19. See A. Ulanov and B. Ulanov, *Cinderella,* chap. 6.

20. See C. G. Jung, "The Transcendent Function," in *CW* 8, and *Mysterium Coniunctionis, CW* 14, 200, 203, paras. 257, 261. See also Norah Moore, "The Transcendent Function and the Emerging Ego," *Journal of Analytical Psychology* 20, no. 2 (1975).

21. "This primordial pair of opposites symbolizes every conceivable pair of opposites that may occur: hot and cold, light and dark, north and south, dry and damp, good and bad, conscious and unconscious." See C. G. Jung, *Psychology and Alchemy, CW* 12, trans. R. F. C. Hull (New York: Pantheon, 1953), 144, para. 192.

22. For a further example of the doubling up of vision a man experiences when he sees his anima's point of view, see A. B. Ulanov, "Transference/Countertransference," in Stein, *Jungian Analysis,* 79.

23. Ulrich's "self-scrutiny," as Musil terms it, approaches the intensity of an Augustinian inwardness as Ulrich doggedly, but never humorlessly, works to make more and more space within him to confront and understand as much as possible of himself. At the end of volume two of his great saga, "standing . . . for a long time" at a window and looking out of it, he has "within him something of that twinkling, sliding intermutation of all the feelings there were." See *The Man without Qualities* 2:454.

24. Von Franz, *Apuleius,* IV:3, XIII:1.

25. This dream is discussed in A. Ulanov and B. Ulanov, *Witch and the Clown,* 173.

26. See Alfred North Whitehead, *Modes of Thought* (New York: Free Press, 1966), 116–118, 120–121.

27. See C. H. Sisson, *Collected Poems* (Manchester: Carcanet Press, 1984), 202, 204, 188, 323. In the economy of his craft, the poet captures the complicated interaction that Jung notes among Self, anima, and persona in a man. When the Self communicates with a man's ego across the anima bridge, or through the changing personifications of his anima imagery, his way of showing himself to the world (his persona) also changes. Jung goes further to speak of the persona as mediator to the outside world and of the anima as mediator to the archetypal inside world, each moving in counter-action to the other. Thus a pompous man's overly correct persona will be balanced by an unconventional, conspicuously incorrect anima. So it is that Sisson, seized by a daring penetration of the divine (as the Self), assumes the lavish persona of the Magdalen. Again, grasped by the living body of his Lord in the bread of the Eucharist, he both resists and accepts his oneness with Christ. See Jung, *Dream Analysis,* 52, 75, 79ff., and *Psychological Types, CW* 6, 470, para. 808.

28. See Winnicott's review of *Memories, Dreams, Reflections,* 451.

29. See Michael Eigen, "Winnicott's Area of Freedom: The Uncompromisable," in *Liminality and Transitional Phenomena.*

30. See Hannah Segal, *Melanie Klein* (New York: Viking, 1979), 176–181; and Phyllis Grosskurth, *Melanie Klein: Her World and Her Work* (New York: Knopf, 1986), 200, 212-214, 218, 229–230, 242–243, 295, 297.

31. See *The Spontaneous Gesture: Selected Letters by D. W. Winnicott,* ed. F. R. Rodman (Cambridge: Harvard Univ. Press, 1987), 26, 34, 84, 90.

32. See A. B. Ulanov, "A Shared Space," in *Quadrant* (Spring 1985).

33. See Jung, *Septem Sermones Ad Mortuos.*

34. See *C. G. Jung, Emma Jung and Toni Wolff: A Collection of Remembrances,* ed. Ferne Jensen (San Francisco: Analytical Psychology Club, 1982); see also Irene Champernowne, *A Memoir of Toni Wolff* (San Francisco: C. G. Jung Institute, 1980).

35. See *The Penguin Book of German Verse,* ed. Leonard Forster (Hammondsworth, Middlesex: Penguin, 1959), 442–443. The translation here is by Barry Ulanov.

Chapter 7: Anima/Animus and Religious Experience

1. There are quantities of methods for approaching religious experience, some consecrated by association with a religious order, such as the Ignatian, the Carmelite, or the Cistercian; some splendidly idiosyncratic, reflecting the sensibility of a poet such as George Herbert, a painter such as Rubens, or a not-quite-classifiable philosopher-theologian such as Pascal

or Kierkegaard. None of us is too small for such august company, for the defining elements always come to us in our own colors, in mixtures as random and as playful as the pieces of glass in a kaleidescope.

2. No translation can quite catch the nobility of phrase of Dante's Italian or its music, but there is no missing in any language its breathtaking psychological and theological point, circling round the mystery by which Mary becomes daughter to her son, the Christ.

3. See this second of the Holy Sonnets in *The Poems of John Donne,* ed. H. J. C. Grierson (Oxford: Oxford Univ. Press, 1953), 319.

4. See Anne Hébert, *Selected Poems,* trans. A. Poulin, Jr. (Brockport, N.Y.: BOA Edition, 1987), 144–145 (for both the French and the English).

5. We are in the realm of the ineffable in the last cantos of the *Commedia,* but somehow Dante, through that most astonishing of anima figurations, Beatrice, finds words to make the unspeakable speakable. Thus it is that sexuality may on certain graced occasions work to deposit one in the very lap, so to speak, of spirituality.

6. Jung, *Psychological Types, CW* 6, 450, paras. 263–264; see also Jung's *Dream Analysis,* 595–597, and for specific examples of types, 162, 230, 269–273, 278, 311, 319, 454, 459. See also Marie-Louise von Franz and James Hillman, *Jung's Typology* (New York: Spring, 1971), part 1.

7. See James Hillman, *Anima: An Anatomy of a Personified Notion* (Dallas: Spring, 1985), chap. 7; and R. A. Johnson, *We: Understanding the Psychology of Romantic Love* (San Francisco: Harper, 1983), 178.

8. See Verena Kast, *The Nature of Loving,* 96–98.

9. See Jung, *The Archetypes of the Collective Unconscious, CW* 9:1, 56, 59, 65, paras. 115, 120, 134. See also Nathan Schwartz-Salant, "Anima and Animus in Jung's Alchemical Mirror," in *Gender and Soul in Psychotherapy.*

10. See Judith Hubback on creativity in "Reflections on the Psychology of Women," *Journal of Analytical Psychology* 23, no. 2 (1978); see also, in the same journal, 30, no. 2 (1985), Rosemary Gordon's "Losing and Finding: The Location of Archetypal Experience"; and Gordon, "Symbolic Experience."

11. See Jung, "Psychology of the Transference," *CW* 16, 258, 312–316, paras. 468, 533–535; and von Franz's *Redemption Motifs,* 27, 78, where she concludes that the hermaphrodite represents union on too unconscious a level.

12. For an indication of the problems involved in skipping over women and images of the feminine in favor of androgyny, see A. B. Ulanov, *Receiving Woman,* 48–52.

13. See Ernst Cassirer, *An Essay on Man* (New Haven: Yale Univ. Press, 1962), 222–223, 268.

14. See Vladimir Solovyov, *The Meaning of Love,* trans. Jane Marshall (London: Geoffrey Bles, 1945), 78n, 56, 58, 55, 54, 62–63, 77, 81.

15. See John Haule, *Divine Madness: Archetypes of Romantic Love* (Boston: Shambhala, 1990), 83, 111, 120, 200.

16. See Manisha Roy, "Animus and Indian Women," *Harvest* (1979):25.

17. See Bou-Yong Rhi, "Psychological Problems Among Korean Women," in *Virtues in Conflict: Tradition and the Korean Woman Today,* ed. Sandra Mattielli (Seoul: Royal Asiatic Society, 1977); see also by the same writer, "Psychological Interpretation of a Korean Fairy Tale: 'Sister Sun and Brother Moon,' " *Korea Journal* (May 1973); and Hayao Kawai, *The Japanese Psyche: Major Motifs in the Fairy Tales of Japan,* trans. Hayao Kawai and Sachiko Reece (Dallas: Spring, 1988), 3, 21, 26. There are arresting parallels and differences to be found in J. G. Neihardt's *Black Elk Speaks* (New York: Washington Square Press, 1959); and Anne Cameron's *Daughters of Copper Woman* (Vancouver: Press Gang Publishers, 1981).

18. See Jae Hoon Lee, *A Study of "Han" of the Korean People: A Depth Psychological Contribution to the Understanding of the Concept of "Han" in the Korean Minjung Theology* (Ph.D. diss., Union Theological Seminary, 1989), 200; see also 193–195 and chap. 5.

19. See Ponca-Otoe, "Teeth in the Wrong Places," in *American Indian Myths and Legends,* ed. Richard Erdoes and Alfonso Ortiz (New York: Pantheon, 1984). Studies of the variants of anima and animus personification in a great range of cultures, wherever they turn up, seem to support our sense of these contrasexual figures and their persistent function as bridges between ego and Self.

20. For a particularly useful discussion of the Double, see Otto Rank, *The Double: A Psychoanalytic Study,* trans. Harry Tucker, Jr. (Chapel Hill: Univ. of North Carolina Press, 1971). See also R. H. Hopcke, *Jung, Jungians, and Homosexuality* (Boston: Shambhala, 1989), 116–118, for his discussion of Mitch Walker's "The Double: An Archetypal Configuration," from *Spring* (1976); and Jung's "Psychology of the Transference," *CW 16,* 218, para. 419, n. 12, and his *Psychological Types, CW 6,* 470, para. 808. See also, *Same-Sex Love and the Path to Wholeness,* ed. Robert H. Hopcke, Karin Loftus Carrington, Scott Wirth (Boston: Shambhala, 1993).

21. See J. N. Findlay's foreword to G. W. F. Hegel, *Phenomenology of Spirit,* trans. A. V. Miller (New York: Oxford Univ. Press, 1977), xi; and Hans-Georg Gadamer, *Hegel's Dialectic: Five Hermeneutical Studies,* trans. P. C. Smith (New Haven: Yale Univ. Press, 1976), 61–62, 64, 124–125.

22. See Jung, "Psychology of the Transference," *CW* 16, 294, 301–302, paras. 505, 522. See also Emma Jung, *Anima and Animus* (New York: Analytical Psychology Club, 1957); Emma Jung and Marie-Louise von Franz, *The Grail Legend,* trans. Andrea Dykes (New York: Putnam, 1970); Barbara Hannah, *Striving for Wholeness* (New York: Putnam, 1976), chaps. 9, 10; Marie-Louise von Franz on "Anima and Animus" in C. G. Jung, *Man*

and His Symbols (New York: Doubleday, 1964), 177–195; von Franz's *Apuleius,* XI:13, and her *Individuation in Fairy Tales* (Dallas: Spring, 1977), xi, 13ff.; and John Beebe's introduction to *C. G. Jung: Aspects of the Masculine,* ed. John Beebe (London: Ark, 1989), xv–xvi.

23. Russian Orthodox spirituality is richly attuned to the understanding that the God who moves among us is the transcendent deity become immanent. Nicholas Arseniev makes the point tidily: "Immanence and Transcendence given simultaneously: this is based on a fact, and this fact is: the Word among us, manifested in Flesh, having become Flesh—most intimate fusion or rather synthesis of Transcendence and Immanence, but not only in our interior experiences and emotions, but in *a fact,* in that which has really taken place." See "Transcendence and Immanence of God," in Arseniev's *Revelation of Life Eternal* (Crestwood, N.Y.: St. Vladimir's Seminary Press, 1982), 27–37, and especially the concluding paragraph, from which this quotation is taken.

24. See *Meditations to the Holy Spirit,* trans. by a Religious of C.S.M.V. (London: Mowbray, 1957), 9. The author of this prayer, as of the other meditations in this set of selections from a devotional work popular in England in the fourteenth and fifteenth centuries, was in all likelihood an Augustinian Canon of the thirteenth or fourteenth century.

Chapter 8: Anima/Animus in Full Pursuit

1. Johann Peter Eckermann, *Conversations with Goethe,* March 11, 1828. Our citations are from Hermann Weigand's splendid translation of Ludwig Curtius's selection of materials from Goethe, *Wisdom and Experience* (New York: Pantheon, 1949), 105–106. The full conversation can be found in the Everyman edition, trans. John Oxenford (London: Dent, 1946), 245–253; the passage discussed here is on pp. 249–250.

2. See Ann Mankowitz, *Change of Life: A Psychological Study of Dreams and the Menopause* (Toronto: Inner City Books, 1984), for a woman's view of menopause; see also Christine Downing, *Menopause: Journey through a Personal Rite of Passage* (New York: Crossroads, 1989); and Penelope Shuttle and Peter Redgrove, *The Wise Wound: Eve's Curse and Everywoman* (New York: Richard Marek, 1978).

3. For an elaboration of this point, see A. B. Ulanov, *The Feminine,* 176.

4. See A. Ulanov and B. Ulanov, *Witch and the Clown,* chaps. 4–7. See also J. H. Wheelwright, *The Animus for Women Growing Older* (Houston: C. G. Jung Educational Center, 1984); and Barbara Walker, *Crone: Woman of Age, Wisdom and Power* (San Francisco: Harper, 1988).

5. See Martin Heidegger, *Being and Time,* trans. John Macquarrie and Edward Robinson (New York: Harper & Row, 1962), 299–311.

6. See José Ortega y Gasset, *Man and People,* trans. W. R. Trask (New York: Norton, 1957), 136–138.

7. Marie-Louise von Franz, *On Dreams and Death* (Boston: Shambhala, 1986), 60.

8. See E. W. Easton, *The Intimate Interiors of Edouard Vuillard* (Washington: Smithsonian Institution Press, 1989), 38, 52. For a full treatment of this sort of completeness of self-inspection, see A. Ulanov and B. Ulanov, *Witch and the Clown,* 135–140.

9. See von Franz, *On Dreams and Death,* 105–115.

10. For split anima, see A. Ulanov and B. Ulanov, *Witch and the Clown,* 323; and A. B. Ulanov, *Receiving Woman,* 128–136.

11. See Renate Köbler, *In the Shadow of Karl Barth: Charlotte von Kirschbaum,* trans. Keith Crim (Louisville, Ky.: Westminster/John Knox, 1987).

12. See Hannah Tillich, *From Time to Time* (New York: Stein & Day, 1973).

13. See Paul Roazen, *Freud and His Followers* (New York: Knopf, 1975), chap. 9.

14. For discussion of this three-way relationship, see *C. G. Jung, Emma Jung and Toni Wolff,* ed. Ferne Jensen, assisted by Sidney Mullen (San Francisco: The Analytical Psychology Club of San Francisco, 1982); see also Laurens Van der Post, *Jung and the Story of Our Time* (New York: Random House, 1976); and Anthony Stevens, *On Jung* (London: Routledge, 1990), 160–162.

15. See François Roustang, *Dire Mastery: Discipleship from Freud to Lacan,* trans. Ned Lukacher (Baltimore: Johns Hopkins Univ. Press, 1982), 11.

16. See Stan Draenos, *Freud's Odyssey: Psychoanalysis and the End of Metaphysics* (New Haven: Yale Univ. Press, 1982), 108, 63. See also, for the letter to Pfister, Bruno Bettelheim, *Freud and Man's Soul* (New York: Knopf, 1983), 35.

17. See C. G. Jung, *Letters* 2:567, 303–304; 1:413–414, 355, 461.

18. For a study of a split-anima condition in a father and his son and its resolution, see A. B. Ulanov, "Disguises of the Anima," in *Gender and Soul in Psychotherapy.*

19. See A. B. Ulanov, *The Feminine,* 341.

20. Jung writes, "But the fact is that the approach to the numinous is the real therapy and inasmuch as you attain to the numinous experiences you are released from the curse of pathology. Even the very disease takes on a numinous character." *Letters* 1:377.

21. See A. B. Ulanov, "Between Anxiety and Faith: The Role of the Feminine in Paul Tillich's Thought," in *Paul Tillich on Creativity,* ed. Jacqueline Kegley and J. L. Adams (New York: Univ. Press of America, 1989);

see also A. B. Ulanov, "The Anxiety of Being: Paul Tillich and Depth Psychology," in *Paul Tillich,* ed. J. L. Adams and R. L. Shinn (New York: Harper, 1985).

22. See José Ortega y Gasset, *Historical Reason,* trans. P. W. Silver (New York: Norton, 1984), 21.

23. See A. B. Ulanov, *The Female Ancestors of Christ* (Boston: Shambhala Publications, 1993). See also, on the Virgin, M. Esther Harding, *Women's Mysteries, Ancient and Modern* (New York: Putnam, 1971); and John Layard, *The Virgin Archetype* (New York: Spring, 1972).

Chapter 9: Breakdown: The Ego's Side

1. See von Franz, *Redemption Motifs,* 40.

2. Testimony to the centrality of this inner conversation, in which we may retrieve large pieces of what Augustine means by *memoria,* the record of ourselves that we carry around with us always, may be found in many places. One of the clearest is in Joseph Wood Krutch's autobiography, where he reports on the way he wrote the second half of his most famous book, *The Modern Temper.* "Ideas, convictions, and attitudes, which had previously found no adequate expression and of the interconnection between which I was not fully aware, suddenly crystallized into a coherent discourse. I listened to what I had been saying to myself for several years, without being quite aware of the fact, and I simply wrote it down as I listened. Here were the conclusions I had come to as I digested or reacted against all I had read, heard, or discussed from the freshman days at college down to the latest book I had reviewed and the latest conversation in *The Nation* office. For the first time I was prepared to say what I, at that moment, believed; just what, in my opinion, the 'modern ideas' I had met came down to." See Krutch's *More Lives Than One* (New York: William Sloane, 1962), 204.

3. See Soren Kierkegaard, *The Sickness unto Death,* trans. Walter Lowrie (Garden City, N.Y.: Anchor, 1954), 166–182.

4. See Ingmar Bergman, *A Film Trilogy,* trans. P. B. Austin (New York: Orion, 1967), 65, 67, 77–78, 80–82, 92–93, 87, 97, 101–104.

5. For further discussion of this material, see A. Ulanov and B. Ulanov, *Witch and the Clown,* 178. For the case of a daughter caught in identification with a wounded father, see L. S. Leonard, *The Wounded Woman: Healing the Father-Daughter Relationship* (Chicago: Swallow Press, 1982).

6. See Vasily Rozanov, *Dostoevsky and the Legend of the Grand Inquisitor,* trans. S. E. Roberts (Ithaca, N.Y.: Cornell Univ. Press, 1972), 145.

7. See Vasily Rozanov, *The Apocalypse of Our Time and Other Writings,* ed. Robert Payne, trans. Robert Payne and Nikita Romanoff (New York: Praeger, 1977), 38, 99, 277, 134, 51, 106, 36–37, 107, 31–32, 97, 189.

8. See Rebecca West, "The Salt of the Earth," in *The Harsh Voice* (London: Virago, 1983), 171–172.

9. Jung explains: "Animus and anima are natural 'archetypes,' primordial figures of the unconscious, and have given rise to the mythological gods and goddesses. . . . Whenever a projection of these archetypes is destroyed by rational criticism, the disembodied image returns to its origin, the archetype. There it awaits a new opportunity to project itself." See *Integration of the Personality,* 23.

10. See A. Ulanov and B. Ulanov, *Witch and the Clown,* 215.

11. See Esther Harding's "Anima and the Animus," 5–10.

12. See, on making passion permanent, A. B. Ulanov, *The Feminine,* 298–303, 306, 313.

13. For another example of this kind of projective identification, see A. B. Ulanov, "Transference/Countertransference," in Stein, *Jungian Analysis,* 77.

14. See George Eliot's *Middlemarch* in the Everyman edition (London: Dent, 1969), 1:2, 11, 4, 6, 61.

15. On this blank space, see A. B. Ulanov, *Receiving Woman,* 123–126.

16. See D. W. Winnicott, "On Communication," in *Maturational Processes,* 182–183. See also Melanie Klein, *Love, Guilt and Reparation and Other Works* (New York: Delacorte, 1975), 323–327, and in the same volume, "The Oedipus Complex in the Light of Early Anxieties," 395.

17. Winnicott calls this "ego orgasm" to distinguish it from instinctual climax; see "The Capacity to Be Alone" in *Maturational Processes,* 34–35.

18. See Emily Dickinson, *Selected Letters,* ed. T. H. Johnson (Cambridge: Belknap/Harvard Univ. Press, 1971), 171–172.

19. See *The Complete Poems of Emily Dickinson,* ed. T. H. Johnson (Boston: Little, Brown, 1960), 128, 133, 320, 322, 336, 337, 484, 666, 574, 506–507, 338.

Chapter 10: Breakdown: The Self Side

1. The media seem to work in a psychological vacuum, charging through such sexual pageantry as that provided by the trials of the rapists of the New York Central Park jogger and of William Kennedy Smith and the Clarence Thomas-Anita Hill exchanges as if unparalleled candor about real or putative human pathology would have no effect on the collective unconscious or on the psyches of those who stayed so attentively glued, for so long, to their TV screens. Too often, in such reporting, candor becomes prurience. Modern man in repudiation of a soul, one might say, in a play on Jung's *Modern Man in Search of a Soul.*

2. See Jung, *Mysterium Coniunctionis,* 379–380, para. 539.

3. For an extensive treatment of this case, see A. B. Ulanov, *The Wizards' Gate: Picturing Consciousness* (Einsiedeln: Daimon Verlag, 1994) chap. 1. See also von Franz's discussion of the nasty dwarf in *The Feminine in Fairy Tales,* 61–64.

4. See R. D. Laing, *The Politics of Experience* (New York: Pantheon, 1967), chap. 3.

5. See Albert Camus, *The Myth of Sisyphus,* trans. Justin O'Brien (New York: Vintage, 1959), v; Camus's *The Fall,* trans. Justin O'Brien (New York: Knopf, 1957), 56, 81, 38–39, 69–70, 104, 121–122, 125–126, 139, 128–130, 135, 147; and *Notes from the Underground,* in *The Short Novels of Dostoevsky* (New York: Dial Press, 1945), 222.

6. Von Franz takes up the fairy tale "Sleeping Beauty" in *The Feminine in Fairy Tales,* chap. 2 et seq.

7. See K. M. Abenheimer, "The Ego as Subject," in *The Reality of the Psyche,* ed. J. B. Wheelwright (New York: Putnam, 1968), chap. 6.

8. See Otto Kernberg, *Borderline Conditions and Pathological Narcissism* (New York: Jason Aronson, 1975), 41–42.

9. Jung, *Mysterium Coniunctionis,* 95, 148, 181, paras. 113, 175, 230.

10. The bitter irony of the last line of the play, spoken by that master of corruption, seduction, and blackmail, Judge Brack, says everything about Hedda in life and in death: "But people don't do such things!" But of course they do, if they are pursued unto death by a world the wounded animus woman sees as united in hostility to her, as Ibsen explained to an actress, speaking of Hedda's husband, his aunts, and an old servant: "To Hedda they appear like a strange and hostile power, aimed at her very being." See Ibsen, *Letters and Speeches,* ed. Evert Sprinchorn (New York: Hill & Wang, 1964), 299.

11. At a crucial moment in Act II of *When We Dead Awaken,* Rubek exults over finding Irene again. His creativity has returned, he thinks. "You shall see the dawn of day looming for us both, bringing us light," he says to her. She tells him not to believe that, but he insists: "I do believe it! I know it—now that I have found you again!" Irene agrees: "Resurrected!" Rubek wants to go farther. "Transfigured!" he cries. No, Irene must say, "Only resurrected . . . not transfigured." A man's anima, in or out of the flesh, can bring him alive again to confront and make use of his imagination; it cannot produce his sculpture for him or sanctify him. That is both good psychology and good theology. See *The Late Plays of Henrik Ibsen,* trans. Arvid Paulsen (New York: Harper, 1973), 409. "To have any vital meaning, an artist's greatness, comparative or absolute, must be intuitively experienced," Hermann Wiegand says at the end of his finely reasoned book *The Modern Ibsen* (New York: Dutton, 1960). That is true for Rubek, for the reader or viewer of the drama, and for Ibsen himself, as *When We*

Dead Awaken, the last of his plays, declares to us in the inescapable application of its events, its people, its fantasies to the playwright that everywhere in the play we are led to make.

12. See Jung, *Aion, CW* 9:2, 8–11, paras. 13–19. See also *The Archetype of the Shadow in a Split World,* ed. M. A. Mattoon (Einsiedeln: Daimon, 1987), and J. L. Henderson, *Shadow and Self: Selected Papers in Analytical Psychology* (Wilmette, Ill.: Chiron, 1990), sect. 2.

13. See John Haule, *Divine Madness: Archetypes of Romantic Love* (Boston: Shambhala, 1990), 98, 107, 114, 131; Marion Woodman, *Addiction to Perfection: The Still Unravished Bride* (Toronto: Inner City Books, 1982), chap. 7; and L. S. Leonard, *On the Way to the Wedding* (Boston: Shambhala, 1987), chap. 5. Sometimes the whole of the male sex is felt as a collective persecutory demon to be dealt with only by exclusion. Mary Daly, in a lecture given at Union Theological Seminary in April 1978, would not allow men to ask questions or make comments in the discussion period that followed her lecture. The impression given was of a woman so inwardly crushed by a persecutory animus and so outwardly victimized by misogynist attitudes in church and academy that the masculine had to be utterly repudiated. No differentiation of self could occur until this great weight could be lifted.

14. See Elizabeth Madox Roberts, *Black Is the Color of My True Love's Hair* (New York: Viking, 1938), 22–23, 70–71.

15. See Marion Woodman, *Addiction to Perfection* and *The Owl Was a Baker's Daughter* (Toronto: Inner City Books, 1980), for discussions of food addictions; see also L. S. Leonard, *Witness to the Fire: Creativity and the Veil of Addiction* (Boston: Shambhala, 1989).

16. See Louis MacNeice, *The Burning Perch* (London: Faber, 1963), 11, 13, 18, 30, 34, 35, 42, 48–53; *Collected Poems* (London: Faber, 1949), 209; *Ten Burnt Offerings* (London: Faber, 1952), 40; *Time Wasting: The World of Louis MacNeice,* ed. Terence Brown and Alec Reid (Dublin: Dolmen Press, 1974), 8; Louis MacNeice, *Goethe's Faust, Parts I and II: An Abridged Version* (New York: Oxford Univ. Press, 1981), 303; *Ten Burnt Offerings,* 91–93, 96, 58; and *The Burning Perch,* 58.

17. Discussed on "60 Minutes," CBS Television, 6 February 1983.

18. Hans Loewald provides a useful and notably lucid description of the principles of mental functioning in his *Psychoanalysis and the History of the Individual* (New Haven: Yale Univ. Press, 1978), 56.

19. For scapegoating, see A. B. Ulanov, "The Double Cross," in *Lingering Shadows: Jungians, Freudians, and Anti-Semitism,* ed. Aryeh Maidenbaum and Stephen Martin (Boston: Shambhala, 1992).

20. See M. Masud R. Khan, "The Use and Abuse of Dream in Psychic Experience," in *The Privacy of the Self* (New York: International Universi-

ties Press, 1974); and "Beyond the Dreaming Experience," in *Hidden Selves: Between Theory and Practice in Psychoanalysis* (New York: International Universities Press, 1983).

21. See Friedrich Schiller, *Essays Aesthetical and Philosophical* (London: George Bell, 1910), 371.

22. For an understanding of the gap and the ways available to us for filling it, see A. Ulanov and B. Ulanov, *The Healing Imagination: The Meaning of Psyche and Soul* (Mahwah, N.J.: Paulist Press, 1991), chaps. 2, 8.

Chapter 11: Transference, Countertransference

1. For discussions of many aspects of transference, see Jung, "The Psychology of Transference," *CW* 16, and Lecture 5 of his "Tavistock Lectures," *CW* 18. See also Michael Fordham, "Jung's Conception of Transference," *Journal of Analytical Psychology* 19, no. 1 (1974); Loewald, *Psychoanalysis and the History of the Individual,* chap. 2; H. Racker, *Transference and Countertransference* (London: Hogarth Press, 1968); H. F. Searles, *Countertransference* (New York: International Universities Press, 1979); A. B. Ulanov, "Follow-Up Treatment in Cases of Patient/Therapist Sex," *Journal of the American Academy of Psychoanalysis* 7 no. 1 (1979); and her "Transference/Countertransference," in Stein, *Jungian Analysis;* D. W. Winnicott, "Hate in the Countertransference," in *Through Paediatrics to Psychoanalysis* (New York: Basic Books, 1975), 194–203, and his *The Piggle: An Account of the Psychoanalytic Treatment of a Little Girl* (New York: International Universities Press, 1977).

2. For vivid examples of the bath motif, see the illustrations in Jung, *Psychology and Alchemy, CW* 12, 72, 115, 224, 253, 287, 385.

3. See Immanuel Kant, *Critique of Pure Reason,* trans. J. M. D. Meiklejohn (London: Dent, 1964), 107, n. 2, 108 (from "Transcendental Deduction of the Pure Conceptions of the Understanding"), and Henri Bergson, *The Two Sources of Morality and Religion,* trans. R. A. Audra and Claudesley Brereton (New York: Holt, 1935), 59.

4. Jung, "Psychology of the Transference," *CW* 16, 250, para. 460. For an understanding of the two methods, the reductive and the prospective, see Jung, *Psychological Types, CW* 6, 252, para. 427.

5. See, for example, Frances Wickes, *The Inner World of Childhood* (Boston: Sigo, 1988), chap. 7.

6. See Klein, *Envy and Gratitude,* 208–211. See also Winnicott, *Playing and Reality,* 73–75; and "A Note on a Case Involving Envy," 76–78, and "Melanie Klein: On Her Concept of Envy," in *Psychoanalytic Explorations.*

7. See Barbara Hannah, "The Problem of Women's Plots in 'the Evil Vineyard' " (London: Guild of Pastoral Psychology, 1964), 51; and her *Striving Toward Wholeness* (New York: Putnam, 1976), chaps. 9, 10.

8. See, for example, Jung, *Dream Analysis,* 52, 75, 79ff.; his *Two Essays,* *CW* 7, 192–200, paras. 305–322; and *Psychological Types, CW* 6, 470–471, para. 808.

9. See Marcel Proust, *Remembrance of Things Past,* trans. C. K. Scott Moncrieff (New York: Random House, 1932), 1:39 (*Combray*), 599–600 (*Within a Budding Grove*); 2:733, 759, 773 (*The Sweet Cheat Gone*), 524, 525 (*The Captive*).

10. See Patrick White, *The Twyborn Affair* (London: Cape, 1979), 14, 25, 171, 240, 293, 296, 311, 322, 328, 422, 430–432. See also Barry Ulanov, *Jung and the Outside World* (Wilmette, Ill.: Chiron, 1992), chap. 7.

11. On the marriage archetype, see Jung, "Psychology of the Transference," *CW* 16, 167–169, 185, 200, 221–225, 231, paras. 353–361, 381, 423–433, 442. See also Harding, *The "I" and the "Not-I,"* chap. 5; and Verena Kast, *Nature of Loving,* chap. 5.

12. See Honoré de Balzac, *Cousin Bette,* trans. M. A. Crawford (London: Penguin, 1965), 43, 72, 127, 211–212, 288–289, 406–407, 423, 442–444.

Chapter 12: *Acting Out Anima/Animus and Its Alternatives*

1. See Elie Humbert and A. B. Ulanov in the symposium "How Do I Assess Progress in Supervision?" *Journal of Analytic Psychology* 27, no. 2 (1982).

2. See Michael Balint, *The Basic Fault: Therapeutic Aspects of Regression* (London: Tavistock, 1968), chap. 4. See also C. M. Barker, *Healing in Depth* (London: Hodder & Stoughton, 1972); Stein, *Incest and Human Love,* 41–47; Kohut, *How Does Analysis Cure?,* ed. Arnold Goldberg with the collaboration of Paul E. Stephansky (Chicago: Univ. of Chicago Press, 1984). 9–10, 14, 16, 24, 54, 56, 61, 63; and Haule, *Divine Madness,* 63, 80.

3. See Jung, "Psychology of the Transference," *CW* 16, 215, 217–218, 224ff., 262–263, paras. 415, 419, 431ff.

4. Jung, "Psychology of the Transference," 233, para. 445.

5. Jung, "Psychology of the Transference," 243, para. 454.

6. *Thisness* is a translation of *haeccitas,* the absolute concreteness that Duns Scotus insisted upon as the identifying element of a singular individual—person, animal, thing—as distinguished from *quidditas,* the whatness that defines a general species. It is the understanding that gives such life to the people, places, and things in the poems of Gerard Manley Hopkins, who was a devout Scotist.

7. For the Russian text, see the bilingual collection *Modern Russian Poetry,* ed. Vladimir Markov and Merrill Sparks (Indianapolis: Bobbs-Merrill, 1967), 429, 445–447.

8. See Boris Pasternak, Marina Tsvetayeva, Rainer Maria Rilke, *Letters Summer 1926,* trans. Margaret Wettlin and Walter Arndt (London: Cape, 1986), 227, 224, 227–228, 14, 81, 84, 197, 87, 201, 95, 201, 204.

9. See Jung, "Psychology of the Transference," 200, 207, 235–236, 246, 251, paras. 401, 404, 451, 458, 462. See also Joanna Field, *On Not Being Able to Paint* (New York: International Universities Press, 1979), 85.

10. See Jung, "Psychology of the Transference," 195, paras. 395–396. See also Loewald, *Psychoanalysis and the History of the Individual,* 56–57; Winnicott, *Playing and Reality,* chaps. 1, 4; and "Living Creatively," in *Home Is Where We Start From,* 39–54; A. Ulanov and B. Ulanov, *Primary Speech: A Psychology of Prayer* (Louisville: John Knox, 1983), chap. 1; and M. Masud R. Khan, *Hidden Selves,* 49–50, 78, 85–87, 97, 183–184, 186, 188.

11. See A. B. Ulanov, "Follow-Up Treatment in Cases of Patient/Therapist Sex." This article deals exclusively with sexual encounters between male analysts and female patients. That is the usual pairing in these difficult situations. Only rarely has the case of two men or two women come to notice, and never of a female analyst with a male patient. We can speculate on the reasons. The analyst-patient relationship is not between equals, no matter what the interdependencies of transference. The analyst has the edge of power. Hence for a woman therapist to engage sexually with a male patient means a dangerous mixing of drinks: on the one hand she is in charge, carrying a full load of responsibility; on the other, her sexual impulses would be moving her to surrender responsibility. The opposition of these factors inhibits sexual acting-out. Another factor might be a mixture of general modesty and particular daring in a woman: she dares for passion in permanence and thus finds it difficult to surrender to impulse in unprotected situations; she does not want to be an episode. Finally, the power drive in women is not so easily linked to phallic erotic aggression as it may be in men. The power motives attributed to male analysts in sexual encounters with female patients are simply less relevant to female analysts. We might also speculate—*contra* Freud, who found women's sense of justice inferior to men's because of a weaker formation of superego arising from women's less precise termination of Oedipal conflicts—that female analysts show a greater empathy with their patients' plights, arising from a sense of justice characteristically mixed with compassion. That inevitably makes them reluctant to take advantage of their patients' sexuality and thus add to the troubles that have brought the patients to the analysts in the first place. See Esmé Wynne-Tyson, *The Philosophy of Compassion* (London: Vincent Stuart, 1962).

12. See *The Personal Papers of Anton Chekhov,* trans. S. S. Koteliansky and Leonard Woolf (New York: Lear, 1948), 128–131, 30, 32, 33, 36, 56, 83, 46, 57, 110–111, 104, 62.

13. See Douglas, *Woman in the Mirror,* 88–91, who argues that Jung did this with Christiana Morgan.

14. See Luigi Pirandello, *Naked Masks: Five Plays* (New York: Dutton, 1952), 275–276. The translation of *Six Characters in Search of an Author* is by Edward Storer.

15. Henrik Ibsen, *Hedda Gabler and Other Plays,* trans. Una Ellis-Fermor (Middlesex: Penguin, 1972), 206, 259–260. See also the William Archer translation of *John Gabriel Borkman* in Barry Ulanov, *Makers of the Modern Theater* (New York: McGraw-Hill, 1961), and the Ulanov introduction, 9–10.

16. See *The Plays of Strindberg,* trans. Michael Meyer (New York: Vintage, 1976), 2:122–123, 260; 1:467; and *Five Plays of Strindberg,* trans. Elizabeth Sprigge (New York: Anchor, 1960), 345–346.

17. See Samuel Beckett, *Waiting for Godot* (New York: Grove, 1954), 28b.

18. See M. Masud R. Khan, *Alienation in Perversion* (New York: International Universities Press, 1979), 214.

19. Jung, "Psychology of the Transference," 199, para. 400. See also A. B. Ulanov, "The Perverse and the Transcendent." See also, A. B. Ulanov, "Self-Service," in *Cast the First Stone,* eds. Lena Ross and Manisha Roy (Wilmette, Ill.: Chiron, 1994).

20. See Elias Canetti, *The Human Province,* trans. Joachim Neugroschel (New York: Seabury, 1978), 217, 213, 274, 245, 183, 182.

21. Occasionally a given analysis may reach a moment of intimacy that allows that odd experience of reversal of sexual roles (that lovers know so much about) while each of the persons involved still maintains his or her actual identity. Rosemary Gordon gives the example of a male patient who fantasized the pleasure a woman experienced in receiving a penis. Gordon, the analyst, registered sexual excitement, but as a male. She illustrates how such a moment may flow into the real life of the analyst, rather than being lived with the patient, as she theorizes about what has happened. The patient projected onto her the good male role, she thought. While he talked, he was introjectively identified with the woman's role, asking implicitly that the analyst protect in herself the good penis from the ravaging one that he also felt. She concluded that they had shared a symbolic sexual experience that had led to good effects. Unlike the usual undoing that followed sessions for this patient, this one stuck. It built what Jung calls a "hard fact" within him—he could be an agent of pleasure, not just of destruction. See Rosemary Gordon, "The Concept of Projective Identification."

Chapter 13: Borderlines, Bluebeard, and Death

1. See Otto Kernberg, "Treatment of Borderline Patients," in *Tactics and Techniques in Psychoanalytic Therapy* (New York: Science House,

1972), 255–256; and *Borderline Conditions and Pathological Narcissism* (New York: Jason Aronson, 1975). See also Charles Rycroft, *A Critical Dictionary of Psycho-Analysis* (New York: Basic Books, 1968), and Jules Masterson, *Narcissistic and Borderline Disorders* (New York: Brunner-Mazel, 1981).

2. Nathan Schwartz-Salant, *The Borderline Personality, Vision and Healing* (Wilmette, Ill.: Chiron, 1989), 3f.

3. See Moore, "The Transcendent Function and the Emerging Ego." She makes the valuable point that the two, the transcendent function and the ego, grow simultaneously. That was true in the case of this patient.

4. See C. G. Jung, *Symbols of Transformation, CW* 5, trans. R. F. C. Hull (Princeton: Princeton University Press, 1956), 124, para. 180. See also Melanie Klein, "The Importance of Symbol-Formation in the Development of the Ego," in *Love, Guilt and Reparation and Other Works 1921–1945* (New York: Delacorte, 1975), 220.

5. See Michael Fordham, "Defences of the Self," *Journal of Analytical Psychology* 19, no. 2 (1974); for a recent discussion of this paper and suggested ways to handle such defenses, see Nathan Schwartz-Salant, "Vision, Interpretation, and the Interactive Field," and Michael Fordham, "Rejoinder to N. Schwartz-Salant," *Journal of Analytical Psychology* 36, no. 3 (1990).

6. See René Char, "The Library Is on Fire," in the bilingual volume *Contemporary French Poetry,* ed. Alexander Aspel and Donald Justice (Ann Arbor, Mich.: Ann Arbor Paperbacks, 1967), 68, 70, 72, 74, 76. The translation here is by Barry Ulanov.

7. See Yves Bonnefoy, *The Act and the Place of Poetry* (Chicago: Univ. of Chicago Press, 1989), 122.

8. Jung offers a useful interpretation of why these animals turn up in people's dreams: "We know that something is coming up from the unconscious which is not to be influenced by will-power. It is like a fate that cannot be twisted. . . . It is always a sign in dreams that now a level is reached where something is going to happen." See *Dream Analysis, 327.*

9. All the versions of this fairy tale are compelling, we think. See, for example, the familiar one in *Bluebeard and Other Fairy Tales of Charles Perrault,* introduced by Simone de Beauvoir, trans. Richard Howard (New York: Macmillan, 1964); "The Robber Bridegroom" and "Fitcher's Bird," in *Grimm's Fairy Tales* (New York: Pantheon, 1944); "The 'Forbidden Chamber' Motif," in Kawai, *The Japanese Psyche,* chap. 1; and for the possibly historical figure upon which the Bluebeard legends and tales are based, Leonard Wolfe, *Bluebeard: The Life and Times of Gilles de Rais* (New York: Crown, 1980).

10. See Von Franz, *Apuleius,* XIII: 11; and *The Feminine in Fairy Tales,* 65–67.

11. See Guntrip, *Schizoid Phenomena,* 28–35, 45.

12. Jung, *The Visions Seminars,* 1:46.

13. See Melanie Klein, *Narrative of a Child Analysis* (New York: Delacorte, 1961), 65, 89, 91, 95, 123, 314. See also Bruno Bettelheim, *The Uses of Enchantment: The Meaning and Importance of Fairy Tales* (New York: Knopf, 1976), 7, 10, 12, 16, 113, 120, 207–215, 249–251, 272, 299–303.

14. See the unpaged text accompanying the recording of Bartók's *Duke Bluebeard's Castle* by the London Philharmonic Orchestra under Georg Solti (London: Decca, 1980).

15. See George Steiner, *In Bluebeard's Castle* (New Haven: Yale Univ. Press, 1971), 3, 121–124.

16. This dream is discussed at some length in A. B. Ulanov, "Transference/Countertransference," in Stein, *Jungian Analysis,* 81–84; and even more fully in her "Disguises of the Anima," in *Gender, Soul and Psychotherapy.*

17. See A. B. Ulanov, *Wizards' Gate.* See also J. H. Wheelwright, "Analysis with the Aged," in Stein, *Jungian Analysis;* and her book *The Death of a Woman* (New York: St. Martin's Press, 1981).

18. The *locus classicus* for philosophy as an apprenticeship to death is Montaigne's essay "To Philosophize Is to Learn to Die" (*Essays* 1:20), where in addition to Cicero he adduces texts from Horace, Lucretius, Virgil, and Ovid, among others, to support his point: "I verily beleeve, these fearefull lookes, and astonishing countenances wherewith we encompasse it, are those that more amaze and terrifie us than death [itself]" (in Florio's handsome sixteenth-century translation).

19. See Theodor Haecker, *Journal in the Night,* trans. Alick Dru (New York: Pantheon, 1950), 96.

20. See Jeremy Taylor, quoted in Barry Ulanov, *Death: A Book of Preparation and Consolation* (New York: Sheed & Ward, 1959), 48.

Chapter 14: Repair from the Ego Side

1. For a discussion of the *albedo* stage, see Marie-Louise von Franz, *C. G. Jung: His Myth in Our Time,* trans. W. H. Kennedy (New York: Putnam, 1975), 223; and her *Alchemy: An Introduction,* 256. See also Jung, "The Spirit Mercurius," in *Alchemical Studies, CW* 13, 214, para. 263; and his *Mysterium Coniunctionis, CW* 14, 238ff., paras. 319ff.

2. The association of the Don Juan figure with death is firm; as Otto Rank points out, the Stone Guest, the father who arises from the grave to avenge his daughter's betrayal by Don Juan, appears in the subtitle of many versions of the story. The corpse-demon brings death to the Don, but also, if only at the point of death, an awakening of conscience. See Otto Rank,

The Don Juan Legend, trans. and ed. D. G. Winter (Princeton: Princeton Univ. Press, 1975), chap. 5. We add here the role of Don Juan in the anima/ animus world as a figure that rouses one from inner emptiness.

3. See Gaston Bachelard, *The Poetics of Space,* trans. Maria Jolas (New York: Orion, 1964), xix.

4. See Gaston Bachelard, *The Right to Dream,* trans. J. A. Underwood (New York: Orion, 1971), 206–208, 212–213.

5. Heinz Kohut stresses the importance of the analyst's allying with an emerging structure, here the strengthening ego, rather than a traumatic wound. See Kohut, *The Analysis of the Self* (New York: International Universities Press, 1971), 29–31. See also A. B. Ulanov, *Receiving Woman,* chap. 6, for a discussion of moves by the ego to emerge from states of identity with others, to reclaim its projections, and turn toward its wounded places—to let life finally fill in the blank spaces behind anima or animus armor and to bind up its splits.

6. Melanie Klein suggests that our ego will often find more bearable a defined external danger onto which we can project our inner fears of an outer danger of a kind that knows no bounds. See her "Early Stages of the Oedipus Conflict and of Super-Ego Formation," in *The Psychoanalysis of Children,* trans. Alix Strachey (New York: Delacorte, Seymour Lawrence, 1975), 147; and in the same volume, "The Relations Between Obsessional Neurosis and the Early Stages of the Super-Ego," 166; and "The Effects of Early Anxiety-Situations on the Sexual Development of the Girl," 202.

7. For exhibitionism as self-validation, see Irvine Schiffer, *The Trauma of Time* (New York: International Universities Press, 1978), 158–159.

8. Winnicott gets at this split anima (and, we would add, at the split image of woman as mother and sex partner) by tracing the development in all of us as children of the need to integrate our instinctive reactions to our parents with our dependency upon them. The best way to do that is in relation to a good-enough mother who can receive (and survive) her child's use of her for at least initially ruthless instinctual attacks, and, alongside this, her child's need for her to provide a holding environment. It is crucial that the mother survive the excitement the child draws from these connections with her, and survive them out of her own resources. If the child feels that it must withhold such instinctual displays in order to protect the mother, the child begins to split off spontaneous expression of instinct. We need loving connection to another person to fuse our aggression and eros. That fact of psychic life should help us understand how healing the effects of a good love affair can be: it can mend the old split if the lover proves to be both dependable and welcoming of our instinctual responses. Unfortunately, a love affair can have devastating consequences if the lover reinforces the old split, either by refusing our dependency or rejecting our

instinctual advances. See Winnicott, "On Communication," in *Maturational Processes,* 182–183; and in the same volume "Ego Distortion in Terms of True and False Self," 145–148. See also A. B. Ulanov, "The Disguises of the Anima," in *Gender and Soul in Psychotherapy,* 36–37, 46, for an example of the knitting back together of such anima splitting.

9. See F. Scott Fitzgerald, *The Last Tycoon and The Great Gatsby* (New York: Scribner, 1941), 295–296, 277–278; and *The Letters of F. Scott Fitzgerald,* ed. Andrew Turnbull (New York: Scribner, 1963), 358, 480.

10. Jean Bazaine, as gifted an analyst of painting as he is a painter, says of Matisse that his "forms are less terms of knowledge [of his subjects] than they are pathways for his passion." His is "not the curiosity of the promenader, but the ardent and blind itinerary of a lover who does not *think* haunch, flower, or face, but identifies with them." Bonnard, says Bazaine, "if he paints a face as a fruit basket, a woman's body as a flowering countryside, it is because these fruits and flowers are all the more [as a result] face and flowers." This is the way Bonnard plumbs the depths of reality and goes far into things, transforming, for example, "a breast-apple into a breast raised to the nth power." See Jean Bazaine, *Le Temps de la peinture* (Paris: Aubier, 1990), 67, 49–50.

11. See A. B. Ulanov, "Transference/Countertransference," in Stein, *Jungian Analysis,* 79.

12. See Loewald, *Psychoanalysis and the History of the Individual,* chap. 2.

13. See von Franz, *Redemption Motifs,* 14–16.

14. See *Judith,* in *The Anchor Bible,* vol. 40, trans. C. A. Moore (Garden City, N.Y.: Doubleday, 1985), 244.

15. See Jean Giraudoux, *Judith,* trans. J. K. Savacool, in *The Modern Theatre,* ed. Eric Bentley (Garden City, N.Y.: Anchor, 1955), 3:218, 223, 228, 230, 233.

16. Winnicott discusses breast potency in an interesting way in *Human Nature* (London: Free Association Press, 1988), 74, 103.

17. For the important distinction between being and doing in psychological terms, see Winnicott, *Playing and Reality,* chap. 5. See also Guntrip, *Schizoid Phenomena,* chap. 9.

18. See A. Ulanov and B. Ulanov, *Primary Speech: A Psychology of Prayer,* chaps. 4, 5; and their *Healing Imagination,* chap. 1.

19. See Barry Ulanov, "The Song of Songs: The Rhetoric of Love," in *The Bridge: A Yearbook of Judaeo-Christian Studies,* ed. J. M. Oesterreicher (New York: Pantheon, 1962), 4:89–118.

20. See Jean Giraudoux, *The Song of Songs,* trans. Herma Briffault, in Barry Ulanov, *Makers of the Modern Theater,* 474–475, 477–478.

21. See Teresa of Avila, *The Interior Castle,* in *The Complete Works of*

St. Teresa, trans. E. A. Peers (New York: Sheed & Ward, 1957), vol. 2, *passim;* see also Stephen Clissold, *St. Teresa of Avila* (London: Sheldon Press, 1979), chaps. 5, 6.

22. Etty Hillesum, *An Interrupted Life: The Diaries of Etty Hillesum,* trans. Arno Pomerans (New York: Pantheon, 1983), 36.

Chapter 15: Ego and Other

1. Werner Jaeger's summation of the meaning of *apeiron* for its early philosophical appropriators is applicable here: "The best ancient expositors follow Aristotle in taking this word of many meanings to denote the endless, inexhaustible reservoir or stock from which all Becoming draws its nourishment, not that which is qualitatively undetermined, as certain modern writers have described it. As a matter of fact, the word *apeiron* points unequivocally to boundlessness as the real meaning of this conception." See Jaeger, *The Theology of the Early Greek Philosophers,* The Gifford Lectures 1936 (Oxford: Clarendon Press, 1960), 24.

2. For the role of archetypal images in the making of diagnoses, see A. Ulanov and B. Ulanov, *Witch and the Clown,* 16–21.

3. See Rainer Maria Rilke, *Selected Works,* trans. J. B. Leishman (Norfolk, Conn.: New Directions, 1960), 32, 33, 35, 85, 328.

4. See *Duino Elegies,* trans. J. B. Leishman and Stephen Spender, in Rilke, *Selected Works,* 225, 226, 234, 237, 239, 245.

5. See Rilke, *Letters to Merline,* trans. V. M. MacDonald (London: Metheun, 1951), 42, 129, 149.

6. See Rilke, *Selected Works,* 246, 248.

7. This translation of the last lines of Sonnet 29 of *The Sonnets to Orpheus* is by Barry Ulanov. The letter to Countess Mirbach, which contains Rilke's explanation of the dense concentration of the *Elegies* and the *Sonnets,* is in an appendix to Stephen Mitchell's translation of the *Sonnets* (New York: Simon & Schuster, 1985), 161.

8. See Haule, *Divine Madness,* 111, 120, 142, 148. See also A. B. Ulanov, *The Feminine,* 298–310.

9. See Erik Erikson, "Reality and Actuality," *Journal of the American Psychoanalytical Association* 10 (1961): 451–474, as cited in Schiffer, *The Trauma of Time,* 131.

10. See A. B. Ulanov, *Receiving Woman,* 57–71.

11. See Winnicott, *Playing and Reality,* chap. 6.

12. See Andrei Bitov, *Life in Windy Weather,* ed. Patricia Meyer, trans. C. G. and Richard Luplow (Ann Arbor, Mich.: Ardis, 1986), 121, 138–140, 143–144. A matching wisdom about anima visitations arises fitfully in Bitov's novel *Pushkin House,* trans. Susan Brownsberger (New York: Farrar,

Straus & Giroux, 1987), where the protagonist, Lyova, a figure Gogol might have created, struggles to make some sense out of his feelings about the women in his life, as he does about his responses to the Russian Revolution, the fiftieth anniversary of which is the occasion for the novel's events. Women fall into his life as bewildering incarnations of his fantasies, always so much harder to take in the flesh than the imagination: "For the first and last time, there arose before him the innate image of external love whose embodiment he had so insistently wished on the first woman to come along. This was She—and he promptly said goodbye to her forever, no longer dreaming of what does not happen in life" (p. 184). Bitov's point, made many different ways in the novel, is that it is exactly what we cast off from our dreams—men, women, ideologies—that we cannot ever get rid of, all the more if they represent "what does not happen in life."

13. See Boris Pasternak, *Poems,* trans. E. M. Kayden (Kent, Ohio: Kent State Univ. Press, 1970), 294–295.

14. See *The Time of the Spirit,* ed. George Every, Richard Harries, and Kallistos Ware (Crestwood, N.Y.: St. Vladimir's Seminary Press, 1984), 80.

15. See Jung, *The Undiscovered Self, CW* 10, 278–279, paras. 540–542.

16. See Emmanuel Levinas and Richard Kearney, "Dialogue with Emmanuel Levinas," in *Face to Face with Levinas,* ed. R. A. Cohen (Albany: State Univ. of New York Press, 1986), 27–28.

17. See S. L. Frank, *Reality and Man: An Essay in the Metaphysics of Human Nature,* trans. Natalie Duddington (New York: Taplinger, 1966), 144–145.

Chapter 16: Repair from the Self Side

1. Jung makes much of the compensatory relation of the unconscious to consciousness. See his *Two Essays on Analytical Psychology, CW* 7, 104, 109ff., 112, 171, 177, 180–181, paras. 107, 182ff., 190, 264–265, 274, 283, 285–286; see also "The Practical Use of Dream-Analysis," in *The Practice of Psychotherapy, CW* 16, 153ff., paras. 330ff.

2. See Jung, *Dream Analysis,* 299, 400; see also the example of such a long-running series in his *Psychology and Alchemy, CW* 12, part 2ff.

3. See Anthony Trollope, *Ayala's Angel* (London: Oxford Univ. Press World's Classics, 1968), 51–52, 103, 149–150, 436, 237, 239, 540, 593–594.

4. This dream is also reported in A. B. Ulanov, *Wisdom of the Psyche,* 89–90.

5. See Julian of Norwich, *The Revelations of Divine Love,* trans. James Walsh (London: Burns & Oates, 1961), chaps. 53, 57.

6. See Boethius, *The Consolation of Philosophy,* trans. I. T. (1609), revised by H. F. Stewart (London: Loeb Classical Library, 1926), 129, 131, 167, 294, 317, 319, 411. The verse fragment translation is by Barry Ulanov.

7. For a further elaboration of this point about plots, see A. B. Ulanov, *The Wisdom of the Psyche,* chap. 2. See also Barbara Hannah, "The Problem of Women's Plots in 'the Evil Vineyard,' " and A. Ulanov and B. Ulanov, *Cinderella,* chaps. 1, 2, 6.

8. "He emptied himself of his divinity," Simone Weil says. "We should empty ourselves of the false divinity with which we were born." She goes on:

> Once we have understood we are nothing, the object of all our efforts is to become nothing. It is for this that we suffer with resignation, *it is for this that we act,* it is for this that we pray.
> May God grant me to become nothing.
> In so far as I become nothing, God loves himself through me.

See Weil, *Gravity and Grace,* trans. Emma Crauford (London: Routledge & Kegan Paul, 1963), 30.

9. See Aniela Jaffé, *Was C. G. Jung a Mystic?,* trans. Diana Dachler and Fiona Cairns (Einsiedeln: Daimon, 1989), chap. 1. Jung, she says, disliked being called a mystic because he saw himself as an empirical scientist, in this case subjecting mystical experience to critical examination.

10. See *The Book of Privy Counsel,* in *The Medieval Mystics of England,* ed. Eric Colledge (London: John Murray, 1962), 157, 180, 161–162, 181.

11. See Karl Jaspers, *Philosophy of Existence,* trans. R. F. Grabau (Philadelphia: Univ. of Pennsylvania Press, 1971), 27–28.

12. See *Noah's Ark,* in Hugh of Saint-Victor, *Selected Spiritual Writings,* trans. by a Religious of C.S.M.V. (London: Faber, 1962), 50–51.

Chapter 17: Self and Other

1. Jung, "Psychology of the Transference," *CW* 16, 260, para. 469.

2. Christopher Bollas investigates this orientation to reality by means of his idea of the transformational object, namely, that in a child's earliest life its mother's processes of managing the infant are introjected by the child; as it grows up, they become its idiom for transforming its environment into livable form. Therapy offers an opportunity to bring these processes into consciousness and to explore them. Bollas, in the fashion of object-relations theorists, investigates our ways of orienting ourselves to Being by tracing them to our early experiences of objects in the world outside us. Jung, in contrast, investigates objects that arise autonomously from the archetypal layers of the psyche and incarnate in our object relationships, in our problems, and in the links we have to the numinous, wherever it may incarnate in our individuation process. See Bollas, *The Shadow of the Object: Psychoanalysis of the Unthought Known,* chap. 1.

3. See chapter 6 of this volume, p. 109.

4. See the *I Ching or Book of Changes,* trans. Richard Wilhelm and C. F. Baynes (New York: Pantheon, 1950).

5. See Paul Celan, *Speech-Grille,* trans. Joachim Neugroschel (New York: Dutton, 1971), 101–102; and *Poems of Paul Celan,* trans. Michael Hamburger (New York: Persea, 1989), 112–113, for the German and for English translations somewhat different from those we have made here.

6. See Geoffrey Hill, *Tenebrae* (Boston: Houghton Mifflin, 1979), 42–44.

7. See *Dark Soliloquy: The Selected Poems of Gertrud Kohmar,* trans. H. A. Smith (New York: Crossroads, 1975), 34, 59, 63f., 67f., 87f., 99f., 113f., 209f.; and Irina Ratushinskaya, *Beyond the Limit,* trans. F. P. Brent and C. J. Avins (Evanston, Ill.: Northwestern Univ. Press, 1987); and her *Pencil Letter* (New York: Knopf, 1989).

8. Barbara Hannah, in her speculations about Emily Brontë, does justice to Catherine Earnshaw, the central female figure in Brontë's *Wuthering Heights,* as an anima-woman, without reducing her to the terms of jargon-haunted literary psychoanalysis. Whatever the precise sources of Catherine in Emily Brontë's relationship with her father, or elsewhere, it seems fair to say, as Hannah does, that "at all events, the voice of Emily's soul or psyche produces a marvelous image of a woman who is blessed or cursed with the faculty of receiving the projection of a man's anima." Both the men in Catherine Earnshaw's life, her husband, Edgar Linton, and the foundling, Heathcliff, "are so completely fascinated by Catherine," Hannah goes on, "that they are willing to endure almost anything—even each other—for her sake. She is well aware of her power over them and is very probably capable of maintaining a balance between the two." That conclusion, appropriately hedged about with full consideration of Catherine's limitations, and especially those that are the result of her unlived life, takes the novel a long distance from the shallow judgments of those, whether sympathetic or unsympathetic, who cannot resist the language of diabolism or Gothic romance to explain the lure of the book. See Barbara Hannah, *Striving Towards Wholeness,* 231.

9. Jung writes: "The union of the conscious mind or ego personality with the unconscious personified as anima produces a new personality compounded of both. . . . Since it transcends consciousness it can no longer be called 'ego' but must be given the name of 'self.' . . . The self too is both ego and non-ego, subjective and objective, individual and collective. It is the 'uniting symbol' which epitomizes the total union of opposites. . . . The self is not a doctrine or theory but an image born of nature's own workings, a natural symbol far removed from all conscious intention." See "Psychology of the Transference," *CW* 16, 264, para. 474. Jung also writes, on the same material: "Animus and anima are images representing archetypal fig-

ures which mediate between consciousness and the unconscious. Though they can be made conscious they cannot be integrated into the ego-personality, since as archetypes they are also autonomous. They behave like the God-image, which while objectivating itself in the world nevertheless subsists of itself in the Unus Mundus." See *Letters* 2:342–343.

10. For the Augustinian Trinity of *memoria, voluntas,* and *intelligentia,* see Books X and XV:11 and 12 of the *De Trinitate;* for *munus,* or gift, see IV: 29, V:12, and XV: 29–46. Books X and XV appear in the selections from the *De Trinitate* in vol. 7 of The Library of Christian Classics, *Augustine: Later Works* (Philadelphia: Westminster, 1935), in John Burnaby's excellent translation. The standard edition, in which the great work appears in its entirety, is vol. 3 of series 1 of the *Nicene and Post-Nicene Fathers,* translated by A. W. Haddan and W. G. T. Shedd (Grand Rapids, Mich.: Eerdmans).

11. See Hans-George Gadamer, *Truth and Method* (New York: Seabury, 1975), 379–381.

12. See A. Ulanov and B. Ulanov, "Intercession," in *Religion and the Unconscious,* chap. 11. See also Jung, "Psychology of the Transference," *CW* 16, 232–234, paras. 444–449.

13. See von Franz, *Alchemy: An Introduction* 237ff.

14. For active imagination, see Janet Dallett, "Active Imagination in Practice," in *Jungian Analysis;* Barbara Hannah, *Encounters with the Soul: Active Imagination as Developed by C. G. Jung* (Santa Monica, Calif.: Sigo, 1981); Norah Moore, "The Transcendent Function and the Emerging Ego," *Journal of Analytical Psychology* 20, no. 2 (1975); and von Franz, *Redemption Motifs,* 102.

15. See C. G. Jung, "The Transcendent Function," *CW* 8, 67–92, paras. 131–193, and *Mysterium Coniunctionis, CW* 14, 200, 203, 495, 528–530, paras. 257, 261, 706, 753–755.

16. See C. G. Jung, Foreword to *Seelenprobleme der Gegenwart,* 1st ed., in *The Symbolic Life, CW* 18, 558, para. 1292.

17. See Jung, *Mysterium Coniunctionis, CW* 14, 155, para. 181.

18. See the discussion of this dream in A. B. Ulanov, "The Holding Self: Jung and the Desire for Being," in *Fires of Desire,* ed. Frederica Halligan and John Shea (New York: Crossroads, 1992).

19. For the role images play in religious life, see A. B. Ulanov, "Picturing God," in *Picturing God.*

20. See Jung, *Psychology and Religion, CW* 11, 8, paras. 8–9. See also Von Franz, *Apuleius,* VII: 7, X: 8, XI: 5–8; her *Individuation in Fairy Tales,* 34, 41; and her *Redemption Motifs,* 20; and Harding, *Women's Mysteries,* 236–237.

21. See Jung, "Psychology of the Transference," *CW* 16, 316, para. 531.

22. See Lorenzo de' Medici, *Comento sopra alcuni de' suoi sonetti,* in *Opere,* ed. Attilio Simioni (Bari: Laterza, 1939), 11, 24, 66, 88, 110.

Bibliography

Allenby, Amy. "The Father Archetype in Feminine Psychology." In *Fathers and Mothers*. Edited by Harry Wilmer. Wilmette, Ill.: Chiron, 1990.

Arseniev, Nicholas. *Revelation of Life Eternal*. Crestwood, N.Y.: St. Vladimir's Seminary Press, 1982.

Aspel, Alexander, and Donald Justice, eds. *Contemporary French Poetry*. Ann Arbor, Mich.: Ann Arbor Paperbacks, 1967.

Augustine, *De Trinitate*. Vol 7, *The Library of Christian Classics*. Translated by John Burnaby. Philadelphia: Westminster Press, 1935.

———. *De Trinitate*. Vol. 3, *The Nicene and Post-Nicene Fathers*. Translated by A. W. Haddam and W. G. T. Shedd. Grand Rapids, Mich.: Eerdmans, 1956.

———. *Selected Letters*. Translated by J. H. Baxter. London: Loeb Classical Library, 1953.

Bachelard, Gaston. *The Poetics of Reverie*. Translated by David Russell. New York: Orion, 1969.

———. *The Poetics of Space*. Translated by Maria Jolas. New York: Orion, 1964.

———. *The Right to Dream*. Translated by J. A. Underwood. New York: Orion, 1971.

Balint, Michael. *The Basic Fault: Therapeutic Aspects of Regression*. London: Tavistock, 1968.

Balzac, Honoré de. *Cousin Bette*. Translated by M. A. Crawford. London: Penguin, 1965.

Barker, C. M. *Healing in Depth*. London: Hodder & Stoughton, 1972.

Baudelaire, Charles. *The Intimate Journals.* Translated by Christopher Isherwood. Boston: Beacon Press, 1959.

———. *Paris Spleen.* Translated by Louise Varèse. New York: New Directions Books, 1970.

Bazaine, Jean. *Le Temps de la Peinture.* Paris: Aubier, 1990.

Beckett, Samuel. *Waiting for Godot.* New York: Grove, 1954.

Beebe, John, ed. *C. G. Jung: Aspects of the Masculine.* London: Ark, 1989.

Bentley, Eric, ed. *The Modern Theater.* Garden City, N.Y.: Anchor Publishing, 1955.

Bergman, Ingmar. *A Film Trilogy.* Translated by P. B. Austin. New York: Orion, 1967.

Bergson, Henri. *The Two Sources of Morality and Religion.* Translated by R. A. Audra and Claudesley Brereton. New York: Henry Holt, 1935.

Bernard of Clairvaux. *On the Song of Songs.* Translated by a Religious of C.S.M.V. London: Mowbray, 1952.

Bettelheim, Bruno. *The Uses of Enchantment: The Meaning and Importance of Fairy Tales.* New York: Alfred A. Knopf, 1976.

Bitov, Andrei. *Life in Windy Weather.* Translated by C. G. Luplow and Richard Luplow. Ann Arbor, Mich.: Ardis, 1986.

———. *Pushkin House.* Translated by Susan Brownberger. New York: Farrar, Straus & Giroux, 1987.

Boethius. *The Consolation of Philosophy.* Translated by "I. T." (1609) and H. F. Stewart. London: Loeb Classical Library, 1926.

Bollas, Christopher. *The Shadow of the Object: Psychoanalysis of the Unthought Known.* London: Free Association Books, 1987.

Bonnefoy, Yves. *The Act and the Place of Poetry.* Chicago: Univ. of Chicago Press, 1989.

Bradway, Katherine. "Gender Identity and Gender Roles: Their Place in Analytical Practice." In *Jungian Analysis.* Edited by Murray Stein. Wilmette, Ill.: Chiron Publications, 1982.

Broch, Hermann. *The Spell.* Translated by H. F. Broch de Rothermann. New York: Farrar, Straus & Giroux, 1987.

Bunting, Basil. *Collected Poems.* Mt. Kisco, N.Y.: Moyer Bell, 1985.

Cameron, Anne. *Daughters of Copper Woman.* Vancouver: Press Gang Publishers, 1981.

Camus, Albert. *The Fall.* Translated by Justin O'Brien. New York: Alfred A. Knopf, 1957.

———. *The Myth of Sisyphus.* Translated by Justin O'Brien. New York: Vintage, 1959.

Canetti, Elias. *An Essay on Man.* Translated by Suzanne Langer. New York: Dover, 1946.

———. *The Human Province.* Translated by Joachim Neugroschel. New York: Seabury Press, 1978.

————. *Language and Myth*. Translated by Suzanne Langer, New York: Dover, 1946.

Celan, Paul. *Poems*. Translated by Michael Hamburger. New York: Persea, 1989.

————. *Speech-Grille*. Translated by Joachim Neugroschel. New York: Dutton, 1971.

Champernowne, Irene. *A Memoir of Toni Wolff*. San Francisco: C. G. Jung Institute, 1980.

Chasseguet-Smirgel, Janine. *Sexuality and the Mind: The Role of the Father and the Mother in the Psyche*. New York: New York Univ. Press, 1986.

Chekhov, Anton. *The Personal Papers of Anton Chekhov*. Translated by S. S. Koteliansky and Leonard Wolfe. New York: Lear, 1948.

Clissold, Stephen. *Saint Teresa of Avila*. London: Sheldon Press, 1979.

Colledge, Eric. ed. *The Medieval Mystics of England*. London: John Murray, 1962.

de Beauvoir, Simone. *Bluebeard and Other Tales by Charles Perrault*. Translated by Richard Howard. New York: Macmillan, 1964.

Deutsch, Helene. *Psychology of Women*. New York: Grune & Stratton, 1944.

Dickinson, Emily. *The Complete Poems of Emily Dickinson*. Edited by T. H. Johnson. Boston: Little, Brown, 1960.

————. *Selected Letters*. Edited by T. H. Johnson. Cambridge: Belknap/Harvard University Press, 1971.

Donne, John. *Poems*. Edited by H. J. C. Grierson. Oxford: Oxford Univ. Press, 1953.

Dostoyevsky, Feodor. *The Short Novels of Dostoyevsky*. New York: Dial Press, 1945.

Douglas, Claire. *The Woman in the Mirror: Analytical Psychology and the Feminine*. Boston: Sigo Press, 1990.

Dourley, John. *Love, Celibacy, and the Inner Marriage*. Toronto: Inner City Books, 1987.

Downing, Christine. *Menopause: Journey through a Personal Rite of Passage*. New York: Crossroads, 1989.

Dranos, Stan. *Freud's Odyssey: Psychoanalysis and the End of Metaphysics*. New Haven, Conn.: Yale Univ. Press, 1982.

Easton, E. W. *The Intimate Interiors of Edouard Vuillard*. Washington: Smithsonian Institution Press, 1989.

Edinger, E. F. *The Anatomy of the Psyche: Alchemical Symbolism in Psychotherapy*. La Salle, Ill.: Open Court, 1985.

Eliot, George. *Middlemarch*. London: Everyman, 1969.

Erdoes, Richard and Alfonso Ortiz, eds. *American Indian Myths and Legends*. New York: Pantheon, 1984.

Erikson, Erik. "Reality and Actuality." *Journal of the American Psychoana- lytical Association* 10 (1961).

Every, George, Richard Harris, and Kallistos Ware, eds. *The Time of the Spirit.* Crestwood, N.Y.: St. Vladimir's Seminary Press, 1984.

Fierz-David, Linda. *The Dream of Poliphilo: The Soul in Love.* Dallas: Spring Publications, 1987.

———. *Women's Dionysian Initiation: The Villa Mysteries in Pompeii.* Dal- las: Spring Publications, 1988.

Fitzgerald, F. Scott. *The Last Tycoon and the Great Gatsby.* New York: Charles Scribners Sons, 1941.

———. *The Letters of F. Scott Fitzgerald.* Edited by Andrew Turnbull. New York: Scribner, 1963.

Fordham, Michael. "The Androgyne: Some Inconclusive Reflections on Sexual Perversions." *Journal of Analytical Psychology* 33, no. 3 (1988).

———. "Defenses of the Self." *Journal of Analytical Psychology* 19, no. 2 (1974).

———. "Jung's Conception of Transference." *Journal of Analytical Psy- chology* 19, no. 1 (1974).

———. "Rejoinder to Nathan Schwartz-Salant." *Journal of Analytical Psy- chology* 36, no. 3 (1990).

Forster, Leonard, ed. *The Penguin Book of German Verse.* Harmondsworth, Middlesex: Penguin, 1959.

Fowles, B. K. "Thoughts About the Tomgirl." *Journal of Analytical Psychol- ogy* 23, no. 2 (1978).

Fox, Matthew. *Meditations with Meister Eckhart.* Santa Fe, N.M.: Bear & Co., 1983.

Frank, S. L. *Reality and Man: An Essay in the Metaphysics of Human Na- ture.* Translated by Natalie Duddington. New York: Taplinger, 1966.

Freud, Sigmund. *The Ego and the Id.* Translated by Joan Riviere and James Strachey. New York: W. W. Norton, 1960.

———. *Three Essays on the Theory of Sexuality.* Standard Edition, vol. 7. Translated by James Strachey. London: Hogarth Press, 1974.

Gadamer, Hans-Georg. *Hegel's Dialectic: Five Hermeneutical Studies.* Translated by P. C. Smith. New Haven, Conn.: Yale Univ. Press, 1976.

———. *Truth and Method.* New York: Seabury Press, 1975.

Goethe, J. W. von. *Wisdom and Experience.* Edited by Ludwig Curtius. Translated by Hermann Weigand. New York: Pantheon, 1949.

———. *The Sufferings of Young Werther.* Translated by Harry Steinhauer. New York: W. W. Norton, 1970.

Goldenberg, Naomi. "A Feminist Critique of Jung." *Signs: A Journal of Women in Culture and Society* 2, no. 2 (1976).

Gordon, Rosemary. "The Concept of Projective Identification." *Journal of Analytical Psychology* 10, no. 2 (1965).

———. "The Symbolic Experience as Bridge between the Personal and the Collective." *Journal of Analytical Psychology* 22, no. 4 (1977).

———. "Losing and Finding: The Location of Archetypal Experience." *Journal of Analytical Psychology* 23, no. 2 (1978).

Grimm's Fairy Tales. New York: Pantheon, 1994.

Grosskurth, Phyllis. *Melanie Klein: Her World and Her Work*. New York: Alfred A. Knopf, 1986.

Guggenbühl-Craig, Adolph. *Marriage—Dead or Alive*. Translated by Murray Stein. Zurich: Spring Publications, 1977.

Guntrip, Harry. *Schizoid Phenomena, Object Relations, and the Self*. New York: International Universities Press, 1969.

Hacker, Theodore. *Journal in the Night*. Translated by Alick Dru. New York: Pantheon, 1950.

Hannah, Barbara. *Encounters with the Soul: Active Imagination as Developed by C. G. Jung*. Santa Monica, Calif.: Sigo Press, 1961.

———. "The Problem of Contact with the Animus." London: Guild of Pastoral Psychology, 1962.

———. *Striving Toward Wholeness*. New York: G. P. Putnam's Sons, 1976.

Harding, M. Esther. "The Anima and the Animus: A Curtain Lecture." New York: Kristine Mann Library of the C. G. Jung Foundation, 1951.

———. *The "I" and the "Not-I"*. New York: Pantheon, 1965.

———. *Psychic Energy: Its Source and Its Transformation*. New York: Pantheon, 1965.

———. *The Way of All Women*. New York: G. P. Putnam's Sons, 1970.

———. *Women's Mysteries: Ancient and Modern*. New York: G. P. Putnam's Sons, 1971.

Haule, John. *Divine Madness: Archetypes of Romantic Love*. Boston: Shambhala Publications, 1990.

Hébert, Anne. *Selected Poems*. Translated by A. Poulin, Jr. Brockport, N.Y.: BOA Editions, 1987.

Heidegger, Martin. *Being and Time*. Translated by John Macquarrie and Edward Robinson. New York: Harper & Row, 1962.

Heisler, Vera. "Individuation Through Marriage." *Psychological Perspectives*, Fall 1970.

Henderson, Joseph. *Shadow and Self: Selected Papers in Analytical Psychology*. Wilmette, Ill.: Chiron Publications, 1990.

Hill, Geoffrey. *Tenebrae*. Boston: Houghton Mifflin, 1979.

Hillesum, Etty. *An Interrupted Life: The Diaries of Etty Hillesum*. Translated by Arno Pomerans. New York: Pantheon, 1983.

Hillman, James. *Anima: An Anatomy of a Personified Notion*. Dallas: Spring Publications, 1985.

———. *The Myth of Analysis*. San Francisco: Harper, 1972.

Hopcke, Robert H. *Jung, Jungians, and Homosexuality.* Boston: Shambhala Publications, 1989.

——, Karin Loftus Carrington, and Scott Wirth. *Same-Sex Love and the Path to Wholeness.* Boston: Shambhala Publications, 1993.

Hubback, Judith. "Reflections on the Psychology of Women." *Journal of Analytical Psychology* 23, no. 2 (1978).

Hugh of St. Victor. *Selected Spiritual Writings.* Translated by a Religious of C.S.M.V. London: Faber & Faber, 1962.

Humbert, Elie. *C. G. Jung.* Translated by R. G. Jalbert. Wilmette, Ill.: Chiron Publications, 1988.

——. "How Do I Assess Progress in Supervision?" *Journal of Analytical Psychology* 27, no. 2 (1982).

Ibsen, Henrik. *Hedda Gabler and Other Plays.* Translated by Una Ellis-Fermor. Harmondsworth, Middlesex: Penguin, 1972.

——. *The Late Plays of Henrik Ibsen.* Translated by Arvid Paulsen, New York: Harper, 1973.

——. *Letters and Speeches.* Edited by Evert Sprinchorn. New York: Hill and Wang, 1964.

Ingarden, Roman. *The Cognition of the Literary Work of Art.* Translated by R. A. Crowley and K. R. Olson. Evanston, Ill.: Northwestern Univ. Press, 1973.

Ivanov, Vyacheslav. *Freedom and the Tragic Life: A Study in Dostoevsky.* Translated by Norman Cameron. New York: Noonday Press, 1952.

Jaeger, Werner. *The Theology of the Early Greek Philosophers.* Oxford: Clarendon Press, 1960.

Jaffé, Aniela. *Was C. G. Jung a Mystic?* Translated by Diana Dachler and Fiona Cairns. Einsiedeln, Switzerland: Daimon Verlag, 1989.

Jaffe, D. S. "The Masculine Envy of Woman's Procreative Function." In *Female Psychology.* Edited by H. P. Blum. New York: International Universities Press, 1977.

Jaspers, Karl. *Philosophy of Existence.* Translated by R. F. Grabau. Philadelphia: Univ. of Pennsylvania Press, 1971.

Jensen, Ferne. *C. G. Jung, Emma Jung, and Toni Wolff: A Collection of Remembrances.* San Francisco: Analytical Psychology Club, 1982.

Johnson, Robert A. *We: Understanding the Psychology of Romantic Love.* San Francisco: Harper, 1983.

Judith. Vol. 40 of *The Anchor Bible.* Translated by C. A. Moore. Garden City, N.Y.: Doubleday, 1985.

Julian of Norwich. *Revelations of Divine Love.* Translated by James Walsh. London: Burns and Oates, 1961.

Jung, C. G. *Aion.* Vol. 9:2 of *The Collected Works of C. G. Jung.* New York: Pantheon, 1959.

————. *Alchemical Studies. CW* 13. Princeton, N. J.: Princeton University Press, 1967.

————. *The Archetypes and the Collective Unconscious. CW* 9:1. New York: Pantheon, 1959.

————. *Civilization in Transition. CW* 10. New York: Pantheon, 1964.

————. *Dream Analysis.* Princeton, N.J.: Princeton Univ. Press, 1984.

————. *Dream Analysis: Notes of the Seminars in Analytical Psychology, 1928–1929 and 1929–1930.* 2 vols. Zurich: 1958.

————. *The Integration of the Personality.* Translated by Stanley Dell. New York: Farrar, Straus & Rinehart, 1939.

————. *Letters.* Edited by Gerhard Adler and Aniela Jaffé. Translated by R. F. C. Hull. 2 vols. Princeton, N. J.: Princeton Univ. Press, 1973 and 1975.

————. *Memories, Dreams, Reflections.* Edited by Aniela Jaffé. Translated by Richard Winston and Clara Winston. New York: Pantheon, 1963.

————. *Modern Man in Search of a Soul.* Translated by C. F. Baynes and Stanley Dell. New York: Harcourt Brace, 1933.

————. *Mysterium Coniuntionis. CW* 14. New York: Pantheon, 1963.

————. *The Practice of Psychotherapy. CW* 16. New York: Pantheon, 1954.

————. *Psychological Types. CW* 6. Princeton, N. J.: Princeton Univ. Press, 1971.

————. *Psychology and Alchemy. CW* 12. New York: Pantheon, 1953.

————. *Psychology and Religion: West and East. CW* 11. New York: Pantheon, 1958.

————. *Septem Sermones ad Mortuos.* Translated by H. G. Baynes. London: Watkins, 1963.

————. *The Structure and Dynamics of the Psyche. CW* 8. New York: Pantheon, 1960.

————. *The Symbolic Life. CW* 18. Princeton, N. J.: Princeton Univ. Press, 1976.

————. *Symbols of Transformation. CW* 5. New York: Pantheon, 1956.

————. *Two Essays of Analytical Psychology. CW* 7. Princeton, N. J.: Princeton Univ. Press, 1953.

————. *The Vision Seminars: Two Books.* Zurich, Switzerland: Spring Publications, 1976.

Jung, Emma. *Anima and Animus.* New York: Analytical Psychology Club, 1957.

————, and Marie-Louise von Franz. *The Grail Legend.* Translated by Andrea Dykes. New York: G. P. Putnam's Sons, 1970.

Kant, Immanuel. *Critique of Pure Reason.* Translated by J. M. D. Meikeljohn. London: Everyman, 1964.

Kast, Verena. *The Nature of Loving: Patterns of Human Relationships.* Translated by Boris Matthews. Wilmette, Ill.: Chiron Publications, 1986.

Kawai, Hayao. *The Japanese Psyche: Major Motifs in the Fairy Tales of Japan.* Translated by Hayao Kawai and Sachiko Reece. Dallas: Spring Publications, 1988.

Kay, D. L. "The Paternal Psyche and the Emerging Ego." *Journal of Analytical Psychology* 26, no. 3 (1981).

Kay, G. R. ed. *The Penguin Book of Italian Verse.* Harmondsworth, Middlesex: Penguin, 1950.

Kernberg, Otto. *Borderline Conditions and Pathological Narcissism.* New York: Jason Aronson, 1975.

———. *Tactics and Techniques in Psychoanalytic Therapy.* New York: Science House, 1972.

Khan, M. Masud R. *Alienation in Perversion.* New York: International Universities Press, 1979.

———. *Hidden Selves: Between Theory and Practice in Psychoanalysis.* New York: International Universities Press, 1983.

———. *The Privacy of the Self.* New York: International Universities Press, 1974.

Kierkegaard, Soren. *Sickness unto Death.* Translated by Walter Lowrie. Garden City, N. Y.: Anchor, 1954.

Klein, Melanie. *Envy and Gratitude and Other Works, 1946–1963.* New York: Delacorte Press, 1975.

———. *Love, Guilt, and Reparation and Other Works 1921–1945.* New York: Delacorte Press, 1975.

———. *The Psychoanalysis of Children.* Translated by Alix Strachey. New York: Delacorte Press, 1975.

Koebler, Renate. *In the Shadow of Karl Barth: Charlotte von Kirschbaum.* Translated by Keith Crimm. Louisville, Ky.: Westminster/John Knox, 1987.

Kohut, Heinz. *The Analysis of the Self.* New York: International Universities Press, 1971.

———. *How Does Analysis Cure?* Edited by Arnold Goldberg. Chicago: Univ. of Chicago Press, 1984.

Kolmar, Gertrude. *Dark Soliloquy: The Selected Poems of Gertrude Kolmar.* Translated by H. A. Smith. New York: Crossroads, 1975.

Krutch, Joseph Wood. *More Lives Than One.* New York: William Sloane, 1962.

Labé, Louise. *Sonnets.* Translated by G. D. Martin. Austin: Univ. of Texas Press, 1972.

Lagerlof, Selma. *The Story of Gosta Berling.* Trans. Robert Bly. New York: Signet, 1967.

Laing, R. D. *The Politics of Experience.* New York: Pantheon, 1967.

Layard, John. *The Virgin Archetype.* New York: Spring Publications, 1972.

Lee, Jae Hoon. *"A Study of 'Han' of the Korean People: A Depth Psychological Contribution to the Understanding of the Concept of 'Han' in the Korean Minjung Theology."* Ph. D. diss. Union Theological Seminary, New York, 1989.

Leonard, Linda Schierse. *On the Way to the Wedding: Transforming the Love Relationship.* Boston: Shambhala Publications, 1987.

———. *Witness to the Fire: Creativity and the Veil of Addiction.* Boston: Shambhala Publications, 1989.

———. *The Wounded Woman: Healing the Father-Daughter Relationship.* Boston: Shambhala Publications, 1986.

Levinas, Emmanuel. *Face to Face with Levinas.* Edited by R. A. Cohn. Albany: State Univ. of New York Press, 1986.

Loewald, Hans. *Psychoanalysis and the History of the Individual.* New Haven, Conn.: Yale Univ. Press, 1978.

Lowell, Robert. *Life Studies.* New York: Farrar, Straus & Cudahy, 1959.

———. *Notebook.* New York: Farrar, Straus & Giroux, 1970.

MacNeice, Louis. *The Burning Perch.* London: Faber & Faber, 1963.

———. *Collected Poems.* London: Faber & Faber, 1949.

———. *Goethe's Faust, Parts I and II: An Abridged Version.* New York: Oxford Univ. Press, 1981.

———. *Ten Burnt Offerings.* London: Faber & Faber, 1952.

Mankowitz, Ann. *Change of Life: A Psychological Study of Dreams and the Menopause.* Toronto: Inner City Books, 1984.

Markov, Vladimir and Merrill Sparks, eds. *Modern Russian Poetry.* Indianapolis: Bobbs-Merrill, 1967.

Marvell, Andrew. *The Poems and Letters.* Edited by H. M. Margoliouth. Oxford: Clarendon Press, 1952.

Masterson, Jules. *Narcissistic and Borderline Disorders.* New York: Brunner-Mazel, 1981.

Medici, Lorenzo de'. *Opere.* Edited by Attilio Simioni. Bari, Italy: Laterza, 1939.

Meditations to the Holy Spirit. Translated by a Religious of C.S.M.V. London: Mowbray, 1957.

Merleau-Ponty, Maurice. *Phenomenology of Perception.* Translated by Colin Smith. London: Routledge and Kegan Paul, 1962.

Miller, Jean Baker. *Toward a New Psychology of Women.* Boston: Beacon Press, 1976.

Milner, Marion. *On Not Being Able to Paint.* New York: International Universities Press, 1979.

Monk, Ray. *Ludwig Wittgenstein: The Duty of Genius.* New York: Free Press, 1990.

Moore, Norah. "The Transcendent Function and the Emerging Ego." *Journal of Analytical Psychology* 20, no. 2 (1975).

Mattoon, Mary Ann. *The Archetype of the Shadow in a Split World.* Einsiedeln, Switzerland: Daimon Verlag, 1987.

Musil, Robert. *The Man without Qualities.* Translated by Eithne Wilkins and Ernst Kaiser. 3 vols. London: Secker and Warburg, 1960.

Needham, Rodney. *Circumstantial Deliveries.* Berkeley, Calif.: Univ. of California Press, 1981.

Neihardt, John G. *Black Elk Speaks.* New York: Washington Square Press, 1959.

Neumann, Erich. *The Great Mother: An Analysis of the Archetype.* Translated by Ralph Mannheim. Princeton, N. J.: Princeton Univ. Press. 1955.

Obolensky, Dimitri, ed. *The Penguin Book of Russian Verse.* Harmondsworth, Middlesex: Penguin, 1965.

Ortega y Gasset, José. *Historical Reason.* Translated by P. W. Silver. New York: W. W. Norton: 1984.

———. *Man and People.* Translated by W. R. Trask. New York: W. W. Norton, 1957.

Pasternak, Boris. *Poems.* Translated by E. M. Kayden. Kent, Ohio: Kent State Univ. Press, 1970.

———. Marina Tsvetayeva, and Rainer Maria Rilke. *Letters, Summer 1926.* Translated by Margaret Wettlin and Walter Arndt. London: Cape, 1986.

Philo. "On the Contemplative Life." In *Philo.* Loeb Classical Library, vol. 9. London: Heinemann, 1960.

Pieper, Josef. *About Love.* Translated by Richard and Clara Winston. Chicago: Franciscan Herald Press, 1974.

Pirandello, Luigi. *Naked Masks: Five Plays.* New York: E. P. Dutton, 1952.

Plath, Sylvia. *Winter Trees.* New York: Harper & Row, 1972.

Polanyi, Michael. *Knowing and Being.* Chicago: Univ. of Chicago Press, 1969.

———. *Personal Knowledge: Towards a Post-Critical Philosophy.* Chicago: Univ. of Chicago Press, 1962.

Popper, Karl. *Unended Quest: An Intellectual Autobiography.* La Salle, Ill.: Open Court, 1976.

Proner, B. "Envy of Oneself: Adhesive Identification and Pseudo-Adult States." *Journal of Analytical Psychology* 33, no. 2 (1988).

Proust, Marcel. *Remembrance of Things Past.* Translated by C. K. Scott Moncrieff. New York: Random House, 1932.

Racker, Heinrich. *Transference and Countertransference.* London: Hogarth Press, 1968.

Rank, Otto. *The Don Juan Legend.* Translated and edited by D. G. Winter. Princeton, N.J.: Princeton Univ. Press, 1975.

———. *The Double: A Psychoanalytic Study.* Translated by Harry Tucker, Jr., Chapel Hill, N.C.: Univ. of North Carolina Press, 1971.

Ratushinskaya. Irina. *Beyond the Limit.* Translated by F. P. Brent and C. J. Avirs. Evanston, Ill.: Northwestern Univ. Press, 1987.

————. *Pencil Letter.* New York: Alfred A. Knopf, 1989.

Reuther, Rosemary Radford. *Sexism and God-Talk: Toward a Feminist Theology.* Boston: Beacon Press, 1983.

Rhi, Bou-Yong. "Psychological Problems Among Korean Women," in *Virtues in Conflict: Tradition and the Korean Woman Today.* Edited by Sandra Mattielli. Seoul: Royal Asiatic Society, 1977.

Rilke, Rainer Maria. *Letters to Merline.* Translated by V. M. MacDonald. London: Metheun, 1951.

————. *Selected Works.* Translated by J. B. Leishman. Norfolk, Conn.: New Directions, 1960.

————. *The Sonnets to Orpheus.* Translated by Stephen Mitchell. New York: Simon and Schuster, 1985.

Roazen, Paul. *Freud and His Followers.* New York: Alfred A. Knopf, 1975.

Roberts, Elizabeth Maddox. *Black Is the Color of My True Love's Hair.* New York: Viking, 1938.

Rodman, F. R. *The Spontaneous Gesture: Selected Letters by D. W. Winnicott.* Cambridge, Mass.: Harvard Univ. Press, 1987.

Rosenthall, Michael. "Notes on Envy and the Contrasexual Archetype." *Journal of Analytical Psychology* 8, no. 1 (1963).

Roy, Manisha. "Animus and Indian Women." *Harvest* 25 (1979).

Roustang, Francois. *Dire Mastery: Discipleship from Freud to Lacan.* Translated by Ned Lukacher. Baltimore: Johns Hopkins Univ. Press, 1982.

Rozanov, Vasily. *The Apocalypse of Our Time and Other Writings.* Edited by Robert Payne. Translated by Robert Payne and Nikita Romanoff. New York: Praeger, 1977.

————. *Dostoevsky and the Legend of the Grand Inquisitor.* Trans. S. E. Roberts. Ithaca, N.Y.: Cornell Univ. Press, 1972.

Ruff, M. A. *Baudelaire.* Translated by Agnes Kertesz. New York: New York Univ. Press, 1966.

Rycroft, Charles. *A Critical Dictionary of Psycho-Analysis.* New York: Basic Books, 1968.

Samuels, Andrew. "Beyond the Pleasure Principle: A Post-Jungian Viewpoint." *Harvest* 34 (1988–1989).

————, ed. *The Father: Contemporary Jungian Perspectives.* New York: New York Univ. Press, 1986.

Schiffer, Irvine. *The Trauma of Time.* New York: International Universities Press, 1978.

Schiller, Friedrich. *Essays Aesthetical and Philosophical.* London: George Bell, 1910.

Schwartz-Salant, Nathan. "Anima and Animus in Jung's Alchemical Mirror." In *Gender and Soul in Psychotherapy*. Edited by Nathan Schwartz-Salant and Murray Stein. Wilmette, Ill.: Chiron Publications, 1991.

———. *The Borderline Personality: Vision and Healing*. Wilmette, Ill.: Chiron Publications, 1989.

———. "Vision, Interpretation, and the Interactive Field." *Journal of Analytical Psychology* 36, no. 3 (1990).

———, and Murray Stein, eds. *Liminality and Transitional Phenomena*. Wilmette, Ill.: Chiron Publications, 1991.

Scott-Maxwell, Florida. *The Measure of My Days*. New York: Alfred A. Knopf, 1968.

Segal, Hannah. *Melanie Klein*. New York: Viking, 1979.

Seinfeld, Jeffrey. *The Bad Object: Healing the Negative Therapeutic Reaction in Psychotherapy*. Northvale, N. J.: Jason Aronson, 1990.

Sexton, Anne. *Love Poems*. Boston: Houghton Mifflin, 1969.

Shuttle, Penelope and Peter Redgrove. *The Wise Wound: Eve's Curse and Everywoman*. New York: Richard Marek, 1978.

Singer, June. *Androgyny: Toward a New Theory of Sexuality*. Boston: Sigo Press, 1989.

Sisson, C. H. *Collected Poems*. Manchester, England: Carcarnet Press, 1984.

Solovyov, Vladimir. *The Meaning of Love*. Translated by Jane Marshall. London: Geoffrey Bles, 1945.

Stein, Murray, ed. *Jungian Analysis*. LaSalle, Ill.: Open Court, 1982.

Stein, Robert. *Incest and Human Love: The Betrayal of the Soul in Psychotherapy*. New York: Third Press, 1973.

Steiner, George. *In Bluebeard's Castle*. New Haven: Yale Univ. Press, 1971.

Stevens, Anthony. *On Jung*. London: Routledge, 1990.

Strindberg, August. *The Plays of Strindberg*. Translated by Michael Meyer. New York: Vintage, 1976.

Taylor, Charles. *Sources of the Self: The Making of the Modern Identity*. Cambridge, Mass.: Harvard Univ. Press, 1989.

Teresa of Avila. *The Complete Works of St. Teresa*. Translated by E. A. Peers. New York: Sheed and Ward, 1957.

Tillich, Hannah. *From Time to Time*. New York: Stein and Day, 1973.

Tillich, Paul. "Remarks." In *Carl Gustav Jung, 1875–1961: A Memorial Meeting*. New York: Analytical Psychology Club, 1961.

———. *The Shaking of the Foundations*. New York: Charles Scribner's Sons, 1948.

Trollope, Anthony. *Ayala's Angel*. London: Oxford Univ. Press, 1968.

Truffaut, Francois. *The Films in My Life*. Translated by Leonard Mayhew. London: Allen Lane, 1980.

Ulanov, Ann Belford. "The Anxiety of Being: Paul Tillich and Depth Psychology." In *Paul Tillich.* Edited by J. L. Adams and R. L. Shinn. New York: Harper, 1985.

———. "Between Anxiety and Faith: The Role of the Feminine in Paul Tillich's Thought." In *Paul Tillich on Creativity.* Edited by Jacqueline Kegley and J. L. Adams. New York: Univ. Press of America, 1989.

———. "Disguises of the Anima." In *Gender and Soul in Psychotherapy.* Edited by Nathan Schwartz-Salant and Murray Stein.

———. "The Double Cross." In *Lingering Shadows: Jungians, Freudians, and Anti-Semitism.* Edited by Aryeh Maidenbaum and Stephen Martin. Boston: Shambhala Publications, 1992.

———. "Fatness and the Female." *Psychological Perspectives* 10 (Fall 1979).

———. *The Female Ancestors of Christ.* Boston: Shambhala Publications, 1993.

———. *The Feminine in Jungian Psychology and in Christian Theology.* Evanston, Ill.: Northwestern Univ. Press, 1971.

———. "For Better *and* for Worse." *Psychoanalytic Review* 76 (Winter 1986).

———. "The Holding Self: Jung and the Desire for Being." In *The Fires of Desire: Erotic Energies and the Spiritual Quest.* Edited by F. R. Halligan and J. J. Shea. New York: Crossroads, 1992.

———. "How Do I Assess Progress in Supervision?" *Journal of Analytical Psychology* 27, no. 2 (1982).

———. "The Perverse and the Transcendent." In *Chicago 92, The Transcendent Function: Individual and Collective Aspects.* Edited by Mary Ann Mattoon. Eisiedeln, Switzerland: Daimon Verlag, 1993.

———. *Picturing God.* Cambridge: Cowley Publications, 1986.

———. *Receiving Woman: Studies in the Psychology and Theology of the Feminine.* Louisville, Ky.: Westminster, 1981.

———. "The Search for Paternal Roots." In *Fathering: Fact or Fable?* Edited by E. V. Stein. Nashville, Tenn.: Abingdon, 1977.

———. "A Shared Space." *Quadrant,* Spring 1985.

———. "Transference/Countertransference: A Jungian Approach." In *Jungian Analysis.* Edited by Murray Stein.

———. "Self-Service." In *Cast the First Stone.* Edited by Lena Ross and Manisha Roy. Wilmette, Ill.: Chiron, 1994.

———. *The Wizards' Gate: Picturing Consciousness.* Einsiedeln, Switzerland: Daimon Verlag, 1994.

Ulanov, Ann and Barry. *Cinderella and Her Sisters: The Envied and the Envying.* Louisville, Ky.: Westminster, 1983.

———. *The Healing Imagination: The Meeting of Psyche and Soul.* Mahwah, N. J.: Paulist Press, 1991.

———. *Primary Speech: A Psychology of Prayer.* Louisville, Ky.: John Knox, 1982.

———. *Religion and the Unconscious.* Louisville, Ky.: Westminster, 1975.

———. *The Witch and the Clown: Two Archetypes of Human Sexuality.* Wilmette, Ill.: Chiron Publications, 1987.

Ulanov, Barry. *Death: A Book of Preparation and Consolation.* New York: Sheed and Ward, 1959.

———. *Jung and the Outside World.* Wilmette, Ill.: Chiron Publications: 1992.

———. *Makers of the Modern Theater.* New York: McGraw Hill, 1961.

———. "Mysticism and Negative Presence." *Gaster Festschrift, Journal of the Ancient Near East Society of Columbia University,* vol. 5 (1973).

———. "The Song of Songs: The Rhetoric of Love." In *The Bridge: A Yearbook of Judaeo-Christian Studies.* Edited by J. M. Oesterreicher. New York: Pantheon, 1962.

Van der Post, Laurens. *Jung and the Story of Our Time.* New York: Random House, 1976.

Von der Heydt, Vera. "On the Father." In *Fathers and Mothers.* Edited by H. A. Wilmer. Wilmette, Ill.: Chiron Publications, 1990.

von Franz, Marie-Louise. *Alchemy: An Introduction to the Symbolism and the Psychology.* Toronto: Inner City Books, 1980.

———. "Anima and Animus." In *C. G. Jung: Man and His Symbols.* New York: Doubleday, 1964.

———. *Apuleius' Golden Ass.* New York: Spring Publications, 1970.

———. *C. G. Jung: His Myth in Our Time.* Translated by W. H. Kennedy. New York: G. P. Putnam's Sons, 1975.

———. *The Feminine in Fairy Tales.* New York: Spring Publications, 1972.

———. *Individuation in Fairy Tales.* Dallas, Tx.: Spring Publications, 1977.

———. *Interpretation of Fairy Tales.* New York: Spring Publications, 1970.

———. *On Dreams and Death.* Boston: Shambhala Publications, 1986.

———. *Projection and Re-collection in Jungian Psychology.* Trans. W. H. Kennedy. La Salle, Ill.: Open Court, 1980.

———. *The Psychological Meaning of Redemption Motifs in Fairy Tales.* Toronto: Inner City Books, 1980.

———. *Puer Aeternus.* New York: Spring Publications, 1970.

———, and James Hillman. *Jung's Typology.* New York: Spring Publications, 1971.

Walker, Barbara. *Crone: Woman of Age, Wisdom, and Power.* San Francisco: Harper, 1988.

Walker, Mitch. "The Double: An Archetypal Configuration." *Spring,* 1976.

Weigand, Hermann. *The Modern Ibsen.* New York: E. P. Dutton, 1960.

Weil, Simone. *Gravity and Grace.* Translated by Emma Craufurd. London: Routledge and Kegan Paul, 1963.

West, Rebecca. *The Harsh Voice.* London: Virago, 1983.

Wheelwright, J. B. *The Reality of the Psyche.* New York: G. P. Putnam's Sons, 1968.

Wheelwright, J. H. "Analysis with the Aged." In *Jungian Analysis.* Edited by Murray Stein. LaSalle, Ill.: Open Court, 1982.

———. *The Animus for Women Growing Older.* Houston: C. G. Jung Educational Center, 1984.

———. *The Death of a Woman.* New York: St. Martin's Press, 1981.

White, Patrick. *The Twyborn Affair.* London: Cape, 1979.

Whitehead, Alfred North. *Modes of Thought.* New York: Free Press, 1966.

Wickes, Frances. *The Inner World of Childhood.* Boston: Sigo Press, 1988.

Wilhelm, Richard and C. F. Baynes. *I Ching, or Book of Changes.* New York: Pantheon, 1950.

Williams, Charles. *Descent into Hell.* London: Faber & Faber, 1937.

Wilmer, Harry. "Jung: Father and Son." In *Fathers and Mothers.* Edited by Harry Wilmer. Wilmette, Ill.: Chiron Publications, 1990.

Winnicott, D. W. *The Child, The Family, and the Outside World.* Harmondsworth, Middlesex: Penguin, 1975.

———. *Home Is Where We Start From.* New York: W. W. Norton, 1986.

———. *Human Nature.* London: Free Association Press, 1988.

———. *The Maturational Processes and the Facilitating Environment.* New York: International Universities Press, 1965.

———. *The Piggle: An Account of the Psychoanalytic Treatment of a Little Girl.* New York: International Universities Press, 1977.

———. *Playing and Reality.* London: Tavistock, 1971.

———. *Psychoanalytic Explorations.* Edited by Clare Winnicott, Ray Shepherd, Madeleine Davis. London: Karnac, 1989.

———. Review of *Memories, Dreams, Reflections* by C. G. Jung. *International Journal of Psychoanalysis* 45, 2 & 3 (1964).

———. *Through Paediatrics to Psycho-Analysis.* New York: Basic Books, 1975.

Wisdom, J. O. "The Perversions: A Philosopher Reflects." *Journal of Analytical Psychology* 33, no. 3 (1988).

Wittgenstein, Ludwig. *Culture and Value.* Translated by Peter Winch. Oxford: Basil Blackwell, 1989.

———. *On Certainty.* Translated by Denis Paul and G. E. M. Anscombe. New York: Harper, 1972.

Wolfe, Leonard. *Bluebeard: The Life and Times of Gilles de Rais.* New York: Crown, 1980.

Woodman, Marion. *Addiction to Perfection: The Still Unravished Bride.* Toronto: Inner City Books, 1982.

Wynne-Tyson, Esme. *The Philosophy of Compassion.* London: Vincent Stuart, 1962.

Credits

The authors thank the following publishers for permission to reprint material copyrighted or controlled by them.

BOA Editions Limited for permission to quote from Anne Hébert, "Original Earth." English translation copyright © 1980 and 1987 by A. Poulin, Jr. Reprinted from *Anne Hébert: Selected Poems,* with the permission of BOA Editions, Ltd., 92 Park Ave., Brockport, N.Y. 14420.

Carcanet Press for permission to quote from *Collected Poems* by C. H. Sisson.

Faber and Faber Ltd for permission to quote from *The Collected Poems of Louis MacNeice* edited by E. R. Dodds, and from *Goethe's Faust* translated by Louis MacNeice.

HarperCollins Publishers for permission to quote from "Three Women" from *Winter Trees* by Sylvia Plath. Copyright © 1968 by Ted Hughes. Reprinted by Permission of HarperCollins Publishers, Inc.

Harvard University Press for permission to quote from Emily Dickinson's poems. Reprinted by permission of the publishers and the Trustees of Amherst College from *The Poems of Emily Dickinson,* Thomas H. Johnson, ed. Cambridge, Mass.: Belknap Press of Harvard University Press, Copyright © 1951, 1955, 1979, 1983 by the President and Fellows of Harvard College.

The Houghton Mifflin Company for permission to reprint excerpts from *The Complete Poems of Anne Sexton,* copyright © 1981 by Linda Gray Sexton. Reprinted by permission of Houghton Mifflin Company. All rights reserved.

Kent State University Press for permission to quote from *Poems by Boris Pasternak* translated by Eugene M. Kayden (Kent, Ohio: The Kent State University Press, 1970).

New Dimensions Publishing Corporation for permission to quote from Rainer Maria Rilke, *Selected Works Vol. II.* Copyright © 1960 by The Hogarth Press Ltd. Translated by J. B. Leishman. Reprinted by permission of New Directions Publishing Corporation.

Oxford University Press for permission to quote from *Basil Bunting: Collected Poems* (Oxford: Oxford University Press, 1978). Used by permission of Oxford University Press.

Penguin Books Ltd for permission to quote from "Tenebrae" from *Collected Poems* by Geoffrey Hill (Penguin Books, 1985). Copyright © Geoffrey Hill 1978.

Diligent efforts were made to obtain necessary permissions for portions of works quoted in this book. The authors wish to express their gratitude for the use of material quoted in cases where efforts to contact copyright holders were unsuccessful.

Index

C. G. Jung Foundation Books

Absent Fathers, Lost Sons: The Search for Masculine Identity, by Guy Corneau.

Closeness in Personal and Professional Relationships, edited by Harry A. Wilmer. Foreword by Maya Angelou.

Cross-Currents of Jungian Thought: An Annotated Bibliography, by Donald R. Dyer.

Ego and Archetype: Individuation and the Religious Function of the Psyche, by Edward F. Edinger.

The Eternal Drama: The Inner Meaning of Greek Mythology, by Edward F. Edinger.

The Female Ancestors of Christ, by Ann Belford Ulanov.

The Feminine in Fairy Tales, Revised Edition, by Marie-Louise von Franz.

Gathering the Light: A Psychology of Meditation, by V. Walter Odajnyk.

The Golden Ass of Apuleius: The Liberation of the Feminine in Man, by Marie-Louise von Franz.

A Guided Tour of the Collected Works *of C. G. Jung,* by Robert H. Hopcke. Foreword by Aryeh Maidenbaum.

In Her Image: The Unhealed Daughter's Search for Her Mother, by Kathie Carlson.

The Inner Lover, by Valerie Harms.

Knowing Woman: A Feminine Psychology, by Irene Claremont de Castillejo.

Lingering Shadows: Jungians, Freudians, and Anti-Semitism, edited by Aryeh Maidenbaum and Stephen A. Martin.

Masculinity: Identity, Conflict, and Transformation, by Warren Steinberg.

The Old Wise Woman: A Study of Active Imagination, by Rix Weaver. Introduction by C. A. Meier.

Power and Politics: The Psychology of Soviet-American Partnership, by Jerome S. Bernstein. Forewords by Senator Claiborne Pell and Edward C. Whitmont, M.D.

*Psyche and Matter, by Marie-Louise von Franz.

*Psychotherapy, by Marie-Louise von Franz.

The Way of All Women, by M. Esther Harding. Introduction by C. G. Jung.

Witches, Ogres, and the Devil's Daughter: Encounters with Evil in Fairy Tales, by Mario Jacoby, Verena Kast, and Ingrid Riedel.

*Published in association with Daimon Verlag, Einsiedeln, Switzerland.